FREEDOM OF SPEECH

FREEDOM OF SPEECH

ERIC BARENDT

CLARENDON PRESS · OXFORD
1985

Oxford University Press, Walton Street, Oxford OX2 6DP

London New York Toronto
Delhi Bombay Calcutta Madras Karachi
Kuala Lumpur Singapore Hong Kong Tokyo
Nairobi Dar es Salaam Cape Town
Melbourne Auckland

and associated companies in
Beirut Berlin Ibadan Mexico City Nicosia

Oxford is a trade mark of Oxford University Press

Published in the United States
by Oxford University Press, New York

British Library Cataloguing in Publication Data
© Eric Barendt 1985
Barendt, Eric
Freedom of speech.
1. Freedom of speech
I. Title
323.44'3   JC591
ISBN 0-19-825381-8

Library of Congress Cataloging in Publication Data
Barendt, Eric.
Freedom of speech.
Includes index.
1. Freedom of speech.   I. Title.
K3254.B37 1985   342'.0853   85-7100
ISBN 0-19-825381-8   342.2853

51, 982

Set by Latimer Trend & Company Ltd, Plymouth
Printed in Great Britain
at the University Press, Oxford
by David Stanford
Printer to the University

Preface

COMPARATIVE civil liberties law is a subject of growing interest in Britain. This is largely attributable to our participation in the European Convention on Human Rights and to the anxiety of many judges, politicians, and commentators whether the common law can and does afford adequate protection for fundamental freedoms. Yet strangely there are relatively few books exploring topics in this area of law in any depth. I have tried in this book on freedom of speech to fill part of this gap in legal literature. It contains a comparative treatment of free speech law in the United Kingdom, the United States of America, West Germany, and under the European Convention. Occasional reference is also made to important court decisions in Commonwealth countries, particularly Australia and Canada.

Freedom of speech is of course a subject of much philosophical and political debate. Frequent reference is made throughout this book, and especially in the first chapter, to recent philosophical and jurisprudential writing on the topic. Perhaps this needs a word of explanation. One of my major themes is that the more difficult free speech questions can only be answered after reflection on the reasons of principle why free speech is valued so highly (and in many jurisdictions given constitutional protection). For example, the issue whether commitment to free speech entails the provision of some rights of access to speak on the media, or the dispute whether pornography or commercial advertising should be treated as 'speech' for the purposes of legal protection, cannot necessarily be resolved by the processes of textual interpretation. Courts, and in particular constitutional courts, must sometimes examine political and moral arguments when determining whether some legislation or executive act infringes a free speech clause. These arguments cannot be sharply distinguished from relevant legal arguments, at any rate in jurisdictions which give fundamental rights some measure of constitutional protection.

The closeness of the relationship between legal and philosophical reasoning may not be so apparent in British cases; the courts here have no powers of constitutional review and are bound to apply Acts of Parliament and follow precedents. But how often are the legal materials and

their impact on freedom of speech (recognized as a common law principle) really clear in the difficult cases that come before the appellate courts? Attempts by the judiciary to prevent general arguments of political principle from influencing 'the law' may prove intellectually futile, and appear a little disingenuous, as evidenced by the direction of the judge in the recent *Ponting* secrets case. There is ample opportunity for British judges to take free speech seriously if they want to. The evidence from areas of law, such as contempt of court and breach of confidence, is that they frequently prefer to give more weight to other values. This preference may often be justified, but less explicable are the failure on occasion of the courts to do justice to free speech considerations and, worse, the pretence in a few leading cases that free speech is not in issue at all when it is patently relevant. These lapses would be even rarer if we had a written constitution or if British judges were more willing to explore the implications of our general, if loose, commitment to the value of freedom of speech.

This book is as much concerned to discuss the legal questions in the context of fundamental free speech principles, as it is to give a detailed account of the law in the various jurisdictions. A comprehensive treatment would in any case require a much longer treatise. Although I have written from a British standpoint, discussion of the United States case law dominates some of the chapters. This is inevitable in view of the wealth of material in this jurisdiction; the American courts have been exploring the meaning and scope of the First Amendment for most of this century. The decisions of the European Commission and Court of Human Rights, of increasing importance for the protection of fundamental freedoms in this country, have also been fully treated where relevant. The discussion of German case law is less comprehensive, except in one or two areas such as libel law where the comparisons with the British and American positions are particularly striking.

I am indebted to many people for their comments on various chapters of the book: David Bentley, Paul Davies, John Finnis, John Gray, Christopher McCrudden, Geoffrey Marshall, Gillian Peele, Jack Pole, Martin Shapiro, Brian Simpson, and Anthony Thornton. Their suggestions were most valuable, but of course I am entirely responsible for any errors of law or fact, omissions and idiosyncrasies that remain. I have also been stimulated by the thoughts of many graduate students during the seminars on free speech that I have held in Oxford. I would like to thank Nerys Jefford for her help in researching and classifying Germany decisions. Finally I am indebted to Audrey Hiscock, who with good humour typed the manuscript at various stages.

It is perhaps not essential for a book of this character to be as up to date as possible. But I have endeavoured to take account of materials available in the Bodleian Library at the end of October 1984. This date, of course, preceded by several months the acquittal of Clive Ponting on a charge under section 2 of the Official Secrets Act 1911 and the ban imposed by the IBA (a prior restraint) on the showing of a programme about MI5 surveillance. I regret my inability to discuss these developments, but it is some compensation that the issues covered in this book have been shown so dramatically to be of great political moment.

April 1985   ERIC BARENDT

Contents

A Note on Abbreviations

MOST of the abbreviations used in the notes in this book will be familiar to British and American readers. References to German and European Convention decisions may need some explanation, so a short list of the most common abbreviations is appended.

British readers may at first find the frequent references in the text to 'the Court' puzzling. This is standard shorthand in American legal writing for 'The United States Supreme Court', and it is so convenient that it is used frequently in this book. In some cases another court may be the object of the reference, but this is (I hope) always clear in the context.

German abbreviations

BVerfGE   Entscheidungen des Bundesverfaßungsgerichts (Decisions of the German Constitutional Court).

BVerwGE   Entscheidungen des Bundesverwaltungsgerichts (Decisions of the German Administrative Court).

BGBl.   Bundesgesetzblatt (Statute-book).

European Convention abbreviations

Coll. Dec.   Collected Decisions of the Commission, vols. 1–46 (1960–74).

D. & R.   Decisions and Reports of the Commission (1975–).

EHRR   European Human Rights Reports (selected decisions of the European Court and the European Commission of Human Rights).

Table of British Cases

Table of United States Cases

Table of German Cases

Principal References are shown in bold type

Constitutional Court

Table of Decisions of the European Commission and Court of Human Rights

Principal References are shown in bold type

Miscellaneous Cases from other Jurisdictions

I
Why Protect Free Speech?

1. INTRODUCTION

WRITTEN Constitutions and Bills of Rights invariably protect freedom of speech as one of the fundamental liberties guaranteed against state suppression. Even in Britain where such liberties lack constitutional protection, politicians and law reformers regard freedom of expression as a basic value which should always be respected. It is not an absolute right, unless of course the speech is made in the course of Parliamentary proceedings; but powerful reasons are generally required before its restriction by legislation is accepted as justified.[1] There is probably in fact widespread public support for the free speech principle, the coherence of which has been debated by political philosophers in the last two or three hundred years: that is, the principle that speech, even speech which causes some measure of harm to the public, is entitled to a special degree of immunity from government restraint not afforded to conduct which might cause a similar amount of damage.[2] Under this rule, for example, speech which offends the majority of people could not legitimately be prohibited, while there would be no comparable inhibition in restraining public conduct—love-making or leaving litter in Hyde Park—which has similar offensive characteristics.

Public political debate in Britain and other Western democracies about free speech is now more concerned with its scope and meaning than with the merits of the general principle. One question, for instance, is whether pornography qualifies as 'speech' for the purposes of the presumption against state control. Another issue, frequently raised by Labour politicians in Britain, is whether commitment to freedom of speech requires the provision of some right of

---

[1] For discussions of principle in Britain, see the Williams Committee Report on Obscenity (1979), Cmnd. 7772, paras. 5.15–5.25, and Law Commission Working Paper no. 84, 'Criminal Libel', para. 7.7.

[2] See F. Schauer, *Free Speech: A Philosophical Enquiry* (Cambridge, 1982), ch. 1.

access to the media or a right to reply to hostile articles in the press. These questions become legal problems in jurisdictions like the United States and West Germany where courts are required to uphold freedom of expression against government control. The First Amendment to the United States Constitution provides that 'Congress shall make no law . . . abridging the freedom of speech, or of the press. . . .' The text appears simple, but it is left to the courts to decide what constitutes 'speech' and whether a state statute compelling a newspaper editor to provide a right of reply does or does not 'abridge' the freedom.

A threshold question, to which this chapter is partly addressed, is the extent to which resolution of difficult free speech issues such as these should be influenced by the arguments of political and moral philosophy. In particular, an examination of the theories underlying the free speech principle may suggest solutions to the problems which confront both legislatures and courts. It goes without saying that politicians and governments may choose merely to act on whim or under electoral or party pressure, but surely only the most cynical would deny that arguments of principle do, or should, influence the decision to legislate and the content of the statute-book. It may be a less obvious, however, that judges should concern themselves at all with these philosophical questions, even in jurisdictions where they do have the power to strike down legislation infringing basic rights. The courts' task, it might be said, is to interpret the text, albeit in the light of the constitution as a whole, rather than to indulge in philosophical speculations.

The functions of courts in constitutional cases raises notoriously difficult questions, discussed at length in several recent books.[3] But some indication may be given here of the problems which make it almost impossible to draw a clear line between legal and philosophical (or political) argument for the disposition of such litigation. The literal approach to textual interpretation, of some serviceable use in the construction of detailed statutes, is of little assistance in elucidating the meaning of constitutions. The courts are perhaps limited to the range of meanings which can be supported on a reading of the text—they cannot supply an interpretation which is wholly unwarranted—but the range of possibilities is so broad in most cases that

---

[3] See, for example, in the United States context, J. H. Ely, *Democracy and Distrust* (Harvard, 1980), M. J. Perry, *The Constitution, the Courts, and Human Rights* (Yale, 1982), and P. Bobbitt, *Constitutional Fate* (New York, 1982).

the limitation is of little importance. Thus, Black J., the member of the United States Supreme Court who is most associated with a literal (and, therefore, absolutist) interpretation of the First Amendment still had to decide the meaning of 'speech', a matter on which the Constitution provides no help whatever.[4] Naturally problems are fewer if the free speech clause is more specific, as is Article 5 of the German Basic Law or Article 10 of the European Convention on Human Rights. But the courts' task when construing these provisions remains fundamentally different from that imposed in the process of ordinary statutory interpretation.

An alternative approach, sometimes advocated, is to consider what the framers of the constitution intended. Did the Founding Fathers of the American Constitution, for example, have in mind that only previous restraints, applied before publication, be prohibited or did they also intend the Amendment totally to outlaw penal sanctions for speech and writing?[5] For rather obvious reasons this technique cannot really be sustained. It is rarely clear what the drafters of a constitution did intend. Preparatory documents frequently evidence conflicting views and aspirations, difficulties which are even more manifest in the case of international conventions. Even when it is possible to infer a particular intent, it should not necessarily be decisive for litigation arising some decades or centuries after the framing of the constitution. Political and social circumstances will have changed so radically that it would be absurd to be limited to the particular conceptions of a freedom entertained by the members of a constitutional assembly. How much guidance can be obtained, for example, on the issue whether freedom of speech entails a legal right of access to appear on the media by examining the views of delegates to the 1787 Philadelphia Convention?

Partly because of these difficulties, it has been urged that constitutional texts should be viewed as embodying moral and political *concepts* rather than specific *conceptions*.[6] On this approach a constitutional provision may reflect commitment to a particular concept of a freedom, such as freedom of speech, which may best be elucidated by examination of the political reasons justifying the protection of that freedom and an appreciation of its significance in the constitution as a

---

[4] This problem is the subject of ch. II.
[5] See D. S. Brogen, 'The Origins of Freedoms of Speech and the Press' (1983) 42 *Maryland LR* 429, 439–44.
[6] R. M. Dworkin, *Taking Rights Seriously* (London, 1977), 132–7.

whole. Moreover, underlying the specific freedoms set out in a Bill of Rights, there may be even broader concepts concerning immutable basic human rights—the rights to equality of concern, dignity, life, and so on. Against this background, the scope of the particular freedom and its meaning in a specific context may be determined through rational argument, more akin to philosophical reasoning than to conventional legal techniques such as the drawing of inferences from precedents. To some extent, then, evidence about the general ideas originally conceived as justifying a particular constitutional provision may be of some help in its interpretation. These ideas are likely to be of a loose, open-ended character, very different from the detailed aims which characterize much modern social legislation. Philosophical and political arguments about the justifications for a free speech principle are, therefore, on this approach highly relevant to constitutional interpretation, in so far as they assist in elucidation of the concept incorporated in the text.

This is, however, not to suggest that judges ought to resolve hard constitutional cases on the basis of abstract philosophical argument. For a start, the constitution may be designed to reflect one particular philosophical or moral perspective rather than another. For example, the protection of freedom of expression in most modern Constitutions is probably more closely connected with a view about the desirability of an informed electorate than it is with the nineteenth-century liberal theories concerning the discovery of truth. So, not all arguments for a free speech principle may be equally relevant, or of equal weight in a particular context. This conclusion may emerge more clearly from a look at the overall structure of the constitution than from surmises about the intentions of the framers and the philosophical concepts which influenced them. Let us consider a hypothetical constitution, in which the right to freedom of speech is set out in a general chapter entitled 'Political Freedoms', and in conjunction with the right to vote, the freedom to form political parties, and rights of access to government information. In that case, it would be hard to deny that freedom of expression is only concerned with political speech, and that consequently commercial speech and obscenity are not covered. The point may also be illustrated by reference to the German Basic Law. The Constitutional Court has to some extent been influenced in its interpretation of Article 5 by the specific protection of political parties in Article 21 of the *Grundgesetz*, and so has afforded political speech a more significant degree of immunity from government regulation than that it has recognized for other types of communication.[7]

There is then a difference between the purely philosophical arguments which assert or deny the case for a free speech principle, and the more specific arguments which may be relevant in the context of constitutional litigation. Judicial consideration of the former must be tempered by the constraints imposed by the text, and must further be substantially moulded by the concepts adopted by the framers of the constitution as revealed in its general structure. Constitutional interpretation can be seen, therefore, as a subtle process in which abstract arguments of principle mingle with historical and institutional factors. The respective weight of all these considerations will naturally vary from one constitution to another. The more specific the legal text and the more detailed and complex the constitution is as a whole, the greater will be the role played by textual and 'structural' arguments.[8] The German Basic Law and the European Convention on Human Rights offer more guidance to the courts than does the United States Bill of Rights, and consequently they leave less room for the abstract contentions of political philosophy.

Some consequences flow from this difference between political theorizing about freedom of speech and constitutional adjudication in this area. Political philosophers sometimes regard the liberty as a *natural right* of individuals as against the state, which must be recognized whether or not, either in general or in particular cases, it is for the benefit of society as a whole. The right is on some versions of this approach regarded as integrally connected with fundamental concepts of human dignity and the right of each person to equal respect and concern.[9] Other arguments for a free speech principle are more obviously utilitarian in spirit. This seems particularly true both of Mill's argument from truth and the argument for the importance of free speech to a democracy. Courts are only secondarily concerned with this dispute. It could indeed be said that they are simply concerned to determine whether on the interpretation of the free speech provision, the individual has a legal right (or immunity), and that this will generally be a conclusion dependent on the weighing or

[7] See 61 BVerfGE 1, 9–11 (1982).

[8] The use of 'structural' arguments to elucidate the meaning of constitutional texts is discussed by Bobbitt *Constitutional Fate*, ch. 6.

[9] Dworkin, *Taking Rights Seriously*, 266–78. Also see his essay, 'Liberalism', in *Public and Private Morality*, ed. S. Hampshire (Cambridge, 1978).

balancing of the various public interests, including the claims of free speech. That, however, is too simple an account. The court will also have initially to determine whether the provision is to be read as recognizing some right to free speech, and whether that right is absolute, at least against public policy considerations; and if it is not, it must then assess the general circumstances in which it may be limited. Again, arguments of abstract political philosophy must be tempered by textual and structural constraints. For judges the question is not whether freedom of speech is in principle a matter of rights or of utility, but what theory or view of the matter is taken by the constitution, as revealed by its text, history, and legal precedent. Article 10 of the European Convention provides that 'Everyone has the right to freedom of expression', but the European Court may not treat this as recognizing the strong right to free speech claimed by some theorists in view of the many exceptions and reservations to the freedom permitted by Article 10(2).

Further, the free speech principle must for philosophers be at some level an independent political principle, distinguishable from general libertarian claims. Speech is entitled to (at least) a degree of immunity from government regulation because of some special quality or value to be attributed to communication and expression. (These terms, 'speech', 'expression', and 'communication', are used interchangeably throughout this book, unless the context indicates otherwise.) Although the case for free speech protection may be associated with, or rest on, more fundamental claims about human dignity or opportunities for self-fulfilment and development, the principle is only coherent to the extent that speech can be distinguished from other areas of human conduct and activity. And further a right to free speech must be isolated from other fundamental liberties that could be, and sometimes are, incorporated in a written constitution, for instance, rights to privacy or to choose a sexual life-style, or property rights. When constitutions are drawn up, the framers presumably have some intuitive ideas about which freedoms should be independently covered and at this stage theoretical arguments perhaps play some part, though they may be outweighed by political considerations and the practical requirements of the draftsman. However, at the stage of constitutional interpretation by the courts, the independence of the free speech principle may be considerably qualified. First, the free speech provision may be so drafted that rights (for example, to attend trials or obtain information), which could not easily be supported by reference to a free speech principle on purely theoretical arguments, are expressly or implicitly covered by it. And secondly, the courts may be inclined on structural grounds to interpret the clause more broadly than the free speech principle would warrant, because it is associated with provisions guaranteeing other, loosely related freedoms. Courts may, for instance treat some forms of street protest as 'speech' for constitutional purposes, when the freedom of expression provision or other articles of the constitution refer to rights of assembly or the right to petition the government.[10] Such decisions might not be warranted by reference to an abstract free speech principle, but this would not be a decisive objection to them.

With these reservations, considerable scope remains for the consideration by the courts of theoretical philosophical issues in free speech cases. As the rest of this chapter will show, the different justifications urged for a free speech principle carry divergent implications for the scope of legal protection. One theory, for example, may suggest it is the right of the speaker or publisher which is paramount, while others may place more emphasis on the interests of the recipient or the public interest in open communication. If the constitutional text does not make plain that both speaker's and recipient's rights are covered, the court must decide for itself whose interests are to be recognized or given priority, a determination which may on occasion be decisive for the disposition of the litigation.[11]

Moreover, the jurisprudence of the courts may shed considerable light on the coherence and contemporary relevance of the competing free speech theories. For instance, a weakness of Mill's argument from truth may be the difficulty with which it is applied to varieties of communication, e.g. some types of sexually explicit material, which are usually characterized as 'speech' and typically enjoy a measure of constitutional protection. Legal experience may reinforce (or negative) more abstract intellectual criticism. But as the emphasis of this book is on the legal interpretation of free speech provisions and principles, there is room for only a short and inevitably over-simplified account of three prominent free speech theories. After considering these, I discuss the extent to which recognition of the

---

[10] The First Amendment covers all these rights, while in the West German Basic Law there is separate provision for freedom of assembly (art. 8) and for the right of petition (art. 17).

[11] See the discussion in ch. III on the question whether free speech provisions embrace a right to acquire information from an unwilling 'speaker'.

separate speaker, audience, and public interests may affect our understanding of freedom of speech. The last part of the chapter sets out the principal legal provisions discussed in the book, relating them to some of the theoretical issues considered earlier.

2. THREE FREE SPEECH THEORIES

(i) Mill's argument from truth

Historically the most durable argument for a free speech principle has been based on the importance of open discussion to the discovery of truth. If restrictions on speech are tolerated, society may prevent the ascertainment and publication of true facts and accurate judgments. The case is particularly associated with John Stuart Mill, but it was also made two centuries earlier by Milton, and it has played some part in the theorizing of American judges.[12] There are a number of versions of the argument. Truth may be regarded as an autonomous and fundamental good, or its value may be supported by utilitarian considerations about the development of society. Mill's theory appears to rest on the assumption that the truth of certain beliefs can be determined in the long run, but before his thesis is considered an alternative view based on the opposite assumption should be mentioned.

This approach, associated with the famous judgment of Holmes J. in *Abrams* v. *US*, asserts that all truths are relative and they can only be judged 'in the competition of the market'.[13] It would be arrogant for government to interfere in this process, because it could only properly do so on the assumption that absolute truths can be determined. Holmes J. felt that the United States Constitution shared this sceptical and gloomy conclusion. That may be the case, though no evidence was given to support this view of the framers' intentions. In any event this version of the 'truth' argument rests on somewhat shaky grounds. If it can never be properly claimed that one proposition is stronger than another, the notion of 'truth' becomes more or less empty. And why should society leave the acceptability of various political or moral arguments to be judged purely through unregulated competition? It is at least just as

---

[12] See J. S. Mill, *On Liberty* (Everyman edn., 1972), ch. II; J. Milton, *Areopagitica: A Speech for the Liberty of Unlicensed Printing* (1644; in *Prose Writings*, Everyman edn., 1958). For relevant American judgments, in addition to that of Holmes J. in the *Abrams* case, see Brandeis J. in *Whitney* v. *California* 274 US 357, 375–8 (1927), and Frankfurter J. in *Kovacs* v. *Cooper* 336 US 77, 95–7 (1949).

[13] 250 US 616, 630–1 (1919).

likely, perhaps more probable, that the utility or value, however these concepts are interpreted, of particular contributions to public discussion can best be assessed by the elected representatives of the public, who could then choose which ones to permit and which it was wisest to prohibit or restrict. Preference for the market-place, as opposed to governmental regulation, in this context can be justified on many grounds, for example, suspicion of government or the harm and outrage felt by individuals when their speech is suppressed; but such a choice seems wholly unrelated to Holmes J.'s eccentric views on the impossibility of discovering truth.[14]

The more usual assumption behind this rationale for the free speech principle is that it is generally possible to distinguish between truth and falsehood, or at least between good and bad claims, even though certainty can rarely, if ever, be attained. Mill puts forward different contentions, dependent on whether the expression which might be suppressed is possibly true or (almost certainly) false. Prohibition of the former category of speech is undesirable because it entails an unwarranted 'assumption of infallibility' on the part of the state. Government naturally acts on its view of what is right when it proscribes certain conduct, for example, unfair business practices and anti-competition agreements, but (Mill argues) it is only because the opponents of such measures are free to challenge their wisdom that the government can ever be confident that its policies are right and that it is appropriate to legislate.[15] Alternatively, speech may be suppressed because it is objectively false. It is still wrong to take this step since people holding true beliefs will no longer be challenged and forced to defend their views. They 'ought to be moved by the consideration that, however true it may be, if it is not fully, frequently, and fearlessly discussed, it will be held as a dead dogma, not a living truth'.[16]

The criticisms of Mill's theory are too familiar to warrant a full statement here. His argument first assumes that in all circumstances (short of an imminent emergency) the publication of a possibly true statement is the highest public good. But there are many situations where legal systems may prefer to protect other values. For example, it is conceivably true that some races are intellectually superior to others. Yet British legislation outlaws the publication of insulting speech likely to

---

[14] See F. Schauer, *Free Speech* ch. 4, especially 19–21.
[15] Mill, *On Liberty*, 81.
[16] Ibid., 95. The US Supreme Court accepted this point in *New York Times* v. *Sullivan* 376 US 254 (1964).

cause racial hatred, a prohibition which might well cover such pseudo-scientific statements.[17] A society is arguably entitled to take the view that for the foreseeable future racial harmony is such an important goal that an absolute tolerance of free speech is too great a luxury. Mill's argument that the utility of an opinion cannot be divorced from its truth is unpersuasive; it is perfectly plausible to hold that the publication of some (possibly true) propositions should be banned, because their dissemination is inimical to the welfare of society. Moreover, the interests of truth are to some extent protected if the wisdom of the ban can be freely debated.[18] A legal system may, for instance, protect privacy against the disclosure of true facts, while permitting the press to campaign against the utility of this restraint on free speech.

A related criticism is that Mill overvalued intellectual discussion, and the need for all individuals to be able to debate public affairs vigorously. This feature emerges most clearly in his claim that it would be wrong to prohibit even false speech, because in the absence of opposition the ability to defend true and valuable beliefs will decline. This may be correct, but a government worried that inflammatory speech may provoke disorder is surely entitled to elevate immediate public order considerations over the long-term intellectual development of the man on the Clapham omnibus. At any rate the risk of immediate damage which may occur from the acceptance of falsehood should be balanced against the long-term benefits of constant, uninhibited debate.

One question which seems to have been relatively little explored in discussion of Mill's theory is whether his argument applies equally to all types of expression, and in particular whether a distinction should be drawn between on the one hand the disclosure of, or allegations about, facts and on the other the expression of opinion. The coherence of this distinction is a matter of both philosophical and constitutional debate, and the theme is touched on frequently in this book.[19] Mill clearly considered the argument from truth, or at least that aspect of it concerned to justify the tolerance of false opinion, to be more relevant to discussion of political, moral, and social affairs than to mathematical or scientific propositions.[20] His treatment does not explicitly refer to other

[17] See below, ch. V, s. 4.
[18] C. L. Ten, *Mill on Liberty* (Oxford, 1980), 131–2, and see also H. J. McLoskey, 'Liberty of Expression—Its Grounds and Limits' (1970) 13 *Inquiry* 219, 226–7, cf. D. H. Monro, ibid., 238, 252–3.
[19] See e.g. p. 17 below (in the context of the argument from self-fulfilment), pp. 57–8 (commercial speech), and pp. 178–9 (libel).
[20] Mill, *On Liberty*, 96.

modes of expression, such as commercial advertising or pornography, which may consist of both information and ideology or fit into neither category.

There is perhaps something paradoxical about Mill's thesis. The argument for a free speech principle from truth is said to be particularly applicable to types of expression, which can only rarely, if ever, establish truths with the same degree of assurance that obtains in mathematics or the natural sciences. 'Truth', of course, is not to be equated with 'certainty', and the fact that there are better and worse arguments in political and moral discourse is enough to substantiate Mill's conclusion that the prohibition of such discussion by the government is (at least generally) wrong on the 'truth argument'. Less clear is the status of speech which does not assert any coherent proposition or make a claim which could ever be objectively tested. Personal abuse, some emotive political speech (perhaps the 'Fuck the Draft' slogan upheld as constitutionally protected speech in *Cohen* v. *California*)[21] and pornography all appear to fall outside the categories of expression which Mill had in mind when he formulated the argument from truth. Yet the legal systems we are considering protect these modes of expression to a certain extent.[22] This may either reflect a judicial view that the free speech provision is to be construed in the context of rationales other than the truth justification, or alternatively a reluctance to attempt to segregate rational discourse, which might contain some element of truth, from purely emotive expression. In any event, Mill's theory is difficult to apply to types of expression where it seems absurd even to look for an element of truth, or to propositions which are quite obviously factually false, like 'the moon is made of green cheese'.

A much more important question is how relevant the argument from truth is to the publication of government secrets or confidential commercial information. Both United States and German law, as well as less surprisingly British law, tolerate numerous restrictions on the disclosure of such information. In some cases even prior restraints are countenanced, with the result that truthful information never reaches the general public at all.[23] Yet a serious commitment to Mill's arguments would seem to entail a virtual absence of restraints (prior or penal) in these cases. The fact that even the most liberal democracies here adopt compromise solutions can be explained in a number of ways. Various

---

[21] 403 US 15 (1971).
[22] See chs. VII (public order) and IX (obscenity).
[23] See ch. IV (prior restraints).

important interests, for example, in state security, the maintenance of confidence between members of a government and its civil servants, or the desire to protect the fruits of industrial and commercial research, outweigh the interest in the free distribution of even accurate information.[24] This balancing process may alternatively indicate that the relevant free speech provisions and principles are shaped by rationales other than Mill's argument from truth. Finally, it may be that he did not intend his argument to apply to most assertions of fact, as opposed to expressions of opinion.

Some points can be made in support of this last conclusion. A government which suppresses or restricts the publication of facts may well be over-secretive, and on other free speech arguments such control might be wrong and unconstitutional. It is, however, not necessarily acting on 'an assumption of infallibility'. The disclosure of information, say, by a civil servant to a newspaper, is not outlawed because it is thought, rightly or wrongly, to be false, but because it is, on the contrary, accurate; it reveals facts which may be regarded as in some sense the government's own property, or trade secrets belonging to a particular industry. Mill's case can only be made relevant if the accurate communication is suppressed on the ground that it contributes to what is thought to be a generally false campaign or set of communications. This may partly explain incidentally why courts are rightly more reluctant to uphold restrictions imposed by government on the disclosure of state 'secrets' than they are to protect private people and industry in comparable circumstances.[25] Often revelation of the former is prevented purely to deter effective anti-government speech. No equivalent aims lie behind the rules protecting commercial secrets or private information. The argument about the discovery of truth would justify recognition of unlimited rights to acquire such knowledge only if it were reformulated in terms of some right of everyone to an equal opportunity to use every type of information for his chosen purposes. This would be a radical distortion of Mill's case that freedom of discussion is to be protected because it is conducive to social progress.

Mill's argument then applies most clearly to speech stating beliefs and theories about political, moral, aesthetic, and social matters. The position

---

[24] The weighing of interests may be required explicitly or implicitly by the constitutional text, or alternatively (as in the United States) may be the result of judge-made doctrines: see the last section of this chapter.

[25] For example, see the attention paid to free speech in *Att.-Gen.* v. *Jonathan Cape* Ltd [1976] QB 752, and in the Australian case, *Commonwealth of Australia* v. *John Fairfax & Sons Ltd* (1980) 32 ALR 485, discussed further below, ch. IV, s. 3.

within his theory of factual propositions and scientific or mathematical formulae is less well established. However, this reservation does not seem to affect the judicial interpretation of free speech provisions. Courts are influenced by the other justifications for a free speech principle, especially the argument from its importance in a democracy, which do apply to much factual information. Moreover, some constitutions, such as the German Basic Law, and the European Convention explicitly cover the right to receive (and perhaps also impart) information, in addition to ideas.[26]

Even in those areas, such as political and moral discourse, where the search for truth is most rigorous and constant, there is one further difficulty in Mill's argument. He assumes that truth is more likely to emerge from uninhibited discussion than from the exercise of freedom subject to occasional government restraint or regulation. Experience shows that this is too optimistic. It seems facile to argue that in all circumstances the best remedy against evil speech will be more or better speech. Admittedly even elected governments are not always to be trusted to discriminate between good and bad speech, or to determine that some intemperate and inflammatory discourse makes no attempt to present a truth. Judicial reluctance to tolerate such categorizations shows itself in many ways: some false speech may be permitted, as long as it is not malicious, so that genuine attempts to contribute to public discussion are not inhibited, and secondly, some abusive speech without any truth-content may be allowed.[27] These decisions, however, owe far more to the courts' fear of unreasonable suppression rather than a simple application of the argument from truth.[28]

Some regulation of the free speech market-place must surely be conceded, if any expression is to be communicated effectively. The discovery of truth does require some minimal government intervention, if only to prevent simultaneous speech—on the streets, on airwaves, at public meetings. Everyone admits this.[29] It is much more controversial

[26] Basic Law, art. 5(1); European Convention on Human Rights, art. 10(1), both of which are set out in full in the last section of this chapter.

[27] These principles underly the leading United States cases, *New York Times* v. *Sullivan* 376 US 255 (1964), affording a First Amendment immunity for non-malicious defamation of public officials, and *Cohen* v. *California* 403 US 15 (1971) holding 'offensive' speech constitutionally protected.

[28] See Schauer, *Free Speech* ch. 6, and an article by the same author, 'Social Foundations of the Law of Defamation: A Comparative Analysis' (1980) 1 *Jo. Media Law and Practice* 3.

[29] Especially, for example, A. Meiklejohn, a leading commentator on the First Amendment, who rules out restrictions on the content of speech: his views are summarized later in this chapter. For a more enthusiastic defence of governmental regulatory powers, see J. Tussman, *Government and the Mind* (New York, 1977).

whether a state should be free to choose among types of speech and draw distinctions with regard to their content. Suppose a state honestly (and on some sound sociological evidence) decides severely to restrict the dissemination of pornography because it thinks its widespread consumption has deterred political discourse and the discovery for that society of important truths. This course seems objectionable, though much less so than a prohibition of extreme political views within the class of public affairs discussion. Yet it is not easy to ground objections to such prohibitions on Mill's thesis, unless the search for truth is viewed purely in terms of the market-place, the sceptical perspective of Holmes J. In fact the United States Supreme Court has—until one or two recent decisions—set its face firmly against contents-based restrictions on speech, even in borderline areas such as obscenity.[30] Its case-law shows perhaps that the argument from the importance of truth, as Mill presented it, has played a relatively minor role in First Amendment theory. However, Mill's thesis does shed some light on distinctions often drawn by legislation and judicial decision: between comment and fact, between contentions which may possibly be true and those which are definitely false or which have no truth-value whatsoever, and between political and moral discourse on the one hand and scientific propositions on the other.

(ii) Free speech as an aspect of self-fulfilment

A second major theory of free speech sees it as an integral aspect of each individual's right to self-development and fulfilment. Restrictions on what a man is allowed to say and write, or (on some formulations of the theory) to hear or read, inhibit the growth of his personality. People will not be able to develop intellectually and spiritually, unless they are free to formulate their beliefs and political attitudes through public discussion, and in response to the criticisms of others. The argument asserts that there is an individual right to freedom of speech, even though its exercise may be inimical to the welfare and development of society. Unlike the theories which relate free discussion to the discovery of truth or to the maintenance of a democracy, this rationale is not really utilitarian in form—though doubtless it might be defended in utilitarian terms. It is also debatable whether the theory treats freedom of speech as an independent or intrinsic good, or as somehow related to more fundmental concepts of human dignity.[31] But such controversy is irrelevant to

---

[30] See chs. V (political speech) and IX (obscenity).
[31] Schauer, *Free Speech*, chs. 4 and 5: the discussion here is much indebted to his book.

constitutional and legal adjudication. The provision of a right to free speech in a constitution suggests strongly that the freedom is specially valued, and in one way set apart from other liberties which might equally be thought crucial to personal development; these also might, of course, be constitutionally guaranteed, as, for example, are the rights to privacy and family life in the European Convention on Human Rights.[32]

Nevertheless, the relationship of freedom of speech to other liberties does raise both philosophical and legal difficulties. These become particularly acute if the right to free speech is justified by reference to arguments about the development of the individual personality. In terms of abstract moral theory, one relevant question is: why is free speech particularly important to a person's self-fulfilment? It is far from clear that unlimited free speech is necessarily conducive to personal happiness or that it satisfies more basic human needs and wants than, say, adequate housing and education. Yet, unless some reasons can be given for treating expression as particularly significant, the case for a free speech principle becomes hard to distinguish from general libertarian claims. Perhaps there is something uniquely valuable in intellectual self-development, but this assumption would support the recognition of rights to education and free foreign travel as much as the right to free speech.[33] On the other hand, there are understandable practical reasons why this latter right should be singled out for constitutional protection and distinguished from these other freedoms similarly related to intellectual and moral growth. Freedom of speech is primarily a liberty against the state, or a 'negative freedom', and largely for this reason is more capable of judicial interpretation and enforcement than positive rights to, say, an adequate education. There are legitimate doubts on the competence of courts to fashion appropriate remedies to secure such social rights, while free speech can to a considerable extent be secured by the restrictive interpretation or annulment of laws infringing the freedom.[34] These ideas are further developed in Chapter III; here, it is enough to point out that there is a respectable practical case for giving special constitutional protection to free speech because of its role in encouraging intellectual maturity for individuals, whatever the philosophical weaknesses of the argument.

---

[32] Under art. 8(1).

[33] Schauer, *Free Speech*, 53–8.

[34] See D. L. Horowitz, *The Court and Social Policy* (Brookings Institution, 1977). Of course, a free speech clause may be interpreted to confer positive claim-rights to information or to the use of facilities for speech: see the discussion in ch. III.

The problems which confront the courts in this context are rather different. Assuming that the 'background' right to self-fulfilment is a relevant justification for the particular constitutional provision they are required to interpret, difficulties will occur in distinguishing between genuine assertions of a right to free speech and claims to other freedoms, which may equally be supported by reference to this background right. Problems are most acute in determining the meaning of 'speech', a topic considered in the next chapter.[35] Are, for instance, claims to be free to advertise goods and services or to make unlimited donations to political campaign funds really free speech claims or only assertions of economic or associational freedoms? At first glance, they might appear to be supported by arguments about self-fulfilment at least in a material sense, but on closer inspection they surely have very little connection with the particular view of intellectual and moral development underlying a rights-based view of free speech. Similar issues arise in deciding whether pornography qualifies as 'speech' for the purposes of the First Amendment or other comparable free speech provision. Claims for constitutional protection which rest on the widespread demand for such material and the role it plays in satisfying sexual curiosity appear in essence to be grounded on a general freedom to moral autonomy, also connected with the background right to personal development, but perhaps without much relevance to free speech arguments.[36]

These problems are not removed if, as argued by Professor Dworkin, the case for free speech protection is grounded on fundamental background rights to human dignity and to equality of concern and respect.[37] Again, this does not appear to provide any clear basis for distinguishing a free speech principle from general libertarian claims concerning, say, the choice of a dress or sexual life-style which might be favoured by individuals. Moreover, unlimited speech may well be contrary to a respect for human dignity. The restrictions imposed by libel and obscenity laws can easily be justified by reference to this value. Indeed, the German Constitutional Court in one of its most important rulings on Article 5 of the Basic Law has held that there was no right to publish a satirical novel defaming a dead person, because artistic freedom was to be

---

[35] See in particular pp. 51 and 56.

[36] It is interesting that some critics now argue for a right to read pornography on the basis of broad freedoms to moral independence and personal choice: see, e.g., R. M. Dworkin, 'Is there a Right to Pornography?' (1981) 1 *Oxford Jo. of Legal Studies* 177, and L. H. Tribe, *American Constitutional Law* (New York, 1978), 905–10.

[37] Dworkin, *Taking Rights Seriously*, 266–78, 364–8.

interpreted in the light of the inviolable 'dignity of man', guaranteed by Article 1.[38]

Quite apart from these criticisms levelled at the intellectual coherence of the theory, there are some grounds for doubting its significance in the development of relevant legal principles. On the versions of the theory considered up to this point, it would be hard to justify the application of the free speech principle to the disclosure of *information*, in contradistinction to the dissemination of *ideas* and *opinions*. This point is even more apparent if emphasis is placed on the rights or interests of the speaker. While an unlimited, or at least very wide, freedom to communicate one's own views may be considered an integral aspect of self-development or human dignity, it is surely far-fetched to make the same claim for news and information, unless perhaps the communicator has assembled or is in some way responsible for it. But the law frequently brings such factual material under a free speech principle (or constitutional provision). Such coverage is better explained under a theory, like the argument from democracy, which emphasizes the interests of the recipients of communications. Similarly the extension of free speech rights to legal persons, such as corporations, makes little sense in terms of self-fulfilment theories, and the same can be said of the application of the principle to the press and other media.[39] These reservations do not, however, apply to the variant of this argument put forward by Thomas Scanlon.

His thesis proceeds from the premiss, 'that the powers of a state are limited to those that citizens could recognize while still regarding themselves as equal, autonomous, rational agents'.[40] A person is only autonomous if he is free to weigh for himself the arguments for various courses of action that others may wish to put before him. The government, Scanlon asserts, is therefore not entitled to suppress speech on the grounds either that its audience will form harmful beliefs or that it may indulge in harmful acts as a result of these beliefs. The first limb of this conclusion is very similar to that reached by J. S. Mill; Scanlon indeed refers to his own thesis as 'the Millian Principle', though unlike the

---

[38] *Mephisto* case, 30 BVerfGE 173 (1971), discussed in ch. VI, s. 2.

[39] Under this theory it is also hard to justify the protection of 'proxy' speech, where the expenditure of funds collected from a mass of individuals is treated as the speech of those individuals, despite the fact they play no part in drafting any communication: see *Common Cause* v. *Schmitt* 512 F. Supp. 489 (1980), and L. A. Powe, 'Mass Speech and the Newer First Amendment' [1982] *Sup. Ct. Rev.* 243.

[40] 'A Theory of Freedom of Expression' (1972) 1 *Phil. and Public Affairs* 204, reprinted in *The Philosophy of Law*, ed. R. M. Dworkin (Oxford, 1977), 153, 162.

earlier argument it does not rest on any assumption that truth will emerge from open discussion. Another difference from Mill's theory is that the thesis is clearly in its effect rights-based rather than consequentialist. The individual has a right to hear views and to consider acting on them, even though this process will damage society—though Scanlon does concede that some limits may be imposed during times of extreme emergency. On the other hand, unlike other versions of the self-fulfilment case, it focuses on the rights or interests of the recipients of speech. One other point is worth noting. Scanlon emphasizes that the Millian Principle does not exhaust the arguments for freedom of expression; other theories might, for example, justify a wide right of access to the means of expression. His case is simply that under the Principle the government is unable to use certain grounds for limiting speech.

Compared with some other free speech theories, this argument provides a relatively coherent explanation of much judicial interpretation of free expression provisions. It should be noted incidentally that it is not based on the history and structure of the United States Constitution, and so it may shed light on any free speech clause in any constitution. One important point is that the argument is not limited to political speech, but applies to all speech (or expressive conduct) which provides the audience with information and opinion relevant to the formation of its own beliefs. This is reflected in the case-law of all the jurisdictions we are considering; although political speech may be accorded some special degree of protection, artistic and moral discourse, and to some extent commercial speech, are also covered. A concern with the legitimacy of the government's reasons for restricting speech can be found in much American case-law; measures aimed at the content of particular ideas or discriminating between varieties of political and social communication are carefully scrutinized.[41] Scanlon's theory also distinguishes between the communication of information relevant to the development of political and moral beliefs (to be protected against regulation) and the revelation of technical information which merely provides the audience with the means to acomplish harmful acts, e.g. military and scientific secrets.[42] This distinction may have some value in explaining the low degree of

[41] Tribe, *American Constitutional Law*, 580–4. But the Court does increasingly draw contents-related distinctions, e.g. between political and commercial speech, and between rational and emotive speech, to determine the extent of protection afforded by the First Amendment; see F. Schauer, 'Codifying the First Amendment: New York v. Ferber [1982] *Sup. Ct. Rev.* 285, 299–317.

[42] T. Scanlon, 'A Theory of Freedom of Expression', in *The Philosophy of Law* (ed. R. M. Dworkin), 159–60.

protection afforded scientific and commercial speech. Finally, the exceptions and qualifications implicit in the theory—that full free speech
protection lapses in times of emergency or when the audience lacks time
for rational reflection on the message communicated—offer some insight
into the rationales for the limits imposed on political speech, particularly
on public order grounds.

The theory has been criticized, largely because of the weaknesses of
the notion of personal autonomy which lies at its root.[43] Moreover,
Scanlon himself has reconsidered its soundness. In a more recent article
he has doubted whether the audience's interest in having a good
environment for the formation of its attitudes really justifies the broad
autonomy principle.[44] Some restrictions on free speech, for example, on
saturation advertising by a candidate for office, could be justified in order
to foster a climate for rational thought by the public. In some circumstances, Scanlon now argues, speech may legitimately be restricted on
paternalistic grounds, while his original theory had left no room for
limitations on, say, cigarette advertising. Perhaps the autonomy thesis
can be rescued by refining what it means to 'restrict' speech, so as to leave
ample scope for broad time, manner, and place regulation whenever this
is in the interests of the audience. A more fundamental objection to the
autonomy thesis is that it does not really do justice to the interests of the
speaker.[45] It seems bizarre, for example, to justify the protection of
unpopular speech (for example, street demonstrations or underground
literature) entirely by reference to the interests of a more or less wholly
unreceptive audience or non-existent readership, and ignore the more
obvious claims of the demonstrator or publisher. And Professor Dworkin
has pointed out that much conventional, political speech hardly offers
fresh information or ideas for the public to reflect on and, therefore,
would not appear to be covered by the Millian Principle.

These qualifications certainly dilute the strength of the Principle as a
background theory, which could invariably be used in the interpretation
of free speech provisions. In any case, it is probably too uncertain in
scope and too difficult to apply in practice. That does not mean, however,
that it may not shed light on some areas of free expression jurisprudence,
as will be seen in later chapters.[46] In contrast, difficulty of comprehension
is not a weakness affecting the final theory of free speech to be

[43] Schauer, *Free Speech*, 67–72.
[44] 'Freedom of Expression and Categories of Expression' (1979) 40 *U. Pittsb. LR* 519.
[45] Dworkin, *The Philosophy of Law*, 14–16.
[46] See below, pp. 160 and 206.

considered: the argument justifying constitutional protection because of its contribution to the democratic process.

(iii) The argument from citizen participation in a democracy

This is probably the most attractive and certainly the most fashionable free speech theory in modern Western democracies. A representative judicial view is this extract from Brandeis J.'s judgment in *Whitney* v. *California*:

Those who won our independence believed that the final end of the State was to make men free to develop their faculties; and that in its government the deliberative forces should prevail over the arbitrary .... They believed that freedom to think as you will and to speak as you think are means indispensable to the discovery and spread of political truth; ... that the greatest menace to freedom is an inert people; that public discussion is a political duty; and that this should be a fundamental principle of American government.[47]

In the United States the argument is now particularly associated with the writings of Alexander Meiklejohn.[48] He thought the primary purpose of the First Amendment is to protect the right of all citizens to understand political issues so as to be able to participate effectively in the working of democracy. The Amendment represented the commitment of the people to representative self-government. In some of its leading judgments the German Constitutional Court has similarly recognized the crucial role of freedom of expression in the formation of public opinion on political questions, and as a result Article 5 has been particularly broadly construed in this area.[49]

The argument is attractive largely because it is easy to understand. To a considerable extent it rests on the values and commitments embodied in the particular constitutional document rather than on the more abstract philosophical theorizing which characterizes the arguments from truth and rights to self-fulfilment. For courts concerned with legal interpretation this feature is an asset, and any conceptual shortcomings of the argument are less troublesome. One or two obvious aspects and consequences are worth noting. It is firmly utilitarian or consequentialist in

---

[47] 274 US 357, 375–8 (1927).

[48] See in particular *Free Speech and its Relation to Self-government*, reprinted in *Political Freedom: The Constitutional Powers of the People* (New York, 1965), and 'The First Amendment is an Absolute' [1961] *Sup. Ct. Rev.* 245.

[49] For example, 12 BVerfGE 113 (1961) (article by a judge replying to criticism of his political attitudes held immune from libel proceedings); 43 BVerfGE 130 (1976) (press article about two politicians similarly immune); 61 BVerfGE 1 (1982) (an exaggerated attack on CSU party held to be protected political speech).

spirit, although in form it may be expressed in terms of citizens' rights. This probably has some awkward repercussions, for the view could be taken that sometimes the values of a democracy, including its long-term commitment to free speech, can best be preserved by the temporary suppression of some speech. Unlike the case for free speech based on its relationship with fundamental human rights, this argument does not appear necessarily to trump counter-arguments that the exercise of free speech may in particular situations be contrary to the public welfare. It is, of course, possible to make further utilitarian arguments in rebuttal of this point: in the long run the maintenance of a confident democracy is best guaranteed by protecting freedom of speech in all (or almost all) circumstances, for temporary regulations may induce political unrest, undermine the acceptability of other laws, and so on.[50] Whether a constitution does adopt the view that restraints are more or less totally undesirable is, of course, one of the hardest free speech questions which courts have to answer.

This difficulty is one aspect of the central weakness of the Meiklejohn position. If the maintenance of democracy is the foundation for free speech, how is one to argue against the regulation or suppression of that speech by the democracy acting through its elected representatives? As Schauer puts it, 'the very notion of popular sovereignty supporting the argument from democracy argues against any limitation on that sovereignty, and thereby argues against recognition of an independent principle of freedom of speech.'[51] Philosophically the case has to be recast if it is to meet this objection; moreover, this entails some borrowing from the other free speech arguments already discussed. It might first be said that society should recognize a free speech principle and accept limits on the rights of the majority, because only through open discussion of forms of government and political ideas will better institutions, legislation, and administration result. This is, of course, a variety of the argument from truth applied to political discourse. Alternatively, the democracy theory could be presented as resting on arguments about the equal rights of all citizens to participate in the processes of government, rights so fundamental that, perhaps like the right to life, they cannot be waived or surrendered to the power of a temporary majority.[52] The case is then difficult to distinguish from the self-fulfilment and dignity arguments canvassed in the previous section.

---

[50] See D. H. Monro, (1970) 13 *Inquiry*, 249–53.

[51] Schauer, *Free Speech*, 41.

[52] Ibid., 41–4.

These problems can up to a point be evaded by constitutional courts. They might assume that the free speech provision is intended to safeguard minorities and to keep alive the possibilities of political change.[53] When the speech clause is combined with explicit protection of freedom of the press, it is particularly tempting to infer that both provisions are designed to protect criticism of the government. But this does not remove all difficulties for the democracy argument. On this approach, only hostile political comment should be covered by the freedom of expression clause. There could be no constitutional objection to the regulation of commercial speech, or censorship of the arts and pornography, as long as people are free to make political arguments against the wisdom of these restraints. Yet the text of both the German Basic Law and the European Convention clearly indicate that some non-political speech is covered by the freedom of expression Articles; and although it has been argued that the purpose of the First Amendment is to guarantee political speech alone, this is not how it is construed these days by the Supreme Court in Washington.[54]

This suggests it would be wrong to see the argument from democracy as a sufficient sole explanation for modern free speech jurisprudence. Too many areas of law—in Britain as well as in countries with constitutional freedoms—show that other justifications for the protection of free speech are regarded as relevant in addition to that singled out by Meiklejohn in the United States. But the argument may still be regarded as the primary justification for free speech protection. In all the jurisdictions considered in this book, political speech is given a special status, a more significant degree of protection than that accorded other types of expression. Moreover, there are other respects in which constitutional provisions and case-law seem more securely linked to this theory than the others. For example, the protection of both opinion and information can be justified on this argument, and it also appears to recognize equally the interests of speaker and recipient. Neither the argument from truth nor that from self-development is so satisfactory in this way. Finally, the theory emphasizes the protection of free speech *against the government*, a feature it shares with Scanlon's autonomy thesis. Constitutions typically protect freedoms against state infringement and less fully against interference by private individuals.[55]

---

[53] This approach has been advocated by J. H. Ely, *Democracy and Distrust*, ch. 5.

[54] See the interpretation of the First Amendment to cover some commercial speech, pp. 58–9 below and to some pornography, pp. 249–54 below.

[55] The complex United States doctrine of 'state action' and the equivalent concept in the European Convention are discussed briefly in ch. III.

My conclusion then is that, although it has to be reformulated to meet some theoretical objections, the argument from democracy has been the most influential theory in the development of twentieth-century free speech law. The fact that to some extent obscenity and commercial speech, in addition to political discourse, are held to be covered by the freedom of expression provision does not disprove this conclusion. The extension of constitutional protection to these types of expression has been—as the discussion in Chapters II and IX shows—extremely controversial. But courts are understandably reluctant to countenance the regulation of some varieties of non-political speech, largely because they distrust the ability of the legislature to distinguish it from genuine discussion of public affairs, or because they fear that the latter will be inhibited by any significant restrictions on freedom of expression. Later chapters will discuss whether categories of 'speech' can be distinguished; distinctions of this sort, or that between 'speech' and 'conduct', are best made by reflecting on the purposes of a free speech principle, and here again the argument from democracy offers the most helpful tool for analysis. Judges are admittedly often influenced in their interpretation of free speech provisions by other rationales for their existence. This is right, for no argument has a monopoly of truth and constitutional provisions are indeed framed in the light of various philosophical perspectives.[56] But case-law shows the central importance of political speech, and this in its turn indicates, it is suggested, the pre-eminence of this third argument for free speech.

3. FREE SPEECH INTERESTS

Another approach to analysis of the justifications for free speech, and determination of its scope, is to explore the interests of the people involved in acts of expression. The discussion may afford philosophical insights, but here also the emphasis is on the relations between these interests and legal rules. Free speech may be looked at from the perspective of the speaker, the audience, or recipient of the publication, and finally, the public's interest. To some extent this section develops points touched on earlier in the chapter and anticipates fuller treatment of some issues in later chapters.

---

[56] See Schauer, *Free Speech*, 85–6, and the same author in [1982] *Sup. Ct. Rev.* 285, 308–17. A similar pluralist approach to the purposes of art. 5 of the Basic Law may be found in a leading commentary: Maunz-Dürig, *Kommentar zum Grundgesetz* (Munich, 1982), paras. 3–12 of the treatment of art. 5.

Intuitively the speaker's interests seem paramount. This appears most obvious if rights to free speech are linked with fundamental rights to self-fulfilment and development, and the speaker as participator in the political process equally clearly has important interests recognized by the argument from democracy. What exactly is his interest? Scanlon has argued that it lies in his ability to bring ideas and propositions to the attention of a wide audience (though not necessarily the widest possible).[57] The formula, however, raises a large number of questions. Should, for example, the interests of a publisher or distributor be equated with those of the speaker and author, as they appear to be here?

Further investigation of the speaker's real motives and purposes is surely necessary to determine whether the interest should properly, or fully, be taken into account in deciding whether free speech protection is appropriate. He may publish something to make a commercial profit, to enhance his own standing, or to contribute to political or social discussion. Obviously speech published with this last aim is the archetypal expression which should be covered by a free speech provision; but there are difficulties in denying a publication any protection, merely because the author was not entirely disinterested. A rigorous examination of motives to exclude speech made for profit would leave little immune from regulation. Moreover, the interests of the recipient must be considered as well. It is of no concern to him that the author was influenced by the prospect of self-advancement, if the speech contains valuable ideas or information. This point is particularly relevant to political speech, where clearly it should make no difference to the degree of legal protection whether it is disinterested or not. And governments are not to be trusted to make this sort of judgment. On the other hand, an economic motive on the part of a publisher might lead to the forfeiture of legal guarantees in other contexts. One of the major arguments for denying commercial speech and obscenity the degree of legal protection afforded political discourse is that much of it is published purely for gain; and further, reservations concerning the state's ability and integrity in drawing lines here appear less significant.[58]

These factors are also relevant to another pertinent question: should a company or corporation be able to claim freedom of speech? Related questions also arise in the case of newspapers, political parties, and groups, though often the issues here are clarified (and to some extent

---

[57] (1979) 40 *U. Pittsb. LR* 519, 521.

[58] The 'slippery-slope' argument against any tolerance of a state ban on any type of publication has been much used, however, in the context of obscenity; p. 249 below.

complicated) by separate provision in the constitution for freedom of the press and of association.[59] If the right to free speech is primarily viewed as the speaker's right, linked to ideas of human dignity and self-fulfilment, it is hard to see any justification for the protection of corporate speech. But legal systems, such as the West German and the American, do consider it covered by the freedom of expression articles.[60] In the leading United States case, the majority of the Supreme Court, invalidating a Massachusetts law prohibiting banks and business corporations from (generally) making contributions to influence referendum campaigns, found the recipients' interests decisive in the decision to extend the protection of the First Amendment:[61] 'The inherent worth of the speech in terms of its capacity for informing the public does not depend upon the identity of its source, whether corporation, association, union or individual.' The decision shows how important it is to examine interests, other than those of the speaker or publisher, in determining whether to apply a free speech provision.

Recipient (or the public's) interests are particularly relevant in the case of information in contradistinction to opinion and ideas. Restrictions on the free flow of political information are suspect because they invade the audience's interests in having enough material before it to make informed choices and to participate fully in the democratic process. An argument against the validity of official secrets laws based on the civil servants' interests in disclosing the contents of government files is much less attractive. On the other hand, the speaker's interest is more involved, if the legislature decides to proscribe controversial or extremist political publications—in which few members of the public may be interested.[62]

These considerations show how wise it is for free speech provisions, like Article 10 of the European Convention on Human Rights and Article 5 of the German Basic Law, to cover the interests of both speaker and recipient. Each has rights which can be asserted in appropriate cases. In most situations they will be equally affected by restrictions on expression. But sometimes one is in a better position to assert a right, say to receive

---

[59] See ch. II, s. 6, and ch. X.

[60] Domestic German companies enjoy the protection of art. 5; see art. 19(3) of the Basic Law and 21 BVerfGE 271 (1967). The more prevalent view seems to be that foreign corporations may also benefit from its protection; see I. von Münch, *Grundgesetz-Kommentar* (Munich, 1981), 703.

[61] *First National Bank of Boston* v. *Bellotti* 435 US 765, 777 (1978).

[62] Nor would it be an argument against free speech protection that the particular communication offers no fresh ideas or information, and, therefore, is of no interest to the audience; see Dworkin, *The Philosophy of Law*.

information, than the other is to claim the right to speak. For example, the speaker may be physically outside the jurisdiction, or unable (or perhaps unwilling for various reasons) to face the challenge of initiating litigation. These circumstances do not present any particular legal difficulties, at least where the constitutional (or statutory) text recognizes that both speaker and audience have rights to protect.

The position is much less straightforward where there is an audience interest, but no real or legitimate speaker interest at issue. The converse case can also occur (the speaker wishes to communicate something which absolutely nobody is interested in hearing), but this does not really pose any problems: there is almost always someone who could be said to have an interest in receiving the communication, and it is clear anyhow that there is no right to compel someone to listen to a speaker. But might there be a free speech right to compel the government, or anyone else for that matter, to disclose information it wishes to keep secret? Attention to the audience's interest alone would suggest that such a free speech right should be upheld. In fact the jurisdictions we are considering in this book are unwilling generally to derive a constitutional right to know, or to acquire information, from the free speech clause, though many countries now have freedom of information statutes.[63] This reluctance can be defended on principle. It is one thing to recognize a right to receive information (as an aspect of freedom of speech) when the speaker is unable or unwilling to assert his rights, or even to protect it when the speaker has forfeited his right (because he is malicious or speaks from an environment, such as prison or a military base, where the freedom is tightly restricted).[64] It would surely, however, be a distortion of a free speech principle to invoke it where there is no willing speaker at all. Furthermore, the government or company has in these situations an interest in not disclosing its information, and this should be recognized in the formulation and interpretation of free speech provisions.

Finally, the public interest must be considered in framing and applying a free speech rule. This may sometimes be hard to distinguish from the audience interest, as is shown by the passage from the judgment in the United States corporate speech case.[65] Mass communications are not aimed at a particular group of people separable from the general public. The argument from democracy could indeed be framed either in terms of the right of individuals to receive information and views

[63] See ch. III, s. 5.
[64] See p. 109 below.
[65] See n. 61 above.

pertinent to their political choices, or in relation to the general public interest in the disclosure of such information. More usually, however, this interest is seen as limiting the circumstances in which expression may legitimately be made. Scanlon distinguishes between the bystanders' interest in preventing harmful side-effects of speech, such as noise, litter on the streets, and so on, and the more weighty public interest in stopping the harms that may occur as a result of the audience reacting to speech, for example, by rioting or leaving the armed forces.[66] These interests—and the weight which should be given to them—are the subject-matter of later chapters dealing with particular areas of law. Two general observations are offered here.

First, it is far from clear whether a neat distinction can be drawn between the (assumedly harmful) consequences of an audience reaction to speech and harmful side-effects independent of such reaction. How, for example, should the consequences of speech invading privacy be characterized? Or take the case of a passer-by reacting angrily to a street demonstration largely because it is holding up the progress of his car rather than because he dislikes the cause supported by the procession: is his violent response to be treated as an incidental side-effect or a harmful reaction to speech? These comments perhaps only matter if the legal system is more willing to countenance time, manner, and place restrictions on speech to prevent deleterious side-effects than it is to tolerate regulation inspired by hostility to its contents. United States courts and commentators frequently advocate this distinction in discussing the constitutionality of limits on free speech, but it is much harder to apply than to state in abstract.[67] A second and rather obvious point is that limits may be placed on speech to protect the public interest or a private right. Public order and national security limitations clearly represent general third-party interests, but expression is also frequently restricted to secure other private rights which are seen to be stronger—either generally or in the particular circumstances. Rights to reputation, privacy, and a fair trial are instances of these competing rights. Their weight may depend, of course, on whether they are also constitutionally protected, or only exist under statute or at common law.

---

[66] Scanlon (1979) 40 *U. Pittsb. LR* 528.

[67] See Ely, *Democracy and Distrust*, 105–16, where this distinction is urged. But there is a fine (and to some, invisible) line between restrictions on public speech designed to prevent noise or preserve privacy—frequently upheld (see *Kovacs v. Cooper* 336 US 77 (1949))—and restraints on 'offensive' speech, now unconstitutional (see *Cohen v. California* 403 US 15 (1971)). Also see the difficulty in characterizing the prohibition in *US v. O'Brien* 391 US 367 (1968), considered below, ch. II, s. 2.

The existence of a public interest in the speech can, however, also be seen as a necessary condition for its legal protection. Meiklejohn doubted whether purely private speech, in the sense of a publication which is of no concern to the people at large, is covered by the First Amendment.[68] Thus, a defamatory remark about a barmaid's chastity, for instance, would not raise free speech issues. The interests of third parties are also relevant in a more straightforward way. Surely it is necessary on any free speech rationale for the expression to be available to the public, or a section of it? Speech—here the term does seem to refer almost entirely to verbal speech—which is only communicated to one person or a small group should not be entitled to legal protection under the free speech principle. The arguments for democracy and Mill's thesis are clearly irrelevant to it. Only the self-fulfilment argument might justify application of the free speech clause, but one of its principal weaknesses is particularly relevant in this context. The rationale, as we saw earlier in the chapter,[69] does not make clear why speech is to be treated differently from other goods or values, and free expression claims made on this basis are hard to distinguish from claims to other liberties. The case, for instance, that homosexual conduct should be constitutionally protected as an expression of feelings between the participants fails because it is not really a free speech claim, but is rather an argument about alleged rights of privacy or a (doubtful) right to sexual autonomy.[70] The positive requirement of a public interest in the communication also explains why the revelation of state secrets to another member of a subversive organization, let alone an enemy agent, does not even begin to raise free speech issues. The publication is clearly 'speech' in the dictionary sense, but the furtive nature of the disclosure and the absence of any third-party interest in its publication precludes serious argument against prosecution—quite apart from the other strong public interests favouring limitation of free speech in this context.

4. FOUR LEGAL SYSTEMS

This book explores the treatment of free speech in four legal systems. In Britain there is no constitutional protection for freedom of expression, so the liberty is at most recognized as a principle of the common law and its scope developed from case to case without the guidance of any general

[68] Meiklejohn, *Free Speech and its Relation to Self-government*, 79.
[69] See above, p. 16.
[70] See the European Commission's decision in 7215/75, *X* v. *UK* 19 D. & R. 66, 80.

principles. Both the United States and West Germany guarantee the freedom, but the constitutional provisions are markedly different, those in the latter country being much more detailed in their exposition of the interests at stake and explicitly permitting some derogation from the right. Finally, the European Convention on Human Rights sets out a full list of objects, the pursuit of which may justify the imposition of restrictions on free expression. The interpretation of an international convention by a supra-national court such as the European Court of Human Rights obviously creates legal problems distinct from those which face federal constitutional courts.[71]

(i) Great Britain

The absence of any constitutional or legislative statement of a freedom of speech means that the liberty is largely residual. In other words the freedom exists where statute or common law rules do not restrict it. This feature of British (or English) law was stressed by Dicey in his classic study of the constitution.[72] He noted that in contrast to French and Belgian law, which frequently made special provision for the protection (or regulation) of the press, English law took little or no notice of such concepts as 'freedom of speech' and 'liberty of the press'. Legal commentary was then as silent, it may be added, as the statute-book: Blackstone, for example, did not mention freedom of speech in his discussion of personal liberties, and the classic passage on freedom of the press occurs in his section dealing with wrongs and libel.[73] Dicey then concluded: 'Freedom of discussion is . . . in England little else than the right to write or say anything which a jury, consisting of twelve shopkeepers, think it expedient should be said or written.' The implications of this for the publication of minority and unorthodox opinion were ignored.[74] He appears to have been satisfied that political speech, approved or tolerated by the majority, was most unlikely to be suppressed.

---

[71] In particular there is the question whether it is appropriate to impose supra-national standards in matters on which societies sharply differ, for example, the acceptability of pornography: See ch. IX, s. 4.

[72] A. V. Dicey, *Introduction to the Study of the Law of the Constitution* (10th edn., London, 1964), ch. VI. For some reason Dicey always referred to 'English' law in this work.

[73] Blackstone, 4 *Commentaries on the Laws of England* (16th edn., London, 1825), 152. The nearest Blackstone got to dealing with free speech in his treatment of 'Rights of Persons' in the first Book is when he mentioned the right to petition the King or the Houses of Parliament for the redress of grievances: 1 Comm. 143.

[74] See I. Jennings, *The Law and the Constitution* (5th edn., London, 1959), 267–9.

Although Dicey's statement of British constitutional principles remains for the most part (and perhaps regrettably) authoritative, something can be added to his treatment of free speech. First, courts now frequently invoke a common law principle of freedom of speech (or of the press) to limit the scope of other common law rules which inhibit the freedom. This is particularly true in the contexts of contempt of court, libel, and actions to restrain breach of confidence.[75] To some extent judges are influenced by British participation in the European Convention, although its Articles and the case-law of the European Court are not regarded as directly binding on them.[76] Moreover, a presumption in favour of free speech may on occasion be used to restrict the scope of an Act of Parliament which might otherwise be construed to limit the freedom unduly.[77] A third point is that the freedom of speech principle may play a decisive role in dissuading the courts from developing new rules of law or exercising discretionary powers in a novel way. Thus, in a wardship case the Court of Appeal refused to grant an injunction to restrain the publication of a book containing details of the ward's father's degrading conduct.[78] The judges emphasized the importance of not adding to the numerous restrictions on the circulation of true information.

It is, however, very unusual for British judges to discuss the philosophical justifications for recognizing a free speech principle or interest. Theoretical discussion can, however, be found to some extent in political debates concerning the legitimacy of restraints—for example, during the passage of legislation creating the offence of incitement to racial hatred.[79] And the recent Williams Committee Report on the reform of obscenity laws contains a short, but first-class discussion of free speech arguments in this context. But owing to the absence of a constitutional right and the (probably consequent) reluctance of British courts to allow arguments of political and moral philosophy to influence their decisions, the United Kingdom contribution to the difficult questions posed by adherence to a free speech principle has been small. But in many areas—for example,

---

[75] See A. Boyle, 'Freedom of Expression as a Public Interest in English Law' [1982] *Pub. L.* 574.

[76] For judicial discussion of the effect of the European Convention on this area of English law, see, *Att.-Gen.* v. *BBC* [1981] AC 303 (Lords Fraser and Scarman), and *Schering Chemicals Ltd* v. *Falkman* [1982] QB 1 (Lord Denning MR).

[77] See Lord Reid's speech in *Cozens* v. *Brutus* [1973] AC 854, construing the word 'insulting' in Public Order Act 1936, s. 5.

[78] *In re X (A Minor) (Wardship: Jurisdiction)* [1975] Fam. 47.

[79] See 711 HC Deb. (5th ser.), cols. 953–7 (P. Thornycroft MP).

public order restraints on speech and meetings—the results of the case-law may be profitably compared with those found in other jurisdictions, despite the differences in constitutional background.

(ii) The United States of America

It will be helpful to set out the relevant part of the First Amendment: 'Congress shall make no law . . . abridging the freedom of speech, or of the press, or the right of the people peaceably to assemble, and to petition the Government for a redress of grievances.' Rarely has such an apparently simple legal text produced so many problems of interpretation. The extent to which solutions have been influenced by various free speech theories, or can be justified by reference to them, is explored in later chapters. The richness of the Supreme Court case-law shows, among other things, the reluctance of the judges to commit themselves to any one of these theories. As has already been suggested, the argument from democracy has been the most popular, its influence being shown by the significant degree of protection given to political speech, in comparison with commercial speech and pornography. But some support can be found for the 'importance of truth' rationale, and more recently, commentators have found attractive rights-based arguments stemming from fundamental rights to dignity and self-fulfilment.[80]

The text itself appears by mentioning free speech alongside rights of assembly and petition to emphasize the former's role in safeguarding the interests of the opposition and minorities. But relatively little reliance has been placed on this point, except in the development of the linked freedom of association.[81] Textual arguments have been ignored in other respects. The First Amendment literally only applies to the laws of Congress, but it has never seriously been suggested that executive and police orders are immune from judicial review,[82] and even more crucially, since the important ruling of the Court in *Gitlow* v. *New York* in 1925 it has been accepted that freedom of speech and of the press are fundamental personal rights protected from invasion by the *states*, as well as the

---

[80] In addition to the writings of R. M. Dworkin, see D. A. J. Richards, 'Free Speech and Obscenity Law: Toward a Moral Theory of the First Amendment', (1974) 123 *U. Pa. LR* 45, and C. E. Baker, 'Scope of the First Amendment Freedom of Speech', (1978) 25 *UCLA LR* 964.

[81] See ch. X, especially pp. 280–1.

[82] In the famous *Pentagon Papers* case (403 US 713 (1971)), it was not even argued that the text did not cover an application by the President to the courts to proscribe a publication.

Federation, under the Due Process Clause of the Fourteenth Amendment.[83]

The other way in which the courts have departed from a literal or strict constructionalist approach is of more general interest for comparative free speech jurisprudence. Despite the frequent promptings of Black J., a member of the Supreme Court from 1937 to 1971, the Court has never taken literally the injunction 'shall make no law ... abridging the freedom of speech ...'. The objection to the absolutist position, advocated by Black and Douglas JJ., is not only that it is difficult to sustain in the real world, where courts are necessarily conscious of the vital interests that may be threatened by unrestricted speech. It is also untenable because it ignores the argument that regulation, and on occasion prohibition, of such speech may be justified in order to protect the free speech rights of others. Even Meiklejohn, who took a very wide view of the protection to be afforded political speech under the First Amendment, recognized that addresses at public meetings could be regulated and cut short on valid free speech grounds. Absolutists can try to defend their corner by asserting that 'abridging' does not cover all forms of regulation and that 'the freedom of speech' is not the same as 'speech', so that rightly understood the term does not exclude restrictions on some modes of expression.[84] But really the game is up, the poverty of literalism laid bare.

What is left is the process of balancing, a technique developed by the United States Supreme Court over the last fifty years without constitutional guidance.[85] Other interests, such as public order, national security, and the protection of children, are weighed in the scales with free speech, and if found 'compelling' or perhaps 'substantial' may justify the restriction. One form of balancing test is the famous 'clear and present danger' formula, which at least has the merit of emphasizing the presumption in favour of freedom of speech and narrowing the circumstances in which it may be curtailed to those where there is an imminent risk of a serious evil.[86] 'Balancing' need not be incompatible with a strong adherence to the free speech principle, though there is an obvious risk

---

[83] The observation of Stanford J. in *Gitlow* 268 US 652, 666 (1925) to this effect was first applied to invalidate state legislation in *Fiske* v. *Kansas* 274 US 380 (1927).

[84] Meiklejohn, *Free Speech and its Relation to Self-government*, 19–28. Also see J. Feinberg, *Social Philosophy* (New Jersey, 1973), 94–7.

[85] The foremost judicial exponent of this approach has been Frankfurter J. See, for example, his judgment in *Dennis* v. *US* 341 US 494 (1951).

[86] Further discussed, ch. V, s. 2.

that judges will treat the speech interest as just one factor to be weighed with others.

Further consideration of these approaches, all of them controversial, must be left until later. Here the general point should be made that their adoption compels the courts to consider the fundamental principles underlying the free speech clause within the context of particular facts. It is one thing to decide in abstract that, say, the argument from democracy entails the coverage of political speech by the First Amendment. The process is much more complex when judges have to apply this general principle to libel actions or in prosecutions for public order offences. Balancing then requires reflection on the implications of the underlying principles in order to determine the meaning of 'political speech', whether it is at issue in the particular litigation and whether it should be protected on the facts. The coherence and scope of general political principles is as much tested as the wisdom of the judiciary.

(iii) West Germany

Article 5 (Freedom of expression) of the Basic Law provides:

(1) Everyone shall have the right freely to express and disseminate his opinion by speech, writing and pictures and freely to inform himself from generally accessible sources. Freedom of the press and freedom of reporting by means of broadcasts and films are guaranteed. There shall be no censorship.

(2) These rights are limited by the provisions of the general laws, the provisions of law for the protection of youth, and by the right to inviolability of personal honour.

(3) Art and science, research and teaching shall be free. Freedom of teaching shall not absolve from loyalty to the constitution.

The detailed character of these provisions, in contrast to the bald prohibitions of the American First Amendment, is immediately striking. Not only, as might be expected from a Constitution drafted in 1949, are there references to novel forms of communication, and a particular provision for academic and artistic freedom, but the rights of speaker and recipient are separately recognized. The relationship between the freedom to express opinions (*Meinungsfreiheit*) and the right to receive information (*Informationsfreiheit*) has been much discussed by the Federal Constitutional Court and in academic commentaries.[87] In parti-

---

[87] See in particular 27 BVerfGE 71 (1969), where the Karlsruhe Court held that *Informationsfreiheit* is not just a component part of the freedom to express opinions, but an independent right, and see Maunz-Dürig, *Kommentar*, paras. 81 ff.

cular there is uncertainty whether the former freedom covers the communication of *facts* as well as the expression of *opinions*; the predominant view now is that a distinction between facts and opinions can be drawn only with difficulty and that it leads to problems concerning the transmission of information from private sources.[88] The Court in different contexts has emphasized the contribution of the freedoms to the development of the individual personality and their importance to the development of public opinion on political matters. Thus, some recognition has been given to both the second and third arguments for a free speech principle considered in this chapter.[89]

The Basic Law (*Grundgesetz*) is a much more complicated constitutional document than the United States Constitution and Bill of Rights. There is, therefore, more room for construing fundamental rights provisions in conjunction with one another and with other basic principles of the Federal Republic's legal order. For example, freedom of expression must be interpreted subject to the fundamental right to 'the dignity of man' (Art. 1) and in the light of Article 20 stating, *inter alia*, the basic principle that Germany is a democratic and social federal state; neither of these provisions can be amended.[90] Also relevant are separate Articles for 'the right to the free development of . . . personality' (Art. 2), freedom of faith and conscience (Art. 4), freedom of assembly and of association (Arts. 8 and 9), and for the place of political parties in forming 'the political will of the people' (Art. 21). The existence of these textual and structural aids means there is less need for the courts to fall back on abstract moral argument, but this is far from absent, and (as has been mentioned) the Karlsruhe Court has adopted the 'democracy' rationale in according political speech some special degree of protection.

Article 5(2) makes it plain that an absolutist view of the freedom is precluded. From the text it would have been open for the Constitutional Court to hold that freedom of expression was confined to the area unaffected by the general laws—a position analogous to that in Britain. However, in its leading decision in the *Luth* case (1958), it held that these

---

[88] *Informationsfreiheit* only covers material available from general sources: see Maunz-Dürig, *Kommentar*, paras. 51–3.

[89] See the *Luth* case, 7 BVerfGE 198 (1958), where the Court referred to the importance of free speech to the development of public opinion, especially on political and social questions, and also to its role in encouraging human development. Both arguments were used to support the recognition of the independent *Informationsfreiheit* in 27 BVerfGE 71, 81–2 (1969). And see 54 BVerfGE 129, 136–7 (1980), where the Court stressed the particular importance of the self-fulfilment rationale for verbal speech.

[90] Basic Law, art. 79(3).

laws must themselves be interpreted in the light of the fundamental values enshrined in Article 5.[91] The result in effect is that the Constitutional Court balances or weighs the interests of free expression and of the particular law (whether public or civil) in a manner resembling the usual approach of the American Supreme Court. It is in this process that the German Court is able to place differing weights on the values of political, literary, and commercial speech in the light of the Article's purposes.

(iv) The European Convention on Human Rights and Fundamental Freedoms

Article 10 provides:

(1) Everyone has the right to freedom of expression. This right shall include freedom to hold opinions and to receive and impart information and ideas without interference by public authority and regardless of frontiers. This Article shall not prevent States from requiring the licensing of broadcasting, television or cinema enterprises.

(2) The exercise of these freedoms, since it carries with it duties and responsibilities, may be subject to such formalities, conditions, restrictions or penalties as are prescribed by law and are necessary in a democratic society in the interests of national security, territorial integrity or public safety, for the prevention of disorder or crime, for the protection of health or morals, for the protection of the reputation or rights of others, for preventing the disclosure of information received in confidence, or for maintaining the authority and impartiality of the judiciary.

The most obvious feature is the extensive list of circumstances in which limitations to the freedom of expression may be upheld. On a superficial view it might appear that Article 10(2) virtually removes the right purportedly guaranteed by the first paragraph. But this is not the European Court's approach. In addition to the requirement that any permissible restriction must be 'prescribed by law', which excludes arbitrary restraints lacking in legal certainty,[92] the limit must be *necessary in a democratic society* to further the stated aims and goals. The balancing, therefore, starts with a presumption in favour of freedom of expression, the exceptions to which must be narrowly construed. Moreover, in terms similar to those employed by the American Supreme Court, the European Court has ruled that an interference with speech

---

[91] 7 BVerfGE 198, 212 (1958).
[92] *Sunday Times* case [1979] 2 EHRR 245, 270–3; the case is discussed in detail in ch. VIII.

will only be upheld if there is a 'pressing social need' for it in the particular circumstances.[93]

Unfortunately, relatively few cases on Article 10 have reached the Court, and most applications have only received the more cursory legal attention of the Commission. That body decides initially whether the application is admissible, and if it is, the case is referred to the Court or the Committee of Ministers. If the case is referred, the Commission submits a report on its merits, which may be published subsequently. Although relatively slight, the material is adequate to enable a few broad conclusions to be stated. Since the principal value underlying the Article is thought to be the preservation of political freedom, political speech enjoys a higher degree of protection than commercial advertising.[94] The Commission has also been prepared to draw implications from the distinction in the text between 'information' and 'ideas'. It is the *public*'s interest in receipt of information which is crucial, rather than the communicator's freedom.[95] Philosophical arguments have played a very small role in determining the scope of the freedom and of the permissible restrictions; on the other hand, frequent reference is made to the text of the Article and its relationship with other provisions, in particular Article 9 (freedom of thought, conscience, and religion) and Article 11 (freedom of assembly and association). As is the case with the West German Basic Law, the more detailed the text is, the less recourse there need be to abstract political and moral theories of free speech.

[93] Ibid., at pp. 275–7.

[94] 7805/77, *X & Church of Scientology* v. *Sweden* 16 D. & R. 68.

[95] See 5178/71, Report of the Commission to the Committee of Ministers, *De Geillustreerde Pers* v. *Holland* 8 D. & R. 5.

II

The Meaning of Speech

I. INTRODUCTION

What exactly should be covered by a rule protecting freedom of speech? The question is, of course, not only of concern to political philosophers, but has to be answered by those courts, such as the United States Supreme Court or the West German Constitutional Court, which are required to interpret constitutional guarantees of freedom of expression. Almost everyone would agree that an oral or printed attack on the government or other institutions of state should be immune from legal regulation—except perhaps when it is made in circumstances where an immediate outbreak of violence is likely to occur. If the free speech principle does not extend that far, it is difficult to see its point at all. But other types of 'speech' create more problems: for example, nobody thinks perjury or dishonest commercial advertising should be constitutionally protected, and for many critics the status of pornography under a free speech principle is far from clear.[1]

It is also difficult to categorize various forms of behaviour and activity, the purpose or effect of which may be to convey ideas more generally transmitted by discussion and writing. Opposition to nuclear weapons may be communicated not only by speeches at the hustings and in Trafalgar Square, but by marches and sit-ins, and by ordinary people wearing CND badges as they go about their daily business. While it is relatively easy to equate these forms of protest with conventional 'speech', such as an editorial in the *Guardian* or the *New York Times*, we may instinctively bridle if the same claims are made in the case of mass picketing, the wearing of political uniforms, or the burning of draft-cards and other government documents. Yet in some contexts and jurisdictions, modes of conduct such as these have been treated as covered by a freedom of expression rule.

One thing at least is clear. It will not do simply to ask whether the

---

[1] See ch. IX, s. 2.

communication—verbal speech, writing, or conduct—falls under the dictionary meaning of 'speech'. The printed word is clearly covered, although this is not 'speech' in the ordinary sense of that word. (It is sometimes argued that there is in this respect a difference between 'speech' and 'expression',[2] the latter term being somewhat broader, but there is no evidence that courts draw any distinction. At any rate, the two words are used interchangeably in this book.) Conversely, some oral communications are not generally regarded as covered by a free speech principle: for example, incitement to murder, perjury, and fraudulent statements inducing a contract. 'Speech' is really a term of art when used in constitutions, and courts should ask whether, in the light of the reasons for protecting expression from legal regulation and so adopting a free speech principle, the type of communication in issue should be covered by the principle.

As Frederick Schauer has pointed out, however, coverage by the free speech principle does not mean that the particular communication should be protected from regulation in the circumstances of the case.[3] For example, political speech is the archetypal kind of communication which is covered by the principle, but often its exercise may be limited, perhaps when an inflammatory statement is made during a time of national emergency or immediately before a likely riot.[4] This distinction between coverage and protection has a significant consequence. It enables courts to treat some types of communicative conduct, or 'symbolic speech' as it is often described in the United States, as 'speech', without thereby being committed to its protection in every conceivable situation. In contrast, judges like Black J. who take an absolutist view of the construction of a free speech provision—all 'speech' is absolutely immune from abridgement—have to rely on a clear distinction between 'speech' and 'conduct'; otherwise it would be difficult to uphold the regulation of anti-social behaviour—for example, the distribution of dangerous drugs and street riots—which could conceivably be treated as an exercise of free speech rights.

In fact the trend of recent judicial decisions, particularly in the United States of America, reveals a broader approach to the scope of free speech coverage. Fewer types of 'speech' are now excluded from the protection of the First Amendment than used to be the case in, say, the 1930s and 1940s. Some libel and commercial speech is now covered, while the

---

[2] See, e.g., F. Schauer, *Free Speech: A Philosophical Enquiry* (Cambridge, 1982), 50–2.
[3] Ibid., 89–92.
[4] Ch. VII, s. 2.

definition of 'obscenity' which the states may regulate without constitutional hindrance was appreciably narrowed in the leading case, *Roth* v.
United States.[5] The majority of the Court has, however, consistently
rejected the view that the most extreme hard-core pornography is
entitled to benefit from First Amendment coverage.[6] A similar development has occurred in the context of abusive personal speech. In
Chaplinsky v. *New Hampshire*, decided in 1942, the Court unanimously
enunciated a 'fighting words' doctrine, under which certain personal
insults were ruled wholly outside the Free Speech clause of the
Constitution: 'such utterances are no essential part of any exposition of
ideas, and are of such slight social value as a step to truth that any benefit
that may be derived from them is clearly outweighed by the social
interest in order and morality'.[7] This principle has, however, been
progressively narrowed in the last twenty years or so, although the actual
decision in *Chaplinsky* has not been overruled.[8] The interesting question
is whether the underlying rationale for the ruling is still supportable.

On one view the primary reason for protecting free speech from
legislative control is that there is some special value in the unfettered
dissemination of intellectual ideas and of information of political and
social importance. Certainly on the basis of the argument from democracy and Mill's infallibility thesis (considered in Chapter I), the case for
including purely emotive speech in the coverage of the free speech
principle seems relatively weak. This might suggest that only discourse of
a political and social character engaging the listener's intellect should be
covered. However, while there is much to be said for treating this
type of communication as the archetypal category of 'speech', the
exclusion of all emotive, non-rational expression from the coverage of the
principle would be a mistake. For a start, it will often be hard to
disentangle such matter from associated rational discourse. The most
opprobrious insult may form part of an otherwise serious criticism of
government or of a political figure. But even if it were possible to separate
the emotive content from the other parts of a particular publication, it
would be wrong to allow its proscription. If speakers can be punished
each time they include some colourful, non-rational epithet in their
publication or address, much valuable speech will be inhibited. Some
margin should be allowed for invective and exaggeration, even if this

[5]   354 US 476 (1957).
[6]   See Ch. IX, especially s. 4.
[7]   *Chaplinsky* v. *New Hampshire* 315 US 568 (1942).
[8]   The case-law is discussed in ch. VII.

means that some apparently worthless comments are as fully protected as a carefully balanced argument. This principle has been accepted by both the United States Supreme Court and the West German Constitutional Court.[9] Moreover, human beings are not entirely rational. Many people may only be able to communicate in emotive terms, and we are almost all in some circumstances influenced by arguments presented in this way. It may, therefore, be right for even the most vapid of political slogans ('Fuck the Draft')[10] to be immune from legal control. Otherwise the deepest feelings of the less articulate could not be lawfully communicated. While society may not value this sort of expression as highly as a *Times* editorial, it is both right and in its interests to afford it the same legal protection. The benefit of a free speech principle is not the prerogative of the intellectual elite.

This is not, however, to deny that some kinds of non-propositional or non-rational speech should be excluded from the coverage of the principle. Outside the area of political and moral discourse, it may be possible to isolate some types of publication which are not entitled to any protection at all under the free speech principle, precisely because they contain no information or ideas. Hard-core pornography and extreme personal insults (not addressed to the victim as a public official) are probably examples of such speech. The weakness of the *Chaplinsky* ruling was that it did not succeed in distinguishing these categories from emotive political speech, such as group libel, which probably ought to be covered by the First Amendment,[11] and it is for this reason that it has properly been distinguished so often in the last twenty years.

In the light of these general observations we can now proceed to examine some areas where the application of any free speech provision is bound to be controversial, because it can be claimed that there is no real 'speech' involved. In the next section of the chapter, we look at the 'speech–conduct' distinction, and see how useful it is in this context. Then we examine in Section 3 the relationship between payment of money and speech. Section 4 discusses the extent to which it is right to protect commercial speech from regulation. Another question is whether someone may claim a right not to speak under a freedom of expression

---

[9] See, e.g. the libel case, *New York Times* v. *Sullivan* 376 US 254 (1964), where free speech protection was conferred on untrue, though non-malicious, defamation of a public official; a narrower rule would inhibit speech which ought to be protected, viz., critical comment on government and its officers. For relevant German cases, see 54 BVerfGE 129, 139 (1980) and 60 BVerfGE 234, 241 (1982).

[10] *Cohen* v. *California* 403 US 15 (1971).

[11] For further discussion of group libel, see ch. V, s. 4.

provision. This aspect of the right to conscientious objection is treated briefly in Section 5. Finally, we look at the relationship between freedom of speech and freedom of the press; the latter right is often separately protected in a constitution, and there are important questions whether it then covers activities which would not fall under freedom of speech.

2. SPEECH AND CONDUCT

It does seem natural to draw a sharp distinction between 'speech' and 'conduct' when determining the scope of a free speech constitutional provision. Yet courts are prepared to hold that some forms of activity, designed to communicate opinions, are covered by these provisions. Many commentators go so far as to deny that there is really any intelligible distinction between 'symbolic speech' and verbal communication: 'The crucial question . . . is simply whether meaningful symbols of any type are being employed by one who wishes to communicate to others.'[12] The somewhat pedantic point is made that in pure speech cases the communication of written messages, perhaps even oral ones, does involve some use of symbols, which are conventionally understood as conveying ideas and information.[13] From this it follows that other, non-linguistic symbols—badges, uniforms, styles of appearance, and gestures—should in some contexts be regarded as a mode of communication. So the United States Supreme Court has ruled that the wearing of black armbands in school to protest against the Vietnam war was so closely akin to pure speech as to be covered by the First Amendment (and in the circumstances constitutionally immune from prohibition),[14] though it has refused to review decisions upholding the suspension from school of students wearing long hair, perhaps because this conduct is not so obviously designed to communicate any idea.[15]

The contrast between these cases indeed shows that it would be wrong to equate action or behaviour with speech. All conduct is admittedly in a sense able to communicate some idea or information to its observers. While generally this 'message' will be without interest or importance, sometimes it will be dramatic and of great political significance; the IRA terrorist campaigns are as much designed to influence opinion in Britain

---

[12] M. B. Nimmer, 'The Meaning of Symbolic Speech under the First Amendment' (1973) 21 *UCLA LR* 29, 61–2.

[13] Ibid., 33–5. Also see L. H. Tribe, *American Constitutional Law* (New York, 1978), 599, for the view that all speech involves some element of conduct.

[14] *Tinker* v. *Des Moines School District* 393 US 503 (1969).

[15] *New Rider* v. *Board of Education* 414 US 1097 (1974).

about the future of Ulster as they are to kill and wound. But surely nobody would suggest that terrorism and political assassination are entitled to free speech protection?[16] Yet if the crude distinction between speech and conduct is to be discarded, some tests or criteria must be formulated to determine when behaviour is entitled to benefit from a constitutional guarantee of free speech.

Before discussing what these criteria might be, a distinction should be drawn between the 'symbolic speech' cases and cases where 'speech' in the conventional sense is transmitted by conduct. The courts are frequently confronted by circumstances which clearly contain some 'pure speech', but also involve an element of physical conduct: leafleting and canvassing, demonstrations and many forms of picketing constitute examples of these situations. They should perhaps be treated more benevolently than 'symbolic speech' which is not accompanied by verbal or literary communication. The justification for this discrimination is that in the former group of cases there is a clearly understood intention to transmit information or opinions, and the difficulties only arise because the object is achieved by, or in conjunction with, some linked activity, which may create a social nuisance or harm unrelated to the content of the speech. For instance, it may be reasonable to regulate or even prohibit leafleting in some areas because of the obvious risk of litter on the streets or in parks. But it cannot be doubted that this is a situation involving free speech issues, and that to draw distinctions based on the content of the leaflet—a local authority might permit the distribution of religious, but not party political pamphlets on the streets—would be wholly indefensible.[17]

This type of case does not seem to produce much difficulty. It falls within the free speech guarantees, a conclusion which is even more obviously true if the relevant constitutional articles also explicitly refer to freedom of assembly and other associated rights, which cover more than 'pure speech'. The only significant difference from the most straightforward free speech litigation is that the governmental interest here in restricting the expression may be much stronger because of the linked element of conduct. This at any rate is broadly the approach adopted by

---

[16] But an idle threat to assassinate the President is protected speech: *Watts* v. *US* 394 US 705 (1969).

[17] See, for example *Schneider* v. *State* 308 US 147 (1939) and *Martin* v. *Struthers* 319 US 141 (1943), which establish that not only are content-based restrictions on leafleting and the distribution of circulars unconstitutional, but so are limitations which are wider than necessary to prevent noise, litter, or other public nuisance.

the Supreme Court in what are sometimes known as 'speech plus' cases.[18]
Of course, the facts of the particular litigation may bring the case very
close to the category of 'symbolic speech': it is, for example, hard to know
exactly how to classify a completely silent march or sit-in. Classification
assumes great significance if the court is committed to the view that
'speech' can never, or only rarely, be restricted. Black J. was therefore
inclined to adopt a narrow view of the scope of 'pure speech' or 'speech
plus' cases and was ready to find a sufficient element of conduct to take
the case out of the First Amendment.[19] Non-absolutists need not draw
such sharp lines, and can afford to weigh the elements of speech and
conduct according to the particular circumstances.

This approach is naturally adopted in Britain, where free speech
counts only as a principle used to construe statutes and to aid the
resolution of difficult common law disputes. Sometimes a judge's
recognition of the close relationship between speech and associated action
will influence his approach to a case which does not only present 'free
speech' issues. In *Hubbard* v. *Pitt*, for example, where the plaintiffs
secured an injunction to restrain a picket outside their offices, Lord
Denning MR in his dissent considered the right to demonstrate and
protest in this way so closely analogous to the exercise of free speech that
the judicial prior restraint was inappropriate.[20] In essence the plaintiffs
were complaining about the contents of the defendants' placards and
leaflets. The majority of the Court of Appeal, however, took the view that
the nuisance aspect of the defendants' activity was more important than
its communicative effect which was merely incidental. In the United
States a characterization of this conduct as 'speech' would be decisive,
since the strong presumption against prior restraints (considered in
Chapter IV) would then be applied to prohibit the court's injunction.

The so-called 'symbolic speech' cases pose greater problems precisely
because the speech element is harder to detect and may well be absorbed
in conduct which the state has a legitimate interest in regulating. The
actor's desire to communicate an idea cannot itself be sufficient to render
the behaviour 'speech'—otherwise political assassination might be
covered by a free speech provision (though, of course, it would not be

[18] A leading example is *Cox* v. *Louisiana* 379 US 536 (1965), where the Court applied a
lower standard of protection to street demonstrations than to 'pure speech'. The distinction
has been criticized by H. Kalven, 'The Concept of the Public Forum' [1965] *Sup. Ct. Rev.*
1, 23: all speech is communicated through conduct, and so could be treated as 'speech plus'.
[19] See his dissents in *Cox* v. *Louisiana* 379 US 559 (1965) and in *Street* v. *New York* 394
US 576 (1969).
[20] [1976] 1 QB 142, 178–9; see below, pp. 91 and 143, for further references to this case.

protected). Nor should it be enough that the action was understood as a communication by the particular people to whom it is addressed; there must be a general understanding on the part of the public that it contained information or an idea. Whether it does will depend on the surrounding circumstances. An English case shows how the courts can approach the question, though the result was inimical to freedom of speech.[21] Under the Public Order Act 1936 it is an offence to wear a 'uniform signifying . . . association with any political organization or with the promotion of any political object . . .'.[22] The issue for the Divisional Court was whether the offence was committed by defendants who wore black berets and dark glasses at the funeral of an IRA member who had died on hunger strike. The court upheld their conviction because berets were generally recognized as the uniform of people in association for militant Republican purposes, an understanding which was reinforced in the circumstances by the speeches and other events at the funeral. The American Supreme Court would probably use these criteria to hold that the wearing of the uniform was 'speech' for the purposes of the First Amendment; at any rate the Illinois Supreme Court and lower federal courts have ruled that the wearing of Nazi uniforms and display of the swastika do constitute political speech.[23]

It is fairly easy to see that there are free speech questions in the political uniform cases, not only because the wearing of these uniforms in public is clearly appreciated as conveying a message, but also because the object of the relevant legislation is to prevent ideological offence to the majority of people and possible consequent disorder. And these interests are not enough—at least in the United States—to warrant the restriction of free expression.[24] The same considerations are relevant in the numerous 'flag desecration' cases, which figure so prominently in the Supreme Court Reports.[25] Statutes prohibiting the mutilation or destruction of the national flag are clearly designed to elevate one view of this important national symbol over less reverential attitudes. They have generally been held void for vagueness, or their application has been considered unconstitutional in the case of defendants who burned or otherwise

[21] *O'Moran* v. *DPP* [1975] QB 864.

[22] s. 1.

[23] *Skokie* v. *Nat. Socialist Party* 373 NE 2d. 21 (1978) and *Collin* v. *Smith* 447 F. Supp. 676, aff'd. 578 F 2d. 1197, 1200 (1978).

[24] *Cohen* v. *California* 403 US 15 (19721). For a comparable British case, see *Cozens* v. *Brutus* [1973] AC 854 (HL).

[25] For example, *Street* v. *New York* 394 US 576 (1969), *Smith* v. *Goguen* 415 US 566 (1975), and *Spence* v. *Washington* 418 US 405 (1974).

abused the flag as a matter of political protest. It perhaps remains an open question whether the Court would, or should, reach the same conclusion if the same act were done for fun at the end of a suburban barbecue—when the political content of the gesture might be, to say the least, obscure.

It is much more difficult to disentangle the issues in the leading American speech–conduct case, *United States* v. *O'Brien*.[26] The respondent was charged with burning his draft-card under an amendment to the Universal Military Training and Service Act which had made it an offence to destroy or mutilate this document. The majority of the Court, reversing the First Circuit Court of Appeals, first decided that the behaviour could not be characterized as 'speech' for First Amendment purposes merely because the actor intended to communicate his opposition to conscription for the war in Vietnam. This conclusion is correct. As suggested earlier, the actor's intention to communicate is probably a necessary, but not a sufficient, condition for his conduct to be treated as speech. But in the context the gesture was almost certainly so understood, at least by some members of the public. The Court therefore went on to consider the case on the footing that it did involve a combination of speech and conduct, or 'symbolic speech'. On this basis Warren CJ held that government regulation was valid if it furthered an important state interest 'unrelated to the suppression of free expression; and if the incidental restriction on alleged First Amendment freedom is no greater than is essential to the furtherance of that interest'.[27] The government had a legitimate concern to safeguard the draft registration system, and so there was nothing unconstitutional in the controversial amendment. The respondent was punished for frustrating the registration scheme, not for communicating opposition to the war in a particularly dramatic fashion.

The decision has been criticized on a number of grounds.[28] It is arguable that the 1965 amendment was so narrowly drafted as to make it plain that Congress's real object was indeed to restrict speech: if the purpose had been to safeguard the registration scheme, the Act would have made a simple failure to produce the certificate to the relevant official a criminal offence. More fundamentally, the Court's application of the formula that the restriction on expression be no greater than is

[26] 391 US 367 (1968).
[27] Ibid., 377.
[28] See Tribe, *American Constitutional Law*, 594–8, Nimmer, 'Meaning of Symbolic Speech' (1973) 21 *UCLA LR* 38–44, and L. Henkin, 'On Drawing Lines' (1968) 82 *Harv. LR* 63.

necessary to achieve the state's interest seems more restrictive of the free speech interest in this context than it is in other types of case where speech is accompanied by conduct, e.g. the street leafleting and canvassing cases. There the prohibition can equally be regarded as essential to prevent a serious social harm—litter on the street—but this is not regarded as an adequate justification for a total suppression of a *familiar mode* of communicating opinions. It may be that the Court is really approving broader controls on what can be characterized as a form of civil disobedience which is partly conduct and partly expression. Again this it may be thought wrong to treat novel and unorthodox types of communication less favourably than a public speech or the printed word. This however begs the question whether draft-card burning should be viewed predominantly as a novel mode of communication. In borderline cases such as *O'Brien* it seems perfectly reasonable for the Court to adopt its conservative approach, particularly in view of the fact that there were numerous other ways in which opposition to the draft could be communicated. It is immaterial that more conventional forms of protest would be less effective, for there is no general right under a free speech principle to put over an opinion in the most newsworthy or dramatic way.

Other jurisdictions too have restrictively defined 'speech' or 'expression' so as to exclude some forms of expressive conduct. The German Constitutional Court has ruled that the call of some powerful publishers for an economic boycott by retailers of all newspapers printing details of East German television programmes went beyond the freedom of expression covered by Article 5 of the Basic Law; the boycott call was backed up by threats to break off business relations with retailers who did not co-operate.[29] A call to readers to stop taking the offending newspapers would have been covered, because this is a mode of intellectual argument, appealing to their sense of moral and political responsibility. In a later case, the Karlsruhe Court has also made it plain that the motive for the boycott may influence its view of the constitutional position.[30] A call made primarily to protect sectional economic interests will be less sympathetically viewed than one which is made to bring political and social concerns to everyone's attention. Similarly, the European Commission of Human Rights has rightly refused to accept the argument that physical homosexual relations are covered by Article 10 of the Conven-

[29] 25 BVerfGE 256 (1969). Compare the *Luth* case, 7 BVerfGE 198 (1958), discussed below, p. 150.
[30] 62 BVerfGE 230 (1982). Compare *NAACP* v. *Claiborne Hardware* 102 S. Ct. 3409 (1982) (speeches calling for boycott of White merchants protected).

tion as a mode of expressing feelings.[31] Even if this activity could be regarded as 'expression', such an intensely private communication—of no interest to the public—should fall outside the scope of any free speech provision.[32]

Therefore, while a sharp line between speech and conduct cannot easily be drawn, courts should not wholly ignore the distinction. Most conduct is equivocal in that it can be construed as asserting some proposition and yet at the same moment it constitutes an act with physical effects. It will only rarely be appropriate to characterize it as solely, or even primarily, communicative. Relevant criteria for this characterization are in summary the intention of the actor and (as the military uniform cases show) generally understood conventions concerning the significance of the behaviour and its role as a means of non-linguistic communication. In some circumstances the actor's behaviour may be objectively so odd that it can only be construed as expressing some proposition, and should be treated as 'symbolic speech'.[33] For example, camping outside a nuclear base is intrinsically a bizarre activity, only comprehensible as a means of protesting against the arrival of missiles or nuclear war. (This does not, of course, mean that it should be protected under a free speech provision, for there are obviously important governmental interests to be weighed against it, but it is certainly some form of speech, if perhaps not very pure.) On the other hand, styles in personal appearance, such as the wearing of long hair or pigtails, cannot so easily be characterized as a mode of expression; we must all choose short or long hair, conventional or unusual clothes, according to taste and so on, and there is generally no reason to think that anyone is asserting anything much with his choice.

Moreover, the state will more often have a legitimate and pressing interest in restricting conduct (even though it also incidentally regulates associated speech) than it does in prohibiting pure speech. Admittedly this point does entail that there will be a greater degree of protection for the spoken and written word than for less traditional means of expression. I see no reason, however, to retreat from this conclusion. There are dangers in trying to extend the scope of a free speech principle too far. A

---

[31] 7215/75, *X.* v. *UK* 19 D. & R. 66.

[32] See ch. I, s. 3.

[33] But conduct may be so opaque that no message can be inferred: see *Davis* v. *Norman* 555 F 2d. 189 (8th Cir. 1977), where the defendant argued unsuccessfully that the parking of a demolished car outside his house was 'speech' protesting against police conduct responsible for the damage.

wide view of its coverage might lead to the protection of civil disobedience (as, for example, would have been the result if the *O'Brien* case had been decided in the defendant's favour), a course which would probably weaken popular support for free speech generally. Moreover, the further the free speech principle is stretched, the more it becomes a general libertarian claim for freedom from state interference. It would consequently lose intellectual coherence as a special reason for limiting state action.[34] Perhaps, however, it does not matter very much whether we conclude that most conduct is outside the coverage of a free speech provision altogether, or alternatively that there is much 'symbolic speech' which is covered to some extent, but which can properly be restricted when there is good reason. On either approach, the distinction between 'speech' and 'conduct' is relevant.

3 . SPEECH AND MONEY

Money talks, but is it 'speech'? This question, on one perspective an aspect of the relationship between speech and conduct, is particularly important in the context of election laws regulating campaign expenditures. It is common in modern Western democracies to limit the amount of money which may be spent by election candidates or on their behalf by outsiders, first, to prevent corruption and secondly, to ensure (so far as possible) that the richer candidates and groups do not have disproportionately more resources with which to influence the outcome of an election.[35] British law imposes limits on the amount that may be spent by individual candidates at both Parliamentary and local elections, though there is somewhat inconsistently no national limit on the expenditures of political parties.[36] The Representation of the People Act also prohibits expenditure by persons (other than the candidate, his agent, and authorized persons), which is incurred 'with a view to promoting or procuring the election of a candidate at an election' for the organization of meetings and displays, the issue of advertisements and circulars, and

---

[34] See above p. 6, for the distinction between a free speech principle and general libertarian arguments.

[35] For German law, see 8 BVerfGE 51 (1958) where the second object was approved by the Court, when it upheld a constitutional attack under art. 3 of the Basic Law (equality before the law) on a provision allowing contributions to political parties to be deducted from income for tax purposes. Some remarks of the Court, 8 BVerfGE 51, 68 suggest that such contributions might be covered by art. 5.

[36] See the Bill introduced in 1983 by some Labour backbenchers to limit the election expenditure of each party to £3,000,000.

for otherwise advocating a candidate or disparaging another candidate.[37] This ban has been construed not to cover expenditure on national publicity which is concerned to promote the interests of a party generally in all constituencies.[38] The result is that there is nothing to stop the Conservative Party nationally from taking advantage of its infinitely superior financial resources, while a wealthy individual candidate is severely limited in the amount he may spend on his campaign. Election expenditure laws such as this can raise a variety of constitutional issues, in particular whether the financial restrictions improperly abridge freedom of political speech.

The Supreme Court addressed these questions in the landmark case of *Buckley* v. *Valeo*.[39] The litigation involved, among other things, challenges, first to those provisions of the Federal Election Campaign Act 1971 (amended in 1974) limiting the *contributions* which could be made to the campaign of a candidate for office to 1,000 dollars, and secondly, to the serious restrictions on the *expenditures* which could be incurred by or on behalf of a particular candidate. In an extremely controversial ruling the Court upheld the contributions limitations, but invalidated the provisions of the Act imposing limits on campaign expenditure. Both restrictions were regarded as limitations on speech rather than merely on conduct, although the contribution limitation was considered less onerous a restraint because 'the transformation of contributions into political debate involves speech by someone other than the contributor'.[40] In contrast the expenditure restrictions entailed, in the Court's view, substantial restraints on the quantity and diversity of political speech. At the outset the Court refused to equate expenditure with conduct such as the destruction of the draft-card in *O'Brien*. It then went on somewhat mysteriously to argue that the dependence of speech on money did not itself introduce an element of 'conduct' into the situation or reduce the exacting scrutiny of legislation which courts must conduct to ensure compliance with the First Amendment. Moreover, even if the *O'Brien*

---

[37] Now the Representation of the People Act 1983, s. 75(1). In *DPP* v. *Luft* [1977] AC 962, the House of Lords construed the quoted words to cover the distribution of leaflets opposing a National Front candidate, but not advocating the election of another particular candidate.

[38] *R.* v. *Tronoh Mines Ltd* [1952] 1 All ER 697 (McNair J.).

[39] 424 US 1 (1976).

[40] Ibid., 21. But see *Common Cause* v. *Schmitt* 512 F. Supp. 489 (1980), where District Court of Columbia held that contributions to political committees should be treated as 'speech' of the contributors, and so expenditure on their behalf by the committee could not be limited.

test, appropriate to cases of 'symbolic speech', were employed, the relevant government interests (restricting campaign expenditures) involved the suppression of communication; it was not a case where there was some other legitimate purpose for the legislation which only incidentally affected freedom of speech.

Almost all of this reasoning seems highly questionable. The expenditure of money certainly enables more speech to be made, or disseminated on the media. But this does not mean that expenditure should be treated as 'speech' or as its equivalent. The payment of contributions and the incurring of expenditure do not as such communicate any message or information. When a cheque is written, money changes hands, but no idea is transmitted. The Court somehow seemed to be under the impression that it was dealing with a 'pure speech' case, where the dependence of the speech on money at most introduced a trivial element of conduct. It is surely more plausible to view the case as involving the constitutionality of limits on the expenditure of money, which would admittedly affect the nature of electoral campaigns. On this perspective the difference between expenditure and contributions is slight, if not illusory, for both uses of money make speech possible or enable it to reach more people. However, a number of attributes and facilities have these effects, yet it is rarely suggested that their possession or use necessarily falls under a free speech provision. Progressive tax laws equally, if rather indirectly, prevent the wealthy from dominating public debate as much as they would do in a completely liberal economy. But they only infringe the First Amendment if they are directed at speech as such, or the institutional press.[41] It will not do to argue that the restrictions in *Buckley*, in contradistinction to income or wealth tax laws, are aimed at the quantity or range of 'speech', as the electoral legislation's supporters can still counter with the claim that it was designed to limit *expenditure*, not speech.

The best point made by the Court was that the expenditure of money should not be limited, 'because virtually every means of communicating ideas in today's mass society requires the expenditure of money'.[42] Money not only enables speech, it is necessary to it. There is a suggestion here that freedom of speech means more than a liberty to talk and write, and also entails an ability to reach the majority of the people through mass communication. Thus, the Court pointed out that the expenditure limits would make it difficult, perhaps impossible, for individuals to place

---

[41] See, e.g., *Grosjean* v. *American Press* 297 US 233 (1936).
[42] 424 US 1, 19 (1976).

political advertisements in metropolitan newspapers. But does this restrict free speech or only a freedom to spend money so that speech is more effective? In other cases the Court has rejected the idea that there is some strong constitutional right to speak to the people through access to the press and media.[43] If this principle is right, *Buckley* v. *Valeo* may lead to the unattractive conclusion that the wealthy have a First Amendment freedom to communicate by purchasing time and space on television and in the press, which is effectively denied other groups in society. The Court's distinction between the expenditure and the contribution restrictions seems to reinforce this discrimination, since the latter, upheld by the judges, prevented donations of more than 1,000 dollars to campaign funds—a more realistic mode of participation in electoral campaigns for middle-income groups.

The Court also said that the restrictions would limit the quantity of political speech published during an election period. This seems far from clear, at least without a more precise explanation of what is covered by the term 'political speech'. The range of ideas and issues could be communicated by other means—door-to-door canvassing, public meetings, publicly financed television broadcasts—without significant loss.[44] The government in fact argued that the expenditure limitations enabled the less affluent groups or parties to make a more effective contribution to the political debate. But the Court did not think this was a permissible basis for the legislation, even though it might have followed that the variety and range of political speech would have been extended. Another point in favour of the restrictions is that they did not discriminate between individuals' and parties' expression on the basis of content; they were essentially neutral in this respect.[45] In short, it is hard to believe that the restrictions would have prevented any political idea from reaching the public, so the argument from democracy is not really applicable here in support of the contention that money should be treated as 'speech'. Large-scale expenditure in support of an electoral campaign may register the intensity of the spender's feelings, as well as the depth of his pocket; but the argument for a free speech principle from self-expression and

---

[43] See below, ch. III, s. 4.

[44] In a 'pure speech' case a limit on the manner of speech cannot be justified on the ground that there are alternative means of communication, but it is not clear that this principle applies to cases on the borderline between 'speech' and 'conduct'; see Harlan J. in *US* v. *O'Brien* 391 US 367 388–9 (1968).

[45] J. Skelly Wright, 'Politics and the Constitution: Is Money Speech?' (1976) 85 *Yale LJ* 1001, 1009.

fulfilment can hardly be deployed, for they all too obviously in this context collapse into general libertarian claims.

There are, therefore, considerable difficulties in accepting the reasoning in *Buckley* v. *Valeo*. But the decision is most unlikely to be overturned, and indeed the underlying principles have been applied and extended in subsequent cases. In *Bellotti*,[46] a bare majority of the Court held that a Massachusetts law prohibiting banks and business corporations from spending money on referendum campaigns (other than on issues which materially affected their interests) infringed the First Amendment. The decision largely turned on the question whether corporations were entitled to benefit from the free speech clause, and the issue whether the expenditure of money was to be treated as 'speech' was relegated to a footnote indicating support for the *Buckley* decision. Though there is probably little risk of corruption through corporate expenditure on referendums, there is every reason to believe it can distort the balance of views presented to the public. And the ban on corporate expenditure does not prevent the communication of any idea or opinion to the public by individual officers and members of the company. It is difficult to see that any of the arguments for the free speech principle justify the interpretation of the First Amendment to cover such expenditure. Arguments from the importance of self-expression as a means to the full development of the individual are clearly irrelevant, as White J. pointed out in his dissent,[47] while the application of the arguments from truth and from democracy to this situation is far from obvious. The most relevant underlying argument is probably the fear that the government will be able to exercise too much political power, unless rival institutions, including private corporations, are free to put over their views as effectively as possible. But as pointed out in Chapter I, it is not clear whether this apprehension really justifies special protection for free speech, or only supports claims for general institutional autonomy. The Court has now extended the *Buckley* principle to outlaw limits on financial contributions to committees organizing support for, or opposition to, local measures.[48] The fact that the contributions would assist

---

[46] *First National Bank of Boston* v. *Bellotti* 435 US 765 (1978).

[47] Ibid. 804–8.

[48] *Citizens against Rent Control* v. *Berkeley* 102 S. Ct. 434 (1982). Also see *Common Cause* v. *Schmitt*, n. 40 above. The courts are prepared to find a closer link between such contributions and the contributors' views than they are in the case of contributions to political candidates' funds. The recent contribution cases prompt the question whether tax rules discriminating in favour of contributions to charities might be constitutionally suspect, because such laws reveal a contents-based preference for certain types of 'speech'!

speech by someone other than the contributor was ignored. Again in dissent, White J. pointed out that the assertion, 'money is speech', proves too much, because much other associated conduct might equally qualify for free speech protection on the ground that it is necessary to mass communication; moreover, the state has a legitimate content-neutral interest in safeguarding the fairness of the electoral process.

There is perhaps a broader dimension to this discussion which is also present in the other controversial areas—commercial speech and the meaning of press freedom—which I am considering in this chapter. Free speech claims may be asserted by people and organizations, whose real interest is not primarily to communicate information or an opinion for consideration and appreciation, but to achieve some other end which has nothing to do with the reasons for a free speech principle.[49] A wealthy individual (or corporation) spends a lot of money during an election campaign on saturation advertising and on a well-organized campaign, so that the favoured candidate is returned to office. It is a matter of secondary concern to him whether any ideas or information are circulated in this enterprise. The same can be said of some commercial speech, published to secure profits rather than to provide information. It is admittedly true that much political speech, for example, an election speech by a candidate, is in a sense self-serving, and this factor is then entirely disregarded. Nobody suggests that in this type of case the court should investigate the speaker's real motives before deciding to confer the protection of a free speech provision. (However, in both Britain and the United States, defences to a libel action may be unavailable when it is shown that the speaker was actuated by malice—so motive is not always irrelevant.)[50] Whatever the speaker's motives, the audience's and the public's interests in receiving the communication support the case for coverage.[51]

The controversial cases considered in this chapter should, however, be treated differently from instances of pure, typically political, speech. It has first to be decided whether the ambivalent action is within the coverage of the free speech provision. The actor's intentions are relevant to this determination, a point already made in the context of the flag-desecration and the draft-card burning cases. This factor should also be considered in deciding how to characterize the expenditure of money. In reaching its decision in *Buckley* v. *Valeo*, the Court seems to have paid

---

[49] See below, p. 56 (commercial speech) and p. 252 (obscene publications).
[50] See ch. VI, s. 2.
[51] See ch. I, s. 3, for the interests relevant to protection of free speech.

little or no attention to this point; at the outset it had decided that the litigation was to be treated more or less as an archetypal speech case.

4. COMMERCIAL SPEECH

Until the last few years it has generally been assumed that commercial and professional advertising falls outside the scope of a free speech provision. Not surprisingly the theoretical issues have never been discussed in Britain, where advertising is subject to a battery of tort and administrative remedies, as well as to possible criminal prosecution under the Trade Descriptions Act 1968 or other legislation. Commercial advertising is further controlled informally and extra-legally by an Advertising Standards Authority, which attempts to enforce a code of practice proscribing false and misleading claims.[52] Much professional advertising, whether of primarily informational or promotional content, is restricted by the rules of the professional bodies concerned. For example, doctors, lawyers, architects, and accountants are all subject to rules of varying strictness, which may prevent them from informing the public what particular skills they have to offer. Many institutions still seek to uphold these restrictions, though there has been some relaxation recently.[53] It is further illegal to publish an advertisement on behalf of a parent wishing to have a child adopted or for a prospective adoptive parent.[54] On the other hand, there do not seem to be any restrictions in Britain on publicizing the availability of advice about contraception or abortion facilities; prohibitions of such publicity have given rise to constitutional litigation in the United States.

It is only in the last decade that the American Supreme Court has reconsidered the traditional exclusion of commercial speech from the coverage of the First Amendment. The justification for this exclusion had never really been explored. Thus, in *Valentine* v. *Christinsen* the Court without discussion upheld the application of a New York city ordinance—which forbade distribution on the streets of commercial advertising—to the owner of a ship who was touting for visitors.[55] It made no

---

[52] Under the Code of Practice, an advertisement must be legal, decent, honest, and truthful. The Code goes well beyond legal controls, for example, in forbidding advertisements which cause grave or widespread offence.

[53] There is an excellent summary of the variety of professional restrictions in the 1970 Monopolies Commission Report on restrictive practices in the supply of professional services, Cmnd. 4463, ch. 6. Architects, quantity surveyors, and solicitors have all relaxed their restrictions in the last few years.

[54] Adoption Act 1976, s. 58.

[55] 316 US 52 (1942).

difference that the circular also contained a protest against the city's refusal to allow his boat mooring facilities. In the circumstances it was right that this feature did not affect the result, for otherwise it would have been too easy to evade the commercial speech exclusion. On the other hand, if a case does substantially involve political (or perhaps artistic) speech, the fact that this is incorporated in an advertisement does not remove the protection it is otherwise entitled to enjoy.[56] Further, there are some cases where it is hard to know whether to characterize the publication as 'commercial' rather than speech of political or social importance; this is particularly true in the case of service advertising, for example, for medical or welfare assistance.

As with the other controversial areas discussed in this chapter, the coherence and scope of the commercial speech exclusion should be considered in the context of the purposes of the free speech principle. The argument that bases the principle on the desirability of a fully informed population, able to play an intelligent and active role in the working of democracy, does suggest that the case for covering commercial speech is relatively weak. Or at least it indicates that the degree of protection afforded by the principle should be less than that conferred on political speech. The Supreme Court did point out in *Virginia State Board of Pharmacy* v. *Virginia Citizens Consumer Council*, one of the recent cases discarding the commercial speech exception, that the particular consumer's 'interest in the free flow of commercial information . . . may be as keen, if not keener by far, than his interest in the day's most urgent political debate'.[57] Information concerning drug prices, held in that case to be covered by the First Amendment, is indeed of crucial importance to many people. This point, however, is not decisive. The question remains whether the material really is 'speech', bearing in mind that the term is not to be given its simple dictionary meaning. The mere strength of consumer demand for commercial information does not determine that its disclosure is covered by the free speech principle any more than enthusiasm for the revelation of government secrets or for the publication of pornography dictates the recognition of a right to look at that material.[58] The argument from democracy implies that some types of information are more worthy of constitutional protection than others; on this basis, therefore, the case for excluding commercial speech is quite strong.

[56] *New York Times* v. *Sullivan* 376 US 254 (1964).
[57] 425 US 748, 763 (1976).
[58] See below, p. 245, for this argument in the context of obscenity.

The argument from truth is also difficult to apply to commercial speech without serious modification. In political, social, and moral inquiry, we can never be certain that the right answer has been obtained. If we prescribe what can be said and written, and prohibit alternative views, we assume an 'infallibility of judgment' (as Mill put it), which is never warranted.[59] This reasoning does not really apply to commercial advertising. We can often be sure that a particular produce does or does not possess certain qualities. A claim that the daily consumption of baked beans guarantees 'long life' is so obviously false that this part of Mill's theory is quite irrelevant. This example brings out another related reason for excluding at least some commercial speech from coverage by the free speech principle. Much advertising is inherently misleading, promising results in terms that are at best vague and at worst clearly false. Even factual statements by doctors or lawyers concerning the range and quality of services offered will often require supplementary information if they are not to give false impressions—a reason, incidentally, for the professions' traditional hostility to advertising.[60] This point has two legal implications. First, in so far as it is easy for an advertiser to know whether the claim for his product is accurate or not, there can be little objection to the proscription of false descriptions; there is no danger here that speech which ought to be covered by a free speech provision will be inhibited. Secondly, it may be reasonable for the government to require the provision of additional information and disclaimers in conjunction with the advert to prevent misleading impressions. These points indicate that, even if some commercial information should be covered by the free speech principle, for example, disclosure of the prices of goods and the addresses of retail outlets, the degree of protection should be significantly lower than that afforded most political speech. This position now seems to have been adopted by the Supreme Court in some recent decisions.

The status of commercial speech is, however, most vulnerable when viewed in the context of the argument that free speech should be protected because of its central importance to the development of the individual personality. One position is that the profit motive breaks the crucial link between the real beliefs of the producer or advertiser and his speech, so that the latter cannot be considered a serious manifestation of

---

[59] See above, pp. 9–13.

[60] This does not provide a good reason for the total prohibition of such advertising, only for its regulation: see Monopolies Commission Report, paras. 269–70, and Blackmun J. in *Bates* v. *State Bar* 433 US 350, 372–5 (1977).

his attitudes. It is, therefore, unworthy of legal protection.[61] The advertiser is trying to market a product, not to communicate an idea. If he wanted to express his true beliefs, he would write a book extolling the merits of his wares. Against this argument, it can be urged that newspapers, journals, and books are frequently published to make money, yet it is rarely doubted that what is written in such publications qualifies as 'speech'. (Of course, the press is often covered, as in the United States and West Germany by a separate constitutional provision, so there may be no need for it to rely on a free speech clause: see below, section 6.)[62] The more important objection to the argument is that it is wrong to concentrate on the author's profit motive, and ignore the recipients' interests in the acquisition of information. The issues here are the same as those which have already been touched on in the discussions of the speech–conduct distinction and of the appropriate classification of expenditure.[63] Although the existence of a profit (or some other ulterior) motive does not necessarily exclude a publication from constitutional protection, it should be taken into account in borderline areas.

Whichever rationale for the free speech principle is thought most persuasive, there does seem to be some difficulty in accommodating all commercial speech within the area of constitutional protection. Some truthful information concerning prices, the nature of services provided, or the details of personnel may be regarded as 'speech', while unsubstantiated commercial puffs and personal solicitation, purely or primarily designed to win custom for the business, should almost certainly not be so treated. Alternatively, the courts should adopt a benevolent attitude to the justifications given by the government for restricting, or imposing conditions on, commercial speech. This pragmatic approach is similar to that recommended by the British Monopolies Commission in 1970,[64] when it suggested some liberalization of the restrictions imposed by professional bodies on their members. The Commission drew a distinction between informational and promotional advertising, advocating the removal of any limits on the former, while admitting that there might in

---

[61] C. E. Baker, 'Commercial Speech: A Problem in the Theory of Freedom' (1977) 62 *Iowa LR* 1.

[62] Privileged treatment of the press, compared with other bodies and corporations, has been denied by Burger CJ in *First National Bank of Boston* v. *Bellotti* 435 US 765, 799 (1978).

[63] See above, pp. 43 and 53.

[64] Cmnd. 4463.

some circumstances be good reasons for inhibiting advertisements designed to create custom. There has recently been considerable liberalization of the advertising rules for solicitors; the change reflects this distinction.[65]

In the United States the Supreme Court has moved cautiously since its initial decisions in 1975 and 1976 reversing the commercial speech rule. The first of these, *Bigelow* v. *Virginia*,[66] involved an advertisement for abortion services in New York and could be regarded as not really a typical 'commercial speech' case, while the *Virginia State Board of Pharmacy* ruling concerned freedom to publish true information about prices.[67] The First Amendment was then held to cover the publication of lawyer's fees, but the Court specifically refused to commit itself on the position of advertisements about the quality of services.[68] The suggestion in Blackmun J.'s majority judgment in that case that the Court would take a different view of personal solicitation was borne out in *Ohralik* v. *Ohio State Bar*, where a state statute banning canvassing of clients by lawyers was unanimously upheld.[69] This sort of speech was treated as a subordinate element in a business transaction, and although not considered to be entirely outside the scope of the First Amendment was afforded a significantly lower degree of protection. Indeed, it now seems that most, if not all, commercial speech enjoys only a limited measure of protection compared with political speech, while false and misleading advertising remains wholly outside the free speech clause.

American courts must, therefore, first decide whether the publication amounts to 'commercial speech', or is an example of straightforward political or social speech entitled to full First Amendment protection. This issue is not easy to resolve where the advertisement is a mixture of propaganda on important social and moral issues, e.g. the desirability of birth control, and the promotion of a particular product, e.g. a contraceptive pill.[70] The Supreme Court has recently said that the producer's economic motivation and the reference in the advertisement to a specific product are factors indicating that the speech is 'commercial'.[71] If this

[65] See (1984) 81 *Law Soc. Gazette* 1266 for details of the proposals approved by the Council of the Law Society; also see 8600/79, *X* v. *UK* (*Solicitors' Advertising*) (1981) 4 EHRR 350 for a challenge to the previous rules, rejected on procedural grounds.
[66] 421 US 809 (1975).
[67] 425 US 748 (1976).
[68] *Bates* v. *State Bar* 433 US 350 (1977).
[69] 436 US 447 (1978).
[70] *Carey* v. *Populations Services International* 431 US 678 (1977).
[71] *Bolger* v. *Youngs Drug Products Ltd* 103 S. Ct. 2875, 2880–1 (1983).

conclusion is reached, the court must then determine what degree of protection is appropriate; advertisements for services, the use of which is itself protected constitutionally (such as contraception or abortion assistance), enjoy a high standard of protection, particularly if it is plain that the reason for their restriction is purely to prevent information reaching the public.[72] Other types of commercial speech may be restricted more easily, whenever the government can show substantial justification for this course, or are left more or less wholly outside the First Amendment (as is the case with deceptive advertising). There are, as we have said, good reasons for treating commercial speech less favourably than political speech, but the present constitutional position in the United States is, to put it mildly, very confusing.

There is relatively little German case law on the question how far commercial speech and advertising are covered by Article 5 of the Basic Law. In what is perhaps its leading pronouncement, the Federal Constitutional Court ruled that press advertisements detailing employment opportunities abroad could not be prohibited.[73] Advertisements may be covered, even though they do not normally assert an opinion or idea (*Meinung*); at least when they provide information, they fall under the right to press freedom. Article 5 does specifically cover press freedom and the freedom of people to gain information from commonly available sources (*Informationsfreiheit*), so there is strong textual argument for holding at least some kinds of commercial speech to be constitutionally protected. However, in a later case the Karlsruhe Court without much discussion held that the advertisement by a chemist of non-professional goods, contrary to *Land* professional rules, was not covered by Article 5 because it did not assert an opinion.[74] It is possible that the Court was influenced by the chemist's economic motives for advertising; he was hardly seeking to contribute to the shaping of public opinion, which is generally regarded as the principal purpose of Article 5.[75] Elsewhere the Court has made it plain that the Basic Law's protection of free speech is not removed merely because the publication of an opinion is designed to bring the publisher financial profits,[76] but as in the United States this

---

[72] See *Linmark Associates* v. *Willingboro* 431 US 85 (1977), where a city ordinance prohibited the public display of 'For sale' or 'Sold' signs in order to prevent people realizing that property was being sold and so stop panic selling by whites hostile to the integration of the area.

[73] 21 BVerfGE 271 (1967).

[74] 53 BVerfGE 96 (1980).

[75] See the *Luth* case, 7 BVerfGE 198, 208–12 (1958) discussed further ch. V, s. 2.

[76] 30 BVerfGE 337, 352–3 (1971).

factor may still influence the courts in controversial commercial cases.

The case law under the European Convention makes the distinction, found in other jurisdictions, between promotional advertising and commercial speech providing information. In *Church of Scientology* v. *Sweden*[77] the Commission ruled inadmissible an application that the Swedish Marketing Improper Practices Act 1970 had been improperly used to restrain commercial advertisements for an instrument connected with the practice of scientology. Commercial ideas were not wholly outside the scope of Article 10 of the Convention, but they were entitled to less protection than political speech, the guarantee of which was said to be the principal object of the provision. This distinction was achieved here by applying the formula—'restrictions . . . necessary in a democratic society'—more generously where commercial speech is in issue. In this case the injunction had been taken out reasonably to protect the interest of consumers. In an earlier case the Commission had drawn a distinction between protection of freedom of expression and the defence of a newspaper's commercial interests, when it refused to support the claim that a journal had a right under Article 10 to publish copyrighted material.[78] This suggests that at least in some contexts commercial speech will not be protected at all, because the publisher's communicative intent will be treated as subordinate to his profit motive, and the latter will take the case wholly outside the scope of Article 10.

On the other hand, an interview given by a vet to a Hamburg evening paper in which he called for a more comprehensive veterinary night service is regarded as a type of expression fully protected under Article 10. In the *Barthold* case[79] the Commission found that the restrictions on publicity imposed by the applicant's Professional Rules (sanctioned by the civil courts under the unfair competition legislation) could not properly be applied in these circumstances. The case did not concern an advertisement in the usual sense; the applicant was providing the public with important information about the state of veterinary services and was not attempting to publicize his own clinic. The Commission also ruled that the requirement of anonymity could not be justified as 'necessary in a democratic society', for the disclosure of the applicant's identity was an essential element in his exercise of his freedom of expression. Importance was also attached to the truth of the statements he made in the interview concerning his own clinic and practice:

[77] 16 D. & R. 68.
[78] 5178/71, *De Geillustreerde Pers* v. *Holland*, 8 D. & R. 5.
[79] 8734/79, *Barthold* v. *Germany* (1984) 6 EHRR 82.

Even if there might be some publicity effect, the Commission finds it cannot reasonably be considered as necessary in a democratic society to suppress true statements which are expressed in fair and moderate language and which are appropriate to back up legitimate criticism expressed in relation to a state of affairs of public concern.

The Commission's Report was adopted unanimously, and it is likely that the Court, to which the case has been referred, will also hold that there was a violation of the applicant's right to freedom of expression.

A difference in the degree of protection between commercial and political speech can be satisfactorily achieved in the formulation of the balancing tests: does the government have to have a compelling, or only a substantial or reasonable interest, in regulating the publication? And the interests which are taken into account in applying this test may be much broader in the case of commercial speech. For example, it is right to protect consumers from deceptive advertising (even though it may be literally true), whereas it would make nonsense of a free speech provision for a court to attempt the same degree of control in the case of misleading political speeches.[80] One particular argument for restricting commercial speech merits further discussion. A government may wish to discourage use of a particular substance or facility—for example, cigarettes, alcohol, gas, or electricity. There is almost certainly no constitutional obstacle to achievement of this end by straightforward prohibition or strict regulation. But are there free speech objections to attempts to accomplish this goal by restrictions on advertising these products? The American courts have not found any objection to restrictions on cigarette advertising.[81] And in *Central Hudson Gas and Electricity Corp.* v. *Public Service Commission*, the majority of the Court intimated that it would countenance a ban on promotional advertising by an electricity company if this were shown to be necessary to reduce energy consumption.[82] In the case itself, the Commission's order went far beyond what was appropriate to achieve this goal, because it also suppressed information about services that would not increase energy consumption, but only three members of the Court considered there were First Amendment objections to any control on sales promotion.

The majority view in this case is surely right. If it is constitutionally open for a government to ban, say, the use of a dangerous drug, such as heroin or cigarettes, it would be bizarre if it could not take the moderate

---

[80] For the different approaches to the protection of untrue libels, see ch. VI, s. 2.
[81] *Capital Broadcasting* v. *Mitchell* 333 F. Supp. 582 (1971).
[82] 447 US 557 (1980).

step of discouraging consumption by outlawing promotional advertising. (A book which argues on scientific medical grounds that these drugs are quite harmless would be a different matter.) If this is accepted, we have another instance of the law drawing a distinction between political and commercial speech. Although states can, of course, legitimately take steps to suppress actual outbreaks of violence, the advocacy of militant protest and even of insurrection is not prohibited (certainly in the United States and probably under the modern sedition law in Britain[83]) unless there is a serious chance of imminent violence. Put more simply, the law will only intervene at the last minute; until then free speech is tolerated. The distinction between the treatment of political speech and commercial advertising in this respect can be justified on the ground that the latter makes no appeal to the audience's own judgment or intellect. Even if to some extent it can be characterized as 'speech', it is only entitled to a weak degree of protection.

One further type of restriction may be briefly mentioned here, though it is by no means confined to commercial speech; indeed it is more relevant to the arts. The law of copyright has rarely been considered to raise serious freedom of expression problems, although of course it enables the copyright holder to retain a monopoly right to communicate information or an idea in a particular form.[84] The similarity to commercial advertising is that those who propose to violate copyright restrictions generally do so for much the same reason as advertisers—to make money. The public already have access to the information from another source of supply. Fair dealing defences cover most circumstances where there is a good case for permitting other people to reproduce the copyrighted material, though there is much controversy in Britain over the scope of this defence.[85] In *De Geillustreerde Pers NV* v. *Netherlands*[86] the European Commission went so far as to deny that there was any free expression issue at all in a case covered by copyright laws: it held that only the person who assembled the facts, in the actual case the details of television programmes, enjoys the freedom under Article 10 of the Convention to impart that information. In the case of facts, as distinct from ideas and opinions, the more important interest is that of the

---

[83] See ch. V, s. 3.

[84] See Tribe, *American Constitutional Law*, 649.

[85] See Copinger and Skone James, *The Law of Copyright* (12th edn., London, 1980), paras. 510–25.

[86] 8 D. & R. 5.

recipients;[87] here they already had access to the information from the copyright holder.

The experience in the United States in the last decade does not indicate that it was wrong to bring some commercial speech within the First Amendment. But both the Supreme Court and the European cases show that courts should proceed with great caution. There remain sound arguments against equating advertising with political and social speech. In particular, promotional slogans and canvassing which make no attempt to appeal to the reason of the people addressed and provide no information should have little or no constitutional protection. Such advertising can more naturally be characterized as an aspect of business conduct which government is perfectly free to control, subject only to the restraints of the political process. Other communications, which do provide factual information about such matters as outlets and prices, should be treated as 'speech', though even they may not be entitled to the degree of protection enjoyed by political and moral discourse.

5. A RIGHT OF SILENCE

In 1943 some Jehovah's Witnesses challenged the constitutionality of a state requirement that children in public schools salute and pledge loyalty to the United States flag. Their case was principally that the regulation violated the 'free exercise of religion' clause of the First Amendment, but the Supreme Court upheld the challenge on the ground that the students had a right not to be compelled to affirm beliefs they did not hold. In one of the most quoted passages in the history of the Supreme Court, Jackson J. declared:

If there is any fixed star in our constitutional constellation, it is that no official, high or petty, can prescribe what shall be orthodox in politics, nationalism, religion, or other matters of opinion or force citizens to confess by word or act their faith therein.[88]

There are references in the Court's judgment to a 'right of self-determination' and 'freedom of the mind', but it seems fairly clear that Jackson J. considered that a right not to speak, in particular a right not to be forced to say what a person does not accept, is an integral aspect of freedom of speech. A flag salute was treated as an established form of

---

[87] See ch. I, s. 3.
[88] *West Virginia State Board of Education* v. *Barnette* 319 US 624, 642 (1943).

'symbolic speech', a feature of the ruling which influenced the reasoning in the flag desecration cases discussed earlier in this chapter.

A right to stay silent can be invoked in many circumstances which appear far removed from the situations where freedom of speech is in issue. For example, it can be claimed by the defendant in a criminal trial. It is then upheld either under the common law privilege against self-incrimination (as in Britain) or under a specific constitutional right of silence (as under the Fifth Amendment to the Constitution of the United States).[89] Doctors, priests, journalists may refuse to give evidence or to help the police on the ground of professional privilege, and the press may use the argument that if it is not allowed this privilege, its sources of information will dry up. This particular claim attempts to benefit from the protection granted by a freedom of speech provision in an apparently paradoxical way: the journalist claims a right not to divulge information to the authorities on the ground that if he did, his ability to gather news and publish his findings would be hampered.[90] Such an immunity (discussed later in this chapter) is very far removed from the right not to speak established by the Court in the *Barnette* case, and the contrast may shed some light on the scope of this latter right. It rests on an underlying freedom of belief and conscience, which is seriously compromised by any requirement to enunciate opinions which are not in truth held by the individual. The freedom may in fact be separately protected in a constitution. Thus Article 9 of the European Convention guarantees the right to freedom of thought, conscience, and religion. In the absence of a provision such as this, the right not to speak must be inferred from the freedom of positive speech.

The connection is very easy to establish. The students in the *Barnette* case clearly had a constitutional right to say and write what they thought about the flag. It would be nonsense to protect this freedom, yet to deny an accompanying liberty not to adopt in public the officially approved attitude. The distinction between the communication of opinions and the disclosure of factual information is relevant to the scope of this negative freedom. The right to transmit *ideas* and *views* is primarily that of the speaker; the justification for its protection is to some extent that the right is necessary to ensure the development of his individual personality.[91] We have seen that in contrast it is the recipient, and also the general public,

---

[89] R. Cross, *Evidence* (5th edn., London, 1979), 275 ff.
[90] See, *Branzburg* v. *Hayes* 408 US 665 (1972), and further, s. 6 of this chapter.
[91] See above, pp. 14–20, where this basis for the free speech principle is discussed.

who are the principal beneficiaries of the freedom to communicate *information*.[92] It follows that a right not to speak can properly only be claimed for ideas and opinions, as in the *Barnette* case itself. A right not to divulge information would often conflict with the public's more weighty interest in the disclosure of the information, and could therefore only relatively rarely be successfully asserted under a free speech provision. That is why some of the United States cases on the refusal to answer questions put in the course of legislative investigation seem more satisfactorily to turn on the Fifth Amendment privilege against self-incrimination rather than on the First Amendment.[93] Recently the German Constitutional Court has ruled that the requirement to complete a census form did not violate the applicants' freedom of expression, since *negative Meinungsfreiheit* only covered views and opinions.[94]

The substance of the right then is the freedom not to be forced to publish opinions or to subscribe to propositions, which the person does not really hold or accept, as if they were his own. Classic examples of its exercise are the 'loyalty oath' cases in which the Court has often struck down requirements that state employees affirm allegiance to the national and state constitutions and disclaim membership of the Communist Party and other 'subversive' organizations.[95] The European Commission has similarly ruled admissible an application that a German *Land*'s requirement for civil servants, including schoolteachers, to take a loyalty oath (disclaiming *inter alia* support of undemocratic parties) infringed Article 10.[96] The applicant argued successfully that prima facie there might be a violation of her right to remain silent concerning her views on the German Communist Party. A political party may not be denied a place on state ballot forms because it refuses to take an oath swearing it does not advocate overthrow of government. Such advocacy, falling short of an incitement to immediate lawlessness, is covered by the First Amendment, and it was therefore unconstitutional to compel the party to deny that it engaged in it.[97]

The right is not infringed merely because the person (or institution) is required by law to publish a proposition he does not agree with. It is only

---

[92] See ch. I, s. 3.

[93] See Tribe, *American Constitutional Law*, 709–10, for discussion of the relationship of First and Fifth Amendment claims.

[94] 65 BVerfGE 1, 40–1 (1984). But the Court did find that the requirement violated the right of privacy protected under art. 2(1) of the Basic Law: see [1984] *Pub. Law* 199.

[95] *Keyishian* v. *Board of Regents* 385 US 589 (1967).

[96] 9228/80, *X.* v. *Germany* (1983) 5 EHRR 471.

[97] *Communist Party of Indiana* v. *Whitcomb* 414 US 441 (1974).

invaded if he is compelled to say or write something in circumstances in which it would appear to a reasonable bystander that he believes in its truth. In the former situation the individual's conscience is not compromised to the same degree, because there is no apparent connection between what is published and the publisher's true beliefs. Thus, the requirement exacted of newspaper editors in some European countries to publish replies by people who have been subjected to personal criticism in their journals does not really infringe the freedom not to speak; the reply can be published in such a way as to make it quite clear that it is the correspondent's version of the truth and does not represent the newspaper editor's own view. The Supreme Court has, however, held that such a right of reply law does violate the editor's First Amendment rights, though the constitutional issue in the United States is complicated by the fact that the Amendment also refers to 'freedom of the press', which may cover 'activities' which go beyond free speech.[98] It is also important for the court to be satisfied that the right asserted is a right not *to speak*, rather than a right not to engage in a particular course of *conduct*. Both the Supreme Court and the European Court have held that in some circumstances individuals may have a right not to be compelled to finance trade union political activities. The weakness of these rulings—more fully discussed in Chapter X—is that they assume that the payment of money is to be treated as a mode of speech, when, as we have seen in this chapter, it might more appropriately be regarded as an activity preparatory to speech.[99] This latter characterization is particularly suitable for the payment of union subscriptions, because it is far from clear what a member could be construed as saying when he pays them; he may be an active supporter of the union, including its political causes, or he might contribute out of group loyalty or mere habit.

Some of these difficulties arose in an entertaining case, *Wooley* v. *Maynard*,[100] where the constitutional issues were as subtle as the facts were trivial. The respondents, again Jehovah's Witnesses contributing to First Amendment jurisprudence, objected to a New Hampshire statutory requirement that all non-commercial motor vehicles bear the state motto, 'Live Free or Die', on their licence plates. So they covered it up. The Court held with two members dissenting on the point of substance, that New Hampshire was compelling car owners to carry the state's ideologi-

---

[98] *Miami Herald Publishing Co* v. *Tornillo* 418 US 241 (1974), discussed further, ch. II, s. 6, and ch. III, s. 4.
[99] See above, p. 50.
[100] 430 US 705 (1977).

cal message, and that this requirement unconstitutionally abridged their right not to speak. Rehnquist J. pointed out in his dissent, first, that it was far from clear that carriage of the motto was conventionally understood as a mode of 'speech', and second, that in any case nobody would understand the car owner as subscribing to the particular political philosophy so cryptically summarized by it. This second point seems well made. So either the *Wooley* case was wrongly decided, or the rule now is that the state may not require anyone to transmit another person's or the state's own views. The majority indeed went so far as to say that an individual has a First Amendment right to refuse to foster any idea he finds objectionable. Such a right might conceivably entitle him not to pay taxes which are used to finance government propaganda.[101] Surely the Supreme Court would not recognize this immunity, but the possibility shows the danger of extending the right not to speak beyond the circumstances of a case like *Barnette*.

6. FREEDOM OF THE PRESS

Constitutions generally refer to a 'freedom of the press' in association with the right to freedom of speech or expression. The drafting naturally varies somewhat from one country to another: sometimes the two freedoms are covered by the same sentence,[102] sometimes in different sentences or even in different paragraphs.[103] But since constitutional interpretation places relatively little weight on textual nuances, these details are not crucial. The question for courts is whether 'press freedom' means merely that the institutional press enjoys the same liberties and immunities as every individual does under the free speech provision, or whether the press has wider (or perhaps narrower) rights. In fact the United States Supreme Court has not really come to terms with the issue, though some judges, particularly in their extra-judicial pronouncements, have clearly favoured the latter position.[104] The West German Consti-

---

[101] Tribe, *American Constitutional Law*, 590. The point also shows the difficulties courts can get into if non-payment of money is regarded as equivalent to an exercise of a right not to speak under the *Buckley* principle.

[102] USA Constitution, First Amendment; Canadian Charter of Rights and Freedoms 1981, s. 2; Constitution of Japan, art. 21.

[103] German Basic Law, art. 5, 1; the Constitution of Ireland, art. 40. 6. 1. i. refers to the press's liberty of expression in a sub-paragraph of the Article guaranteeing the right of citizens to freedom of expression.

[104] Stewart J., 'Or of the Press' (1975) 26 *Hast. LJ* 631; Brennan J., (1979) 32 *Rutg. LR* 173, 176–82.

tutional Court appears in some respects to treat press freedom as a distinct constitutional freedom, perhaps because it is covered in a separate sentence of Article 5 in conjunction with the freedom of reporting by broadcasts and films. (Freedom of the broadcasting media, and its difference from press freedom, is discussed in Chapter III.) But it is far from plain to what extent *Pressefreiheit* does confer wider privileges and immunities than the right of individuals to express their opinions freely, and the Court usually construes the press freedom clause in the light of the general objectives of the Article as a whole.[105] The European Convention makes no special provision for freedom of the press, but the European Court has observed that the principles applicable to freedom of expression are of particular importance to the press.[106]

Are there then good arguments for giving some special meaning to a 'freedom of the press' clause? If textural and historical arguments—what did the founders of the Constitution intend?—are of limited assistance, courts must ask whether there are good reasons of constitutional principle for distinguishing free speech and freedom of the press. This inquiry necessitates some reflection on the purposes and significance of the freedoms in the context of the constitution as a whole. Some of the arguments for a free speech principle hardly apply at all to the institutional press, or alternatively fail to provide any justification for conferring on it rights or freedoms not covered by the free speech clause. For example, arguments from self-fulfilment and personal development which focus on the interests of the speaker are irrelevant to national newspapers and journals, though they may play some role in supporting the rights of fringe or underground papers. Mill's argument for freedom of discussion are not particularly pertinent to newspapers. On the other hand, the argument from democracy may suggest that the press should now be given special status and rights, in view of its particular responsibilities in keeping the public informed. Freedom of the press may mean not only the freedom of newspapers to publish information and opinion, but may also entail certain rights of investigation, and rights of access to public institutions. On a more radical view, it can be contended that the framers of a constitution have recognized the unique value of the press as a check on government by its specific mention in the document; and it is for the courts then to give effect to this status by recognizing rights which enable it to discharge its responsibilities. We are

---

[105] See, e.g., 10 BVerfGE 118, 121 (1960); 20 BVerfGE 162, 174–6 (1966); 34 BVerfGE 269, 282–3 (1973).
[106] *Sunday Times* v. *UK* (1979) 2 EHRR 245, 280.

on this approach far removed from free speech and its immediate implications.[107]

To some extent there may seem to be special rules for the press, including certain immunities, in the legal systems we are considering: for example, there is a right to found a newspaper free from a licensing system and to run it free from discriminatory taxation on profits or turnover.[108] But these rules only involve the application to the press of general free speech principles. Thus the invalidity of a licensing system is an application of the widespread hostility towards censorship of speech. In fact, the courts in the United States and Germany have stopped short of the more radical position canvassed at the end of the previous paragraph. Although it is not precluded by the text or spirit of the relevant constitutions, it is equally not required by them. The press does indeed perform a crucial role in modern democracies, but, as the British Royal Commission concluded in 1977, it is questionable whether it should be given a wide set of legal privileges which would set it apart from ordinary individuals.[109] A legal problem which would arise from the admission of special status is the definition of the 'press' for this purpose. Should books, weekly journals, specialist magazines, and the underground press be included, or only the daily national and local newspapers?[110] The argument from democracy discussed in the last paragraph suggests that the status should be reserved for the latter, but this discrimination may be considered élitist and reinforces the objections to the grant of legal privileges. German law incidentally adopts a wide definition for the purpose of the Article 5 guarantee of *Pressefreiheit*.[111]

A further argument against recognition of a distinct constitutional right of press freedom, separate from freedom of speech, is that there may be conflicts between the two rights. How should a legal system concerned to enhance free speech resolve a claim by a person attacked in a newspaper article that he has a right to reply to it? The individual's free speech interests here conflict with the editor's freedom to control what is printed in the newspaper. Resolution of the question may partly depend on the nature of freedom of speech, in particular the extent to which it may entail positive claim-rights to have speech published in certain

[107] If 'free speech' does encompass wide claim-rights of access—see below, ch. III—the significance of a separate freedom of the press is less than it is if the former freedom is only a set of liberties and immunities.

[108] See ch. IV for these types of control on speech, especially p. 123.

[109] Cmnd. 6810, para. 19.7.

[110] See D. Lange, 'The Speech and Press Clauses' (1973) 23 *UCLA LR* 77.

[111] *Grundgesetz-Kommentar*, ed. by I. von Münch (2nd edn., Munich, 1981), i. 251.

circumstances. The legal position is, therefore, discussed in Chapter III, which is largely concerned with the question: is freedom of speech a mere liberty or does it also consist of some strong or claim-rights?[112] But it can here be pointed out that the issue is complicated if the newspaper's free speech or press interests (or rights) are thought to be threatened by recognition of a correspondent's free speech right to have his reply published. In the previous section of this chapter, it has been suggested that a paper's freedom of speech, or rather freedom not to speak, is not really infringed if it is required to publish a contribution by a particular individual.[113] Clearly, however, editorial freedom would be restricted by the imposition of such a requirement. If there is a separate constitutional right of press freedom, the untrammelled ability of an editor or owner to determine the contents of the newspaper would almost certainly be considered a necessary implication from that right. But the recognition of this right would run contrary to the weight of the free speech arguments; the public, as well as the potential correspondent, has an interest in the letter's publication. This difficulty is one reason why we should be cautious in accepting the claim that there is a right to press freedom, separate from freedom of speech.

Similar difficulties have occurred in determining whether the press is entitled to claim immunities from the application of anti-monopoly legislation. The United States Supreme Court has held that the Sherman Act may constitutionally be applied to press agencies: the First Amendment does not protect a 'freedom to combine to keep others from publishing . . . .'.[114] The 1962 British Royal Commission cited the ruling in support of its conclusion that legislation to control press mergers and monopolies does not necessarily raise freedom of the press objections.[115] The Secretary of State for Trade has since 1965 possessed powers to refer newspaper mergers and acquisitions to the Monopolies Commission, which must then report whether the transfer is contrary to the public interest, taking into account the need for free expression of opinion.[116] There has been some controversy concerning the exercise of the Secretary of State's power to refer and the adequacy of the Commission's jurisdiction, but the argument that their existence constitutes an infringement of freedom of the press is now rarely heard.[117] There has

---

[112] See below, ch. III, s. 4.
[113] See above, p. 66.
[114] *Associated Press* v. *US* 326, US 1, 20 (1945) *per* Black J.
[115] Cmnd. 1811, para. 337.
[116] See now Fair Trading Act 1973, ss. 57–61.
[117] G. Robertson, *People against the Press* (London, 1983), 120–31.

recently been a furore in France over the Mitterrand government's Press law under which severe restrictions have been imposed on the concentration of press ownership.[118] The better view, however, as the German Constitutional Court has indicated, is that there is no constitutional objection to such laws, provided their object and effect is to ensure that a wide range of opinion reaches the public.[119] Often arguments against such legislation on grounds of press freedom conceals opposition which is really concerned to protect vested property rights. However, antimonopoly legislation, which is aimed at silencing particular views would infringe freedom of speech and the press, as would discriminatory tax legislation.

A final difficulty, emerging to some extent from the previous paragraphs, is this: would a separate freedom of the press be the freedom of the owner, the editor, or the journalist? This has rarely been adequately discussed by proponents of a distinct institutional freedom for the Fourth Estate. One constitutional conundrum would be whether legal recognition of an owner's power to dismiss an editor for writing leaders, which run contrary to the former's views, is required by or contrary to press freedom? The question is difficult enough if one examines it simply in terms of a free speech provision. The answer is almost certainly that there is no constitutional right to exercise free speech rights in a particular private employment, so that subject to the jurisdiction's rules of labour law, the editor may properly be dismissed.[120] Recognition of a separate freedom of the press, with its general implications of a right of editorial freedom in such contexts as the 'right of reply' controversy, only makes the issue more complicated. The usual view in Germany, where the question of internal press freedom (*innere Pressefreiheit*) has more often been canvassed than in the United States and Britain, is that the Basic Law affords no clear answers to these problems; press freedom neither requires nor precludes legal control of an owner's powers.[121] Certainly the Constitutional Court studiously avoided any definite pronouncement in a case concerning the legality of an editor's dismissal from his post.[122] Press

[118] Some provisions in the original Bill were ruled by the Conseil constitutionnel to be incompatible with the Declaration of the Rights of Man 1789: see P. Morigin, 'Loi du 23 octobre 1984', *Juris-Classeur Penal* 2, commentary on arts. 283–94.

[119] 20 BVerfGE 162, 176 (1966).

[120] It is different if the employment is public, where the state itself imposes the sanction; see for USA, *Pickering* v. *Board of Education*, 391 US 563 (1968), and under the European Convention, 9228/80, *X.* v. *Germany* (1983) 5 EHRR 471.

[121] *Grundgesetz-Kommentar*, 256–7.

[122] 52 BVerfGE 283 (1979) (held that art. 5 did not preclude a statutory obligation to grant works council a hearing before dismissal of editor).

freedom, as already mentioned, does mean the freedom to found a newspaper, free from licensing restrictions and discriminatory taxation; it probably follows that the founder, and subsequent owners, should enjoy some management prerogatives to determine the newspaper's ideology. It is questionable, however, whether it is necessary or useful to invoke distinctive constitutional arguments in this context.

Although, therefore, the case for separate press rights remains unproven, there are a few circumstances in which it is legitimate for practical reasons to recognize some degree of privilege. In later chapters of this book, there is some discussion of rights of access to government institutions, such as prisons, or to attend criminal trials, which may be regarded as necessary aspects of freedom of speech.[123] It would obviously be impossible for everyone to exercise such a right. In these circumstances the press, or representative members of it, might be given special facilities on behalf of the public. It makes more sense to allow journalists rights of access than to confer them on interested individuals or pressure groups, because the former are in a better position to communicate the information to the public. To that extent journalists might be accorded greater rights of *free speech* than other members of the population.

Sometimes, it is argued, there is a First Amendment right to acquire information relevant to the conduct of government. It is difficult to support this on the basis of freedom of speech, largely because there is something paradoxical, to say the least, about a claim to secure information from an unwilling speaker.[124] The press can try instead to assert such a right under the 'freedom of the press' limb of the First Amendment or other pertinent constitutional provision, on the ground that it is a vital function of the press to obtain, and then disclose, government information. But its recognition by the court does then depend on a willingness to grant pressmen legal privileges. On the other hand, if everyone has a constitutional 'right to know' (in addition to the statutory right which may be created by freedom of information legislation), the press should be in exactly the same position as the public; unlike the situations considered in the previous paragraph, there are no practical arguments for giving it some preferential treatment.

Rights of access and rights to know as possible aspects of freedom of speech are further discussed in some detail in the next chapter. Two related legal problems are mentioned here to illustrate the consequences which would follow from recognition of such separate claim-rights of the

---

[123] See below, ch. III, s. 5, and ch. VIII, s. 5.
[124] The point is further discussed below, p. 82.

press. Do journalists have a right to refuse to disclose the names of their sources on the ground that this would handicap news-gathering, and does the press have some immunity from search warrants, the execution of which would enable the police to look through press files and may similarly deter the supply of news by the public? The Supreme Court by a bare majority denied the former right in *Branzburg* v. *Hayes*.[125] Reporters claimed a privilege under the First Amendment to refuse to appear before, and answer questions at, grand jury investigations into various serious offences. For the Court majority, White J. refused to recognize that the press enjoyed any special privileges either with regard to access to information or for the claimed immunity from answering questions during the course of a criminal investigation. Moreover, any First Amendment interest that did exist was outweighed by the government's strong interest in detecting crime. Emphasizing the close connection between free speech and press freedom, White J. stated that the case involved 'no intrusions upon speech and no command that the press publish what it prefers to withhold'.[126] In contrast the German Constitutional Court has stated that freedom of the press may enable newspapers to protect their sources' confidentiality and to refuse to answer questions.[127] These immunities cannot, however, be invoked regardless of the circumstances. For example, a reporter was not entitled to refuse to answer questions concerning the identity of suspects, who had claimed to him that they had been promised sums of money by the law enforcement authorities for talking to the press. In this situation important state interests, in particular in the prevention of corruption by public officials, outweighed any possible right to keep the sources of information secret.[128]

The treatment of these issues in Britain has a chequered history. Two cases decided in 1963 showed that the press had no common law immunity from the general obligation to disclose sources of information, when this is relevant to proceedings in a court of law or a tribunal of inquiry.[129] Against this, newspapers (and the broadcasting media) have enjoyed for over a hundred years a privilege not to disclose the names of their informants during the interlocutory stage of libel proceedings.

[125] 408 US 665 (1972).
[126] Ibid., 681.
[127] 20 BVerfGE 162, 176 (1966).
[128] 25 BVerfGE 296 (1969). Also see 64 BVerfGE 108 (1983) (privilege does not apply to questions about persons placing advertisements, since this section of a newspaper is not so important to the functions of the press).
[129] *Att.-Gen.* v. *Glough* [1963] 1 QB 773 (DC); *Att.-Gen.* v. *Mulholland* [1963] 2 QB 477 (CA).

Often called 'the newspaper rule',[130] in principle it ought to apply to individual defendants in defamation actions, since British law, partly owing to the difficulties of defining the 'press', generally refuses to accord newspapers legal privileges.[131] In 1980 the House of Lords in *British Steel* v. *Granada Television* refused to recognize any privilege for the press not to disclose its sources of information in an equitable action for discovery. Granada was required to reveal the names of the plaintiff's employees who had supplied it with some confidential documents, quoted in a current affairs programme on a steel strike. Only Lord Salmon in dissent, seeing no sensible justification for limiting the 'newspaper rule' to libel actions, was prepared to apply it to these proceedings. He was moreover willing to recognize that the press enjoyed a special privilege to keep its sources confidential, not shared, for example, by government departments which generally should disclose information when this was relevant to the administration of justice.[132] The other Law Lords, however, were adamant that freedom of the press was not in issue at all, an unqualified assertion that was perhaps made possible by Granada's concession that they would not have been able to resist the grant of an injunction to restrain publication of the documents.[133] At least two members of the majority saw difficulties in treating the media differently from members of the public. Since freedom of the press, like free speech, is in Britain only a common law principle, and not a constitutional right, there is something to be said for this caution. Privileges should not be conferred by judicial decision, particularly if there is no social consensus in their favour.

The law has now been amended by section 10 of the Contempt of Court Act 1981, under which nobody is required to disclose sources of information contained in his publication, unless this disclosure is necessary in the interests of justice, national security, or the prevention of crime. In the first case to discuss the provision the House of Lords has recently ruled that the *Guardian* was not entitled to invoke it as a defence to an action for the return of a copy of a confidential document, the property of the Crown, which had been anonymously sent to the

---

[130] Gatley, *Libel and Slander* (8th edn., London 1981, by P. S. C. Lewis), para. 1216.

[131] See Lord Fraser's discussion of the rule in *British Steel* v. *Granada* [1981] AC 1096, 1197–9, considered by Gatley, *Libel and Slander*, to be wrong.

[132] For example, *Norwich Pharmacal Co.* v. *Customs and Excise Commssrs* [1977] AC 133 (HL), applied by the majority in the *British Steel* case. Usually British judges are sympathetic to claims by the government (or other public bodies) that its sources of information remain confidential.

[133] See the discussion in ch. IV, s. 3.

newspaper.[134] The document had been addressed by the Ministry of Defence to the Prime Minister, and discussed the ways in which the government could best deal with the controversy resulting from the arrival of cruise missiles in Britain. The Lords, unanimously reversing the Court of Appeal on this point, held that the provision in the Contempt of Court Act did cover proceedings for the return of property or documents from which the identity of a source could be discovered, but then, with Lords Fraser and Scarman dissenting, ruled that the Crown had shown that return of the document was necessary in the interests of national security. This was not because the particular leak of the document endangered that interest, but because an informant who was not traced and removed from his position would continue, in the majority's view, to pose a continued threat to national security.[135] But this controversial approach to the weighing of the competing interests— national security and confidentiality of sources—reduces the significance of the balancing required by the section, for strictly speaking the ruling would govern any case where a newspaper published classified infor- mation; however trivial that information might be, it could still be argued that the absence of sanctions might 'encourage' the civil servant on a subsequent occasion to leak information which was appropriately classi- fied as 'secret'. In any case, whatever its significance after this decision, section 10 of the Contempt of Court Act clearly does not confer any privilege on the institutional press; it can be invoked by anybody, whether he is writing for a newspaper, or is publishing any book or tract as long as it is addressed to the public or a section of it.[136]

Immunity from searches can be discussed more briefly. The case for recognition of an immunity seems much weaker, since it is hard to believe that the prospect of searches under warrant in a newspaper office will really deter news-gathering by the press or inhibit people supplying it with information. The Supreme Court refused to provide the press with special protection in this context, when it held in *Zurcher* v. *Stanford Daily*[137] that the government might issue a search warrant to look for pictures and film in newspaper offices, which might constitute evidence

---

[134] *Secretary of State for Defence* v. *Guardian Newspaper Ltd* [1984] 3 WLR 986, affirming the decision of the Court of Appeal [1984] Ch. 156.

[135] Only Lord Scarman refused to give express assent to this proposition. He also emphasized (n. 134 above, p. 1008) the duty of the Court not to accept 'without critical examination' the Crown's argument that national security was implicated.

[136] Contempt of Court Act 1981, s. 2(1).

[137] 436 US 547 (1978).

in a criminal prosecution arising from a demonstration. The argument that the paper should only be liable to a subpoena requiring it to produce specific documents was rejected.

The German Constitutional Court has in principle been prepared to take a more generous approach under the Article 5 protection of *Pressefreiheit*. In the famous *Spiegel* case,[138] the Court considered a challenge to the constitutionality of the issue of search warrants to look for evidence relevant to criminal charges against the publisher and editor of the weekly magazine, *Spiegel*. It had published an article, criticizing the performance of the German army in recent NATO manoeuvres and discussing plans, allegedly contemplated at that time by the Defence Minister, Franze-Josef Strauss, for the equipment of the army with nuclear weapons. The evidence was required to substantiate charges of disclosing state secrets contrary to the treason statute. All the members of the Court considered that press freedom encompassed a degree of immunity from arbitrary searches of newspaper offices and confiscation of their material. This was subject to the limits imposed by general laws, while those laws must be construed in the light of the values protected by the Constitution. Four judges held that in this case the search was not unconstitutional, since it had been designed to look for evidence of a serious crime, in which the occupiers of the premises were suspected of being participants. The press only enjoyed those immunities which were compatible with the general constitutional order and the well-being of the state. The other four judges—in effect, the dissenting opinion because of the rule that a majority is needed to reverse a lower court's decision[139]—thought the press enjoyed greater freedom to publish military secrets than ordinary people, particularly when the publication involved, as arguably the *Spiegel* article did, the presentation and analysis of information which was already available elsewhere.[140] Moreover, they considered that the lower court had not fully considered whether there were other means of discovering evidence when it upheld the issue of the search warrants.

Whatever the statements of principle may suggest, in practice the constitutional position in Germany seems similar to that in the United

---

[138] 20 BVerfGE 162 (1966). See the note by H. Bernstein, (1966–7) 15 *Am. Jo. Comp. Law* 547.

[139] Gesetz über das Bundesverfaßungsgericht, 1951 BGBl. S. 243, s. 15(2).

[140] This point has arisen in the USA: see *US* v. *Progressive* 467 F. Supp. 990 (1979), where much of the information contained in the defendant's projected article concerning the manufacture of H-bombs was admitted by the government to be already in the public domain; see below, ch. IV, s. 3, for further discussion of this case.

States. In both jurisdictions free speech or free press interests must be taken into account in determining the constitutionality of the search warrant, but neither recognizes an absolute immunity on the basis that the press enjoys particular constitutional status. There is little to support the proposition that searches (which are otherwise constitutionally and legally valid) may endanger press freedom. Of course there may be other constitutional issues concerning freedom from arbitrary searches and rights of privacy, and perhaps where the press itself is accused of an offence the privilege against self-incrimination. The press is as entitled to avail itself of these freedoms as any individual or institution. Moreover, courts are right to scrutinize government action if it attempts to search newspaper premises, when the press itself is not suspected on reasonable grounds of involvement in a serious offence or possession of relevant evidence against a third party. Free speech arguments here do reinforce the conclusion that the search is arbitrary and contrary to some other specific constitutional provision or principle. However, where there are good reasons for the search, it would be wrong to allow the press to claim special privileges and immunities. At the most there is a case for establishing particular procedures for the grant of warrants—as instituted by the recent British Police and Criminal Evidence Act 1984 for 'journalistic material'—in order to prevent abuse.[141] To do more than this would be to confer a privileged status on the press, without any demonstration that this is necessary to enable it to exercise its freedom of speech.

[141] s. 13.

III

The Character and Scope of Freedom of Speech

1. INTRODUCTION

THE preceding chapter examined the meaning of 'speech' for the purposes of legal application of the free speech principle. This chapter is concerned with an equally intransigent subject: what does *freedom* of speech entail? In particular, legislatures and courts must decide whether commitment to the freedom requires only the recognition of a liberty to speak and write, free from governmental restraints, or whether it may also to some extent demand the provision (by the state or even private individuals) of facilities for speech. For example, it is argued, particularly in Britain by Labour politicians and trade unionists, that freedom of speech and of the press will only be properly realized if ordinary people have claim-rights of access to the newspaper columns and to appear on radio and television. Similar arguments have been made in the United States to justify the recognition under the First Amendment of a right to demonstrate on the streets and in other public places.

The debate as to the true character of freedom of speech naturally raises a number of philosophical and political issues. To some extent it is an aspect of the long-running controversy whether political freedom is only a *negative* freedom from state control and regulation, or whether it also comprises *positive* freedoms and rights against the state, because there is only real freedom when everyone has adequate economic and social opportunity to exercise civic rights and participate in the community.[1] At the level of purely philosophical argument, considerable light on the question may be shed by reflection on the reasons why free speech is regarded as worthy of protection in the first place: if the main justification for the free speech principle is the fear of any governmental

---

[1] See I. Berlin, 'Two Concepts of Liberty', in *Four Essays on Liberty* (Oxford, 1969); C. Taylor, 'What's Wrong with Negative Liberty?', in *The Idea of Freedom: Essays in Honour of Isaiah Berlin* (ed. A. Ryan, Oxford, 1979), 175.

regulation, we might be more reluctant to countenance state measures designed to ensure access to the media than we would be if we were concerned primarily to ensure the widest possible dissemination of political information to the electorate—the argument from democracy considered in the first chapter. Constitutional courts, however, must also take into account any indications in the text that positive rights of speech should be recognized. They should, moreover, consider institutional factors, in particular the extent to which regulation of any positive rights is undertaken by independent agencies to minimize the dangers of government control over the content of expression. Similar considerations may influence the form of any legislation enacted to secure facilities for speech or to provide freedom of information. Therefore, even if as a matter of political principle free speech is really a 'liberty' from government intervention and censorship, legal systems may recognize some positive rights as aspects of the freedom. In fact the jurisdictions discussed in this book are unwilling to do this except in certain particular circumstances. Some general arguments are considered in the next section of the chapter, while the other three sections are concerned with various contexts in which the nature of freedom of speech is often debated: the 'right' to hold meetings, access to the press and media, and freedom of information.

A lawyer's approach to this subject may be influenced by the writing of the American jurist, Hohfeld. He categorized all legal relationships into the following correlations: right–duty, liberty–no right, power–liability, immunity–disability.[2] The analysis of broad legal concepts, such as 'the right to trade' or 'the right to work', in terms of these relationships would according to this theory prevent confusion and wrong legal conclusions. One party has a *right* to performance of a contract (or damages in lieu), and the other has a correlative duty to honour the agreement, but 'the right to trade' is really only a *liberty* (or 'privilege' to use Hohfeld's own terminology) since there is no correlative duty not to interfere with someone's trading. So, it has been said that 'freedom of speech, which is a liberty, represents the limits of the duty not to utter defamation, blasphemy, obscenity, and sedition', and further, that there are no correlative duties not to interfere with the liberty.[3] The liberty to speak and write means that the state has no right to intervene. But nobody has a

---

[2] W. N. Hohfeld, *Fundamental Legal Conceptions* (Newhaven, 1919). Hohfeld used the term 'privilege' rather than 'liberty', but the latter is more illuminating in this context.
[3] G. Williams, 'The Concept of Legal Liberty' (1956) 56 *Col. LR* 1129, reprinted in *Essays in Legal Philosophy* (ed. R. S. Summers, Oxford, 1968), 121, 122, and 138–9.

duty to listen, nor is the state (or anyone else for that matter) under a duty to provide facilities for speech. Of course, the liberty may to some extent be protected by various claim-rights, where there are correlative duties, e.g. the right of a person not to be assaulted when he is speaking or the right of a property-owner to hold meetings on his land free from disturbances amounting to the torts of trespass or nuisance, but these rights are only incidentally associated with and not integral to the freedom of speech.[4]

This analysis, however, only states conclusions about the rights and relationships within a particular legal system. Characterization of free speech as only a liberty is generally accurate for the position in Britain, but this is not a universal truth. In the United States, for example, the First Amendment imposes a disability on Congress and confers corresponding immunities on those entitled to assert the freedom of speech. More generally, however, Hohfeldian analysis does not really provide any guidance how free speech (or other civil liberties) provisions ought to be construed. In the absence of clear indications in the relevant text, these questions have to be decided by the courts on the basis of the philosophical and political arguments to be discussed shortly. Further the analysis is hard to apply satisfactorily to rights and freedoms that are claimed against the state and other public authorities; Hohfeld was only concerned with the categorization of jural relationships between individuals.[5]

An assertion that freedom of speech does (on occasion) confer positive claim-rights against the state is itself far from clear. It might mean that the state is under a duty not to interfere—or to tolerate interference by others—with the freedom, so that damages are recoverable if there is such interference. Or it may be argued that the state itself is under a duty to provide facilities for speech, or to compel the provision by some persons or institutions of such facilities. Of course, these uncertainties in the assertion do not mean it is misconceived, and that we should therefore conclude after all that freedom of speech is only a liberty. But they do show that the implications of the broader view of the scope of free speech require more consideration than they have hitherto generally received. In constitutional ligitation, however, this theoretical point is of little importance, for the argument then need only be that freedom of

---

[4] See H. L. A. Hart, 'Bentham on Legal Rights', in *Oxford Essays in Jurisprudence*, 2nd series (ed. A. W. B. Simpson, Oxford, 1973), 171, 179–81.

[5] A. M. Honoré, 'Rights of Exclusion and Immunities against Divesting' (1959–60) 34 *Tul. LR* 453, 459.

speech should be construed to include a specific positive right—e.g. to reply to a personal attack in a newspaper column—rather than a general set of claim-rights.

2. POLITICAL ARGUMENTS CONCERNING CLAIM-RIGHTS TO FREE SPEECH

The general policy arguments for the recognition under a constitutional free speech clause (or by the legislature) of positive free speech rights of access are broadly of two kinds. One resting on the speaker's interests will be considered a little later. The other approach proceeds from the interests of recipients, and is particularly pertinent if the 'participatory democracy' rationale for free speech protection is emphasized in judicial interpretation of the constitutional provision. As mentioned in Chapter I, the freedom to receive information and ideas is explicitly covered in Article 5 of the German Basic Law (*Informationsfreiheit*) and in Article 10 of the European Convention.[6] In the United States recipient interests are frequently taken into account in interpretation of the First Amendment.[7] These interests—in receiving as much information and as wide a range of ideas as possible to enable intelligent political choices to be made—will only be satisfied (it is said) if the recipient is exposed to the views of everyone who wishes to communicate with him. The relevance of this to the discussion about possible rights of access to the media is particularly clear: now that radio and television are the most significant means for influencing public opinion and the most important fora for public debate, the electorate should be able to hear on the media the views of ordinary people in addition to those of politicians and professional broadcasters.

However, the recognition of recipient interests in hearing a wide range of views and in access to information does not compel the grant (either by the legislature or constitutional courts) of individual *rights* to speak on the media or to use public facilities and premises for speech. The argument only constitutes a powerful case for ensuring that the media transmit a variety of opinions. In the case of information, the interest of the public in its receipt does not warrant the conclusion that everyone, or anyone in particular, has a right to transmit it; recipient interests are satisfied if someone is free to communicate the news.[8] Moreover, the freedom to

[6] The texts are set out above, pp. 33 and 35.
[7] See below, pp. 82, 103, and 109.
[8] See 5178/71, *De Geillustreerde Pers.* v. *Holland* 8 D. & R. 5, where the Commission ruled that the public interest in the receipt of information about television programmes did not justify a right on the part of the press to publish it in violation of copyright laws.

receive information, as for instance the German *Informationsfreiheit*,[9] is usually regarded as a liberty (*Abwehrrecht*), so it would be odd to use it as a foundation for the recognition of claim-rights to impart ideas and information. A recent United States case shows the possible implications of a bolder approach. In *Island Trees School District* v. *Pico*,[10] three members of the Supreme Court were prepared to recognize a First Amendment claim-right of school students to read any book once it had been placed in the school library, so that the governing board were under a correlative duty not to remove it on the basis of its 'offensive' contents. The dissent of Rehnquist J. pointed out that the recognition of a right to receive information implies that the communicator has an equally strong right to transmit it.[11] In this case, the argument might lead to the bizarre conclusion that an author or publisher has some right that the school library acquire his work, or at least not delete it from the list. Similarly, it might be said that if listeners have a right not to have a particular programme taken off the radio, the producers should have an equivalent right to transmit it.[12] These results would be regarded by most people as unacceptable. They show, it is suggested, that it is probably unwise to treat the freedom to receive information or ideas as more than a liberty, and also to build strong speaker rights on this foundation.

The most radical use of recipient interests as a basis for the recognition of rights of access arises in a different context from those discussed so far. Free speech, it is sometimes argued, will be valueless if the public does not have an opportunity to acquire enough information from the government (and other public bodies) to enable it to discuss political issues on approximately equal terms with politicians and civil servants. In other words, the 'right to know' is an integral aspect of freedom of expression. The case has a long and respectable ancestry,[13] but it is surely easy to spot a critical weakness: freedom of expression is claimed in circumstances where there is no willing speaker. It might be right to apply a free speech clause to uphold a claim to speak to a mass audience

---

[9] See Maunz-Dürig, *Kommentar zum Grundgesetz* (Munich, 1982), paras. 60–3 and 101 of treatment of art. 5.

[10] 102 S. Ct. 2799 (1982); see further, s. 5 of this chapter.

[11] 102 S. Ct. 2831 (1982).

[12] The Supreme Court has denied a constitutional right of listeners to compel review by the Federal Communications Commission of programme changes: *FCC* v. *WNCN Listeners Guild* 450 US 582 (1981).

[13] For example Milton, *Areopagitica: A Speech for the Liberty of Unlicensed Printing* (1644; in *Prose Writings*, Everyman edn., 1958), 145, and J. Madison, quoted by T. I. Emerson, 'Legal Foundations of the Right to Know' (1976) *Wash. LQ* 1.

on television or even conceivably to prevent a school board (as in the *Pico* case) from interfering with the rights of the author and students, but it is surely far-fetched to invoke it to compel, say, the government or a public enterprise to disclose information against its will.[14] Some of the values underlying freedom of speech probably do justify the recognition of a right to know or access to information. That is, however, not very significant, for equally these values would support legal enforcement of rights to education, minimum standards of living and other goods which foster participation in political debate.

We should now turn to the second argument for recognizing some positive, claim-rights to speak. This focuses on the speaker's interests. It proceeds from an attempt to harmonize the demands of equality in this context with those of liberty. The case is that all people should have equal opportunities to present their views; free speech should not be the privilege of the rich and powerful.[15] The more educated may write books and articles, and the rich may own newspapers and (in some countries) television channels. In contrast, the poor and oppressed can only express their opinions through demonstrations on the streets, and in meetings held in premises they do not own. Since the press and broadcasters predominantly represent (it is claimed) conservative and establishment views, a balance can only be achieved by conferring on minority groups and individuals legal rights of reply to comment in the press and of access to the media. True freedom of speech in short requires the recognition of claim-rights for persons wishing to speak and the imposition of corresponding duties to afford them facilities and grant equal opportunities for the exercise of these rights.

One important consequence may follow from this argument. If freedom of speech is not regarded solely as an absence of government restraint, the powers exercised by private individuals, such as newspaper magnates, or by public agencies like the BBC, to control what is written and broadcast may become subject to legal control under a free speech clause. There may in certain cases be no real difference between state censorship and the private censorship exercised by editors and journalists.[16] If the streets and open land in a community are in private

---

[14] Such compulsion would completely ignore or override the speaker's interests: see the discussion in ch. I, p. 26.

[15] See A. Cox, *The Role of the Supreme Court in American Government* (Oxford, 1976), 42–3; H. Kalven, 'The Concept of the Public Forum' [1965] *Sup. Ct. Rev.* 1, 10–12.

[16] For a more conservative view, generally defending the validity of the distinction, see F. Schauer, *Free Speech: A Philosophical Enquiry* (Cambridge, 1982), 119–28.

ownership, the freedom to demonstrate may equally be subject to an individual's control.

At the philosophical level the debate between advocates of positive free speech rights, and those taking the more traditional view of free speech as a liberty, may turn substantially on the reasons for adopting the free speech principle. The conclusion that the freedom is only a liberty from official restraint and can never found rights against private bodies is inevitable if the main justification for the principle is the fear of government abuse. The proposition is really a tautology. But it may be that the more positive arguments considered in Chapter I have played a significant role in shaping the constitutional right of freedom of speech— whatever their defects as abstract arguments of principle. Moreover, the courts in a particular country may be required to construe the free speech clause in conjunction with other provisions stipulating rights of equality and non-discrimination in the exercise of constitutional rights. These may suggest there should be some recognition of rights of access in certain circumstances.

Traditionalists can easily show that the equality case proves too much. If free speech entails an equal opportunity to appear on television, does it not also require equal education facilities or cash hand-outs from the state to cover the publication costs of journals and articles? Moreover, if a local authority is required to allow any group to use its premises for public meetings and an editor is obliged to print replies to his leading article, might it not follow that a publisher should be under an obligation to produce a balanced list of new titles each year? The recognition of rights and duties in all these situations would require a significant degree of regulation by the government; alternatively, the courts might feel constrained to devise or superintend remedies where the legislature has omitted to act.[17] Intervention on a large scale would indeed pose dangers to general liberty, quite apart from the possible risks to the free speech rights of the editor or broadcaster—a complex issue considered in section 4 of this chapter.

Yet these points do not altogether destroy the case for recognition of claim-rights of free speech in some limited circumstances. A number of factors are relevant in the selection of these situations. The argument from equality seems particularly strong where the government, or public authority, has pursued a discriminatory course of conduct, allowing

---

[17] There are doubts about the courts' competence to devise remedies, even in areas where positive action may be required, for example, to achieve school integration: D. L. Horowitz, *The Court and Social Policy* (New York, 1977).

facilities for some political groups to speak and denying them to others. That is why it is appropriate to uphold a right of equal access to use public buildings for meetings, as is the position under the First Amendment.[18] In this context it seems artificial to draw any distinction between the *liberty* to speak and a *right* to hold a meeting; the convenor of the forbidden meeting has a reasonable expectation that he will be treated in the same way as others who have been given permission. Moreover, it seems reasonable to characterize such discrimination as 'state action' for the purpose of any constitutional doctrine requiring the involvement of government before rights can be asserted, even though in form freedom of speech has been denied through the refusal of the authority to act.[19]

While rights, such as freedom of speech, are ordinarily guaranteed only against state action, there are some situations where private persons and institutions occupy virtual monopoly positions which confer powers more or less equivalent to those possessed by the state. The concentration of the press in the hands of a few owners, privately controlled television channels, and company towns exemplify these circumstances. Private censorship may well constitute as serious a danger to free speech as state control. There is certainly no infringement of free speech if a particular learned journal refuses to publish a scholarly article; but are we quite so sure that free speech rights are not imperilled if the views of a political party or pressure group are never published (or reported) by a press whose owners are uniformly hostile to that group's ideology?

Schauer has pointed out that the evils of private censorship can only be cured by greater state control, which may significantly diminish the newspaper's speech and press freedom.[20] Detailed consideration of this particular question is left to later in this chapter.[21] There is often a risk that any attempt to equalize the opportunities for speech will reduce the freedoms of other people, but it is sometimes acceptable to run it. The degree of the quasi-monopoly, and the importance of the type of speech which is denied by that institution, are clearly relevant factors. Also significant is the extent to which abuse of regulatory power by the state can be prevented by judicial review and through the creation of independent agencies to determine when the private institution should

---

[18] See below, pp. 91–5.
[19] For the complex USA doctrine of 'state action', see L. H. Tribe, *American Constitutional Law* (New York, 1978), ch. 18. It is unclear to what extent rights under the European Convention must be protected against interference by private persons; see F. Jacobs, *The European Convention on Human Rights* (Oxford, 1975), 11–12.
[20] Schauer, *Free Speech*, 122.
[21] See below, s. 4.

concede, say, rights of reply or access. The recognition of some positive free speech rights to enable people more effectively to communicate their views to a mass audience may therefore be justified, where their voice would otherwise be systematically excluded, or where there is some indication of discrimination on the part of public authorities. It is unduly dogmatic to argue that freedom of speech cannot entail such rights in any circumstances; but they should be upheld with caution and with awareness of the accompanying dangers.

3. ACCESS TO PUBLIC FORA: MEETINGS AND PROCESSIONS

The first category of cases where the character of freedom of speech is in issue involves claims that the speaker has a right to use public open spaces or other public facilities for the exercise of this freedom. The most usual contexts are public meetings and processions; demonstrators assert that they have a right to march on the streets, hire premises, or hold meetings in parks and grounds. But a right to free speech may also be asserted by someone wishing to advertise a political cause by posting a notice in a public library or town hall. Alternatively, though less frequently, the claim may be made against the owners of private property. A common element linking these situations is that the interest in issue is primarily that of the speaker. (In contrast, in the access to the media cases and still more in the right to information cases, greater emphasis is placed on the interests of the recipients or the public.) Another feature frequently found in public fora litigation—to use the American terminology—is that the applicant bases his case on the equality and non-discrimination arguments outlined in the previous section. But there are significant differences in the facts of these cases which it is easy to overlook when they are grouped together under the rubric, 'access to public fora'.

One major variable factor is the character of the property on which the applicant claims there is a right to speak. It may be premises or spaces which are specifically dedicated to public meetings or are traditionally used for these purposes. Streets and pathways exist primarily for passage and repassage, though courts are willing to recognize they may lawfully be used for some types of demonstration compatible with this primary function. Alternatively, a convenor may claim a right to hold his meeting on public property, such as parks, army bases, or court-rooms, which are designed for other uses; here the use of the property for speech might conflict with the interests of other individual members of the public or an important governmental interest. Obviously the force of the free speech claim is much weaker in these circumstances than it is in regard to, say, a public meeting-hall. Another relevant factor is the ownership of the property concerned. It may belong to the government, or some public authority or it might be privately owned. Generally it is harder success-fully to argue for a right to hold meetings on private property; there is then some interference with the owner's freedom to regulate the use of his land, and the recognition of free speech rights in this context would pose problems in finding any element of 'state action' that may be required. These are not decisive arguments against ever upholding any such rights, but it is important to recognize the distinction between these claims and a similar claim to use public property. Sometimes the government itself in justifying a ban on speech on its land may urge that it is merely acting as a typical property-owner rather than as the state totally outlawing undesirable publications.[22] But this suggestion is unacceptable if the government (or any public authority) selects particu-lar groups as free to use meeting-halls and denies these facilities to others. There is no real analogy between this discriminatory behaviour and the management of private property by its owner.

Another possibility is that the speaker claims a right to use private property, free from restrictions imposed by the government rather than by the private property-owner. This unusual situation occurred in *US Postal Service* v. *Council of Greenburgh Civic Associations*,[23] where the majority of the Supreme Court declined to recognize a right to deposit unstamped mail in letter-boxes provided and owned by individual house-owners, but subject to regulation by the Postal Service. The Service had banned the use of the boxes for unstamped mail. There was much dispute among the members of the Court whether post-boxes were to be treated as 'public fora', similar to streets and some open spaces, suitable for the exercise of the First Amendment freedom. But Stevens J. dissenting was surely right to say that this was irrelevant; the mail-boxes are private property, and both depositor and (on the evidence) home-owners were willing to use them for unstamped mail. The case should have been examined, as it was by one or two members of the Court, purely in terms of the reasonableness of this content-neutral regulation of the manner of speech.[24] The character of free speech would have been

---

[22] The Court used to recognize an unlimited right of public authorities to ban speech on their property: *Davis* v. *Massachusetts* 167 US 43 (1897).
[23] 453 US 114 (1981).
[24] See the judgments of Brennan J. (concurring) and Marshall J. (dissenting).

relevant if the boxes had been government property or if it had been clear that the house-owners wished to exclude the material, for then it would have been necessary to rule whether the depositor had a claim-right and the box-owner a correlative duty.

A final general point is that the claim in these contexts may either be to the use of already existing facilities or to their provision. When somebody asserts that he is free to conduct a parade along the city's streets or to hold a religious or political meeting in a public park, he does not ask the public authority to do anything for him. Indeed, unless and until he is arrested for obstruction or asked to leave, he is free to be on the land; a free speech claim in these cases could be presented as an argument that the authority should not interfere with one possible use of the area, or, in Hohfeldian terms, that he has a liberty to speak in, say, Hyde Park and an immunity from government regulation (save on narrow grounds). At the opposite end of the spectrum, as it were, would be an extreme claim that the state is under a duty to build premises which are suitable for public meetings. More usual would be claims which put a lesser burden on the state: for example, to permit access to property from which the public is normally excluded, for instance, an army base, purely for the purpose of exercising free speech rights, or to allow the use of an official notice-board (in government offices or a public library) for political messages. There are in fact a bewildering variety of circumstances, in which more or less onerous duties might be imposed on the public authority or sometimes on a private individual. Some of these have emerged in the case-law, particularly from the United States, which is now discussed.

It is a commonplace observation in British constitutional law books that there is no *right* to hold a public meeting, but that meetings and processions are prima facie lawful.[25] This means that the convenor has generally no right to compel a public authority to provide him with facilities for his meeting or to permit him to hold it on the streets or other public open spaces. On the other hand, in the absence of any restriction, it is perfectly lawful to hold a meeting as an exercise of the individual's liberty of speech. There have been one or two recent attempts in the courts to argue for a strong claim-right in this context,[26] but in contradistinction to the result of some litigation in the United States, they have met with little success.

To look at the law in a little more detail, it is clear that nobody has the

---

[25] For example, see de Smith, *Constitutional and Administrative Law* (4th edn. by H. Street and R. Brazier, London, 1981), 495.

[26] In particular in *Hunt* v. *Broome* [1974] AC 587.

right to the use of a public building for a meeting, with the single exception that candidates for parliamentary and local elections are entitled to use schools and public halls for election meetings.[27] Apart from this case permission must be obtained from the owner of the property, and a public authority is as much entitled to refuse consent as is a private landowner. In practice, however, many local authorities readily give permission to political and other groups to hold meetings in town halls and other public property. But since they are exercising ordinary property rights rather than acting under specific statutory powers in allocating the use of their buildings, there is, it would seem, nothing to prevent them from discriminating between various political groups.[28] On the other hand, an authority must honour a contract to allow an extremist political party the use of its premises for a conference; when contractual *rights* are at stake, the law will not allow the authority to pick and choose.[29]

With regard to meetings on public open spaces, such as streets and parks, there is admittedly no general common law power of local authorities to ban them in advance.[30] It would be wrong, however, to infer from this even a limited right of public meeting, for not only are there many restrictions imposed by the criminal law (e.g. the offence of obstruction of the highway under the Highways Act 1980), but frequently local by-laws require the prior permission of the district authority, or on occasion the consent of a government department is needed.[31] It is sometimes said that the law in Britain is more generous with regard to processions than it is for public meetings on the streets. A procession is a use of the highway for its primary purpose of passage, so it is lawful unless it blocks the movement of other users unreasonably.[32] But there is no more a claim-right to process than there is a right to hold a meeting. It may be added that in addition to their powers here to enforce the common law of nuisance, the police have authority to control the route of, or even to apply to a local authority to ban, processions under the Public Order Act 1936. These powers are discussed in Chapter VII in the context of public order, but one point is worth mentioning here.[33]

[27] Representation of the People Act 1983, ss. 95–6.
[28] For further discussion, see *Brownlie's Law of Public Order and National Security* (2nd edn., by M. Supperstone, London, 1981), 41 and 323–5.
[29] *Verrall* v. *Great Yarmouth Council* [1981] QB 202 (CA).
[30] *M'Ara* v. *Edinburgh Magistrates*, 1913 SC 1059.
[31] *Brownlie's Law of Public Order and National Security*, ch. 2 and pp. 316–17.
[32] A. L. Goodhart, 'Public Meetings and Processions' (1937) 6 *Camb. LJ* 161.
[33] See below, ch. VII, s. 3.

Under the present law a ban may not be imposed on a particular procession or on demonstrations by specific groups; it must be comprehensively applied to all processions or at least those of a particular category. This is an unusual instance in British law of a legislative prohibition of discriminatory treatment of persons exercising freedom of expression. It falls short of the 'right of equal access' to facilities recognized in many cases by the Supreme Court, but at least it evidences a principle that might be adopted by an innovative court prepared to regulate the discriminatory exercise of power by public authorities.

The conclusion that in Britain the right of public meeting is really a liberty or 'privilege' (to use the Hohfeldian term) is of course closely connected with the residual character of the freedom in English law: the freedoms of speech and of assembly exist where the law does not interfere.[34] The inability or reluctance of the courts to control the discretionary grant of permits, the allocation of public buildings, and the exercise of police powers both reflect and reinforce this position. If the judges did intervene to ensure the equal treatment of political groups wishing, say, to hire public halls for meetings, and further if they refused to countenance bans on public meetings, save on narrow circumscribed grounds, some claim-rights would in effect be recognized. The present state of British law is attributable to the absence of constitutional protection for free speech and of any judicial recognition of a strong free speech principle rather than to the inherent meaning of freedom of speech. This can be simply illustrated by contrasting two cases in this area. In the English *De Morgan* case,[35] the Divisional Court upheld a by-law which enabled the Metropolitan Board of Works to discriminate between types of meeting when deciding whether to grant permits for gatherings on Clapham Common. No objection was taken either by the Court, or more strangely by the applicants, to the open-ended character of this prior restraint system. On the other hand, in *Kunz* v. *New York*[36] the Supreme Court, by an 8–1 majority, held that a New York ordinance empowering the police commissioner to refuse a meeting on the streets on any ground was an unacceptably broad restraint and violated the First Amendment. A more precise ordinance which precluded arbitrary decisions might have been acceptable. Jackson J. dissenting pointed out that the majority were in effect ruling that the speaker had a right to hold

---

[34] See the discussion in ch. I, p. 29.
[35] *De Morgan* v. *Metropolitan Board of Works* (1880) 5 QBD 155.
[36] 340 US 290 (1951).

a meeting on the streets, until it occasioned disorder when a criminal prosecution could be brought.

One interesting British case where the character of freedom of assembly was discussed is *Hunt* v. *Broome*.[37] The defendant, a strike picket during a building workers' dispute, attempted to stop a lorry-driver entering a building site. His defence to the prosecution for obstructing the highway (an offence under the Highways Act 1959) was that he had a right to cause a temporary obstruction under section 134 of the Industrial Relations Act 1971. This provision made it clear that picketing did not of itself constitute a crime or a tort, but the House of Lords unanimously refused to hold that it afforded a defence to the obstruction charge. According to them the defendant's case was tantamount to a contention that he had a right to stop anyone using the highway and that that person then had a duty to halt and listen. That could not be correct either as a matter of principle—it would interfere with the right to use the highway free from obstruction—or as a matter of statutory interpretation.[38] The decision seems right, even if some of the reasoning is open to criticism. What the defendant was really contending was that he had a right against the state to hold a short meeting on the highway even if this temporarily held up those wishing to enter the site. This claim-right could not be easily inferred from the terms of the 1971 statute, though it could just be argued that without such a right it was not really possible to communicate effectively with lorry-drivers. Recognition of the right on this basis would, however, have placed union pickets in an exceptionally privileged position compared with other members of the public,[39] and it was hardly surprising that the Lords declined to take this step. In a later case the Divisional Court has similarly refused to recognize a right of access to British Airports Authority land for the purpose of picketing.[40]

Any discussion of the comparable American law inevitably starts with the much-quoted judgment of Roberts J. in *Hague* v. *CIO*.[41] The Committee for Industrial Organization, a trade union, challenged a New Jersey city ordinance establishing a licensing system for the holding of

[37] [1974] AC 587.
[38] In Hohfeldian analysis, the right to use the highway is a 'privilege' or 'liberty': see Williams, 'The Concept of Legal Liberty', 139.
[39] Compare *Hubbard* v. *Pitt* [1976] QB 142, where the Court of Appeal granted estate agents an interim injunction to restrain a picket outside their premises, which amounted to a nuisance.
[40] *British Airports Authority* v. *Ashton* [1983] 1 WLR 1079.
[41] *Hague* v. *CIO* 307 US 496 (1939).

meetings on the streets and in its parks and public buildings. City officials had refused the applicant permission to hold a meeting in a public park to explain to workers the meaning of the recently passed National Labour Relations Act. There was no evidence of any apprehended breach of peace; moreover, it was clear that other groups had been given permits to hold meetings in public places. The case was, therefore, that the ordinance was itself void in that it did not preclude arbitrary exercise of licensing powers, and, secondly, that it had been applied in a discriminatory manner. A majority of the Supreme Court rejected the city's submission that it was as entitled to use its property freely as a private property owner, a proposition still generally true of British law. The licensing system was both on its face and as applied void. The decision itself does not perhaps state anything more radical than the *Kunz* ruling and other cases outlawing discriminatory permit systems for street demonstrations, though the principle was here applied to public parks. But a passage in Roberts J.'s judgment has been cited to support a general right of access to public places for the exercise of free speech rights:[42]

Wherever the title of streets and parks may rest, they have immemorially been held in trust for the use of the public and, time out of mind, have been used for purposes of assembly, communicating thought between citizens, and discussing public questions ... The privilege of a citizen of the United States to use the streets and parks for the communication of views on national questions may be regulated in the interest of all; it is not absolute, but relative, and must be exercised in subordination to the general comfort and convenience, and in consonance with good order and peace; but it must not, in the guise of regulation, be abridged and denied.

It is this statement which paved the way for arguments that even non-discriminatory refusals to allow rights of access for free speech may be unlawful under the First Amendment.

In the last twenty years the Supreme Court has explored the implications of these 'Roberts' Rules': do they confer a right of access, or only a right of equal access so that all that is prohibited is discriminatory treatment of various groups? In what sense is the right 'relative' and what interests are compelling enough to take priority over free speech rights? Finally, should the rules be extended beyond streets and open spaces to cover government offices and buildings or in some cases even private

---

[42] Ibid., 515–16.

property? Only a few of the leading cases need be mentioned to illustrate the various problems. In *Edwards* v. *South Carolina*,[43] in the course of reversing a conviction for carrying in an orderly manner anti-segregation banners on state capitol grounds, the Court intimated that there was a right of access to demonstrate in this area. Defiance of a law *reasonably* limiting the hours during which the grounds were open to the public might have led to a different result. A more surprising decision was reached in the later case, *Brown* v. *Louisiana*,[44] where by a bare majority the Court held that there was a protected right under the First Amendment to sit in peaceably in a public library in order to protest against state segregation of the students there. There was no evidence of any disturbance, so the conviction under the state breach of the peace statute was ruled unconstitutional. This provoked a vigorous dissent from Black J. who protested that:[45]

[The First Amendment] does not guarantee to any person the right to use someone else's property, even that owned by government and dedicated to other purposes, as a stage to express dissident ideas. The novel constitutional doctrine of the prevailing opinion nevertheless exalts the power of private non-governmental groups to determine what use shall be made of governmental property over the power of the elected governmental officials.

It may be that Black J.'s remarks read too much into the majority judgment. The case does not establish a right to demonstrate for any conceivable cause in any government building and no matter what the degree of interference with the normal usage of that building. The occupiers in *Brown* were protesting against the segregated facilities in that library, not segregation laws generally or any other political grievance. And there was no evidence of significant interference with normal library use. At any rate other decisions have shown a more cautious approach to the recognition of positive rights to hold meetings on public property.

A year before the library case, the Court in *Cox* v. *Louisiana*[46] had expressly refrained from holding that the uniform, non-discriminatory banning of all processions and meetings on city streets and other public spaces under an obstruction of the highway statute (strikingly similar in terms to the British Highways legislation) would be unconstitutional.

[43] 372 US 229 (1963).
[44] 383 US 131 (1966).
[45] Ibid., at p. 166.
[46] 379 US 536 (1965).

The measure had, however, been held unconstitutional as applied on the facts, because of evidence that the police had enforced it selectively against the protestors who were demonstrating against segregation by department stores. More conclusively the Court has clearly decided there is no absolute right of access to speak and hold meetings on prison grounds[47] or on army bases,[48] though it has recognized a right to exercise First Amendment freedoms, subject to reasonable regulation, in schools, university campuses, and in the areas immediately outside a school and the Supreme Court building itself.[49]

It is not easy to make sense of these apparently conflicting cases. Perhaps the best approach is that suggested by Powell J.'s concurring judgment in *Greer* v. *Spock* to the effect that access rights will be denied where there is a basic incompatibility between the activity carried on in the particular area, e.g. an army base or prison, and the protection of free speech. This probably explains the qualified recognition of the right to demonstration in and near schools and in libraries. Both are fora devoted to the exchange of ideas and information. Moreover, this approach follows the first principle in the Roberts' Rules, that there is at least a right of equal access to use the fora traditionally employed for public discussion, viz. streets and parks.

If the Court has seemed to beat a retreat in the case of publicly owned spaces and buildings, this has been even more evident in the case of possible First Amendment rights to speak, distribute leaflets, and hold meetings on private property which is used for public purposes, principally shopping centres. In the first case, *Marsh* v. *Alabama*[50] distribution of literature in a private company town was held constitutionally protected by the First Amendment. We have seen earlier in the chapter that freedom of speech is only protected against 'state action',[51] but this problem was surmounted through the argument that the company town performed an essentially public function, and, therefore, should be equated with an ordinary municipality. Twenty years later *Marsh* was applied to a case involving the picketing of a store in a private shopping

---

[47] *Adderley* v. *Florida* 385 US 39 (1966).

[48] *Greer* v. *Spock* 424 US 828 (1976).

[49] See *Tinker* v. *Des Moines School Dist.* 393 US 503 (1969) (protest by high-school students inside school constitutionally protected); *Grayned* v. *Rockford* 408 US 104 (1972) (noisy demonstration 100 feet from high school covered by First Amendment, but subject to reasonable regulation); *US* v. *Grace* 103 S. Ct. 1702 (1983) (pavements outside Supreme Court a 'public forum' for leafleting and protest).

[50] 326 US 501 (1946).

[51] See above, p. 85.

centre,[52] but this latter ruling was subsequently distinguished on very similar facts,[53] and has now been overruled in *Hudgens* v. *NLRB*.[54] Picketing in front of an employer's store in a private shopping centre is not to be regarded as protected under the First Amendment. The Court in particular found difficulty with the 'state action' point. Stewart J. who gave the majority opinion emphasized that no redress is provided by the Constitution against a private person or corporation who abridges the free expression of others; only statute or common law could provide a remedy.

However, in an odd twist to this story, the Court has recently held it is permissible under the First Amendment for a state constitution to require a right of access to a private shopping centre for the exercise of free speech rights.[55] The California Supreme Court's construction of the 'liberty of speech' clause in the state Constitution to this effect did not violate the shopping-centre owner's property rights under the Federal Constitution;[56] the United States Supreme Court emphasized that he was free to dissociate himself from any message communicated there and that he had invited members of the public to enter this land. Clearly the recognition of a general right to use other people's private property for speech would infringe property rights, and perhaps the owner's own free speech rights, for he would then be forced to transmit another's ideas.[57] What emerges from this case is that there is no overwhelming libertarian objection to the recognition of some right of access in this context, although the Court is not prepared (as we have seen) to construe the First Amendment as generally demanding such recognition. The decision represents a sensible compromise, enabling (in theory) each state to determine the character and scope of free speech beyond the minimum established by the Supreme Court; we will see that judges frequently adopt a similar approach when determining whether there is a free speech right of access to the media.[58]

Access to public fora problems occur in contexts other than that of public meetings and demonstrations. In the *Lehman* case,[59] the City of Shaker Heights, Ohio, refused the applicant, a candidate for election to

---

[52] *Amalgamated Food Employees Union* v. *Logan Valley Plaza* 391 US 308 (1968).
[53] *Lloyd Corporation* v. *Tanner* 407 US 551 (1972).
[54] 424 US 507 (1976).
[55] *Pruneyard Shopping Center* v. *Robins* 447 US 74 (1980), affirming 592 P. 2d. 341.
[56] There was no 'taking' which violated the Fifth Amendment.
[57] This might violate the First Amendment 'right to silence' discussed in ch. II.
[58] See below, pp. 103–6.
[59] *Lehman* v. *City of Shaker Heights* 418 US 298 (1974).

the State Assembly, advertising space on municipal buses. Advertising by commercial bodies, churches, and civic groups was permitted, but there had been a consistent policy of barring political notices. The Court upheld this by a 5–4 majority. The transit system was not to be regarded as a public forum analogous to streets and parks, and the decision to limit the available space to commercial and non-controversial advertising was reasonable. There would be sensitive administrative problems for the city if it did permit political advertising, for example, whether to allocate the limited space on a 'first come, first served' basis, or perhaps to distribute it on the basis of votes in previous elections (as with television time in Britain and Germany)[60], so that minority candidates could only advertise on the less well patronized routes! Of course, such legal discrimination between types of speech would not be countenanced in other circumstances; it would not be compatible with a free speech clause to limit the type of advertisement which can appear in a newspaper or on a hoarding on private property.[61] The question is whether it is more acceptable where the use of limited public facilities is in issue. The administrative difficulties do not seem much more complex than in those cases where the hire of public premises for meetings is requested, but the difference may have been enough to warrant the conclusion that buses should not be treated as public fora. Moreover, it is surely right to take account of the interests of the transport users, who would find it less easy to avoid the enforced exposure to political advertisements than they do to keep away from meetings and demonstrations.[62]

The principle applied in the *Lehman* case has recently been extended to permit discrimination in the allocation of access to school mail-box facilities.[63] The Court here, in another 5–4 decision, upheld the refusal of a school district authority to allow a non-recognized union the access it had accorded the recognized teachers' association. Naturally this was characterized by the minority as the censorship of a particular viewpoint, normally even less acceptable than discrimination against speech on the

---

[60] For the leading German case on this, see 14 BVerfGE 121 (1962), where it was held that television time should be allocated on the basis of a number of factors, including the parties' votes at prior elections, the duration of each party's existence, and its total membership. The number of candidates, however, is not a factor, while it is in Britain; see H. Street, *Freedom, the Individual and the Law* (5th edn., London, 1982), 93.

[61] In *Metromedia* v. *City of San Diego* 453 US 490 (1981), a majority of the Court struck down an ordinance permitting some billboards to be displayed (commercial advertisements on the business' premises, and some public notices), but banning others.

[62] See the concurring judgment of Douglas J. in *Lehman* 418 US 298, 305 (1974).

[63] *Perry Educational Assoc.* v. *Perry Local Educators' Assoc.* 103 S. Ct. 948 (1983).

basis of its general contents.[64] But an authority is surely entitled to choose which groups enjoy access to special facilities for communication, such as official mail-boxes. They are hardly to be equated with streets, halls, and other places which are open or available to the public and may be regarded as appropriate fora for various types of speech. Some places are more suitable for certain types of communication than others. For example, a social security office might be required to allow the posting of information about welfare assistance, but permitted to forbid political advertisements.[65] In Britain it is common for public libraries to permit cultural groups to give details of their activities on notice-boards, but commercial and political advertising would not generally be tolerated. Similar distinctions can be drawn for hospitals, museums, and galleries.[66]

The United States case-law concerning the recognition of rights of access to speak and hold meetings is, therefore, extremely complex. In some contexts a right of equal access has been consistently upheld, and one or two cases suggest that a total denial of a right to demonstrate on public property will not be countenanced. Other cases such as *Lehman* indicate an approach more familiar to British lawyers. It would also be shared in Germany, where the freedom of expression under Article 5 and the freedom of assembly guaranteed under Article 8 (*Versammlungsfreiheit*) are treated as liberties, not entailing rights to the provision of facilities by the state.[67] Caution in this area is justified. The recognition of claim-rights may interfere with other interests (of the public or the owner) in the use of the relevant property and may require the formulation of detailed rules by the government (or other authority) to regulate the use of a limited space. These are important points, but they do not provide a decisive argument against the acceptance of some access rights, at least where the applicant has a legitimate expectation that he will be treated equally with other groups.

[64] The Court has traditionally been hostile to distinctions on the basis of the particular views or attitudes expressed in speech or writing. But in recent years, it has been more tolerant of regulations which treat some speech, for example, commercial or obscene speech, less favourably than other types: see for instance *Young* v. *American Mini Theatres* 427 US 50 (1976).

[65] In *Albany Welfare Rights Org.* v. *Wyman* 493 F 2d. 1319 (2nd Cir. 1974) the Court of Appeals held unconstitutional a ban on leafleting in a welfare office by a body attempting to assist claimants. Also see *Brown* v. *Louisiana*, n. 44 above, for the same point in the context of sit-ins.

[66] See Blackmun J. in *Lehman* v. *City of Shaker Heights* 304.

[67] Hitherto there has been no decision of the Karlsruhe Court on art. 8, but it is unlikely that the Article will be construed to impose duties on public authorities to provide facilities for speech or to compel such provision by individuals: Maunz-Dürig, *Kommentar*, paras. 20–3 on art. 8.

4. ACCESS TO THE PRESS AND MEDIA

It is in this area that arguments about the character of freedom of speech are sharpest. Traditionalists contend that to construe a free speech provision as providing some rights of access to appear on television or of reply to attacks in the press is unwarranted in principle and creates practical dangers. In particular, the regulation of such positive rights entails government interference, which threatens the freedom of speech of broadcasters and newspaper editors. Others, mainly though not entirely on the political left, argue that neither speaker nor recipient interests are properly accommodated unless all political parties and other groups and individuals have some opportunity to use the means of mass communication. The equality argument discussed earlier in this chapter might be particularly pertinent here. But most legal systems are generally no more inclined to uphold individual rights of access and reply in this context than they are comparable claim-rights in other situations. On the other hand, there is widespread recognition that the concentration of the press and broadcasting faciliities in a few hands poses problems for freedom of speech, and that some special legal regulation is on occasion appropriate.

As might be expected, British law largely reflects the traditional perspective. The press is under no obligation to print letters or articles submitted to them, nor does a person attacked in a newspaper enjoy a legal right to have a reply published. Instead extra-legal remedies for such attacks may be secured through the offices of an informal Press Council, which gives rulings on complaints against newspapers and periodicals. This body was set up in 1953 in response to the recommendations of a Royal Commission.[68] Since 1964 the chairman and a significant (though minority) proportion of its membership have been drawn from outside the press itself. Its principal functions are to protect press freedom and to maintain high professional standards in newspaper reporting and comment; it is in the exercise of this latter role that it considers complaints from members of the public and urges offending newspapers to publish replies to inaccurate items. The Council has in fact produced a formidable body of 'case-law' determining when the 'right of reply', as it is somewhat bizarrely styled, should be afforded. It must, it seems, be made available to a person or organization attacked in a

---

[68] The Press Council is discussed in G. Robertson, *People against the Press: An Enquiry into the Press Council* (London, 1983).

feature which contains disputed assertions of fact.[69] The right cannot be claimed in response to hostile opinions, or to articles, which the complainant dislikes or thinks unbalanced, but which do not attack him.[70] The Council has been criticized for inconsistency and lack of clarity in its adjudications, and certainly a greater attempt might have been made—even by an extra-legal body—to formulate more detailed and precise principles.[71] Perhaps even more important is, of course, the absence of any sanction: a newspaper can defy the recommendations of the Press Council with impunity.

These weaknesses have prompted the introduction of Right of Reply Bills in the House of Commons, one of which (in 1983) was almost given a Second Reading. Modelled on the French rules,[72] it would have entitled any individual or organization to require a newspaper (or broadcasting authority), which had made an inaccurate or distorted report involving the complainant, to publish a reply within a short period: three days in the case of a daily paper and in the next issue of a weekly or monthly periodical. A failure to publish a reply in appropriate cases—to be decided by a panel under the chairmanship of a judge—would have attracted a maximum £40,000 fine. Predictably there was some nonsense talked on both sides of the debate. The Home Office Minister resisted the Bill on the argument that it would be wrong in principle to have special rules for the press. This ignores the fact that there are already some special rules,[73] and more importantly the point that newspapers are clearly in a different position from other persons and institutions in this context. On the other side, it was said that fairness or natural justice requires some right of reply.[74] This, however, is only true if the press is under some moral (or constitutional) duty to be impartial in its treatment of issues and individuals, a position which needs some argument. The case from

---

[69] See the statement in the Chairman's foreword to the 25th Ann. Report of the Council, 1978, 3. Where the mistake of fact is clear, the Council soon established the principle that the newspaper should publish a frank correction and apology: 2nd Ann. Report, 1955, 24.

[70] See rulings in 11th Ann. Report, 1964, 76–7, and in 16th Ann. Report 1969, 34.

[71] Robertson, *People against the Press*, 78–88.

[72] Loi sur la Presse 29. 7. 1881, arts. 12 and 13, discussed in J. Rivero, *Les Libertés publiques* 2, 238–41.

[73] The speech of D. Mellor MP, Under-Secretary of State for Home Office (37 HC Deb. (6th ser.), cols. 624–8) ignored, for instance, the provisions of the Defamation Act 1952, s. 7, under which the media enjoy a special qualified privilege for the publication of certain reports. Sometimes the privilege is lost if the newspaper fails on the plaintiff's request to publish a letter of explanation and contradiction—the closest provision in British law to a right of reply.

[74] 37 HC Deb. (6th ser.), cols. 576–7 (Sir D. Walker-Smith, MP).

natural justice would, moreover, only justify the provision of a right of reply to somebody who has been personally attacked or defamed; the 1983 Bill went much further than this.

The crucial question is whether a right of reply abridges the free speech or press rights of the newspaper editor. If it does not, it is difficult to see any general constitutional argument against it, since it enables individuals to exercise liberty of speech more effectively and provides newspaper readers with a wider range of views. The United States Supreme Court in *Miami Herald Co. v. Tornillo*[75] has, however, unanimously held that a right of reply law, requiring editors to print a reply by a political candidate who had been subjected to adverse comment in the paper, did violate the First Amendment. There was an impermissible interference with freedom of the press in the compulsion to print replies; this might have lead to the omission of other material which the editor wished to publish in the particular edition of the paper, and might in the long term have encouraged him to leave out controversial matter. These undesirable consequences were only conjectural, however, and Burger CJ in the Court's leading opinion did not really explain how the right of reply law abridged the editor's freedom to say what he wanted on all current issues. It may be that the 'freedom of the press' limb of the First Amendment should be construed as covering unlimited editorial freedom to select what is published, but this interpretation, as pointed out in Chapter II, leads to difficulties, in particular the conflict in litigation such as the *Tornillo* case between free speech and free press interests. Moreover, if the veto on publication of a reply is in effect imposed by the newspaper owner, press freedom as understood by the Supreme Court in this case looks more like a quasi-property right than a freedom linked with liberty of speech.

The existence of right of reply laws in France and Germany, as well as the acceptance of informal reply 'rights' in Britain, shows that the American attitude is not universally shared.[76] Absolute positions, for or against reply laws, cannot be easily sustained. It would be ludicrous for legislation to require the *New Statesman* or *New Republic* to publish right-wing replies to feature articles or editorials.[77] Conversely a national newspaper which publishes a factually inaccurate statement about a particular individual ought to provide space for a reply or at least make an apology. The character of the particular journal is relevant because only

[75] 418 US 241 (1974).
[76] For German law, see the Länder Press laws, e.g., s. 11 Bad-Würt. PresseG.; s. 10 Bay. PresseG., discussed in M. Löffler, *Presserecht*, vol. II (Munich, 1968), 204–57.
[77] Schauer, *Free Speech*, 122.

journals with a significant national, or perhaps local, circulation are able to exercise a restraint on the dissemination of information equivalent to that imposed by government. In this situation, private censorship does seriously curtail freedom of speech. Secondly, it is surely better to confine rights of reply to clear misstatements of fact, because it is easier to judge that one has been committed than it is to conclude that an account is generally distorted or contains an unfair attack. Moreover, readers can often judge the latter for themselves. The most difficult issue is whether the right should be afforded by legislation and enforceable by judicial sanctions, or be left to informal regulations as in Britain. On balance the wisest course is to reserve legal remedies for the most serious instances of abuse by the press, that is, when there is an inaccurate statement or report about an individual. Wider rights of reply, as contemplated in the unsuccessful 1983 Bill, should be enforced extra-legally; this course reduces difficult litigation and removes what might otherwise be unacceptable burdens on the press, whether or not they amount to an abridgement of its constitutional free speech and press rights.

This compromise position carries significant implications for the scope of constitutional review. The free speech arguments against the recognition in any circumstances of rights of reply are probably unconvincing, but it may equally be true that courts should not require the provision of such rights under a free speech clause. The demarcation of these rights, in particular the determination of which journals should honour them, should primarily be a matter for legislative judgment—subject naturally to judicial review if the relevant statute is arbitrary or discriminatory. The formulation of positive rights in this context is too sensitive a task for courts to perform. There are differences here from the 'access to public fora' issues considered earlier in the chapter. There the rights are generally claimed to control the exercise of discretion by a public authority, rather than 'censorship' by a newspaper editor, and there is sometimes a powerful equality argument of constitutional status against the denial of facilities for meetings to particular groups. Neither of these features usually applies where a newspaper denies somebody the opportunity to reply. Moreover, there is in most countries a variety of newspapers; thus, a prominent politician of the left refused the 'right' to answer a hostile leading article in *The Times* may have his views published in the *Guardian*. We will now see whether the same points are equally pertinent, where access is claimed to speak on the broadcasting media. There is perhaps a stronger case for treating radio and television as 'public fora'.

In Britain ordinary people and private organizations have no right usually to broadcast on the radio or TV, though this has sometimes been advocated by politicians, such as Tony Benn, as a way of breaking down the monopoly of the BBC and the ITV companies (which put out their programmes under contract with the Independent Broadcasting Authority). Sometimes access has been granted to pressure groups and societies to broadcast their own programmes, but the only extra-legal right of reply is the 'right' of Opposition parties to reply to Ministerial broadcasts, for example, on the annual Budget, under an agreement between the broadcasting authorities and the political parties.[78] Provisions of the Broadcasting Act 1981 require the Independent Broadcasting Authority to ensure 'a proper balance and wide range' in the subject-matter of programmes and also due impartiality on the part of programme contractors in regard to matters of political or industrial controversy.[79] In a Scottish case it has been held that there is a duty to provide a balance of viewpoints, so that an interdict was obtained to restrain broadcasts by four political parties before the Devolution Referendum, three of which would have advocated a 'Yes' vote.[80] The Court of Session recognized that the applicants had standing as voters as well as members of a group campaigning for rejection of the devolution proposals, thereby taking into account recipient interests in hearing all sides of an argument. The decision is not, of course, authority for upholding a right of reply in such circumstances, but there is no obvious reason why this further step should not be taken, at least where one group is denied equal opportunity to present its view on an issue requiring resolution by the public.

British law, therefore, imposes some enforceable legal duties on broadcasting authorities to provide equal opportunities for speech, without thereby recognizing individual rights of access to broadcast on television and radio. The imposition of the duty shows that the broadcasting media are not treated in the same way as the press in that companies, whether private or public, are subject to restraints additional to those imposed by the law of libel, obscenity, and so on. German law, and to some extent United States law, also apply free speech principles differently to the press and the broadcasting media, but in both jurisdictions the justifications for these distinctions are controversial.

---

[78] See Street, *Freedom, the Individual and the Law*, pp. 90–2.
[79] Broadcasting Act 1981, ss. 2(2)(b) and 4(1)(f). The leading monograph discussing these provisions is C. R. Munro, *Television, Censorship and the Law* (Farnborough, 1979).
[80] *Wilson* v. *IBA* 1979 SLT 279.

Freedom of broadcasting (*Rundfunkfreiheit*) is specifically covered in Article 5 of the German Basic Law.[81] In a number of cases the Constitutional Court has recognized the crucial role of the mass media in shaping the development of public opinion and the consequent importance of keeping them, like the press, free from state control.[82] But the Court requires the framing of some positive legal provisions to ensure that a wide range of views is transmitted. The rules must be formulated by the *Land* legislatures and not left to the discretion of their governments.[83] Broadcasting authorities and advisory councils must themselves be drawn from representative groups and institutions to guarantee the equitable enforcement of the legislation. Unlike *Pressefreiheit*, therefore, broadcasting freedom is not only a set of liberties and immunities of the media authorities from state control. According to the *First Television* case decided in 1961, two factors explain this difference.[84] First, the number of wavelengths is severely limited, so in practice few people have any real opportunity to broadcast, unless regulations ensure some distribution of facilities. Second, the cost of instituting private stations, which the Court considered a constitutionally permissible alternative to public broadcasting, prohibited an effective free market. The assumption was that a market exists for the press.

The United States Supreme Court has also considered that the shortage of frequencies justifies a special legal regime for broadcasting. In the *Red Lion* case in 1969,[85] it unanimously upheld the constitutionality of the 'right of reply' requirement imposed by the Federal Communications Commission (FCC) on licensees of broadcasting stations: any licensee who broadcast a personal attack was obliged to send the person concerned a tape of the broadcast and afford him a right of reply at the station's expense. Since there were more prospective broadcasters than wavelengths, it was legitimate to compel licensees to share facilities with others; in this context, the rights of viewers and listeners were more important than the freedom of broadcasters.[86] The Court was not upholding, it should be noted, a *constitutional* right to reply. All that was

---

[81] See above, p. 33, for the text of art. 5.

[82] For example, 12 BVerfGE 205, 259–64 (1961); 14 BVerfGE 121, 130 (1962); 31 BVerfGE 314, 325–6 (1971); 57 BVerfGE 295, 319–21 (1981).

[83] See especially 57 BVerfGE 295, 324–5, 328–9. Under the Basic Law, regulation of broadcasting, as well as the press, is primarily a matter for the Länder: see P. M. Blair, *Federalism and Judicial Review in West Germany* (Oxford, 1981), 176–83.

[84] 12 BVerfGE 205 (1961).

[85] *Red Lion Broadcasting Co. v. FCC* 395 US 367 (1969).

[86] Ibid., 390.

decided was that there was nothing contrary to the First Amendment in the creation of a right by Congress or by the Commission in the exercise of its statutory powers.

Neither reason for distinguishing the treatment of broadcasting from that of the press carries so much conviction in the 1980s. The development of cable and satellite broadcasting, and the greater number of available frequencies, have significantly increased facilities for broadcasting, and the financial investment now required is probably no greater than for the foundation of a newspaper or periodical.[87] The wider range of opportunities allows for a less restrictive legislative framework than that imposed in the 1950s and 1960s. So, it may no longer be incumbent on each broadcaster to provide a balanced range of programmes, and a channel might even be permitted to reveal a political bias, provided that viewers and listeners are able to hear contrary views on other channels and stations. This framework was held by the German Constitutional Court in the *Third Television* case[88] to be an acceptable alternative to the traditional model, under which there is a duty to ensure balance in the subject-matter of programmes. The difference between the two models is now highlighted in British law in the distinction between the duties of the Independent Broadcasting Authority and those of the new Cable Authority established under the 1984 Act to regulate cable services: the latter is not required to see that there is a balance in each particular service's programmes.[89]

One question that the German Court has not yet answered is whether there is a constitutional *right* under Article 5 for private institutions to broadcast in competition with the established public service. (It has been clear since the *First Television* case that there is no objection under the Article to private television.) For the moment the form of broadcasting remains a matter for the *Land* legislature, though the view of one leading commentary is that with the expansion of technical facilities this right must soon be recognized.[90] The European Commission has also reserved for further consideration the compatibility of a state monopoly of

---

[87] See Maunz-Dürig, *Kommentar*, paras. 221–2 on art. 5; L. Bollinger, 'Freedom of the Press and Public Access: Toward a Theory of Partial Regulation of the Mass Media' (1976) 75 *Mich. LR* 1.

[88] 57 BVerfGE 295 (1981).

[89] But under the Cable and Broadcasting Act 1984, s. 7, the Authority is under a duty to take into account, *inter alia*, the range and diversity of programmes an applicant for a licence proposes to include.

[90] Maunz-Dürig, *Kommentar*, para. 236 on art. 5.

national broadcasting facilities with Article 10 of the Convention.[91] Recognition of broad individual rights to broadcast under a constitutional provision—either on particular occasions or generally—would be a bold step for courts to take. Some limitations on the number and quality of services still have to be imposed even in the era of cable broadcasting, and this regulation would be difficult to accommodate with upholding a right of access, as distinct perhaps from some right of equal opportunity to be considered for a licence or permit. This cautious approach at any rate was taken by the United States Supreme Court in *CBS* v. *Democratic National Committee*,[92] where the Democratic Committee and an anti-Vietnam war group unsuccessfully claimed a First Amendment right to broadcast short prepaid editorial advertisements for their policies on the CBS network. The majority of the Court did not deny that it would be permissible for the FCC itself to compel rights to place editorial advertisements; indeed, the opinion of Burger CJ advanced the fact that the Commission was investigating the recognition of some access rights under its Fairness Doctrine as an argument against upholding a constitutional right. The implication is that, while the free speech clause does not mandate rights of access, it equally does not preclude them, a conclusion perfectly compatible with the earlier ruling in the *Red Lion* case.

Two members of the Court in the *CBS* case, Douglas and Stewart JJ, took a more extreme position than the majority, and considered that the free speech and press rights of the broadcasting media would be compromised by the recognition of any access rights. The weakness of their judgments is the same as that of the *Tornillo* ruling: they did not consider whether First Amendment freedoms cover a licensee's right to refuse requests by pressure groups for the limited use of his broadcasting station. In principle, this right seems more analogous to a property right than to freedom of speech; moreover, the licensee's freedom to transmit his own views is not hindered by the imposition of an obligation to afford some access rights to would-be broadcasters.[93] In a more recent case, the Court has reaffirmed the *Red Lion* principle that a statutory right of limited access—in this case for the benefit of election candidates—is constitutional.[94]

---

[91] 6452/74, *Sacchi* v. *Italy* 5 D. & R. 43; 9297/81, *X Assoc.* v. *Sweden* 28 D. & R. 204.
[92] 412 US 94 (1973).
[93] Nor does the *Barnette* principle—above, ch. 11, s. 5—apply, since the broadcaster is not required to present the views as if they are his own.
[94] *CBS* v. *FCC.* 453 US 367 (1981).

Election broadcasts perhaps present a special case in the context of this discussion. Not only is there obviously a strong recipient interest in exposure to the views of all candidates and party leaders, but the latter may invoke equality and non-discrimination arguments to buttress their free speech claims. Thus, although the European Commission declined to recognize an Article 10 right of access to enable the leader of a far right British political party to put across his views by political advertising,[95] it did indicate that in appropriate cases such a right might be protected. An arbitrary refusal to allow a political party broadcasting opportunities during an election campaign or to reply to a Ministerial broadcast would surely violate Article 10, especially if it is considered in conjunction with Article 14 of the Convention (prohibiting discrimination in the enjoyment of the Convention rights and freedoms).

Apart from these circumstances and those cases where a right of access is claimed in order to reply to a personal attack, courts are rightly chary of upholding constitutional rights of access to the broadcasting media. Many of the points already made in the context of rights of reply to the press are equally relevant here. The determination of the scope of such rights is much better left to the legislature, or an independent specialist commission; in this context it is interesting to note that even the dissenters in the *CBS* case, Brennan and Marshall JJ, thought the matter should go back to the FCC for it to formulate detailed rules of access. At most the courts should be more willing to recognize the principle of access rights here than they are in press cases. Generally, however, the special responsibilities of broadcasting bodies should be upheld through legislation which takes into account a broad range of speaker and listener interests in an attempt to achieve a diversity of programmes and viewpoints.[96]

The question remains whether there is still a respectable case for treating press and broadcasting freedom differently in view of the technical and economic developments, which make it virtually as easy for an individual (or at least a body of individuals) to broadcast as it is to publish a newspaper. If the differences are no longer significant, one of two possible inferences could be drawn. We might conclude that broadcasting should be as little subject to regulation as the press. The requirements of a free speech principle would be satisfied simply through guaranteeing the freedom of broadcasters and cable operators to say what they want without state control. Alternatively, we could decide that

[95] 4515/70, *X and Assoc. of Z. v. UK* 38 Coll. Dec. 86.
[96] See *FCC. v. WNCN Listeners' Guild* 450 US 582 (1981).

freedom of the press is now in practice the freedom of a handful of newspaper magnates and their editors, and that on occasion the free speech principle itself justifies some degree of control—by anti-concentration or right of reply laws.[97] Although generalizations are difficult, it does seem that the prevailing trends are to liberalize restrictions on the broadcasting media and, albeit very reluctantly and often extra-legally, to impose some restraints on press freedom—though the United States represents an exception to the latter development. Differences in attitude to the press and media are traditional rather than rational.[98] Historically the press (at least in Britain) has been immune from licensing from the end of the seventeenth century, and press freedom is easily viewed as an extension of the individual freedoms of the orator and the leafleter. In contrast, from its outset broadcasting has been thought to present special problems for free speech theory. The discriminatory treatment may become about as arbitrary as the law's qualified approval of alcohol and its intolerance of cannabis, but it is equally likely to survive as those contrasting attitudes.

5. ACCESS TO INFORMATION

In this final section of the chapter we consider a different type of access right: the right asserted by the press, or members of the public, to acquire information or to attend public meetings and events for information-gathering. The right is now frequently protected in Western democracies by freedom of information statutes.[99] These are justified in terms of the desirability of an informed electorate, able to assess the wisdom of governmental decisions, the same arguments which play an important role in supporting a free speech principle. But we have seen that in principle it is difficult to subsume a broad 'right to know' under a free speech clause, because it will be invoked most often where there is no willing speaker. The claimant may contend, for example, that he has a free speech right to acquire information from a government department or to attend a confidential meeting. Indeed, recognition of a right of access would then be tantamount to the imposition of constitutional

---

[97] See above, ch. II, s. 6. J. Barron, 'Access to the Press—A New First Amendment Right' (1967) 80 *Harv. LR* 1641, argues for greater government regulation to ensure the free exchange of ideas and information.

[98] Bollinger, '*Freedom of the Press and Public Access*', 27–37.

[99] For example, Freedom of Information Act 1966 (USA); Freedom of the Press Act 1949 (Sweden). Relevant extracts from these and other legislation are to be found in the booklet, *An Official Information Act* (Outer Circle Policy Unit, London, 1978).

duties to disclose information. Sometimes, however, the right may be asserted where a willing speaker is reluctant or unable to protect his constitutional rights. For instance, the intended recipient of imported magazines seized on arrival in the jurisdiction may be in a much better position to initiate litigation than the foreign publisher or author.[100] In a situation like this, the right to receive information is a Hohfeldian liberty, and its protection does not appear to pose any difficulties for free speech theory. There is, however, a third intermediate category of case where there is a willing speaker, but the communication cannot be received without recognition of some positive right of access—to attend a criminal trial or to interview a prisoner. Courts, particularly the United States Supreme Court, may be prepared in some of these circumstances to uphold claim-rights.

British law, of course, does not recognize any general 'right to know', though there are numerous statutory provisions requiring public authorities to disclose information to the public or to afford access to their meetings.[101] Court orders for discovery of documents in effect confer rights to information for the limited purpose of the conduct of the trial. In *Home Office* v. *Harman*,[102] where the Lords held a solicitor liable for contempt in allowing a journalist to look at documents which had been disclosed to her on discovery and which had been read in open court, Lord Scarman in his dissent referred to the journalist's right to receive information about the documents.[103] Once documents and information have entered the public domain, anyone in his view is free to use and comment on them. This approach was not shared by the majority, and in any case it does not support a claim-right of access to inspect documents which have been disclosed to a party to court proceedings. The courts refer quite often to the public interest in receiving information, and sometimes even to the value of investigative journalism, as aspects of freedom of speech.[104] Thus, in the *Crossman Diaries* case,[105] one reason

---

[100] See *Lamont* v. *Postmaster General* 381 US 301 (1965) and 27 BVerfGE 71 (1969) for decisions illustrating this point.

[101] For example, Public Bodies (admission to meetings) Act 1960; Local Government Act 1972, s. 100 (admission to local authority council and committee meetings); Education Act 1981, s. 7 (statements of child's special education needs); Local Government, Planning and Land Act 1980, ss. 2–4 (information about housing and planning programmes, and authority's employees).

[102] [1983] AC 280; see ch. VIII, s. 1 for further discussion.

[103] [1983] AC 311.

[104] For example *AG* v. *Times Newspapers Ltd* [1974] AC 273; *Hubbard* v. *Pitt* [1976] 1 QB 142 (Lord Denning MR dissenting); *R.* v. *Savundra Nayagan* [1968] 1 WLR 1761.

[105] *AG* v. *Jonathan Cape* [1976] QB 752; see below, p. 133.

for refusing the grant of an injunction applied for on the ground of public interest was that it would be contrary to the competing public interest in freedom of speech; in the circumstances this was clearly a reference to the legitimate public curiosity in the proceedings of the Cabinet and government. But this and other cases stop well short of upholding a positive, claim-right 'to know'. It is hard to imagine that such a right could be formulated in the absence of a constitutionally protected freedom of speech.

Even the United States courts have hesitated to recognize a general right of access to information. Its existence has been frequently asserted in challenges to the constitutionality of prison regulations prohibiting press interviews with particular prisoners.[106] In this situation, restrictions on the prisoners' own First Amendment rights are readily sustained because of the strong government interests in prison security and in prisoner rehabilitation, but these factors might not be powerful enough to limit any right which the public, or the press on its behalf, might claim to receive information about prison conditions. In two companion cases the majority of the Supreme Court, however, denied that the 'Constitution imposes upon government the affirmative duty to make available to journalists sources of information not available to members of the public generally'.[107] The disagreement between the majority and the dissenters, particularly Powell J, also revolves around an issue integrally connected with the existence and scope of any First Amendment rights of access to information: does the press enjoy any special privilege to gather information under the 'freedom of the press' limb of the First Amendment? There are obviously sound practical reasons for denying that every individual member of the public has a right to interview prisoners, inspect prisons and army bases, or to attend public meetings in the exercise of the right to know. But the press might be accorded such rights as an agent of the public. In fact, for reasons discussed at the end of the previous chapter, the Court has generally refused to confer special privileges and immunities on the press, although its news-gathering role has been recognized.[108]

The question whether there is a First Amendment *right to gather* information was answered in another prison case, *Houchins* v. *KQED*.[109]

---

[106] For example, *Procunier* v. *Martinez* 416 US 396 (1974); *Pell* v. *Procunier* 417 US 817 (1974); *Saxbe* v. *Washington Post* 417 US 843 (1974).
[107] 417 US 817, 834 (Stewart J.).
[108] *Branzburg* v. *Hayes* 408 US 665 (1972); see above, p. 73.
[109] 438 US 1 (1978).

A Californian broadcasting station argued it was entitled to enter a state prison to inspect and take photographs of that part of the gaol where a prisoner had recently committed suicide. The majority of the Court denied the existence of an access right to government information or to information in its control, distinguishing between this claim and the right to communicate information once it has been obtained. Speaking for the three dissenters, Stevens J. considered entry to the prison necessary to protect the public's right to be informed about the conditions there. In their view the right's recognition would not entail the grant of special privileges to the press or media, nor would it amount to a forced disclosure of confidential information. Admittedly the access right asserted in *Houchins* did not involve these difficulties, but it could have been regarded as tantamount to a claim that the media could do anything which made the distribution of information more effective. It is hardly surprising that the case was rejected. Its acceptance might have led to the pressing of novel First Amendment claims, for example, to attend Cabinet meetings or witness army exercises, on a similar line of reasoning. On the other hand, the Court has recognized a First Amendment right to attend criminal trials, irrespective of the wishes of the parties. The justifications for this particular departure from the general line of authority are explored in Chapter VIII.[110]

A right to receive information and ideas has now been upheld by the three members of the Court, who gave the plurality opinion in the recent controversial school library case.[111] This right of school students would be violated by a high school board's decision to remove 'offensive' books from the library. The difficulties in formulating this novel First Amendment right, and correlative duty on the school authorities, were pointed out by the four dissenters. Would not the recognition of such a right also require the authorities to provide books which the students have requested for the library, and can a clear line be drawn between a right to receive ideas in the form of library books and a right to be taught subjects which the students find of interest—or at least those topics the teachers and students agree should constitute the curriculum? Another difficulty was pointed out in Rehnquist J.'s dissent. The plurality derived the students' right to receive ideas from the speaker's First Amendment right to transmit them. But no author or publisher has a right that a school purchase his book for its library, or that any public library buy it for that

---

[110] See below, ch. VIII, s. 5.
[111] *Board of Education, Island Trees Union Free School Dist. no. 26.* v. *Pico* 102 S. Ct. 2799 (1982).

matter. It would be bizarre to uphold a positive claim-right to receive information where the speaker (or author) has none. The alternative basis for the students' right to receive—that the books contributed to the effective exercise of their own free speech rights—is no easier to sustain. As Rehnquist J. said, the state did not deprive them of all access to the books; the claim was that they had to be provided in school.[112] If this were accepted, it is hard to see any ground for denying, say, the existence of a First Amendment right to have public libraries provided by the state at places reasonably accessible to the public or a right to read official information in readily available booklets.

The *Informationsfreiheit* specifically covered by Article 5 of the German Basic Law equally does not confer any constitutional title to acquire information from public authorities. The text makes it plain that the freedom is only to receive information from generally available sources (*aus allgemein zugänglichen Quellen*), and this obviously excludes government information which has not been publicly released. As is the case with the freedom of the speaker or writer protected in the first half of the opening sentence of Article 5(1), the freedom of the recipient is fundamentally a negative right, or in Hohfeldian terms a bare liberty; it does not impose duties on the state to provide information or to ensure its provision by others.[113] The German Administrative Court has left open the question whether in some circumstances the press might have a constitutional right of access to information under the separate *Pressefreiheit* provision in Article 5(1), while rejecting a claim by a journalist to participate in special railway journeys which would have enabled him to become better informed about transport plans.[114] The Court indicated, however, that the exclusion of a particular journalist on the basis of the content of his articles might have raised difficulties under Article 5, in conjunction with the Article 3 prohibition of arbitrary discrimination.

The cautious approach to the character of *Informationsfreiheit* adopted by both courts and commentators is strikingly similar to the reluctance of the United States Supreme Court to recognize First Amendment rights to know. But the Karlsruhe Court has ruled that the recipient's interests, protected by the freedom of information, must be independently weighed by courts. Thus, in the leading case,[115] the Court upheld a constitutional

---

[112] Ibid., 2831.
[113] Maunz-Dürig, *Kommentar zum Grundgesetz*, para. 101; I. von Münch, *Grundgesetz-Kommentar*, vol. 1 (Munich, 1981), p. 250.
[114] 47 BVerwGE 247 (1974).
[115] 27 BVerfGE 71 (1969).

complaint brought against the confiscation of literature imported from the German Democratic Republic supporting the proscribed West German Communist Party, because the lower court had not considered the readers' interest in informing themselves from this source. It did not matter that the source was foreign; indeed, it is in this situation that *Informationsfreiheit* is most likely to be invoked, for the distributor will often be unable to protect his own *Meinungsfreiheit*.

The European Convention also explicitly covers the right to receive information. Unfortunately, there is no indication in the Commission's case-law whether this is to be construed as more than a mere liberty to receive information imparted willingly by a speaker. It would be surprising in view of the Commission's cautious attitude towards rights of access to the media, if claim-rights were upheld in this context. Both the Universal Declaration of Human Rights and the International Covenant on Civil and Political Rights cover the right *to seek* information, and the European Court has apparently ventured the opinion informally that this right is implicit in Article 10.[116] Too much significance should not be attached to this. The right to seek information would probably prevail over restrictions on press interviews or over a discriminatory ban on the access of journalists to public events or buildings; it does not mandate the imposition of any duty on the part of government to provide information. In this context it may be noted that the Committee of Minister's Recommendation advocating the extension of public access to information does not mention Article 10 as part of the relevant legal background.[117]

It is rare then to find judicial acceptance of rights of access to information under a free speech clause. The case for their recognition on this basis is much weaker than the case for upholding the other claim-rights discussed in this chapter. This is partly because the claims are generally made by a recipient against an unwilling speaker, upon whom it is sought to impose a duty to disclose information. It may be added that if such a claim were made against a private person or body, rather than government, that person or body's own First Amendment or privacy rights might be implicated.[118] These particular objections do not apply where the applicant claims a free speech right *to gather* information, as in the *Houchins* case, but the acceptance of such a claim, as we saw, raises

---

[116] See the Report of the Council of Europe on Activities in the Mass Media Field, DH/MM (83) 1, p. 5.

[117] Recommendation no. R (81) 19.

[118] See above, p. 64 (right to silence) and below, pp. 282–7 (freedom of association).

other difficulties. Finally, the equality argument, which is often relevant in the public meeting and access to the media cases, is rarely pertinent where access to information is at issue: all members of the public are denied access to government files, and all non-recognized journalists are refused admission to press conferences. Only in a few circumstances will it be possible to reinforce a (weak) freedom of speech case with non-discrimination arguments.

IV

Prior Restraints

IT is a commonplace observation that the law regards, and is right so to regard, prior restraints on speech and writing with particular hostility. In England licensing of the press was in effect abolished in 1694, when the annual legislation under which the Stationers' Company used to control the publication of newspapers and pamphlets was not renewed.[1] There has been no general censorship of the press since that time. Indeed Blackstone considered freedom of the press 'consists in laying no *previous* restraints upon publications, and not in freedom from censure for criminal matter when published'.[2] While the second part of that definition has often been criticized, the first has been treated as gospel, particularly in the United States, where prior restraints are rarely countenanced. There is a heavy presumption against their constitutional validity, which is difficult to rebut even in cases involving the disclosure of government secrets. And though the Supreme Court has refrained from altogether prohibiting censorship of films and plays, in practice it is now no more common in these cases than for books and newspapers. In Germany censorship is outlawed by Article 5(1) of the *Grundgesetz*.

British law, however, adopts a more pragmatic approach. Under legislation there is a 'system' of film censorship, which at least in principle has been approved by the Williams Committee Report on Obscenity and Film Censorship.[3] Local authorities may enjoy powers to refuse permits for meetings on some public open spaces, and may (subject to the Home Secretary's consent) outlaw public processions for up to three months on an application by a chief officer of police if he believes they would occasion serious public disorder. In some cases the courts have granted injunctions to restrain a future publication without apparently being aware that this is judicial censorship, though in others they are more sensitive to this argument. The reasons for this inconsistency are rarely articulated by the judiciary or, more surprisingly,

---

[1] See W. S. Holdsworth, 'Press Control and Copyright in the Sixteenth and Seventeenth Centuries' (1920) 29 *Yale LJ* 841.

[2] 4. Bl. Comm. (16th edn., London, 1825), 151.

[3] (1979) Cmnd. 7772, ch. 12.

explored by commentators. Lip-service continues to be paid to Black-stone's proposition, but on the whole prior restraint is a rather neglected aspect of free speech arguments in this country.[4] And so far there is little indication from the cases decided by the European Commission and Court that these restraints will be viewed with particular suspicion under the Convention. The last sentence of Article 10(1) expressly permits the *licensing* of broadcasting, television, and cinema; but it would certainly be too much to argue from this that other forms of censorship are as such proscribed.[5]

The initial question, therefore, must be whether the differences between prior restraints and penal sanctions imposed subsequent to publication are sufficiently serious to justify the traditional hostility to the former shown in American jurisprudence. If these differences turn out to be relatively insignificant, there may be something to be said for the less ideological approach to be found in Britain. This question is discussed in the first section of this chapter. The second and third sections respec-tively deal with the censorship of plays and films and with the use of prior restraints to prohibit harmful political speech. The final section of the chapter briefly explores the role of these restraints in two other areas: contempt of court and permits for meetings.

1. THE VARIETIES AND VICES OF PRIOR RESTRAINTS

On one view the distinction between a prior restraint and a subsequent penal sanction is little more than one of *form*; the first prohibits publication before it is issued, while the second operates afterwards. In *substance* their effect is the same in that they both inhibit the exercise of free speech. The 'chilling' effect of prospective penal sanctions may in fact be rather greater, as the publisher faces the twin uncertainties of a possible prosecution and an unpredictable sentence. In contrast a censorship system enables him to have the legality of the book or film determined at comparatively minimal cost; if the work is then cleared by the censor, there is very little chance of subsequent prosecution and the publisher's investment is secure. For these reasons prior restraints may actually be preferred in some circumstances—the best example of this is

---

[4] For example, P. O'Higgins in his book, *Censorship in Britain* (London, 1972) does not emphasize the distinction between prior and subsequent restraints.

[5] The Commission has approved pre-publication restraints in, e.g., 4274/69, *X. v. Germany* 35 Coll. Dec. 158, 4515/70, *X. and Assoc. of Z. v. UK* 38 Coll. Dec. 86, *De Geillustreerde Pers* v. *Holland* 8 D. & R. 5.

the attitude of the major British film distributors who value the commercial certainty afforded by preliminary scrutiny.[6]

Moreover, in some cases it is difficult to determine whether the method of control is really a prior restraint or not. Thus, the minority of the Supreme Court in the leading American decision, *Near* v. *Minnesota*,[7] doubted whether the facts justified the application of Blackstone's principle: under a state statute a County Attorney could apply for an injunction to restrain further publication of scandalous and defamatory newspapers. Unlike censorship in its purest form, the proceedings were judicial in character and could only be instituted after one publication of the paper in question (and the injunction would not be issued if the publisher showed the article was true and written for good motives). Yet, in view of the injunction's broad prohibition of future publication of the newspaper, the majority decision to apply the prior restraint rule was plainly right.

Harder cases have arisen subsequently. If a book has already been published, should an ex-parte injunction to restrain its further publication pending the immediate determination of its obscenity be regarded as a prior restraint? A bare majority of the Court refused to apply the doctrine in this situation,[8] while in the *Bantam Books* case a few years later only Harlan J. dissented from its application when a state Commission warned publishers that their literature was 'objectionable' and would be referred to the Attorney-General for possible prosecution.[9] In this decision the Court in effect characterized an administrative warning without legal effects as an invalid prior restraint, an approach which contrasts sharply with the occasional British use of extra-legal 'censorship', as in the D Notice system.[10] A possible implication of the *Bantam Books* ruling is that a police warning that a book might be prosecuted would be ruled unconstitutional, although it is hard to see how the publisher's position would be prejudiced by this. Another difficult situation to categorize is the suspended sentence. Under this procedure a sentence will not take effect unless the convicted person commits another offence punishable with imprisonment within a particular period of time.[11] This might be regarded as a prior restraint if used in the case of,

---

[6] Williams Committee Report paras. 12.5–12.6.

[7] 283 US 697 (1931).

[8] *Kingsley Books* v. *Brown* 354 US 436 (1957).

[9] *Bantam Books* v. *Sullivan* 372 US 58 (1963).

[10] See below, p. 135.

[11] For suspended sentences in English law, see Sir R. Cross and A. Ashworth, *The English Sentencing System* (3rd edn., London, 1981), 55–61.

say, the publisher of an obscene book or a person convicted of making a speech likely to lead to breach of the peace. Similarly the magistrates' power to issue a warrant to search for and seize obscene articles under the English obscenity legislation might be constitutionally suspect in the United States.[12]

The German Constitutional Court has also had to resolve difficult questions on the meaning of the *Zensurverbot* imposed by Article 5(1). In the leading case, a majority of the Court ruled that it only covered pre-publication restraints (*Vorzensur*) under which materials have to be submitted to the authorities for inspection and approval before distribution is permitted.[13] Thus, the requirement to submit a copy of any film imported from Eastern Europe to a government office within one week of its distribution was not covered by the censorship provision. Its exhibition did not depend on government approval, though all copies of the film might be confiscated subsequently if found to be propaganda against a free constitution. The Court also ruled that the prohibition on censorship was absolute, and that it would be impossible to apply this ban to restraints operating after a publication (*Nachzensur*). It was not impressed by the dissenters' view that the 'chilling effect' of the deposit requirement was the same as that of a formal censorship process. The majority thought this view proved too much, for it would also apply to the threat of criminal sanctions *after* publication—which is certainly not covered by the *Zensurverbot*.

It is arguable that the German Constitutional Court's approach here was too formal. If the effect of a provision is to delay publication or distribution while the government office inspects the material to see whether it is covered by the criminal law, it operates as a prior restraint or censorship system. The Administrative Court has ruled that the censorship provision may cover a system under which films are graded for the purpose of assessing an entertainment tax, since this might in practice deter the release of serious films that were not properly graded.[14] This approach looked more to the substance of the restraint than its form. The more cautious stance of the Karlsruhe Court is, however, understandable. The text of Article 5 imposes an absolute ban on censorship, while

---

[12] The forfeiture procedure under the Obscene Publications Act 1959, s. 3, was at issue before the European Court in the *Handyside* case, below, ch. IX, s. 4. American cases hold that there must be an adversary hearing *before* a warrant is granted: *Marcus* v. *Search Warrants* 367 US 717 (1961), *A Quantity of Books* v. *Kansas* 378 US 205 (1964).

[13] 33 BVerfGE 52 (1972), followed by 47 BVerfGE 198 (1978).

[14] 23 BVerwGE 194, 199 (1966).

generally freedom of expression and *Informationsfreiheit* are weighed against the interests protected by general laws. This difference constitutes a strong reason for a narrow interpretation of censorship. In the United States in contrast a more flexible view of its scope is tenable, because a prior restraint is only viewed with a greater degree of hostility than are penal sanctions.

But these problems may suggest that no sharp distinction can be drawn in all cases between a prior restraint and a subsequent punishment. It might be better instead to analyse the defects of censorship or previous restraints in their most obvious forms, and then determine how far these apply in those borderline cases where it is not clear whether there is really a prior restraint issue. If the procedure in question does suffer from the same vices, then the courts should scrutinize the restriction on free speech with the degree of hostility indicated by Blackstone's precept. The principal general characteristics of a censorship system are surely that control over publication is exercised by an administrative official on vague and imprecise standards, with no right of appeal and little effective judicial review. The writer, publisher, or distributor (as the case may be) is required to submit the book or film in question to the censor for prior inspection; it is further an offence which may be summarily punishable to publish or exhibit without his approval. Moreover, in these summary proceedings the courts may not permit argument about the constitutionality of the censorship system or its application in the particular case. Sometimes, as in *Near* v. *Minnesota*, and many important English cases,[15] a previous restraint on publication is imposed by court injunction. Though this type of control does not share all the features of administrative censorship, it is supported by contempt proceedings in which there is likely to be a similar bar on argument about the constitutionality of the restraint.

It is worth saying a little more about these vices. An administrative censor is likely to adopt a bureaucratic, unsympathetic attitude to the publications he is required to inspect; otherwise, his job would be redundant. This is particularly probable where he is responsible to a body which is politically committed to restricting free speech. In eighteenth-century America some local officials responsible for censorship were ultimately answerable to the Crown, and perhaps for this reason a tradition of hostility to prior restraints emerged.[16] In contrast,

[15] For example, *Att.-Gen.* v. *Times Newspapers, Ltd* [1974] AC 273, *Att.-Gen.* v. *Jonathan Cape* [1976] QB 752, *Schering Chemicals* v. *Falkman* [1982] QB 1 (CA).

[16] This was the view of A. M. Bickel, *The Least Dangerous Branch* (New York, 1962),

since the end of the eighteenth century in both the United States and in Britain, the decision whether a publication is a libel in a criminal prosecution has been for the jury.[17] They are not only independent, but are naturally more aware of contemporary community standards and responsive to public opinion. (It could, however, be argued that these days a jury—at any rate, a middle-aged, middle-class jury—is more likely to impose restrictions on radical speech than an élitist censorship body!) The absence of a jury in British civil cases, and also in applications for interim injunctions in all common law jurisdictions, renders some forms of judicial prior restraint open to the same objection. However, judges should not suffer from the same degree of institutional bias as an administrative censor such as a local official or chief of police.

The difference between administrative and judicial proceedings does not reside, of course, solely in the character of the tribunal. In the latter the burden of proof is on the prosecution or the person seeking the injunction, while there may be no clear rules on this under an administrative censorship system. Moreover, officials will not be limited by rules of evidence and the publisher may not have rights of representation or even an opportunity to defend his work. Most importantly, the censor may work entirely in secret. Anxiety about these features of administratively imposed restraints has led the Williams Committee to suggest procedural improvements in the system of film censorship in Britain.[18] And in the *Freedman* case[19] the Supreme Court emphasized the importance of procedural safeguards—in particular, prompt judicial determination after an adversary hearing—as necessary to validate any such system.

Another common aspect of censorship systems is the relative lack of precise standards by which the official is to assess the publication. Procedurally this makes it harder for the author to argue his case and more difficult to frame rules of evidence. As far as the substance of a publication is concerned, if the criteria in the relevant statute or

---

135–6. But see L. Levy, *Legacy of Suppression* (Cambridge, Mass., 1960), ch. 3, where it is argued that provincial assemblies and courts were as much responsible for restrictions on free speech as the governors and their councils.

[17] Fox's Libel Act 1792 established this in England. Trial by jury for seditious libel was upheld in New York in the famous Zenger case in 1735, but this was exceptional in state law until the end of the eighteenth century: see Levy, *Legacy of Suppression*, 126–33, 203–4. But juries decided all issues of law and fact under the Federal Sedition Act 1798.

[18] Williams Committee Report, paras. 12.21–12.32.

[19] *Freedman v. Maryland* 380 US 51 (1965).

regulations are vague and unclear, it will be all too easy for constitutionally protected speech, e.g. an attack on government policy, to be
censored. In some circumstances, when the case comes to court it will be
so obvious that the speech is constitutionally immune from any type of
control, that it is strictly unnecessary for the judges to invoke the special
prior restraint principles. This would now probably be true of *Near* v.
Minnesota itself, where the publication, an attack on public officials,
would surely be held protected political speech; in 1931 when First
Amendment principles were still very undeveloped, it was understandable that the Court invoked Blackstone's precept.

   In contrast, it is less clear what a court should hold when the speech
which has been restrained is obviously not constitutionally protected. In
the *Pittsburgh Press* case,[20] the majority of the Court refused to apply
prior restraint principles when a Commission issued an order prohibiting
the publication in a newspaper of sexually discriminatory advertisements;
the speech was commercial and related to a course of business conduct,
and so fell outside the First Amendment. The newspaper's advertisement
policy did infringe precise standards, and further the Commission's order
was only effective after a court hearing. So two of the usual reasons for
invocation of the prior restraint doctrine did not apply. The case is some
authority for the view that there is nothing wrong as such, or even
suspect, in a restraint which is prior in form, but does not suffer from its
characteristic vices.[21] Where, however, there is room for any plausible
argument that the standards applied by the censor may permit the
abridgement of constitutionally protected speech, the courts should not
hesitate to apply the prior restraint doctrine. We will see at the end of the
chapter that this approach has been particularly important in cases
arising from the refusal of permits for meetings and demonstrations
under imprecise legislation.[22]

   This discussion may incidentally suggest one way in which some sort
of prior restraint doctrine could be developed under the European
Convention. Article 10(2) provides that the exercise of freedom of
expression may be subject to restrictions 'as are prescribed by law and are

---

[20] *Pittsburgh Press* v. *Human Relations Commission* 413 US 376 (1973).

[21] See W. P. Murphy, 'The Prior Restraint Doctrine in the Supreme Court: a Re-
evaluation' (1976) 51 *Notre Dame Lawyer* 898. F. Schauer, *Free Speech: A Philosophical
Inquiry* (Cambridge, 1982), 148–52, takes the view that even allowing for its characteristic
procedural vices there is no justification for special hostility to prior restraint, but his
argument seems to underestimate the possible (perhaps likely) abuses of censorship
systems.

[22] See below, pp. 142–4.

necessary in a democratic society . . .'. A broad discretionary power of censorship wholly unlimited by precise standards could hardly be considered 'prescribed by law'. In the *Sunday Times* case,[23] the European Court stated that a rule could not be regarded as a 'law' unless it was precise enough to enable a citizen to regulate his conduct, and it hesitated before holding the English common law of contempt sufficiently clear to meet this standard. Even if a censorship system could surmount this hurdle, there is the further obstacle that it might be regarded as unnecessary in view of the alternative availability of penal sanctions after publication.

A further vice of censorship is the comparative ease with which the restrictions may be enforced. It will typically be an offence under the relevant regulations to publish or exhibit without having been granted a permit. The publisher may not be permitted to raise in his defence arguments about the unconstitutionality of the permit system as a whole or its application to the particular book or film. This bar on collateral challenge may also apply where the court has granted an injunction; the defendant cannot then challenge this order in subsequent contempt proceedings, but must seek judicial review immediately after the injunction is issued.[24] Some commentators in the United States have gone so far as to argue that this is now the principal defect of prior restraints, which otherwise would have no more chilling effect on the exercise of free speech than the prospect of a subsequent penal sanction.[25] A court injunction may suffer from another related drawback; it may prohibit not only the particular publication in issue, but also all further publications dealing with the same subject-matter. A classic instance of this occurred in the House of Lords' ruling in the *Sunday Times* contempt case: the newspaper was enjoined from publishing any article which prejudged the issue of negligence or dealt with the evidence relating to any issue arising in any actions brought against Distillers in respect of the thalidomide drug.[26] This is a much more draconian remedy than a criminal prosecution in this respect; a conviction is entered only in respect of a particular 'publication' of the article, and so the accused or another person may republish it somewhere else without necessarily being charged or, if charged, without being convicted.[27]

[23] Decisions of the Court, Series A, no. 30; (1979) 2 EHRR 245.
[24] *Walker* v. *City of Birmingham* 388 US 307 (1967).
[25] See S. R. Barnett, 'The Puzzle of Prior Restraint' (1976) 29 *Stanford LR* 539.
[26] *Att.-Gen.* v. *Times Newspapers Ltd* [1974] AC 273.
[27] See the dissent of Douglas and Black JJ in *Kingsley Books* v. *Brown* 354 US 436, 446–7 (1957).

Of course, most of these defects of prior restraints could be avoided. A decision taken under detailed and precise standards after an open adversary hearing conducted by an impartial tribunal *before* publication would meet many of the objections raised in the preceding paragraphs. It would even be possible to arrange, as Chafee suggested in his classic book, *Free Speech in the United States*, for a 'play jury' to assess a dramatic performance before it was commercially staged.[28] In these eventualities, it is hard to see any significant difference between a previous restraint and a subsequent penalty, unless there is some sort of right to have an idea or piece of information enter the market-place at least once. Such a right hardly seems of great value, and in any case— unless the penalties for refusing to go before the censor are severe—is no more effectively abridged by a prior restraint than by the prospect of a criminal prosecution. But this sort of reformed system of censorship exists only in Utopia. In the real world these improvements lead to the disappearance of the system altogether, because its typical advantages— speed, cheapness, and lack of publicity—are lost. Thus, film censorship in the United States was virtually terminated when the Supreme Court imposed severe procedural requirements in *Freedman* v. *Maryland*.[29] Virtually all types of prior restraint seem inevitably to present some feature—procedural or substantive—which calls for special scrutiny by the courts.

This conclusion is in no way incompatible with the observation that these restraints vary so markedly in their form and effect that it is not good enough to apply a uniformly hostile attitude. As Paul Freund remarked: 'What is needed is a pragmatic assessment of [the doctrine's] operation in the particular circumstances. The generalization that prior restraint is particularly obnoxious in civil liberties cases must yield to more particularistic analysis.'[30] Some of the factors relevant to this analysis have been indicated in the preceding paragraphs. Perhaps the most important of them is the character and procedure of the censoring body. Judicial restraints are generally more tolerable than administrative, but not so much so as to justify the frequent refusal of the English courts to recognize an injunction prohibiting publication as a form of previous restraint. In some circumstances the legislature itself imposes a *de facto* restraint. Special taxes and registration requirements imposed on news-

---

[28] Z. Chafee, *Free Speech in the United States* (Harvard, 1942), 533–40.
[29] 380 US 51 (1965).
[30] 'The Supreme Court and Civil Liberties' (1950) 4 *Vanderbilt LR* 533, 539.

paper publishers may require special scrutiny. Thus the Supreme Court has struck down a Louisiana statute which levied a licence tax on the advertisement receipts of newspapers enjoying a large circulation; it was clearly designed to restrict press freedom rather than raise revenue.[31] In contrast, the Privy Council adopted a more benevolent attitude to a licence fee exacted from newspaper publishers in Antigua.[32] More disturbingly, it also upheld a legislative provision requiring as a condition of freedom to publish the deposit of 10,000 dollars to satisfy possible libel judgments. This was regarded as 'reasonably required for the purpose of protecting the reputations and rights of others' in the terms of an article of the Constitution modelled on the European Convention. The Privy Council wholly ignored the prior restraint aspect of the case, and made no serious attempt even to balance the clear inhibition on ability to publish with the danger of unsatisfied defamation judgments, a risk which would probably only arise after a jury trial.

Another factor of crucial importance in determining the reasonableness of a prior restraint is its duration. The injunction in *Near* perpetually enjoined the newspaper from publishing scandalous and defamatory matter, while the order in the English *Sunday Times* case was framed so as to stifle discussion of the legal issues while the actions remained pending or imminent. Clearly these permanent restraints should be subject to much closer scrutiny than a temporary order which may delay publication by only a few days or weeks. But the delay has to be balanced against the importance and urgency of the postponed communication. The relevance of political information may be entirely lost if its publication is put back by a day or so, while such a ban on pornography may be much more tolerable: as Harlan J. once remarked, 'Sex is of constant but rarely particularly topical interest.'[33] To some extent temporary bans on publication are inevitable for the court properly to examine whether a more permanent injunction can be justified.[34] The only alternative is to outlaw prior restraints altogether—a position which has been adopted only by a minority of the Supreme Court. The total prohibition of such restraints, with certain defined

[31] *Grosjean* v. *American Press* 297 US 233 (1936). Also see *Minneapolis Star and Tribune Co.* v. *Minnesota Comr. of Revenue* 103 S. Ct. 1365 (1983).
[32] *Att.-Gen. for Antigua* v. *Antigua Times* [1976] AC 16.
[33] *A Quantity of Books* v. *Kansas* 378 US 205, 224 (1964).
[34] Thus, a bare majority of the Court in the *Pentagon Papers* case (below, p. 136) granted a temporary stay to restrain publication, while it considered whether to impose a permanent injunction.

exceptions, e.g. for publications threatening the safety of the nation, does not obviate this difficulty; it would still be necessary for the court to grant a temporary injunction while it determines whether the article falls within the exceptional category.

Other considerations material to the justifiability of a prior restraint relate to the particular type of speech which is in issue. In some circumstances restrictions on speech may be justified because of the probable consequences of its dissemination, e.g. a breach of the peace may be likely in view of the character of the audience addressed, or there may be a clear and present danger of civil unrest. It may then be very hard to justify a prior restraint simply because there is not, before the publication, any evidence on which an anticipatory ban could be justified. The reasons for placing restrictions on other types of speech, perhaps contempt of court and obscenity, may be easier to assess divorced from their context; there, provided that the standards governing the censor's discretion are sufficiently precise, a previous restraint may be more tolerable. But it should not be upheld unless there is also some good reason for reliance on this means of control rather than on a penal sanction. There are further some situations where control exercised *before* the speech is really the only means of preventing the harm which the state is entitled to avoid. Two examples are injunctions to restrain the disclosure of highly damaging secret information (relevant to affairs of state or commercial secrets) and the use of permits to prevent the clash of rival meetings and processions when it is clear that violence is inevitable.[35] In these circumstances only absolutist ideologues would rule out the use of prior restraints altogether.

There is one further argument sometimes deployed in favour of censorship which is of more doubtful worth—that publishers may prefer it. A system of prior restraint which can be defended on other grounds may be more attractive if it enjoys the support of those affected. But the argument on its own ignores the interests of those who wish to receive the information or ideas and are denied all access to them by censorship. Moreover, it fails in so far as freedom of speech is based on the broad public interest in the quality of political and social debate.[36] Even if freedom of speech is primarily justified in terms of the *speaker*'s rights, there remains the difficult question whether this is a right which can properly be waived. There does not appear to be any clear authority on

[35] For a general discussion of these factors, see L. H. Tribe, *American Constitutional Law* (New York, 1978), 728–31.
[36] See the discussion in ch. I pp. 20–23.

this question, but in principle there is much to be said for the view that such an important freedom cannot be surrendered, except perhaps by contracts, such as the contract of employment.[37] Further there is the practical point that while a system of censorship may be acceptable to the majority of publishers, it will also affect any more adventurous minority. This point may have been somewhat neglected by the Williams Committee in its discussion of film censorship.[38]

2. THEATRE AND FILM CENSORSHIP

At various times the live theatre and the cinema have been seen as presenting special problems, which justify some measure of previous restraint. This is now almost unknown in Western democracies in the case of stage plays, but cinema censorship is still common, and has recently received the imprimatur of the British Williams Committee on Obscenity and Film Censorship. It is, however, far from clear that plays and films are so different from books or newspapers that any special legal measures of control can be justified. To some extent the reasons for their separate treatment may be historical. New forms of expression may initially be thought more dangerous than those which have enjoyed traditional acceptance. This perhaps explains the current anxiety about video recordings, now subject to licensing by the British Board of Film Censors.[39] Alternatively, these modes of expression may be first be regarded primarily as a means of entertainment rather than as affording a fresh method for the communication of political and social ideas; this was a common view of the cinema in the first decades of this century.[40] These arguments, of course, can hardly have been applied to live drama, a much more ancient art form than the novel or the press column. There the reasons for suspicion would largely be its immediacy of impact and obvious potential for incitement to disorder. Another explanation is that once some means of communication has been made subject to a separate

---

[37] For the view that the more important the right, the less it is alienable, see D. N. MacCormick, 'Rights in Legislation', in *Law, Morality and Society: Essays in Honour of H. L. A. Hart* (Oxford, 1977), 189, 195–9.

[38] (1979) Cmnd. 7772, ch. 12. The same point may also apply to the work of the New Zealand Indecent Publications Tribunal, to which publishers may submit books for preliminary scrutiny; see S. Perry, *The Indecent Publications Tribunal: A Social Experiment* (New Zealand, 1965), 124.

[39] Video Recordings Act 1984, s. 4.

[40] See McKenna J. In *Mutual Film* v. *Industrial Commission of Ohio* 236 US 230, 244 (1915), and see I. H. Carmen, *Movies, Censorship and the Law* (Michigan, 1966), ch. 1.

type of institutional control, it becomes difficult to bring it under the general law, no matter how strong the rational arguments may be for taking this step.

The long survival of theatre censorship in Britain is well known.[41] Put on a statutory basis in 1737 and reformulated in 1843, the powers of the Lord Chamberlain were not abolished until 1968. The Theatres Act followed the recommendations of a Joint Select Committee of the House of Commons and House of Lords, which had found there was no sensible justification for treating plays differently from books.[42] No other form of absolute censorship limited artistic freedom—though it will be seen that control over films does not fall far short of this. The powers exercised by the Lord Chamberlain exhibited many of the characteristic vices of censorship: the standards he applied were uncertain and imprecise, allowing some degree of political censorship, authors had no procedural rights, and there was no appeal. But his ability to produce quick and inexpensive decisions on the suitability of plays for performance was appreciated by theatre managers, an interesting parallel to the support for censorship still provided by many film distributors. The Committee rejected the suggestion that there might be a system of voluntary censorship, under which authors could, if they wished, submit plays to a body, approval by which would secure immunity from subsequent prosecution. One of the reasons for this conclusion was that an advisory body might be less liberal than the Lord Chamberlain had been in practice, though the record of the British Board of Film Censors in the last few years does not suggest this would have been a serious danger.[43] The real objection to the institution of such a body is surely that even if it lacks legal powers, its very existence encourages caution and so inhibits artistic expression.

The Theatres Act 1968 therefore subjects 'plays', naturally subject to careful definition, to the ordinary criminal law of obscenity, incitement to racial hatred, and provocation of a breach of the peace. British law was thus brought into line with the rules applying in other comparable countries. The Committee found that there were no prior restraints in this area in France, West Germany (where it is constitutionally pro-scribed), Canada, New Zealand, and most Australian states.[44] Not surprisingly it has not been countenanced in the United States. Indeed,

---

[41] See G. Robertson, *Obscenity* (London, 1979), 246–50.
[42] (1966) HL 255, HC 503.
[43] Williams Committee Report, ch. 3.
[44] (1966) HL 255, HC 503, Appendix 24.

in one of its bolder decisions the Court ruled that a municipality imposed an invalid prior restraint when it refused a permit for the musical *Hair* to be staged at a civic theatre.[45] The basis for the ruling was that the procedural requirements mandated by *Freedman* v. *Maryland* in the context of film censorship were not observed, but the Court virtually ignored the point that the board was regulating use of its own property and not simply acting as a general theatre censor. In this context the imposition of a subsequent punishment is hardly a viable alternative, so one of the arguments against use of prior restraints is not really applicable.[46]

For a variety of reasons the cinema continues to pose more difficulties. In Britain there is a system of censorship under which in legal form decisions are taken under the Cinematograph Acts by local authorities, but in practice by the informally constituted British Board of Film Censors (BBFC).[47] Film distributors and exhibitors may now be prose-cuted under the Obscene Publications Act 1959,[48] but it seems clear that both the BBFC and local authorities (under guidance issued by the Home Office) prohibit or require cuts to films on broader grounds, e.g. that they are grossly offensive, appear to glorify violence, or degrade women.[49] Before the 1959 Act was applied to films, the Court of Appeal had ruled that it was wrong for the Greater London Council to apply the obscenity test (does the film tend to 'deprave and corrupt'?) rather than the broader indecency criterion when exercising its licensing functions.[50] The Act now prohibits prosecutions in respect of films for any common law offence of indecent or offensive publication, so it might be argued that it is no longer lawful for the BBFC to take these criteria into consideration. It would certainly be odd to tolerate the exercise of censorship powers on grounds which would not support a criminal prosecution.

Despite the reservations in principle to any system of prior restraint, the Williams Committee, which reviewed the law of obscenity and control of the cinema in 1977-9, concluded that film censorship should be continued.[51] Some of its practical points can hardly be denied:

[45] *South-eastern Promotions* v. *Conrad* 420 US 546 (1975).

[46] The Court was really recognizing a right of access to public property for theatrical performances.

[47] N. M. Hunnings, *Film Censorship and the Law* (London, 1967), 29-148.

[48] See Law Commission Report no. 76, paras. 3.60-3.66.

[49] Williams Committee Report, ch. 3. For a criticism of the Committee's approach by one of its members, see A. W. B. Simpson, *Pornography and Politics: the Williams Committee in Retrospect* (London, 1983), 83-4.

[50] *R.* v. *GLC, ex parte Blackburn* [1976] 1 WLR 950.

[51] Williams Committee Report, paras. 12.1-12.11.

whatever its theoretical weaknesses, the system has worked satisfactorily in Britain, and most cinema distributors appreciated its advantages of certainty, speed of decision, and cheapness. Moreover, it is hard to quarrel with the experience of Committee members that some films are exceptionally nasty and sadistic. Its conclusion that they require special treatment because of the medium's unique capacity to disturb and arouse is, however, more controversial; live theatre surely has an equal potential to instil or cultivate violent behaviour. A stronger point, perhaps underemphasized by the Committee because of its élitist connotations, is surely that generally cinema caters for a mass audience, less inclined to be selective about what it watches. Moreover, its relative cheapness and availability pose greater dangers for children. On the other hand, such risks can be met by the display of warnings about the character of the films shown and stricter controls on the age of the audience. There are, therefore, less 'restrictive means' which avoid the necessity of prior restraints. And the argument that 'censorship avoids ... decisions by courts who know nothing of films and are not representative of the film-going public' ignores the point that trial would be by jury.

The Williams Committee did, however, suggest various fundamental reforms to the censorship system. In particular, it recommended the abolition of local authority control. Differing decisions on the films that could be shown in particular localities could not be justified, since there was little evidence that attitudes varied substantially from one area to another. Moreover, the Committee might have added the point that in principle it is wrong for a civil liberty—the interest in communicating and receiving artistic expression—to be more fully respected in some areas than in others.[52] It recommended that the BBFC should be replaced by a statutory body, which would enjoy legal authority and the power to enforce its decisions. The new Film Examining Board would decide the criteria to be applied (subject to restrictions in the reforming legislation) and hear appeals from decisions on particular films taken by its examining staff. Although not entirely clear on this point, the Report does seem to envisage a somewhat more open and formal procedure, with reasons to be given for Board decisions.[53] But it would retain the BBFC's ability to apply broad criteria, going beyond the legal grounds on which a film may be prosecuted. There is no doubt then that the implementation of this part of the Williams Committee Report would remove some of the

[52] This point is particularly important in determining whether it is right to assess 'obscenity' by reference to local community standards: below ch. IX, s. 4.

[53] Williams Committee Report, paras. 12.31 and 12.45.

vices of the existing censorship system. Its arguments for its general retention are, however, unconvincing.

Film censorship remains a common feature of other Western legal systems. In Europe it appears from the Appendix to the Williams Report that only Belgium, the Netherlands, and Denmark manage without it altogether for adults. Germany, however, has a system of self-regulation by bodies representative of the film industry, since formal legal censorship, as we have seen, is prohibited by Article 5 of the Basic Law. In practice this may inhibit artistic freedom just as much as a statutory system, even if it does not suffer from some of the latter's procedural drawbacks. The greatest contrast with the British structure is now provided in the United States, where film censorship is in effect a dead letter. It has in fact never been ruled unconstitutional, though the cinema has enjoyed First Amendment protection since the decision of the Supreme Court in *Burstyn* v. *Wilson*.[54] The old-fashioned view that films were mere entertainment and not vehicles for communicating ideas was then unequivocally rejected. The Court unanimously refused to approve the ban of a film on the ground that it was 'sacrilegious', a term which was so vague as to enable the state to proscribe a documentary or feature which is clearly covered by the First Amendment. Later cases suggest that the body should only be able to ban a film which is obscene or which would fall outside the protection of the Amendment in the event of a criminal prosecution.[56] There has been little danger that censorship boards would be able to proscribe a film on the broad grounds applied by the British Board of Film Censors.

The Court did have an opportunity to outlaw censorship altogether in 1961, but by a bare majority declined to take it.[56] Characterizing the issue as whether there is a constitutional right to show every type of motion picture at least once, the majority refused to invalidate the Chicago ordinance which empowered the commissioner of police to examine all films and ban those offending certain criteria. The exhibitor had refused to submit his film, and so there was no question here about the appropriateness of the ordinance's standards or its application to the picture. The challenge was to the system itself. The leading dissent of Warren CJ defined the central question as the constitutionality of an

---

[54] 343 US 495 (1952).
[55] For example, see *Superior Films* v. *Dept. of Education of Ohio* 346 US 587 (1954), summarily reversing 155 Ohio St. Rep. (1953), and *Kingsley Pictures* v. *Regents* 360 US 648 (1959).
[56] *Times Film* v. *Chicago* 365 US 43 (1961).

ordinance requiring the submission of *all* films for inspection; this formulation suggests that the minority might have been prepared to tolerate some censorship systems. But in fact most of Warren CJ's points, in particular his scepticism that there is any reason for treating films differently from the press, indicate disapproval of all prior restraints in this area. A few years later the Court in effect outlawed administrative restraints by the imposition of rigorous procedural restrictions.[57] First, the censor had to shoulder the burden of proof, second, only a court could order a permanent ban after an adversary hearing, and third, this hearing must take place promptly after the temporary administrative order. These conditions sweep away two of the characteristic advantages of censorship: its informality and lack of publicity. It was, therefore, hardly surprising that a number of states abandoned prior restraints in this area after the *Freedman* ruling.[58]

Now the only form of control in the USA is a voluntary classification system operated by the film industry itself. This is used to grade films, largely to assist parents decide which are suitable for children. The effect is that hard-core pornographic movies are easily accessible to adults, as they are in one or two European countries.[59] Such differences are only partly attributable to the continued existence of censorship in some countries and its abolition in others; the scope of the obscenity laws and the popular attitudes they reflect are at least as important. While it may be conceded that the arguments against film censorship are largely those of principle, and that in practice the British system has worked well, the positive case for treating the cinema in this special way has not really been made out. The Williams Committee itself seemed to admit this when it framed the issue as 'whether we should *abandon* a functioning system'.[60] The negative answer can perhaps be accepted, provided it is not treated as a precedent for censorship in other areas.

3.   OFFICIAL SECRETS AND CONFIDENTIAL INFORMATION

One area where there does seem a good case for the use of some form of prior restraint is the protection of confidential information. This may

---

[57] *Freedman* v. *Maryland* 380 US 51 (1965).

[58] See Carmen, *Movies, Censorship and the Law*, ch. III, and Hunnings, *Film Censorship and the Law*, 14–15, 220–2.

[59] Private cinema clubs in Britain used to be exempt from licensing, but are now within the system: Cinematograph (Amendment) Act 1982.

[60] Williams Committee Report, para. 12.11 (emphasis added).

apply equally to government secrets and confidential commercial information. If the law does not intervene in advance to prohibit disclosure, the damage will be done and subsequent penal sanctions are relatively pointless. The same argument perhaps also justifies restraints on the publication of defamatory material or on a newspaper feature which invades personal privacy. Harmful speech here can not always be satisfactorily remedied by more speech or by an award of compensatory damages. On the other hand, the prospect of penal sanctions or a civil action will in some circumstances be enough to deter unacceptable disclosure of confidential information, etc. Much will depend on such factors as the chance of a prosecution being initiated, and the likely sentence on conviction or the measure of damages in civil proceedings. Thus, quite apart from the other objections to the use of injunctions in this context, the threat of a heavy damages award may well be enough to inhibit newspapers from publishing defamatory material, so rendering prior restraints unnecessary. In contrast the reluctance of juries to convict persons accused of breaches of the official secrets legislation (where the information about to be disclosed is not really material to the security of the state) may explain why governments are sometimes disposed to apply for an injunction to restrain a breach of confidence.

It is in fact impossible to formulate satisfactory general rules here without regard to the particular character of the speech in question. If the information which a newspaper contemplates publishing really does threaten serious damage to the nation's security, only absolutists like Black J. would refuse to countenance a prior restraint. Conversely, neither an injunction nor a subsequent sanction (whether criminal or civil) is appropriate for speech which criticizes the conduct of a public figure. In these cases the real issue is not the form of the restraint, previous or subsequent, but whether any restriction at all is reasonable. However, in other circumstances the justification for any sort of restraint may be far from clear at the stage when an injunction (or prior administrative order) is sought. This may be because the publisher will assert that on the facts there is no crime or civil wrong—hence the rule that an injunction will not be issued to restrain publication of a defamatory article where justification or fair comment is pleaded. Alternatively, there may be a real doubt about the appropriateness of applying the criminal law to a particular publication (as in the *Crossman Diaries* case,[61] to be discussed shortly); then the case for a preliminary

---

[61] *Att.-Gen.* v. *Jonathan Cape* [1976] QB 752.

injunction is very weak. But if there is a strong likelihood of irreparable damage to a vital interest, a prior restraint can be justified, as even the Supreme Court, traditionally hostile to such a remedy, accepted in the *Pentagon Papers* case.[62] Therefore, the form of the restraint is relevant, but rarely decisive, in determining whether publication should be prevented in advance. The character of the speech, and the degree of damage likely to be inflicted if an injunction is refused, must also be considered.

The British courts seem relatively inconsistent in their practice. In libel cases the interests of free speech are always taken into account when judges refuse an injunction to restrain a prima facie defamatory article, the contents of which may be justified or held to be fair comment.[63] A similar principle has been applied in some commercial breach of confidence cases: an injunction will not be granted to restrain disclosure, even in some situations to the press, of information which is of public interest, e.g. concerning the lawfulness of a company's conduct.[64] A full discussion of these issues occurred in *Schering Chemicals* v. *Falkman*.[65] A drug company employed a firm to train some of its executives to counteract the adverse publicity resulting from use of one of its products. Elstein, an employee of the firm, who had received information from the drug company to assist him conduct the training course, prepared a film for Thames Television about the drug and its alleged harmful effects. By a majority the Court of Appeal granted the drug company an injunction to restrain broadcasting of the film on grounds of breach of confidence. Templeman LJ did not think the order interfered with press freedom. The film could have been made and shown, provided the firm's employees did not help in its preparation. This view is plausible on the assumption (which seems to be warranted on the facts of the case) that all the relevant information had already entered the public domain and was freely available. On this footing, the order really only restrained the participation by Elstein in the making of the programme. It is probable, however, that Templeman and Shaw LJJ would have granted the injunction even if it did have the effect of preventing fresh information

---

[62] *New York Times* v. *US* 403 US 713 (1971).

[63] *Bonnard* v. *Perryman* [1891] 2 Ch. 269 (CA).

[64] See in particular *Initial Services* v. *Putterill* [1968] 1 QB 396, 405, *per* Lord Denning MR, and *Woodward* v. *Hutchins* [1977] 1 WLR 745 (CA). Lord Denning's suggestion in *Fraser* v. *Evans* [1969] 1 QB 349, 361 that the defamation rule be applied to actions to restrain breach of confidence was rejected by the Court of Appeal in *Lion Laboratories* v. *Evans* [1984] 3 WLR 539.

[65] [1982] QB 1.

about the drug from reaching the public. Lord Denning MR's dissent emphasized the undesirability of imposing any prior restraint in this situation. Following the approach of the European Court of Justice in the *Sunday Times* contempt case,[66] he urged that disclosure of information of public interest should not be prevented on the ground of breach of confidence unless there is a 'pressing social need'. Such a balancing exercise seems inevitable if the courts are to take proper account of the importance of free speech, including the public interest in receiving information.

Two recent contrasting decisions of the Court of Appeal show how the balancing exercise can be performed. In *Francome* v. *Mirror Group Newspapers Ltd*[67] an interlocutory injunction was granted to restrain the publication by the newspaper of an article, based on the tapes of illegally tapped telephone conversations, which alleged breaches of the rules of racing by the plaintiff. Sir John Donaldson MR, in the Court's leading judgment, was rather disparaging of the defendant's freedom of the press argument; in these circumstances, he argued, the public interest could be best served by sending the tapes to the police or the Jockey Club. On the other hand, a differently composed Court lifted an injunction which had been granted to restrain publication in the *Daily Express* of an article, assembled from confidential documents disclosed to the newspaper by former employees of the plaintiff, alleging defects in a breath-test machine manufactured by the latter.[68] The Court of Appeal here considered that the public interest in the accuracy of the machine outweighed the plaintiff's interest in confidentiality. Moreover, in this case it would not be right to expect the information to be given to the police before publication in the press, for it was the police who were using the machine! By analogy it would not be right to expect the press to refer to a government department any allegations about government misconduct or incompetence before publishing an article containing confidential information.

In recent years the courts have applied the equitable jurisdiction to restrain breaches of confidence in novel contexts. They are willing to grant injunctions to prevent the disclosure of family and political secrets.[69] The ruling in *Att.-Gen.* v. *Jonathan Cape* (the *Crossman Diaries*

[66] [1979] 2 EHRR 245, 281–2.
[67] [1984] 1 WLR 892.
[68] *Lion Laboratories* v. *Evans* [1984] 3 WLR 539.
[69] *Argyll (Duchess)* v. *Argyll (Duke)* [1967] Ch. 202; *British Steel* v. *Granada* [1981] AC 1096, where the Lords *obiter* said it would only be rarely lawful for the press to disclose confidential information about the management of a nationalized industry.

case) is particularly important, affording a striking contrast to the American approach. The Attorney-General applied for an injunction to restrain the publication of diaries kept by a deceased Labour Cabinet Minister. These dealt in some detail with Cabinet discussions, the deliberations of government committees, and the advice received from civil servants. As the revelations concerned matters which had occurred some ten to eleven years before the date of the proposed publication, Lord Widgery CJ did not think disclosure would undermine the relationship of confidence which existed between government Ministers. He would, however, have been prepared to grant an injunction if publication had shortly followed the relevant Cabinet meetings. What is particularly interesting is that, while the judge denied he had power to intervene on broad public interest grounds, largely because of the importance of free speech, he paid little attention to this value in extending the equitable jurisdiction to restrain breaches of confidence: 'I cannot see why the courts should be powerless to restrain the publication of public secrets, while enjoying the *Argyll* powers in regard to domestic secrets.'[70] The distinction is, of course, that the former involves political speech, likely to be of legitimate public interest, while the latter affects privacy interests and is much less obviously of public concern. The point was appreciated in the Australian case, *Australia* v. *John Fairfax*,[71] where Mason J. refused to grant an injunction to restrain breach of confidence merely because the revelations would be embarrassing to the government in the conduct of its foreign policy. Prior restraints should not be outlawed altogether in this situation, e.g. where disclosure might endanger national security or treaty negotiations, but English courts ought to be a little more solicitous of free speech interests than they have hitherto been in actions for breach of confidence.[72]

Another dimension of the *Crossman Diaries* case which causes concern is that apparently the Crown had contemplated the institution of a criminal prosecution under section 2 of the Official Secrets Act 1911. This course was rejected either because it was felt the jury would be reluctant to convict in the circumstances or because of technical difficulties in applying the Act where the author was deceased.[73] In effect the injunction was sought because of doubts about the criminal sanction, and

---

[70] [1976] QB 752, 769.
[71] (1980) 55 ALJR 45.
[72] See the recommendations in the Law Commission Report no. 110, *Breach of Confidence*, paras. 6.77–6.84.
[73] H. Young, *The Crossman Affair* (London, 1976), 32–3.

the publishers were denied the benefit of a jury trial where public assessment of the merits of the prosecution would have been relevant. The repercussions of the case are equally disturbing. Shortly before the proceedings the government had set up a Committee of Privy Councillors to review the law and conventions concerning publication of Ministerial memoirs. That body under the chairmanship of Lord Radcliffe, a former Law Lord, recommended that Ministers (and ex-Ministers) should not be free to disclose confidential discussions for fifteen years or, in the case of advice from a civil servant, during that person's working career.[74] The Committee did not think these conventions should be embodied in statute, nor did it feel that the courts were the right bodies to adjudicate the issues. Rather such conventions should be observed as a matter of honour, with a signature of acceptance required when a Minister assumes office. The government accepted these proposals, although they are more restrictive of political speech than the *Crossman Diaries* judgment. They show the characteristic British indifference to legal rules and distrust of the courts in politically sensitive areas; moreover, the refusal to incorporate them in an Act of Parliament means they have evaded political scrutiny by the House of Commons and, of course, they are not subject to jury enforcement.

The British fondness for extra-legal control is also shown by the D Notice system, under which the Defence, Press and Broadcasting Committee asks editors of newspapers and in television and radio not to print or broadcast certain categories of information regarded as secret for national security reasons.[75] Although clearance by this Committee does not give the press any immunity in law from prosecution under the Official Secrets legislation, in practice it almost always has this effect.[76] As a result there is some evidence that the press in the past has been inclined to rely totally on the Committee's view, and an informal system of censorship has been instituted. It has been remarked earlier that no such system can be justified simply on the ground that it is convenient to, and preferred by, the publishers—otherwise the public interest in receiving information may be entirely ignored. From a constitutional point of view, a voluntary system of censorship accepted by the publishers is surely the very worst; no individual will have an opportunity to challenge it in the

---

[74] Report of the Committee of Privy Counsellors on Ministerial Memoirs (1976), Cmnd. 6386.

[75] See D. G. T. Williams, *Not in the Public Interest* (London, 1965), 80–7; G. Marshall [1967] PL 261.

[76] But see J. Aitken, *Officially Secret* (London, 1971), 111–12.

courts, and particular decisions are effectively insulated from judicial review.[77]

At least until recent times, the law in the United States afforded a complete contrast. Admittedly the possibility of prior restraints in this area was left open in *Near* v. *Minnesota*:

> The protection even as to previous restraint is not absolutely unlimited. But the limitation has been recognized only in exceptional cases. No one would question but that a government might prevent actual obstruction to its recruiting service or the publication of the sailing dates of transports or the number and location of troops . . .[78]

But no proceedings to restrain the publication of secret government information seem to have been taken before the *Pentagon Papers* case arose in 1971.[79] There the government requested an order to restrain publication in the *New York Times* and the *Washington Post* of secret State Department compilations of papers relating to the history of United States involvement in Vietnam. After consideration of the case in a few days, characterized by Harlan J. in dissent as 'almost irresponsibly feverish',[80] the Court, by a majority of 6–3, dismissed the application. All nine justices delivered separate opinions, and as a result the decision is hard to summarize. But the following observations can safely be made. First, with the exception of Marshall J. (whose judgment turns on the lack of any legal basis for an injunction in the absence of legislation), the majority regarded the prior restraint issue as decisive. Second, while the two absolutists, Black and Douglas JJ reiterated their familiar view that the First Amendment wholly precludes any prior restraints, the case is probably only authority for the more moderate proposition that an injunction will only issue if 'disclosure . . . will surely result in direct, immediate and irreparable damage to our Nation or its people'.[81] A third point is that all members of the majority were influenced by the absence of any Congressional statute authorizing the grant of an injunction in these circumstances, although it is not clear why the existence of a statutory basis would have affected the issue. A criminal prosecution under the Espionage Act might have been brought, though one or two

---

[77] A potential reader wishing to challenge decisions under such a system may be met by the arguments that he has no standing, and probably that in the absence of a legally binding decision, there is no justiciable issue for the court to determine: but see *Bantam Books* v. *Sullivan* 372 US 58 (1963).

[78] 283 US 697, 716 (1931) *per* Hughes CJ.

[79] *New York Times* v. *US* 403 US 713 (1971).

[80] Ibid., 753.

[81] Ibid., 730, *per* Stewart J (with whom White J. concurred).

members of the Court were sceptical whether it could have succeeded.[82] In effect the government was, therefore, relying on an inherent power to take proceedings to protect national security, a similar argument to that made unsuccessfully by the British Attorney-General in the *Crossman Diaries* case. The Court was clearly reluctant to impose a prior restraint in the enforcement of such a broad power—in the absence of the clearest possible justification for its exercise.

In fact the prior restraint at issue in the *Pentagon Papers* case lacked many of the remedy's characteristic vices. There was an adversary judicial hearing before an impartial court held very shortly after the government's application; the burden of proof was on the plaintiff and the application, unlike that in *Near*, related to specified materials of a definite character. The difference between these proceedings and a subsequent criminal prosecution lies in the absence here of a jury trial, but it is questionable whether that is enough to justify the markedly stronger presumption against prior restraints in a case involving national security. In effect the Court was protecting a right to publish at least once.[83] And it formulated in this context a more severe test for the validity of a previous restraint (in particular the novel requirement of *immediate* damage) than that employed for film censorship and public meeting permits.

Doubts about the reasoning in this case are reinforced by the more cautious stand adopted by American courts in later litigation. A Federal District Court in *US* v. *Progressive, Inc.*[84] granted an injunction to restrain publication of an article which described in technical detail the manufacture of the H-bomb. On the basis of expert evidence the judge found that the information might enable a medium-power country to make the bomb more expeditiously, and concluded understandably that there was more justification for the government's view that publication would endanger national security than there had been in the *Pentagon Papers* case. The judge emphasized that a statute, the Atomic Energy Act 1954, authorized the government to apply for an injunction against anyone communicating 'restricted data'; this feature, however, would not guarantee an otherwise suspect prior restraint against judicial review. But on the facts the ruling seems unquestionably right.

More difficult are two cases where the courts have sustained restrictions in CIA employment contracts which amount to prior restraints. In

[82] Ibid., at p. 721 *per* Douglas J. (with whom Black J. concurred).
[83] H. Kalven, 'The Supreme Court—1970 Term' (1971) 85 *Harv. LR* 3, 34.
[84] 467 F. Supp. 990 (1979).

the first,[85] a Court of Appeals upheld a clause prohibiting publication by an ex-CIA agent of classified information, while in *Snepp*,[86] the Supreme Court approved as constitutional a contractual provision requiring employees to submit any forthcoming publication for preliminary clearance. It further granted an order imposing a constructive trust for the government's benefit of the profits from the sale of the defendant's book, which had not been submitted for scrutiny. Showing myopia more characteristic of the British courts, the majority here seems virtually to have ignored the prior restraint issue; a term requiring submission for approval of all material, whether classified or not, certainly inhibits speech which is constitutionally protected, and should surely only be upheld if there is no other way of preventing disclosures which create a serious risk of direct and irreparable damage.[87]

These cases, like the British decisions on protection of confidential information, raise the difficult question whether an employee (or a government Minister) may be subject to more severe restraints than ordinary citizens, and the related issue whether contractual restrictions are more tolerable than those imposed by the general law. It may be argued that the speaker here has voluntarily surrendered part of his freedom of expression, and that he has no strong interest in disclosing information which has only been made available to him through his employment. This, however, wholly ignores the interests of the recipients and the public, who on the basis of the argument from democracy might have a strong free speech claim to be informed. These points are taken up again in the discussion of official secrecy laws and of civil servants' association rights.[88] Is there anything in this context particularly heinous in the use of prior restraints to prevent disclosure? As in other circumstances the government may be tempted to use contractual remedies to avoid the embarrassment of a criminal prosecution with trial by jury and, of course a clearance procedure of the type at issue in *Snepp* is conducted in private and without any clear standards. But equally there may well be powerful arguments against the toleration of any disclosure of confidential information and the contractual remedies may provide a more effective means of enforcement than a post-publication criminal prosecution. The justification for the prior restraint

---

[85] *US* v. *Marchetti* 466 F 2d 1309 (1972). The Supreme Court denied *certiorari*, 409 US 1063 (1972).
[86] *Snepp* v. *US* 444 US 507 (1980).
[87] See the dissent of Stevens J. (joined by Brennan and Marshall JJ) ibid., 516.
[88] See below, ch. V, s. 5, and ch. X, s. 2.

cannot easily be considered without attention being given to the character of the particular disclosure.[89]

The cases in both Britain and the United States show how hard it is for the courts to formulate clear rules and apply them consistently in these sensitive areas. An absolutist prohibition on all previous restraints is too dogmatic. It would entail an unqualified right to publish everything once, when what is in question is whether the injunction (or other form of restraint) is an unacceptable restriction on the right to free speech, which in no jurisdiction is regarded as an absolute right. There are sometimes good reasons for treating these restraints with particular suspicion, and judges are equally open to criticism both when they totally ignore these reasons or when (as in *Pentagon Papers*) they formulate extremely severe tests for the restraint to be upheld.

4. TWO OTHER AREAS: CONTEMPT OF COURT AND THE LICENSING OF MEETINGS

There are two other principal areas where prior restraint issues sometimes arise: contempt of court and restrictions on public meetings and demonstrations. Normally proceedings for a contempt are taken after the offending article has been published, and it is relatively rare, at least in Britain, that an application for an injunction is made to restrain publication of a forthcoming article. But this unusual course was taken in the famous *Sunday Times* case after the editor of that newspaper had sent the Attorney-General the draft of a further article he was proposing to publish during his press campaign against Distillers.[90] The newspaper further welcomed the institution of proceedings by the Attorney-General, so in a sense the prior restraint here could be characterized as voluntary. But that, as we have said before, is not a decisive point.[91] In the Court of Appeal, where the injunction was discharged, Scarman LJ drew the contrast between a defamation action and these contempt proceedings: in the former an interlocutory injunction would be refused if fair comment on a matter of public interest was pleaded, while in the latter a prior restraint might be imposed.[92] Yet the public interest in free

---

[89] A prior restraint was upheld in *Brown* v. *Glines* 444 US 348 (1980), where the approval of a commanding officer had to be obtained for the circulation of a petition on an Air Force base or by an officer in uniform. Also see *Greer* v. *Spock* 424 US 828 (1976) above, p. 94.

[90] *Att.-Gen.* v. *Times Newspapers* [1974] AC 273.

[91] See above, p. 124.

[92] [1973] QB 710, 746.

discussion of the issues would be the same. The House of Lords seems to have paid little attention to the prior restraint aspect of the case, though this was accentuated by the extraordinarily wide injunction formulated by the House: all further matter prejudging the issues in the pending trial was enjoined.[93]

The issue arose again in *Att.-Gen.* v. *BBC*,[94] where proceedings were brought to restrain the repeat of a programme about the Exclusive Brethren. It was claimed this would prejudice the hearing of the sect's application for rating relief. The main ground on which the Lords dismissed the contempt proceedings was that a local valuation court was not an inferior court of law for this purpose. But Lord Denning MR in dissent in the Court of Appeal, and Lords Salmon and Scarman in the Lords were aware of the prior restraint issue. Lord Denning MR, said that the Attorney-General was seeking a 'gagging injunction', and this should not be awarded unless there was a 'clear case where there would manifestly be a contempt of court . . .'.[95] Again the comparison between the court's approach to injunctions in defamation and contempt cases was made. Lord Scarman was even more forthright. A prior restraint should only be ordered where there is 'a substantial risk of grave injustice', because it was 'a drastic interference with freedom of speech'.[96] Such language and principles are more characteristic of the American Supreme Court; they show a welcome appreciation of the questions involved in this type of proceeding.

It is, however, far from evident that it is right to treat an application for an injunction more severely than subsequent contempt proceedings. In Britain both types of application are heard by judge alone, and there does not appear to be any significant procedural difference. Arguably the injunction does not really operate as a sanction unless it is enforced by separate civil contempt proceedings if there is a publication in violation of the enjoining order. So it can be urged that the inhibiting effect of an injunction, such as that granted in the *Sunday Times* case, is not necessarily any greater than the prospect of subsequent contempt proceedings. It may be more significant if the penalty for disobedience to the order is greater than that likely to be imposed in the latter type of contempt procedure. In the United States there is another reason why a prior 'gagging order' may be subject to stricter scrutiny than penal

---

[93] [1974] AC 273, 327.
[94] [1981] AC 303.
[95] Ibid., 311 (CA).
[96] Ibid., 362.

contempt proceedings: it may not be permissible to challenge the constitutionality of the 'gagging order' when it is subsequently enforced.[97] If the bar on later collateral challenge were removed, there is little reason for treating preliminary injunctions with so much suspicion.[98] Those who believe, as most English judges seem to do, that publicity before a trial (criminal or civil) is really likely to prejudice the result, will naturally defend such orders as the most effective means of avoiding that prejudice. The argument in Chapter VIII casts doubt on this belief.[99] Such scepticism is even stronger in the case of prior restraints, which may well be imposed at a time when the danger to a fair trial can not properly be assessed. As in other areas of free speech law, the fact that a restraint is previous (as opposed to a subsequent penalty) is one important factor to be taken into account in determining its reasonableness.

The Supreme Court at any rate has had no hesitation in applying its general hostility to prior restraints in this area. In *Nebraska Press Association* v. *Stuart* it unanimously invalidated an order restraining the press and broadcasting media from reporting confessions and other admissions made by a defendant in a murder case and from publishing other facts which implicated him.[100] The judgment of the Court, given by Burger CJ, considered that the heavy presumption against prior restraints had not been rebutted, but implied that it could be if there were no other means by which a fair trial could be safeguarded. In a separate judgment, Brennan J., joined by Stewart and Marshall JJ, considered that this extreme remedy could never be justified in this context. The harm to a fair trial was always speculative, and it was an impossible task for the courts to weigh this risk against the public interest in reading newspaper reports. The categories of permissible prior restraints formulated in *Near* were exhaustive.[101] In fact this approach probably rests on doubts concerning the justification for any sort of contempt proceedings; the argument against judicial balancing applies equally to criminal prosecutions, and certainly is not sufficiently convincing to preclude any use of prior restraints in this context. Publication of a highly prejudicial article about the accused during the course of his trial should surely be prevented by injunction.

---

[97] See above, p. 121.
[98] See Barnett, 'The Puzzle of Prior Restraint'.
[99] See below, ch. VIII, ss. 3 and 4.
[100] 427 US 539 (1976).
[101] Ibid., 589–94.

The Supreme Court has shown a more cautious approach in the second area of law. Although not specifically listed in the *Near* categories, previous restraints have frequently been upheld to control the holding of public meetings and processions. Permit requirements to regulate the time, manner, and place of such meetings are generally approved.[102] On the other hand, an ordinance under which the county or city officials have an unfettered discretion to ban the distribution of literature or a peaceful march on the grounds that they dislike the particular cause of protest will be struck down.[103] Here the ordinance suffers from the characteristic prior restraint vice of lack of clear standards; if not invalidated, constitutionally protected speech may well be prohibited. The cases in which convenors are prohibited from holding a meeting, because on a previous occasion it has led to violence, or because this time the officials fear a hostile audience will cause disorder, pose greater problems. Generally the Supreme Court has disapproved bans made on these grounds.[104] The best justification for this is that other means are available to deal with actual disorder at the event; moreover, if there is a serious likelihood of a breach of the peace, this can often be met by extra policing.[105] Then the argument for the prior restraint becomes one of cost and administrative convenience, and this is certainly not enough to outweigh the free speech right or interest. Further, the risk of disorder may be hard to assess at the time the permit application is made.

There are two other arguments which can be made against the use of permit systems. First, they are administered by officials or police commissioners who are likely to acquire institutional attitudes and who may not observe fair procedural rules. There has been some suggestion that the procedural requirements laid down in *Freedman* v. *Maryland* in the film censorship field should be applied here,[106] but this is not the general rule. They were however applied in one case to strike down the grant of an ex-parte injunction on the application of city officials to restrain the further staging of demonstrations by a far right political party.[107] The case also shows a second reservation about licensing in this area: often it has the effect of postponing or permanently banning

---

[102] *Cox* v. *New Hampshire* 312 US 569 (1941); *Niemotko* v. *Maryland* 340 US 268 (1951).
[103] *Lovell* v. *Griffin* 303 US 444 (1938).
[104] *Kunz* v. *New York* 340 US 290 (1951).
[105] See the exhaustive discussion of the relevant arguments by V. Blasi, 'Prior Restraints and Demonstrations' (1970) 68 *Mich. LR* 1481.
[106] See Harlan J. in *Shuttlesworth* v. *Birmingham* 394 US 147 (1969).
[107] *Carroll* v. *President & Commissioners of Princess Anne* 393 US 175 (1968).

political speech of contemporary and vital interest, where even a delay of a few days will dilute its impact. In this respect there is less justification for the use of censorship here than in the case of films and theatre.

It is less surprising that British law frequently countenances prior restraints in this area. They take a variety of forms. In addition to the standard licensing systems under which a local authority or (in the case of Trafalgar Square) the Secretary of State for the Environment may refuse permission for a meeting in a public place, there are a number of common law and statutory restraints. For example, a property-owner with land adjoining the highway may apply for an injunction to restrain the nuisance occasioned him by a protest demonstration against his business.[108] Under the Public Order Act 1936, a chief officer of police may impose conditions on processions, including the route to be followed, where he believes they are likely to lead to a serious breach of the peace. And if this is not sufficient to avert disorder, he may apply to the local authority for a ban on all processions for three months.[109] The police have preventive powers to stop meetings where the speaker intends to bring about a breach of the peace, or where this is likely.[110] The courts here virtually never seem troubled that the law is imposing a prior restraint, supported by criminal penalties for violation of the order or the obstruction of the police. In one or two Canadian cases, some judges have, however, adopted critical attitudes to broadly drafted by-laws enabling authorities to control the content of leaflets and prevent their distribution. Although the Canadian Constitution did not until very recently outlaw legislation which interferes with freedom of speech, there has been a strong presumption against tolerating antecedent restraints in this area.[111]

One problem is that it may be hard to distinguish between preventive and punitive justice in this area, and the characterization of a restriction as prior may therefore be somewhat artificial. The power of magistrates to bind demonstrators over to keep the peace or to be of good behaviour is a good illustration of this uncertainty. Sometimes a binding-over order is made after a conviction when it could be regarded as part of the sentence, but it is also on occasion made for a person who has been

---

[108] *Hubbard* v. *Pitt* [1976] 1 QB 142 (CA).

[109] Public Order Act 1936, s. 3. The exercise of this power to ban all processions in part of London has been held by the European Commission not to contravene arts. 10, 11, and 14 of the Convention: 8440/78, *Christians against Racism* v. *UK* 21 D. & R. 138.

[110] *Duncan* v. *Jones* [1936] 1 KB 218 (DC).

[111] See *Saumur* v. *City of Quebec* [1953] 2 SCR 299, 329, *per* Rand J.; *Switzman* v. *Elbling & Att.-Gen. of Quebec* [1957] SCR 285.

acquitted, or who has not even been charged with any offence.[112] In a recent case the Divisional Court appears to have recognized that an order made after a conviction for the offence of using insulting words likely to cause a breach of the peace may constitute an unreasonable restraint, when it said: 'A binding over must not be in such terms as effectively to inhibit a convicted person from exercising his right to free speech within the law.'[113] Again the leader of a demonstration convicted of a breach of the peace may shortly afterwards be refused permission to hold another meeting, and this can be regarded as a delayed instalment of the penalty for the disruption. These ambiguities may go some way towards explaining the greater tolerance for prior restraints in this context.

The best justification, however, for the courts' tolerance is that a permit system is much the most satisfactory method of control. Criminal sanctions alone cannot properly deal with the allocation of times and places for meetings, or so easily with the clear risks of confrontation between rival groups when each is planning to demonstrate on the same day and in the same neighbourhood.[114] The community's interest can therefore really only be protected by some censorship system—a proposition which is certainly not true in the case of obscene publication and films, or of breaches of confidentiality in many cases. But there are tremendous risks of administrative arbitrariness conducive to the suppression of valuable political speech. The judiciary should be alert to check this through judicial review of particular decisions, and by careful scrutiny of licensing systems where this is constitutionally mandated.

---

[112] For a general discussion, see D. G. T. Williams, *Keeping the Peace* (London, 1967), ch. 4. There was considerable political debate about the impact on free speech of the binding-over order made on George Lansbury: see *Lansbury* v. *Riley* [1914] 3 KB 229 (DC), and 56 HC Deb. (5th ser.), cols. 2342–5 (J. C. Wedgwood MP). (I am indebted to Dr G. Marshall for this reference.)

[113] *R.* v. *Central Criminal Court, ex parte Boulding* [1984] 2 WLR 321, 325.

[114] L. H. Tribe, *American Constitutional Law* 731.

V

Political Speech

I. INTRODUCTION

PERHAPS the most significant ruling of the United States Supreme Court since the last war on the scope of the First Amendment has been its decision in *New York Times* v. *Sullivan*.[1] It was held that a civil libel action brought by a public official could only be constitutionally sustained if the statement was made with malice, that is, the defendant must know that it was untrue or be reckless as to its truth. The precise reasons for this ruling will be explored in the following chapter, but the fundamental rationale may be found in Brennan J.'s much-quoted dictum:

... we consider this case against the background of a profound national commitment to the principle that debate on public issues should be uninhibited, robust and wide open, and that it may well include vehement, caustic, and sometimes unpleasantly sharp attacks on government and public officials ...[2]

Under this principle, not only civil libel laws, but the rules of seditious and private criminal libel and prohibitions on inflammatory racial speech may well be constitutionally suspect. In other jurisdictions too, the courts are particularly willing to invalidate or narrowly construe such laws under a freedom of speech clause.

An initial question is what justifications there are for treating speech in the political sphere as more worthy of protection than other types of speech. To some extent this entails a reference back to the arguments discussed in Chapter I for according freedom of expression special protection against government interference. Some of these arguments may suggest that political speech should occupy what is referred to in American constitutional jurisprudence as a 'preferred position', and that courts should be less prepared to countenance abridgements of political

---

[1] 376 US 254 (1964). This was certainly the view of H. Kalven, 'The New York Times Case: A Note on "The Central Meaning of the First Amendment"' [1964] *S. Ct. Rev.* 191.

[2] 376 US 254, 270 (1964).

and social discussion than they should restrictions on literature, porno-graphy, or commercial advertising. The implications of this differential treatment can then be explored in three areas of political speech: seditious speech and some related areas of expression (including that prohibited by the British Incitement to Disaffection Act 1934), group libel or racially inflammatory speech, and finally official secrets laws. The relationship of the free speech principle to private libel laws, criminal and civil, is left to the next chapter, where the topic is considered together with some aspects of privacy law.

These topics do not exhaust the areas where the courts' special concern for political speech may be relevant. Many of the public order cases discussed in Chapter VII concern such speech; indeed there is some overlap between the subject-matter of that chapter and one or two of the issues treated in this. Less obviously some of the varieties of contempt of court considered in Chapter VIII, such as criticism of the judiciary, can be regarded as a type of political expression. Attempts to bracket such cases with archetypal instances of political speech, e.g. an attack on the government, show the strength of the view that such speech does enjoy a preferred status. They support one of the major themes of this book: courts do generally recognize this status, and moreover, they are right to do so.

2.   THE PREFERRED POSITION OF POLITICAL SPEECH

We saw in Chapter I that the courts in the United States and West Germany are particularly keen to protect political speech under the relevant constitutional provisions, and that this concern stems from the weight of the argument from democracy.[3] While the rights-based argument concerning the importance of speech to self-development and Mill's argument from truth might suggest that artistic and scientific propositions are equally immune from legislative regulation, the third rationale for free speech clearly elevates political discourse to a special status. An absence of restraint in this area encourages a well-informed and politically sophisticated electorate able to confront government on more or less equal terms; it also, as Brandeis J. pointed out in his celebrated judgment in the *Whitney* case, prevents that stifling of debate on political questions, which in the long term endangers the stability of the community and makes revolution more likely.[4]

---

[3] See above, pp. 20–3.
[4] *Whitney* v. *California* 274 US 357, 376 (1927).

The simple strength of the argument from democracy may be reinforced from a court's point of view by other indications that political speech enjoys a preferred position. Free speech rights may be incorporated in the constitution together with other political freedoms, such as the right to vote and the rights of political parties to play a role in the democratic process. These structural arguments may further be buttressed by observations about the spirit of the constitution, and the commitment of the society, as revealed in that document, to open political debate. More controversially, a court may uphold a 'right' of political debate on the ground that it is inherent to a free society, although no specific constitutional provision guarantees the right: in *Re Alberta Statutes*,[5] three members of the Canadian Supreme Court, which had been asked for an advisory opinion on an Alberta press law, found such a right implicit in the British North American Act, which was thought to reflect the spirit of the unwritten British Constitution.

The preferred status of political speech can also be defended in another way. Constitutional courts and commentators are constantly concerned to justify judicial decisions which appear to conflict with the wishes of the electorate, as represented in the enactments of the democratically elected legislature. How to reconcile judicial review with democracy is a problem which has baffled generations of scholars, and perhaps despite the wealth of legal and philosophical literature has never been satisfactorily resolved.[6] If the legislature has voted to ban abortion or pornography, can it be right for judges, who are not elected or accountable to the people, to interfere with these decisions? The question is particularly pertinent if there is little or no textual warrant for judicial intervention. To confine freedom of expression to political speech (or at any rate to protect it most rigorously in this context) does reduce the scale of the difficulty. Political speech is immune from restriction, because it is a dialogue between members of the electorate and between governors and governed, and is, therefore, conducive, rather than inimical, to the operation of a constitutional democracy. The same is not so obviously true of other categories of 'speech', for which the protection of the free speech clause may be claimed—pornography or commercial advertising.

Sometimes this case is put in the very strong form that the courts should only protect political speech, and that it would be wrong for them

---

[5] (1938) SCR 100, 132–5, 142–6, *per* Duff CJ and Cannon J.
[6] See in particular A. M. Bickel, *The Least Dangerous Branch* (New York, 1962), especially ch. 1, and J. H. Ely, *Democracy and Distrust* (Harvard, 1980), especially ch. 3.

to construe the relevant provision as covering, say, obscenity.[7] This view is, however, unacceptable. It ignores altogether the other arguments for the protection of free speech, in particular the case from individual self-development and autonomy, without which perhaps the argument for democracy lacks complete conviction.[8] Moreover, constitutions expressly insulate other freedoms, for example, rights to privacy or a fair trial, from state control, although they have nothing to do with the preservation of democracy. At all events, the jurisdictions considered in this book clearly give some non-political speech a degree of protection. The Supreme Court of the United States, for instance, has resiled from its view that commercial speech falls outside the First Amendment.[9] And the German Constitutional Court has held that commentary on artistic and social questions is covered by the Basic Law,[10] a conclusion which is hardly surprising in view of the Article 5(3) protection of 'freedom of art and science, research and teaching'.

However, the weight given to free speech interests and the degree of their protection may vary significantly according to the characterization of the expression as political, commercial, artistic, and so on. The American and German courts, and the institutions applying the European Convention, are required to balance the relevant government interests underlying the challenged law against the speech which the state wishes to punish or restrain under that law. The balancing process, as mentioned in Chapter I, may be mandated by the text itself or be (as in the United States) a judicial technique developed in order to avoid the difficulties of the 'absolutist' position.[11] Thus, considerations such as national security or public order will be assessed to determine whether they are sufficiently weighty to justify the suppression or restriction of speech. Often this process merely appears to involve an *ad hoc* calculation of the importance in the particular circumstances of the competing interests, but the courts have also formulated general rules. These may be used to ensure greater consistency in decisions, and may also in some formulations emphasize the presumption in favour of the free speech interest.

Paramount among these rules in the United States law has been the

---

[7] R. Bork, 'Neutral Principles and Some First Amendment Problems' (1971) 47 *Ind. LJ* 1.

[8] See above, p. 21.

[9] See ch. II, s. 4.

[10] See the *Mephisto* case, 30 BVerfGE 173 (1971) and 54 BVerfGE 129 (1980).

[11] See above p. 32.

'clear and present danger' test; this may now briefly be discussed in order to illustrate how the Court balances in the area of political speech. The rule was first formulated by Holmes J. in his judgment for the Court in *Schenk* v. *US*, where the defendants were prosecuted under the Espionage Act 1917 for circulating leaflets, which urged opposition to the draft and participation in the war, among people called up for military service. Upholding the defendants' conviction, he formulated this general rule:

The question in every case is whether the words are used in such circumstances and are of such a nature as to create a clear and present danger that they will bring about the substantive evils that Congress has a right to prevent.[12]

The test has been applied subsequently in many cases, some of which are discussed in this chapter, and it has also been applied extensively to restrict contempt of court proceedings.[13] Despite, perhaps because of, its progressive refinement in later cases, it remains full of uncertainties. The difficulty of most comparative interest is the level at which the test is to be applied: is the court to ask itself whether the legislature could reasonably take the view that a certain type of speech or writing constitutes a clear and present danger to state security (or some other compelling interest), or is it for the court to decide whether there was a patent and imminent danger in the particular circumstances of the case?

Holmes J.'s judgment in *Schenk* suggests the latter approach is correct, but some influential opinions contemplate that at least great deference is due to the legislative assessment, implicit in the statute, that speech of a certain character is *per se* dangerous.[14] One noted example of this view is Frankfurter J.'s judgment in *Dennis* v. *US*, where he said: 'How best to reconcile competing interests is the business of the legislatures, and the balance they strike is a judgment not to be displaced by ours, but to be respected unless outside the pale of fair judgment.'[15] If, as it had done, Congress has determined that the perils to national security from aggressive Communist propaganda outweigh the interests of free speech, the courts should be reluctant to interfere. This approach is no longer typical of the American judiciary. It is open to criticism for failing to respect the constitutionally determined presumption in favour of freedom of speech, and treating the liberty as merely one factor to be

---

[12] 249 US 47, 52 (1919).
[13] See below, ch. VIII, s. 3.
[14] For example, *Gitlow* v. *New York* 268 US 652 (1925); *Whitney* v. *California* 274 US 357 (1927).
[15] 341 US 494, 539–40 (1951).

considered among many. Moreover, it is precisely because the legislature cannot be trusted not to enact broad legislation indiscriminately suppressly speech which is harmless, together with dangerous propaganda, that judicial review is justified.[16]

Certainly both the German Constitutional Court and the European Court have insisted that the interests should be balanced in the context of the particular facts. The Karlsruhe judges have emphasized that the character of the speech, the extent to which it was true or fabricated, and the degree of danger to the relevant state interest must all be considered in this concrete weighing process.[17] In the *Luth* case (1958),[18] still the leading ruling on the principles to be applied under Article 5, the Court concluded that speech designed to contribute to public debate on a matter of legitimate general concern is entitled to a greater degree of protection than expression aimed at a private interest, particularly in the commercial sector. The issue in this case was whether the grant by a lower court of an injunction, which prevented the director of public relations of Hamburg from calling for a boycott of a film made by a former Nazi supporter, violated the director's freedom of expression. The Constitutional Court held that the protection of the film-maker's reputation and economic interests was not a sufficiently important objective to justify restrictions on the boycott call; this was treated as speech intended both to influence public opinion and to show that former Nazi sympathizers could not expect an easy rehabilitation in post-war Germany.

The European Court's approach to balancing is strikingly similar to that adopted by the German Constitutional Court and (generally) the Supreme Court in Washington. Moreover, it enables the judges to show a degree of preference for political speech, although it is clear that both commercial advertising and publications with some 'obscene' content may be covered by Article 10. In the *Handyside* case[19] it was said that the Article was primarily concerned to protect the dissemination of political ideas, while in the *Sunday Times* decision[20] the Court stressed that the extent of each member state's discretion to determine the measures

---

[16] See F. Schauer, *Free Speech: A Philosophical Enquiry* (Cambridge, 1982), ch. 6.

[17] See in particular 34 BVerfGE 269 (1973) (fabricated press interview of no value to the development of public opinion); 20 BVerfGE 162 (1966) and 21 BVerfGE 239 (1967) (risk of danger to state security from disclose of official information to be assessed on the particular facts).

[18] 7 BVerfGE 198 (1958).

[19] (1976) 1 EHRR 737.

[20] (1979) 2 EHRR 245.

necessary to restrict free speech varies according to the character of the state interest involved. In particular, the state has a greater 'margin of appreciation' in framing measures to protect morals than it does in the case of rules required to maintain confidence in the administration of justice. This distinction is controversial, but it can be justified as a consequence of the preferred status of political (or public) speech: articles deploring the conduct of one party to pending litigation are in a loose sense 'political', while it would be far-fetched to characterize most pornography in this way. In the *Sunday Times* case, the Court also expressed its hostility to the *absolute* nature of the English contempt rule, under which all articles prejudging the merits of a forthcoming trial were treated as contempt, no matter what their relevance to matters of contemporary public discussion.[21] Whether restrictions are 'necessary in a democratic society' can only be determined in the particular circumstances. This concrete weighing process not only enables the judges to determine the importance of the relevant state interest and the degree of danger threatened by the expression, but also encourages them to examine the precise character of the speech. It may, for example, as the *Luth* case illustrates, be significant whether it is calculated to contribute to general public discussion, or is alternatively primarily concerned to bring about violence or to intimidate or defame individuals. Only the former should be regarded as 'political' speech.

Even in the common law, where freedom of speech is at most a principle limiting the application of other rights, such as the right to reputation or a fair trial, the political character of the expression may be decisive. As the next section will show, growing appreciation of the importance of public discussion has led to the virtual disappearance of the offence of seditious libel. The same factor has influenced the recognition of defences of qualified privilege to libel proceedings, for example, in the case of the fair reporting of Parliamentary debates.[22] And the scope and application of the 'fair comment on a matter of public interest' defence, discussed in Chapter VI, enables the courts to discriminate between political and other types of public speech on the one hand and purely private character assassination on the other.

Therefore, while constitutions do not confine freedom of speech to political speech, the courts do appear inclined to protect such speech more fully than other categories of expression. The 'balancing' approach virtually universally adopted enables this to be done without difficulty.

---

[21] Ibid., 280.
[22] *Wason* v. *Walter* (1868) 4 QB 73.

So far the meaning of the term, 'political speech', has deliberately been left vague. To some extent its scope can be determined in relation to other types of speech which are not so fully covered, in particular commercial speech and pornography. Reflection on the implications of the argument from democracy may also shed some light, since it underlies the special status of political speech. But it would be wrong to look for very much precision. Courts dislike drawing too many distinctions in this area, probably because they do not wish arbitrarily to discriminate against certain types of expression on the basis of their contents. Even the familiar frontiers between, say, 'speech' and 'conduct', or between political and commercial speech are frequently contested.[23] All that can be said perhaps is that the category is not exhausted by political publications and addresses which seek to influence electoral choices. Rather 'political speech' refers to all speech relevant to the development of public opinion on the whole range of issues which an intelligent citizen should think about. Beyond this generality, we must look to the decisions of the courts, especially those discussed in the remainder of this chapter and in the next chapter dealing with libel.

3. SEDITION AND RELATED OFFENCES

A prominent American lawyer has observed that the existence of the offence of seditious libel is the hallmark of an unfree society.[24] If this is the case, there are remarkably few free countries, for in England and many Commonwealth countries the offence still exists (though prosecutions are nowadays very rare), and there are similar crimes in the codes of European states.[25] Nevertheless, the argument is a serious one, for what used to be regarded as a clear case of seditious libel in both England and the United States is now generally considered to be merely the vehement expression of political opinion, and therefore the classic instance of speech which is constitutionally protected. The elements of the common law crime in English law are far from clear, an obscurity which made use of the charge dangerous when it was frequently brought, but which now probably encourages its obsolescence. The classic definition, approved by Cave J., in his direction to the jury in *R. v. Burns*,[26] is to be found in

---

[23] See above, ch. II, ss. 2 and 4.

[24] H. Kalven, 'The New York Times Case', 205.

[25] See the French Law of the Press, 29. 7.1881, arts. 24 and 30–1, and the German Criminal Code, ss. 90–90b.

[26] (1886) 16 Cox C. C. 333.

Stephen's *Digest of the Criminal Law*,[27] and can be paraphrased as the publication of a speech or writing with intent to bring into hatred or contempt, or excite hostility towards, the Crown, government, Parliament, and administration of justice, or with the aim of inducing reform by unlawful means or of promoting class warfare. Taken literally, this would cover much political argument and oratory, and frequent prosecution and conviction would surely have the effect of stifling any serious criticism of government and other institutions. The offence's survival has only been rendered tolerable in Britain and other Commonwealth jurisdictions by numerous refinements and qualifications.

In its original form the definition of the crime reflects a traditional, conservative view of the correct relationship between state and society. Governments and public institutions are not to be regarded as responsible to the people, but in some mystical way, as under the doctrine of the Divine Right of Kings, are naturally entitled to the respect and veneration of their subjects. At the very most, tentative and discreet suggestions concerning the improvement of government may be tolerated, but not open or vehement attack. This attitude was responsible for the frequent use of the charge of sedition in the eighteenth and early nineteenth centuries in England, and has been contrasted, probably too starkly, with the intellectual climate which accompanied the American Revolution and which led to the drafting of the First Amendment. It used to be generally thought that it was the intention of the framers of the Bill of Rights to proscribe prosecutions for seditious libel, because the spirit of American government is that it exists to serve the people and that the state is responsible to the electorate.[28] Now despite the judicial view that the Sedition Act of 1798 is in contravention of 'the freedom of speech',[29] modern historical scholarship has made a convincing case that the Amendment was only intended to reaffirm the common law's hostility towards prior restraints or, at most, prevent the federal Congress, though not the states, from enacting sedition laws.[30] The Supreme Court has, however, never regarded itself as confined to implementing the intentions of the Founding Fathers, and it may now safely be said that the ordinary common law of sedition, or any statute formulated along its lines, would

---

[27] Ed. by L. Sturge (9th edn., London, 1950), art. 114.

[28] See A. Meiklejohn, *Free Speech and its Relation to Self-government* reprinted in *Political Freedom* (New York, 1965); Z. Chafee, *Free Speech in the United States* (Harvard, 1941), especially ch. 1.

[29] See Brennan J. in *New York Times* v. *Sullivan* 376 US 254, 276 (1964).

[30] L. W. Levy, *Legacy of Suppression: Freedom of Speech and the Press in Early American History* (Harvard, 1960).

be held unconstitutional as a violation of the central meaning of the First Amendment. But a number of other laws proscribing the advocacy of revolutionary change or membership of radical political parties with these aims have given the American courts more difficulty.[31]

Before looking at developments in the law of sedition and at the contemporaneous progress of American law to a more liberal attitude towards the protection of political speech, it is interesting to point out that in other jurisdictions the conservative view of the state is still reflected in the criminal law. The Irish Constitution specifically preserves the offence of seditious libel, perhaps rather paradoxically in the very article in which the state guarantees the citizens' rights to express freely their convictions and opinions.[32] Rather more surprising and revealing is the decision of the High Court of Australia in *Burns* v. *Ransley*,[33] upholding the constitutionality of section 24 of the Federal Crimes Act 1914–16 which proscribes speech expressive of seditious intent. The defendant, a leader of the Australian Communist Party, who had said at a public debate that he would fight on the side of the Soviet Union, contended that the law usurped the power of the states to enact criminal laws. But the Court found that the offence could be validly created under section 51 (xxxix) of the Commonwealth Constitution, enabling the Federal Parliament 'to make laws with respect to matters incidental to the execution of any power vested' in the Commonwealth government. This provision apparently validates the enactment of statutes proscribing incitements to disaffection, on the somewhat conservative view that this course is reasonably incidental to the business of government. Such a decision would be more predictable in French law. There, the law of the press institutes the criminal offences of defamation and contempt of the President of the Republic, Deputies, government ministers and important public officials.[34] During the 1960s there were successful prosecutions against writers of intemperate political attacks, construed as insulting the President.[35]

The common law of sedition has been liberalized in a number of

---

[31] See, for example, the treatment of the Smith Act in *Dennis* v. *US* 341 US 494 (1951), *Yates* v. *US* 354 US 298 (1957), and in *Scales* v. *US* 367 US 203 (1961).

[32] Constitution of Ireland, art. 40. 6 But see J. M. Kelly, *Fundamental Rights in the Irish Law and Constitution* (2nd edn., Dublin, 1967), where it is pointed out that there have been no reported decisions on sedition in Ireland since 1922.

[33] (1949) 79 CLR 101: see also *R.* v. *Sharkey* (1949) 79 CLR 121.

[34] Law of the Press, 29. 7. 1881, arts. 26 and 31. See J. Rivero, *Les Libertés publiques*, II (2nd edn., Paris, 1980), 225.

[35] See DS 1965. J. 645; DS 1967. J. 372.

respects by the judiciary. Stephen's definition itself drew the important distinction between incitement to revolutionary change on the one hand, and on the other advocacy of lawful reform and the removal of grievances. This difference was crucial in *R.* v. *Burns*,[36] where the defendant was acquitted after making a passionate speech at a meeting in Trafalgar Square, calling attention to the plight of unemployed workers in London. A number of English cases stress that the speaker must intend to cause violence for the offence to be committed: 'was the language used calculated, or was it not, to promote public disorder or physical force or violence in a matter of State?'[37] The jury must take into account the character of the audience and the current state of public feeling, considerations which emphasize the circumstantial nature of the offence in the modern law. The approach is similar to the concrete weighing of interests, which occurs in jurisdictions where free speech is protected by the constitution. In the leading Canadian case, *Boucher* v. *R.*,[38] the Supreme Court held that there must be an intent to disturb the government by force; it was not seditious to incite violence between classes or groups of the population—a matter sometimes covered by the group libel laws discussed in the next section of this chapter. The result of all these qualifications, and the changing attitude to the range of permissible restrictions on the expression of political opinion, is that prosecutions for sedition have become virtually unknown, at least in England, so much so that the Law Commission has questioned whether there is any need for the offence.[39]

Nevertheless, at least in theory the common law still draws a distinction between the expression of political opinion and the advocacy or incitement of violent (or in some formulations, unlawful) political action. The American Supreme Court has attempted to make a similar distinction in many of its leading decisions in the area of political speech, though the line is now drawn in a different place, which ensures a wider berth for permissible freedom of expression. In *Gitlow* v. *New York*, a case involving a prosecution under the state criminal anarchy statute which prohibited advocacy of the forcible overthrow of government, the majority of the Court distinguished between the 'expression of philosophical abstraction' and the 'language of direct incitement'.[40] The state

[36] (1886) 16 Cox C. C. 333.
[37] See in particular *R.* v. *Aldred* (1909) 22 Cox C. C. 1, 4 *per* Coleridge J., *R.* v. *Caunt* (1947), noted 64 LQR 203 (Birkett J.).
[38] [1951] 2 DLR 369.
[39] Working Paper no. 72 (1977), paras. 76–8.
[40] 268 US 657, 664–5 (1925) *per* Sanford J.

could constitutionally punish the latter because of its *tendency* to lead to crime and endanger other vital community interests; the Court did not think the 'clear and present danger' test relevant where the legislature proscribed the speech itself, as well as the harmful action to which that speech might lead. In this case, the majority of the Court reasoned, the state legislature had in effect determined that the speech constituted a source of danger. The decision, of course, shows remarkable deference to the legislature's abstract assessment of the possible harmful consequences of some types of political speech.

The substitution of the tendency test for the clear and present danger rule was subjected to withering criticism by Brandeis J. in his concurring opinion in *Whitney*,[41] and it is now firmly established that the courts are entitled to determine themselves whether prohibited speech does constitute a serious and imminent danger to state security or any other government interest that is alleged to justify the restriction of speech. In *Yates* v. *US*,[42] Harlan J., construing the notorious Smith Act of 1940, which made it unlawful to advocate or teach the duty of violent overthrow of the government or political assassination, distinguished between advocacy of abstract political doctrine, and advocacy designed to promote specific action. Only the latter fell within the terms of the statute. A similar test was then given constitutional status by a unanimous Supreme Court in *Brandenburg* v. *Ohio*:

... decisions have fashioned the principle that the constitutional guarantees of free speech and free press do not permit a State to forbid or proscribe advocacy of the use of force or of law violation except where such advocacy is directed to inciting or producing imminent lawless action and is likely to incite or produce such action.[43]

The two absolutists, Black and Douglass JJ, in separate concurring judgments, denied that the 'clear and present danger' rule was compatible with the First Amendment; their position suggests that the majority did have this principle in mind when it formulated this new constitutional requirement for the proscription of inflammatory political speech. There is only a clear and present danger when the advocacy is likely to produce immediate violence or insurrection. The *Brandenburg* test has been applied in subsequent cases, in particular to invalidate a state statute refusing access to the ballot to extreme political parties

---

[41] 274 US 357, 376 (1927).
[42] 354 US 298 (1957).
[43] 395 US 444, 447 (1969).

advocating the overthrow of government by force.[44] The law did not distinguish between abstract support for revolution and incitement to its immediate achievement.

The current United States formula seems somewhat more protective of extremist political speech than the common law of sedition, under which there is no need to prove an incitement to *immediate* violence. It also may be more liberal than some comparable German cases. Comparisons are, however, rather crude in this area, because the *Grundgesetz* in Article 21(2) specifically enables the Federal Constitutional Court to declare unconstitutional political 'parties which, by reason of their aims or the behaviour of their adherents, seek to impair or abolish the free democratic basic order or to endanger the existence of' the Republic. The Article has been applied in two extremely important cases to ban first the neo-Nazi Socialist Reich Party and then the German Communist Party.[45] There was no reference to Article 5 of the Basic Law in the former case; the legal argument turned exclusively on the constitutional status of political parties under Article 21. But the Court did observe that the constant abuse and insults hurled by the leaders of the party against the Bonn government and the German democratic party system were far removed from constitutionally guaranteed free expression.[46] The relationship between free speech and the Court's power to ban totalitarian political parties was fully examined in the *Communist Party* decision. The party argued that Article 21(2) was incompatible with Article 5 and the fundamental principles of a liberal constitution. In particular, the propagation of Marxism was constitutionally protected by Article 5(3), '... research and teaching shall be free'. The Constitutional Court, however, drew a distinction found in many American cases: it was legitimate to preach the inevitable triumph of Marxism and to deny in an abstract way the validity of the present legal order, but an active and aggressive campaign against the Constitution and political system could be proscribed.[47] The interests of free speech and the preservation of the state could, therefore, be reconciled. These cases are as much concerned with freedom of association as free speech itself, but their principles have been applied subsequently to justify the suppression of extremist political speech.[48] In contrast to the *Brandenburg* rule, there is no requirement that

---

[44] *Communist Party of Indiana* v. *Whitcomb* 414 US 441 (1974).
[45] 2 BVerfGE 1 (1952); 5 BVerfGE 85 (1956).
[46] 2 BVerfGE 1, 57–8 (1952).
[47] 5 BVerfGE 85, 141–6 (1956).
[48] 25 BVerfGE 44, 63 (1969).

the speech is likely to lead to immediate insurrection. The experience of the 1930s has taught that it is too late to intervene at the eleventh hour.

No major case has yet been referred to the institutions of the European Convention, requiring them to decide the compatibility of sedition or other comparable laws with the freedom of expression protected by Article 10. The report of the Commission in the *Arrowsmith*[49] case does, however, strongly suggest that such laws would be upheld as necessary restrictions to protect national security and public safety, or to prevent disorder and crime. The case arose out of the successful prosecution of Miss Pat Arrowsmith under the British Incitement to Disaffection Act 1934 for distributing leaflets at an army base advocating that soldiers refuse to serve in Northern Ireland or desert the army.[50] She argued before the Commission that her conviction in effect stifled her freedom of expression in the crucial sphere of political debate: there was no real distinction between the expression of an opinion on troop involvement in Northern Ireland, coupled with the supply of information about the treatment of deserters, and direct advocacy that soldiers refuse to fight. The Commission without much discussion of this argument rejected the applicant's case, and concluded that the prosecution under the 1934 legislation could be regarded as a necessary restriction in view of the *possible* consequences of the applicant's campaign. If the Commission had adopted the *Brandenburg* formula, its report would surely have been favourable to Miss Arrowsmith; the only conclusion that can be drawn is that for the time being it is reluctant to uphold a right of political speech which goes beyond measured criticism of government and other institutions.

What then is the right course for a constitutional court to adopt when called upon to determine the extent to which revolutionary political speech must be tolerated under a free speech provision? Should it protect only measured and reasonable criticism designed to influence the electorate to press for reform by lawful means, or does a right of political free speech embrace the advocacy of unlawful, even violent, revolutionary action? One famous judicial answer is really to deny that there is any plausible distinction between these two modes of speech:

Every idea is an incitement . . . The only difference between the expression of an opinion and an incitement in the narrower sense is the speaker's enthusiasm for the result.[51]

---

[49] 7050/75, *Arrowsmith* v. *UK* 19 D. & R. 5.
[50] [1975] QB 678 (CA).
[51] *Gitlow* v. *New York*, n. 40 above, at 673 *per* Holmes J.

This is eloquent, but not very convincing. Granted that often incitement to action is implicit in political speech, unless perhaps addressed to 'an assembly of professors or divines',[52] the law, even constitutional law, has constantly to draw fine lines which may be hard to justify in abstract philosophical terms. And there seems intuitively a real distinction between criticism, however vehement, of the government on the one hand, and the advocacy of unlawful action and revolution on the other. But does it follow from the truism that a line can be drawn here that this is where the courts should draw it?

Courts may be able to derive substantial assistance in solving this problem from the whole text and spirit of the constitution. Its structure, the historical background, and contemporary political developments, may suggest, for example, that only reasonable and moderate expressions of opinion, not seeking to undermine the common commitment to the democratic basis of the state, is legally protected from government regulation; this does seem to have been the view of the German Constitutional Court in the two political party cases and there are good historical reasons for it. Bork has argued that the same limits on permissible political speech may be imposed under the USA Constitution; advocacy of the overthrow of government, even on a theoretical level, is prohibited because it seeks as its goal the denial of what the majority has democratically decided.[53] The First Amendment does not aim to protect radical speech challenging the conventional political process. Now this view may be in accordance with the framers' intentions, but it hardly reflects the modern jurisprudence of the Supreme Court and it would probably permit prosecutions for sedition. Where the text and other relevant explanatory material does not provide an answer, as is the case with the First Amendment and, it is suggested, the European Convention, courts may have no alternative to determining itself what a commitment to freedom of speech necessarily entails in this context.

This means that the courts must, at least to some extent, examine the philosophical and political arguments which underlie and justify entrenchment of the right to freedom of expression. The argument from democracy, which, we have seen, provides both the best explanation for the protection of speech and also justifies a preferred status for political speech, hardly warrants the application of these guarantees to discourse posing a serious threat to democracy itself. Two caveats must be entered

---

[52] *R.* v. *Aldred* (1909) 22 Cox C. C. 1, 4 *per* Coleridge J.
[53] See Bork, 'Neutral Principles'.

to this proposition. First, it does not justify the maintenance of sedition or other broad offences punishing all inflammatory political speech. Long-term considerations must be taken into account. As Brandeis J. observed in *Whitney* v. *California*,[54] the suppression of speech may bottle up discontent for so long that eventually really serious violence is inevitable. This reservation does not apply in an emergency. But liberal societies are prepared to take the risk of some small-scale disorder as a result of intemperate political speech. The second point is that the danger to democracy and the stability of the state should be assessed by the courts, and not determined simply by legislative (or executive) fiat. Otherwise, it becomes too easy for a repressive, albeit democratic, government to undermine a free speech guarantee, which is concerned to restrict the prerogatives of temporary majorities. For this reason, an *ad hoc* concrete balancing of interests by the courts is generally to be preferred to the deference to the legislature advocated by Frankfurter J. in the *Dennis* case.[55] These arguments may support the 'clear and present danger' rule, with its requirement that the harm must be certain and unavoidable for the restriction on speech to be justified.

Another argument which supports the position now adopted by the United States Supreme Court is that of Scanlon, outlined in Chapter I.[56] Because of the moral autonomy of each individual, the state is not justified in preventing his exposure to inducements to act, including incitements to overthrow the government. On this approach, there is no legitimate place for the law of sedition, the British Incitement to Disaffection Act, or for the criminal anarchy statutes now almost certainly unconstitutional in the USA. It is also possible on this perspective to explain the limited exception to free political speech permitted in *Brandenburg*. Where speech is made to an audience which has no time for reflection before it pursues the course of action urged on it, the persons incited are not to be treated as fully responsible for their conduct, and the 'autonomy' principle does not apply. Disorder is here both imminent and likely. J. S. Mill himself allowed for this exception when he justified the punishment of rabble-rousers for insulting corn-dealers before a mob assembled outside a corn-dealer's house.[57]

---

[54] See n. 41 above.

[55] See above, p. 17.

[56] T. M. Scanlon, 'A Theory of Freedom of Expression' (1972) 1 *Phil. and Pub. Affairs* 204, reprinted in *The Philosophy of Law*, ed. R. M. Dworkin (Oxford, 1977), 153.

[57] *On Liberty* (Everyman edn., 1972), 114.

4. RACIALIST SPEECH

While the common law of sedition has fallen into disuse and in most jurisdictions intemperate criticism of government is now regarded as legitimate, verbal and written attacks on racial and other groups have generally been subjected to greater restriction in the last fifty years. This has been achieved by the creation of criminal offences in group libel statutes and Race Relations legislation. It is not difficult to explain these developments. The repercussions of the vicious abuse of Jews (and other ethnic groups) encouraged by the Nazi regime suggested, to put it mildly, that there are worse evils than suppression of free speech. Then after the war many European countries faced the problems of assimilating immigrants into the native culture. The prohibition of racially inflammatory speech was regarded as necessary to preserve order between different groups. Moreover, it has seemed anomalous to proscribe discriminatory practices, e.g. in employment and housing, and not to restrict speech advocating discriminatory treatment of minority groups or the compulsory repatriation of immigrants. Sometimes, of course, it is hard to determine whether a type of writing, for example, advertising a house 'For Sale: Only Whites may apply', is to be regarded as protected speech or unlawful action.[58] These technical points reinforce the arguments of principle for regulation of speech likely to cause racial hatred.

However, although there are considerable pressures for legal intervention in this area, it is far from clear that this is justifiable in a society with any serious commitment to the principles of free speech. Under the *Brandenburg* formula, advocacy of imminent unlawful action and violence may constitutionally be prohibited; this will cover incitement to race riots where a breakdown of law and order is likely. Group libel laws, however, such as the British Race Relations legislation, typically prohibit speech, even though there is no suggestion that it is likely to lead immediately to violence and disorder. The argument is instead that to tolerate speech abusing racial, ethnic, or religious groups is to lend respectability to racist attitudes, which in their turn may foster an eventual breakdown of public order.[59] But the proponent of free expression may reply that such speech is best met by more speech advocating the moral and cultural superiority of a multi-racial society; moreover, the

---

[58] For an example of a case raising this problem, see *Chicago Real Estate Board* v. *City of Chicago* 224 NE 2d. 793 (1967) (Illinois S. Ct.).

[59] See, e.g., the speech of Sir B. Janner MP on the 2nd Reading of the Race Relations Bill 1965, 711 HC Deb. (5th ser.), cols. 955–62.

suppression of propaganda is in the long run more likely to expose society to the risk of violence than is its dissemination. This, of course, is an essentially pragmatic argument, and many advocates of a liberal free speech position would want to contend that even if it is not accepted, racialist speech laws are indefensible on broader grounds, such as the Scanlon moral autonomy reasoning referred to at the end of the previous section.

Although it may be inconclusive, there is one feature of the pragmatic argument to which attention should be drawn. The real dispute between the advocates and opponents of racial speech proscription is the extent to which legislation affects long-term popular attitudes; the opponent doubts whether it does, and more positively claims that even occasional prosecutions for the offence are likely to lead to bitterness and to fan racial hatred. Conversely, the advocate of such legislation is probably as much concerned to change the climate of opinion as to punish violations of the law. This feature of group libel laws is highlighted by the relative infrequency of prosecutions for their contravention.[60] In Britain, moreover, the consent of the Attorney-General is necessary for proceedings to be taken. Governments perhaps fear that too many prosecutions would undermine respect for these laws, and it is likely that on occasion political considerations have dictated a decision not to take legal proceedings, although the speech fell squarely within the terms of the statute.[61]

In Britain the legislation is defended now in terms of the offence to minority groups occasioned by racialist speech.[62] The difficulty then is to explain why it is appropriate (and constitutional) to proscribe this type of 'offensive' speech, although it would obviously be wrong to outlaw other types of speech on this ground. Commitment to a free speech principle, whether it is constitutionally recognized or not, surely entails the tolerance of publications that a majority, or groups of minorities, find unpleasant or offensive. Nobody would suggest that the offence to Conservatives or Democrats caused by hostile attacks on their parties would be an adequate basis for legislation proscribing such speech. Of course, the argument that a racialist speech causes more offence to the insulted minority than the most vicious attack on members of a political party or Church is not to be dismissed. But this sort of calculation is hard

---

[60] Fifteen people were prosecuted for the offence between 1977 and 1980: see Home Office, *Review of the Public Order Act 1936 and Related Legislation* (1980) Cmnd. 7891, para. 106.

[61] See I. A. Macdonald, *Race Relations: The New Law* (London, 1977), 138–9.

[62] See the Home Office Review of Public Order Act 1936, para 107.

to make, and a legislature which has proscribed some 'offensive' speech may be tempted to widen the terms of the ban. A major justification for a free speech clause is that it prevents any slide down this slippery slope.

The modern legislation in this area filled a gap in the criminal law of common law systems. There was admittedly some old authority that a scurrilous attack on a racial group could amount to ordinary criminal libel.[63] The orthodox definition of sedition certainly covered such writing, but in practice prosecutions for this offence were wholly unsuccessful;[64] in the leading modern case, *Boucher* v. *R.*,[65] almost all the members of the Canadian Supreme Court took the view that it was necessary to show an intent to disturb constitutional authority, and that it was not enough to allege an incitement to class or group violence. Not only was the common law of little use for securing convictions, it also inevitably lacked the declaratory effect of legislation designed to promote racial harmony.

This was the background to Section 6 of the British Race Relations Act 1965; this provision made it an offence to publish written matter or make a speech in public, which was threatening, abusive or insulting, and likely to stir up racial hatred, if the defendant actually intended to cause such hatred. It is also important to see this legislation in the light of the Public Order Act 1936, which had been used to prevent racialist speech in previous years, but which required a probable breach of the peace before the police could intervene.[66] The new Act removed this requirement and largely for this reason was condemned by some critics as an unwarrantable invasion of freedom of speech.[67] Prosecutions during the 1960s and 1970s were relatively rare. It is ironic that the legislation has often been used to convict militant black spokesmen, and of course (as in some obscenity cases), prosecution secured greater publicity for the publication than it would otherwise have achieved.[68]

Largely because of Lord Scarman's critique of the 1965 Act provision in his Report on the disorders in Red Lion Square,[69] it was amended by the Race Relations Act 1976. The new section is now incorporated into

---

[63] *R.* v. *Osborn* (1732) 2 Barn. K. B. 166.

[64] See in particular *Caunt*, n. 37 above.

[65] See above, n. 38.

[66] See ch. VII, s. 2.

[67] For example, see the speech of P. Thorneycroft MP, 711 HC Deb. (5th ser.), cols. 934–6.

[68] P. M. Leopold, 'Incitement to Hatred—The History of a Controversial Criminal Offence' [1977] *Pub. L.* 389, 395–9.

[69] (1975) Cmnd. 5919, para. 125.

the Public Order Act 1936,[70] because many Members of Parliament understandably thought that statute a more appropriate place for a criminal law rule than an Act concerned with the improvement of race relations. But there is something bizarre about adding to public order legislation a provision which in its terms has nothing whatsoever to do with a likely breach of the peace. The principal change is the abandonment of the requirement of intention to cause racial hatred; it is enough if, 'having regard to all the circumstances', hatred is likely to be stirred up against any racial group. It must now be a moot point whether the law does not cover publication in a 'scientific' journal of an article suggesting that one racial group is inherently inferior in intelligence to another, though it should be remembered that the matter must still be found to be abusive or insulting. The amendment does not extend the protection of the law to religious groups, so outside Northern Ireland,[71] a vicious attack on Catholics, Protestants, or adherents of any other faith could be proscribed only under the vague laws of blasphemy or perhaps public mischief.

Some suggestions for further widening the offence to cover any advocacy of discrimination against ethnic groups or of their compulsory repatriation have been made recently. But the Home Office in its Green Paper on the review of the Public Order Act 1936 doubted whether this reform could be defended in principle: 'Such an extension of the offence would penalize the expression of opinion as such'.[72] Nor was the Home Affairs Select Committee of the House of Commons any more sympathetic to these proposals in its report on the 1936 Act.[73] Such caution is entirely justified. British law in this area is already questionable under free speech principles, and any further development would show commitment to the value to be a complete sham.

Interestingly, the French law of the press was amended about the same time as the changes in Britain in order to inhibit racialist attacks. The law of 1 July 1972 prohibits incitement to discrimination, hatred, or violence with regard to any person or group on account of race, nationality, or religion, and also makes group defamation on racial and religious grounds a crime.[74] In this latter offence there is no need for any intent to incite to

---

[70] Public Order Act 1936, s. 5A.

[71] Prevention of Incitement to Hatred (Northern Ireland) Act 1970, discussed by Leopold, 'Incitement to Hatred' 399–402.

[72] Home Office, *Review of Public Order Act* 1936, para 111.

[73] 5th Report of the Home Affairs Committee 1979–80, HC 756, paras. 94–9.

[74] Amendments to Law of the Press, 29. 7.1881, arts. 24 and 32, noted by J. Foulon-Piganiol, DS. 1972, Chron. 261.

hatred; the prosecution only has to show that the defendant made grossly disparaging remarks about a section of the community, and it is, therefore, probable that an article alleging the intellectual inferiority of a racial group would be covered. Under the incitement to hatred provision, a conviction was secured when an editor of a periodical wrote an article to the effect that immigrant workers were economically damaging to France;[75] this is certainly more restrictive of free speech than comparable English cases under the 1965 Act as amended.

German law makes even greater departures from the free speech principle, though there are powerful constitutional and historical explanations for this course. Section 130 of the Penal Code makes it an offence to attack the dignity of other people, in any way tending to disturb the peace, by (*inter alia*) provoking hatred against groups in the population or abusing or ridiculing them. The law does not only protect racial and ethnic minorities against offence; religious communities, members of political parties, and cultural associations are also covered.[76] The key element of 'an attack on human dignity' prevents the institution of prosecutions under the provision to stifle normal democratic political debate. It also immunizes it from constitutional criticism. Article 1 of the *Grundgesetz* provides: 'The dignity of man shall be inviolable. To respect and protect it shall be the duty of all state authority.' All other basic rights are construed subject to this clause and, therefore, speech abusing, say, Jews or blacks would not be protected under Article 5.[77]

There have only been two reported challenges to laws of this kind under the European Convention. In *Glimmerveen* v. *Netherlands*,[78] the applicants, extremist right-wing politicians, complained that their conviction for possessing racialist leaflets violated Article 10 of the Convention. The Commission invoked Article 17 in holding the application inadmissible; this provision is designed to prevent the abuse of the Convention freedoms by groups supporting totalitarian policies. Here it was construed to cover the advocacy of racial discrimination and the repatriation of non-whites from Holland, a policy which contravened Article 14 of the Convention. Group libel laws can also be defended under Article 10(2) itself, on the ground that they are necessary either to

---

[75] DS 1975. J. 468.
[76] See Schönke–Schröder, *Kommentar zum Strafgesetzbuch* (20th edn., Munich, 1980), pp. 1017–20.
[77] Ibid. Also see below ch. VI, s. 2, where the importance of this Article in relation to libel proceedings is discussed.
[78] 8348/78, 18 D. & R. 187.

prevent disorder or crime, or to protect the reputation or rights of the minority groups concerned. In a recent case from Germany, the Commission has upheld the use of defamation laws to prohibit the display of literature denying the historical facts about the holocaust of the Jews; the racialist pamphlets could properly be regarded as a defamatory attack on each individual member of the Jewish community.[79]

Racialist attacks can, therefore, be covered by general libel laws, either civil or criminal, which render the passage of special legislation unnecessary. However, the common law rule is that no individual may sue in defamation for remarks directed against a group or class, unless it is clear they refer to him in particular.[80] The Porter Committee, reviewing the English law of libel in 1948, considered whether this requirement was too restrictive, but concluded that any alteration would seriously interfere with freedom of speech.[81] It thought the law of sedition was the more appropriate sanction for group defamation. But we will see in the next chapter that libel law in England may be used to protect public authorities and officials against defamatory criticism, and that this also may be incompatible with any commitment to free speech.[82]

In the United States legislation prohibiting the publication of racialist speech is treated as a species of libel law. Its constitutionality depends on the shaky precedent of *Beauharnais* v. *Illinois* decided by the Supreme Court in 1952.[83] By a bare majority it upheld the statute under which the president of a Chicago-based organization had been convicted for circulating a leaflet calling for a halt to 'the further encroachment, harassment and invasion of white people, their property, neighbourhoods and persons by the Negro'. Frankfurter J., giving the Court's judgment pointed out that ordinary libel laws were not subject to review under the First Amendment.[84] Since an individual's dignity and reputation was associated with that of the group to which he belonged, there was no justification for treating group libel laws differently from the rules of private libel. Although he then went on to justify the law in terms of its long-term contribution to the preservation of peace, there is no real suggestion that the statute was upheld on public order grounds.

The authority of *Beauharnais* is naturally weakened, now that the Court has held private libel to be covered by the free speech clause, and it

---

[79] 9235/81, *X* v. *Germany* 29 D. & R. 194.
[80] *Knuppfer* v. *London Express Newspaper Ltd* [1944] AC 116 (HL).
[81] (1948) Cmd. 7536, paras. 30–2.
[82] See below, ch. VI, s. 1.
[83] 343 US 250 (1952).
[84] This was true at the time: *Chaplinsky* v. *New Hampshire* 315 US 568 (1942).

has been doubted and distinguished in many recent cases.[85] The most important of these is the decision of the Court of Appeals for the Seventh Circuit in *Collin* v. *Smith*,[86] where it was ruled that an ordinance prohibiting the dissemination of material, which promoted racial or religious hatred, was unconstitutional. *Beauharnais* was regarded as implicitly overruled by the Supreme Court's decisions on private libel; if not, it was to be explained as turning on public order grounds. At all events a law remarkably similar to the British statutory provisions was struck down. With two dissenters, the Supreme Court refused *certiorari*, and thus the apparent incompatibility between *Collin* and its own earlier decision remains unresolved.

The question whether these laws can be reconciled with a free speech principle (or clause) is one of the hardest posed in this book. The policy arguments for suppression of attacks on racial minorities are powerful, and the political pressures for such legislation considerable. But it remains hard to justify the statutes on either public order or offensiveness grounds. As for the former, it should be remembered that the prosecution, at least in Britain and in the USA (so long as *Beauharnais* is good law), need not prove that violence is a likely and imminent result of the speech. It is enough that it may have this general tendency, a criterion which has been found too feeble to justify the intervention of the law in other areas of political speech.[87] The alternative rationale, that the speech is offensive to minorities, is little easier to accept in principle. Racialist propaganda is very wounding to human dignity and sensitivity, but the same can be claimed of sexist literature and blasphemy.[88] These other two abuses of free speech do not, however, arouse so much popular concern; the proscription of racialist speech is, therefore, probably only to be explained, if not justified, in political terms.

5. DISCLOSURE OF OFFICIAL SECRETS

While most people in Britain are now prepared to accept the legitimacy of the restraints on free speech discussed in the previous section, the

[85] *Anti-Defamation League of B'nai B'rith* v. *FCC* 403 F. 2d. 169, 174 (DC Cir. 1968); *Tollett* v. *US* 485 F. 2d. 1087 (8th Cir. 1973).

[86] 578 F. 2d. 1197 (1978), and see the judgment of the District Court, 447 F. Supp. 676 (1978).

[87] See the *Brandenburg* principle, above p. 156.

[88] The common law offence of blasphemy has not fallen into desuetude, as was supposed: see *R.* v. *Lemon* [1979] AC 617. But the Law Commission has tentatively suggested that it should be abolished: Working Paper no. 79 (1977). The Commission did not think the case for the offence was as strong as that for the crime of incitement to racial hatred.

restrictions imposed by the Official Secrets Act 1911 have rarely been more controversial. For some time there has been much criticism of section 2 of that Act, described by the Franks Committee in 1972 as a 'mess'.[89] It makes it an offence for a government employee to communicate any official information to anyone without authorization, and for anyone to receive such information. Prosecutions may be brought to punish any unauthorized disclosure which the government finds embarrassing, even though the information is of great interest to the public and its publication does not endanger national security, the conduct of foreign relations or other important interest. In 1984 there was considerable disquiet when a Foreign Office clerk was sentenced to six months' imprisonment for supplying to the *Guardian* a copy of a confidential memorandum sent by the Secretary of State for Defence to a number of other Ministers, including the Prime Minister, outlining plans for handling public reaction to the arrival of cruise missiles; the *Guardian*, which published the document in the belief that the public had a genuine interest in this aspect of government conduct, could have been prosecuted, but was not.[90]

Current controversy over official secrecy laws is, of course, a major aspect of the campaign in Britain to introduce freedom of information legislation. Under these proposals not only would the disclosure of much official information cease to be an offence, but the public would have a right of access to such information (or at least considerable amounts of it). Whether such a positive right can be derived from free speech arguments is considered elsewhere in this book;[91] here we are concerned with the implications of the free speech principle, and in particular the protection of political speech, for criminal laws penalizing the communication (and receipt) of government information. The use of injunctions to restrain disclosure under confidentiality rules is discussed in Chapter IV, dealing with prior restraints.[92]

One obvious difference between the communication of official secrets and the publication of the political speech considered in the previous sections of this chapter is that the former is concerned with the disclosure of information rather than the assertion of opinion. The distinction

---

[89] *Report of the Departmental Committee on Section 2 of the Official Secrets Act 1911* (1972) Cmnd. 5104, para. 88.

[90] For the civil proceedings against the *Guardian*, which enabled the government to discover the identify of the informant, see above, ch. II, s. 6.

[91] See above, ch. III, s. 5.

[92] See above, ch. IV, s. 3.

between these two categories of speech should not be exaggerated. Most information or news is communicated in a manner which implies a view as to how it is to be interpreted.[93] Government information is leaked in order to influence public opinion or provide ammunition for the opposition. Equally political speech advocating violent opposition to government or hostility to racial and ethnic groups may contain, or assume, some propositions of fact. But it is the case that the disclosures considered in this section are restricted because they reveal *information* which the government wishes to keep secret. Suppression is justified in the cause of national security or some other public interest, these arguments often being supported by an assertion of the government's property rights over its own documents and records. Mill's truth argument is, therefore, not really applicable, since there is no suggestion that disclosure is forbidden because it makes false claims.

Free speech arguments from background rights to self-development or to personal dignity are also hard to employ in this context. This point is associated with another feature of free speech claims here: they are generally made on behalf of the recipient of the disclosure or the general public, rather than for the speaker.[94] As the German Constitutional Court pointed out in a case where the constitutionality of a provision penalizing the disclosure of confidential matters to foreign secret services was upheld, it is difficult to see how the communicator here could assert an individual free speech right derived from a fundamental freedom of self-development.[95] It is little easier to invoke any free expression right of speakers to claim constitutional protection for a civil servant who has leaked confidential information to the press. On the other hand, members of the public have a real interest in receiving as much information as possible to enable them to contribute effectively to political debate. The argument from democracy is indeed the only underlying free speech theory which supports the application of the principle (or constitutional freedom of expression provision) to these cases.

These theoretical points do shed some light on the case law. They explain why the First Amendment (and other comparable constitutional provisions) are wholly irrelevant if a challenge is made to the validity of

---

[93] Although in contexts such as libel the German Constitutional Court recognizes the distinction between fact and comment (see ch. VI), in other circumstances it has refused to accept there is any sharp distinction: see e.g. *The First Television Case*, 12 BVerfGE 205, 260 (1961).
[94] For a general analysis of free speech interests, see ch. I, s. 3.
[95] 57 BVerfGE 250 (1981).

espionage laws and other measures prohibiting communication with foreign powers.[96] Disclosures to enemy agents, or a small group of political associates, are not designed to, and do not, enable anyone to contribute to political discussion. Since they lack any public dimension, private disclosures and conversations of this sort are not 'speech' for constitutional purposes, so there is no need for the court even to ask itself whether there is any state interest justifying espionage laws. On the other hand, the publication by a newspaper or the public disclosure by a politician of confidential government information both seem covered by free speech and press clauses, though the particular publication may not be protected because some competing public interest is strong enough to justify restrictions on disclosure.[97] In these circumstances, both speaker and recipient (the general public) have a genuine free speech interest in the communication and receipt of information, wide awareness of which may well sharpen political debate.

The really difficult issue is whether a communication by a civil servant to a newspaper (or to members of the public) should be regarded as 'speech' for constitutional purposes. As we have just seen, it can hardly be so regarded if the rights of the speaker, derived from an underlying right to self-fulfilment, are considered crucial. Nor is it clear that the civil servant has any real free speech interest in disclosing information entrusted to him in confidence; this is particularly dubious when he reveals the information for financial reward.[98] The best argument for extending the coverage of the free speech principle to disclosure by civil servants is that this is necessary to enable the press to acquire as much information as possible from them, which can be passed on to the public. This case is indeed somewhat similar to that made for the recognition of rights of access (to court-rooms or public meetings) and of the prerogatives of investigative journalism.[99] In this situation the argument for coverage is a little stronger because the speaker does willingly, although improperly, communicate the information.

---

[96] The constitutionality of the United States Espionage Act 1917 was upheld in *US* v. *Rosenberg* 195 F. 2d. 583 (2nd Cir. 1952).

[97] The interest must be exceptionally strong to justify the imposition of a prior restraint in the USA: see ch. IV, s. 3.

[98] The Franks Committee recommended the extension of the existing corruption laws so that it would be an offence for a civil servant to reveal information (not otherwise covered by the legislation proposed to take the place of the Official Secrets Act 1911) for private gain: n. 89 above, paras. 201–5. See Y. Cripps, 'Disclosure in the Public Interest: The Predicament of the Public Sector Employee' [1983] *Pub. L.* 600, 624–31, for a general discussion of the British statute law.

[99] Sec. ch. II, s. 6 and ch. III, s. 5.

Free speech arguments against the application of official secrecy laws to disclosure by civil servants are far from being overwhelming. This conclusion, however, does not warrant the scope of the present British statute, which seems much broader than comparable provisions in Germany and the United States. But the principal grounds for criticism are that it is too vague, that it uses the criminal law unnecessarily when other sanctions would suffice, and that it' reinforces the unfortunate atmosphere of secrecy which pervades British government. These are important points, which stand quite independently of the free speech principle. In this context it is interesting to note that the literature produced by the Campaign for Freedom of Information does not attempt to ground the freedom, or the repeal of section 2 of the 1911 Act, on free speech rights;[100] but some of the arguments for freedom of information, in particular the view that it would strengthen the accountability of government to the public, are also relevant to the justifications of the free speech principle.

In so far as free speech considerations are pertinent to the construction or validity of official secrets legislation, the principal legal issue is what role (if any) the courts should play in balancing the competing interests. The British approach is to permit the executive conclusively to determine whether the disclosure would occasion serious harm to the national interest. The Franks Committee, which recommended that the 1911 Act provision should be replaced by an Official Information Act covering specified types of information, considered that it would be inappropriate to leave these questions to the judiciary;[101] this approach was reflected in the Conservative government's Protection of Official Information Bill 1979, withdrawn in a fit of irrationality after the public revelation of Anthony Blunt's espionage for the Soviet government. One factor influencing the Franks Committee was the reluctance of the judges themselves to pass judgment on the executive's claims to immunity from orders for discovery, when this privilege is said to be necessary to safeguard state security or the conduct of foreign relations.[102]

In contrast, the German Constitutional Court does itself balance the

---

[100] *Our Right to Know* (London, 1984).
[101] *Report on Official Secrets Act*, para. 146.
[102] See *Conway* v. *Rimmer* [1968] AC 910, 952–3 *per* Lord Reid. In principle, however, the courts are prepared to balance the interests of, say, confidentiality and Cabinet secrecy against the importance of the disclosure of documents for the litigation, and order disclosure where this will be of significant assistance to the party seeking it: *Air Canada* v. *Secretary of State for Trade* [1983] 2 AC 394 (HL).

interests of state security or other important public good against the value of free speech or press freedom. This must be done in the context of the particular circumstances, and it involves a judicial evaluation of the danger posed to state security by the disclosure. Thus, in one case the Court emphasized that attention should be paid to the amount of detail about the siting of air-force bases contained in the prosecuted article, when it concluded that the defendant's conviction was not an unconstitutional interference with his *Pressefreiheit*.[103] This approach is consistent with that adopted by the German Constitutional Court (and the American Supreme Court) in other areas of political speech.[104] It is surely right to adopt it here. If the disclosure of official information is covered by a free speech clause—or for that matter, a constitutional freedom of information provision—the courts should have the last word in its enforcement. The British preference is, of course, understandable if one takes the view that government is to be trusted.

[103] 21 BVerfGE 239 (1967).

[104] See s. 2 of this chapter for discussion of the general principles established by the *Luth* case.

VI

Libel and Invasion of Privacy

I. GENERAL PRINCIPLES

FEW areas of law present such baffling problems for the application of a free speech principle as the law of libel. The reasons for this are relatively clear. There is a conflict here between two private rights (or interests): freedom of speech and the right to reputation, the second of these having historically much more venerable ancestry.[1] In all Western societies great importance is still attached to each individual's reputation and his self-esteem. The protection of human dignity, the concern which underlies libel laws, is given special constitutional status in the German *Grundgesetz*.[2] Until recently, a person's reputation has been regarded as one of his fundamental liberties protected by the Due Process Clause of the Fourteenth Amendment to the United States Constitution.[3] The relationship of free speech and privacy rights creates similar problems. Although the common law in Britain has obstinately refused to recognize such rights, they are now well established in the American states and in civil law jurisdictions. Indeed they are often given constitutional status, either explicitly in the texts or by judicial interpretation.[4]

One solution to the problem is to deny that defamation is really 'speech' for the purposes of a freedom of expression provision. This used to be the view of the United States Supreme Court; an attack on an individual's reputation did not contribute to public discussion, but was

---

[1] For the Roman law principle of *iniuria* which covered a variety of wrongs including injury to reputation, see J. K. B. M. Nicholas, *An Introduction to Roman Law* (Oxford, 1962), 215–18. Blackstone, who virtually ignored freedom of speech and of the press, regarded the right to reputation as an aspect of the absolute right to personal security: 1 Black. Comm. 129.

[2] Basic Law, art. 1. Below, p. 184, for further discussion.

[3] In *Paul* v. *Davis* 424 US 693 (1976), the Court in a much criticized ruling held that reputation alone was not enough to constitute a 'liberty' or 'property' interest protected by the Fourteenth Amendment; see H. P. Monagaan, '"Of Liberty" and "Property"' (1977) 62 *Cornell LR* 405, 423–34.

[4] See European Convention, art. 8; the German Basic Law, art. 10 protects privacy of posts and telecommunications, and art. 13 guarantees 'inviolability of the home'.

rather to be equated with an assault.[5] Even absolutists committed to protecting any mode of speech from restriction can explain libel laws as restraints on conduct or action. These fallacies were not finally exposed until the landmark ruling of the Court in *New York Times* v. *Sullivan*.[6] A non-malicious defamatory attack on the conduct of a public official—an Alabama Commissioner of Police—was held to be a form of political speech, the protection of which (as we saw in the previous chapter) is the principal concern of the First Amendment. The crucial step in the Court's reasoning was the analogy drawn between this type of libel and the offence of sedition which was clearly outlawed by the Amendment; if the analogy is correct, it inevitably follows that at least some libels are covered by a free speech clause.

Anyone disposed to question this aspect of the Court's reasoning should first consider whether it is consistent with free political speech to allow a government or local authority to protect its governing reputation by means of an action for libel. In one quite extraordinary English case,[7] the judge ruled that a local authority was entitled to protect its reputation by this means, and so it was awarded £2,000 damages (plus £20,000 costs) against a ratepayer who had circulated a strongly critical pamphlet at a public meeting. American courts have long appreciated that there is no real distinction in this context between criminal prosecutions for sedition and civil defamation actions;[8] indeed, there are good reasons to be more reluctant to tolerate the latter in relation to the free speech principle, for in such proceedings there may be no trial by jury, damages are unlimited, and the onus of proof is lighter. If civil actions by public authorities are incompatible with the protection of political speech, the same is surely also true where a politician or public official seeks to protect his political reputation by initiating defamation proceedings. Certainly no line can be easily drawn in the context of those cases where, as in the *New York Times* case itself, the individual officer is attacked by implication in an article which is for the most part a protest against the general behaviour of a public authority.

The Court's ruling in the *New York Times* case can also be explained as a reasonable application to a modern society of the immunities enjoyed

---

[5] *Chaplinsky* v. *New Hampshire* 315 US 568 (1942).

[6] 376 US 254 (1964).

[7] *Bognor Regis DC* v. *Campion* [1972] 2 QB 169, criticized by J. A. Weir, [1972] *Camb. LJ* 238.

[8] *City of Chicago* v. *Tribune Co.* 139 N. E. 50 (Illinois S. Ct., 1923); *City of Albany* v. *Meyer* 279 P. 213 (Calif. DC of Appeals, 1929).

by the politicians and officials themselves. In Britain Members of Parliament may say anything they like in 'debates or proceedings in Parliament', free from legal challenge.[9] The Supreme Court itself had, only five years before the *New York Times* decision, held that a federal official is absolutely immune from liability in respect of speech made in the course of his official duties.[10] These privileges are considered necessary for the discharge of their holders' public responsibilities, though it may be doubted whether this applies to false statements made maliciously. But the argument from democracy suggests that the criticism of officials and legislators by members of the public is entitled to equal protection under a free speech clause: '. . . it would give public servants an unjustified preference over the public they serve if critics of official conduct did not have a fair equivalent of the immunity granted to the officials themselves'.[11] Just as Members of Parliament and Congressmen may be inhibited from contributing to open debate in the legislature if they fear libel proceedings, so may ordinary people without an immunity from such proceedings be deterred from political discussion regarding the merits of particular public figures.

This argument does of course rest on controversial theories about the nature of a democracy and the desirable modes of conducting public life. It might be said that some sensitive people will be deterred from entering public life if their reputation can lawfully be impugned by non-malicious comment based on unsubstantiated facts.[12] Constant exposure of politicians to such comment may undermine their confidence, while the faith of ordinary members of the public in the political system may gradually be weakened by the publication in the press of defamatory material. Powerful though these points are, they do not show that the decisions in the *New York Times* case and its progeny (discussed in the next section) were misconceived. The First Amendment is based on the assumption that everyone should be free to contribute to political debate and the belief that restraints imposed by government and politicians should be viewed with suspicion. As the previous chapter showed, political speech is protected unless there is an imminent and likely danger to an important state interest, such as internal security or public order. It would hardly be compatible with this line of authority to restrain some political speech

---

[9] Bill of Rights 1689, art. 9. See P. M. Leopold, 'Freedom of Speech in Parliament—its Misuse and Proposals for Reform' [1981] *Pub. L.* 30.

[10] *Barr* v. *Matteo* 360 US 564 (1959).

[11] *New York Times* v. *Sullivan* 376 US 254, 282–3 *per* Brennan J.

[12] See H. H. Wellington, 'On Freedom of Expression' (1979) 88 *Yale LJ* 1105, 1113–15.

because it defames a politician or official. The dangers resulting from such defamation, which have been outlined in this paragraph, are simply too conjectural to warrant restrictions on speech.

This conclusion, however, is only the start of any worth-while analysis of the relationship of libel to the free speech principle. While comment on public officials (and perhaps public figures) should obviously be wholly free, it is not so clear that the free speech principle, even interpreted in the light of the argument from democracy, necessitates constitutional protection for false allegations of fact about such people. As Powell J. has said:[13] 'There is no constitutional value in false statements of fact.' In so far as it is relevant to constitutional adjudication, Mill's truth theory does not seem to demand tolerance of false allegations of fact, as opposed to questionable political and moral opinions.[14] But we will see shortly that there are strong reasons for allowing false claims some degree of protection from libel actions, a position reached by the Supreme Court and to a much lesser extent the German Constitutional Court, but not accepted in British law.[15]

A second problem is that the case for protecting political speech from the spectre of libel actions does not apply to all types of defamatory statement or every publication which invades privacy. The argument from democracy suggests that defamation of politicians, public officials, and some other public figures occupying similar positions is covered by a free speech clause. Thus, the importance of open public debate probably requires that a trade union official, a bishop, and a prominent lawyer or doctor all forfeit (to some extent) their ability to protect their reputation by the initiation of libel proceedings. On the other hand, there is no justification for applying a free speech clause to cover a casual remark in a public bar that the barmaid's morals are not all that they might be. But how should the law characterize libels on, or infringements of the privacy of, film stars, sportsmen, and other people in the public eye, whose activities, however, are of relatively little significance in the conduct of political and public life? And even in the case of statesmen and civil servants, there is the question whether defamation of their *private* character—by, for example, drawing attention to some reprehensible episode in the past before the person became active in public life—should really be treated as an instance of protected 'political speech'.

---

[13] *Gertz* v. *Robert Welch* 418 US 323, 340 (1974).
[14] See above, ch. I, s. 2(i).
[15] See below, pp. 181–7.

The rest of this chapter is concerned with the principles evolved by the courts in determining the extent to which a free speech principle (or constitutional clause) affects the laws of libel and privacy. In all three national jurisdictions, there is an attempt to balance the interests of expression against those of the plaintiff's reputation and privacy rights, though Britain does not recognize any right to protect privacy, partly because it might interfere with press freedom.[16] The results of these weighing processes are, as will be seen, significantly different in the three countries; the United States is much more prepared to limit actions for libel under the First Amendment than Britain is under the common law or through legislative reform. Article 5(2) of the German Basic Law specifically legitimates the imposition of limits on freedom of expression to protect personal reputation. Under this provision, the Karlsruhe judges have evolved a number of guidelines, some of which are similar to the rules formulated by the American Supreme Court.[17]

There is, however, one important difference of approach, which can be commented on before the law is discussed in detail. In this area, the United States courts do not weigh the competing interests in a case-by-case, *ad hoc* way, or within the framework of a general rule such as the 'clear and present danger' test. In other words, it does not assess for each case the gravity of the damage to the plaintiff's reputation or privacy against the value or importance of the particular speech. Instead, the Supreme Court has formulated a number of fairly precise rules to cover actions for libel and for invasion of privacy under which the First Amendment affords greater or less protection for the otherwise unlawful speech. One commentator in a leading article has explained this preference for 'definitional' balancing in terms of the greater predictability of decisions it secures, and has also argued that it enables the courts to give greater weight to speech than is possible under an *ad hoc* approach.[18] Courts would be inclined on this latter approach to place undue emphasis on the particular harm suffered by the plaintiff and so would ignore the long-term effects on free speech brought about by the award of damages. In contrast, the German judges generally look at the particular circumstances of the case and may consequently give less weight to the free speech interest.

---

[16] See the *Report of the Younger Committee on Privacy* (1972) Cmnd. 5012, paras. 651–8.
[17] See below, p. 187.
[18] M. B. Nimmer, 'The Right to Speak from *Times* to *Time*: First Amendment Theory Applied to Libel and Misapplied to Privacy' (1968) 56 *Cal. LR* 935.

2. LIBEL

The English law of civil defamation is widely regarded as unsatisfactory, except perhaps by some libel lawyers and those lucky enough to collect large sums of damages. Unusually in the law of torts, liability is strict; a newspaper may even be liable, although it had no reason to believe that the offending article referred to the plaintiff.[19] Nor need the plaintiff prove any loss if the defamation is written; damage to his reputation is presumed to follow from the publication. Nevertheless, the common law does not wholly ignore free speech considerations. The principal device for balancing this factor against the plaintiff's reputation is the defence of 'fair comment on a matter of public interest'. The range of such matters is relatively wide and certainly extends well beyond the topics of political and public life to cover any subject in which members of the public are properly or legitimately interested, for example, theatrical criticism or local questions.[20] In many cases judges have emphasized the importance of protecting free comment on issues of current political interest.[21] Indeed this aspect of the defence has given rise to little difficulty; it is at any rate wider in this respect than the *constitutional* immunity enjoyed by the press against actions by 'public figures' in the United States.

The defence, however, can only be sustained if the defamation consists of *comment*, rather than an allegation of *fact*. This distinction, easier to state than to apply in practice, is also to be found in German law, where it is relevant to both the application of the pertinent provisions of the Criminal Code and to constitutional argument under Article 5.[22] In English law the distinction is important, because the defendant must prove the truth of libellous factual claims either under the separate defence of justification or as the basis for the plea of fair comment.[23] On the other hand, an expression of opinion falls under the fair comment

---

[19] *Hulton and Co.* v. *Jones* [1910] AC 20 (HL).

[20] For example, *London Artists Ltd* v. *Littler* [1969] 2 QB 375 (CA); *Slim* v. *Daily Telegraph Ltd* [1968] 2 QB 157 (CA).

[21] For example, see Diplock J. in *Silkin* v. *Beaverbook Newspapers Ltd* [1958] 1 WLR 743, 745.

[22] The more serious offences against honour and reputation cover factual allegations, but not abusive and libellous opinion: see ss. 185–7a of the Criminal Code, set out and analysed in Schönke–Schröder, *Strafgesetzbuch-Kommentar* (20th edn., Munich, 1980), 1266–81, especially 1274.

[23] But where fair comment is pleaded, the defendant need not prove the truth of *all* the allegations; it is enough that the factual basis of the comment is accurate: Defamation Act 1952, s. 6.

defence, however obstinate, exaggerated, or prejudiced it is. The crucial criterion is that the view is honestly expressed.[24] The courts are, however, reluctant to hold that an imputation of dishonesty or corrupt motives is protected by the defence, though there must be many occasions when such views about the conduct of one or two public figures could be honestly stated. In the leading English case on this issue, Lord Cockburn CJ said:[25]

It is said that it is for the interests of society that the public conduct of men should be criticised without any other limit than that the writer should have an honest belief that what he writes is true. But it seems to me that the public have an equal interest in the maintenance of the public character of public men; and public affairs could not be conducted by men of honour with a view to the welfare of the country, if we were to sanction attacks upon them, destructive of their honour and character, and made without any foundation.

The Court of Queen's Bench was perhaps suggesting that an allegation of dishonesty is not really comment at all, but rather a factual claim which has to be justified. This is a tenable view in principle. However, the characterization imposes a significant limitation on freedom of political debate in view of the difficulty a defendant has in proving the truth of such allegations. Lord Cockburn's remarks are, of course, a classic expression of the utilitarian view that on balance unrestrained attacks on public figures are contrary to the public interest; adherence to a free speech principle on the other hand rules this sort of calculation out of court.

English law also recognizes the importance of free speech in the defences of absolute and qualified privilege. Many of the privileges exist in the political sphere, e.g. the absolute privilege of speech enjoyed by Members of Parliament in Parliamentary proceedings and of communications between officers of state, and the qualified privilege for non-malicious fair and accurate reports of Parliamentary and judicial proceedings.[26] Judges are sometimes willing to interpret the established heads of privilege broadly in the light of the important recipient free speech interest in access to information on public matters. Thus, in *Webb* v. *The*

---

[24] *Silkin* v. *Beaverbrook Newspapers Ltd*, n. 21 above.

[25] *Campbell* v. *Spottiswoode* (1863) 3 B. & S. 769, 777.

[26] See e.g., *Chatterton* v. *Secretary of State for India* [1895] 2 QB 189 (CA) (absolute privilege for communication from the defendant to the Under-Secretary of State); *Cook* v. *Alexander* [1974] QB 279 (CA) (qualified privilege for fair and accurate 'Parliamentary sketch').

Times Publishing Co. Ltd,[27] Pearson J. held that the privilege for fair reports of judicial proceedings extended to foreign court proceedings in which the English public had a real interest as distinct from an interest 'due to idle curiosity or a desire for gossip'. While in the case of English legal proceedings it was possible to have a general rule conferring the qualified privilege, its application to actions abroad had to be determined in the light of the particular facts—an example of *ad hoc* balancing. But the courts are not prepared to recognize a general privilege to publish 'fair information on a matter of public interest'. The existence of such a defence was denied by the Court of Appeal in *Blackshaw* v. *Lord,*[28] where a newspaper had published the name of a civil servant, associating him with incompetence in a government department which had cost £52 million; the libel action succeeded as a plea of privilege could only be accepted where the public had a legitimate interest in receiving the information and the communicator had a duty to publish it. The judges might have recognized a privilege if the allegations about the plaintiff had had some factual basis, but in the absence of this foundation the defence would have been so broad as to supplant the fair comment plea.[29]

A proposal to create a privilege along the lines rejected in *Blackshaw* had been considered by the Faulks Committee in 1975.[30] The defence would have protected statements on matters of public interest, which the publisher had reasonable grounds to believe were accurate, or which as far as comment was concerned were made in good faith. In effect negligence would have replaced strict liability for certain types of libel, a position now reached as a matter of constitutional law by the United States Supreme Court. The Committee was unenthusiastic about this change. One of its arguments was the apparent absence of evidence that the press was unduly muzzled by the present state of libel law, a surprising view not shared by the Justice Committee (which had made the proposal) or by the Press Council.[31] The American courts, as we will see shortly, take the view that to require the press or other defendants to prove the truth of factual allegations does deter them from publishing material which they might believe to be accurate; the fear of defamation

---

[27] [1960] 2 QB 535.

[28] [1984] QB 1.

[29] Ibid., 36 (Dunn LJ).

[30] *Report of the Faulks Committee on the Law of Defamation* (1975) Cmnd. 5909, paras, 211–15.

[31] See Justice Report, *Law and the Press*, 38; Press Council, *19th Annual Report* (1972), 82.

liability poses an unacceptable 'chilling effect' on freedom of speech. English law ignores this argument. It also appears to adopt the view that the press is normally able to discharge its general responsibilities to alert the public to controversial issues and to expose the misuse of public powers without implicating individuals. Thus, the Court in the *Blackshaw* case thought the journalist could have written an article about government incompetence, which avoided speculation on the involvement of an individual.[32] But often this will not be possible. The law of defamation, with its imposition of strict liability and the complex law of innuendoes which enables a plaintiff to claim that he is libelled, although he is not expressly referred to, may impose significant restrictions on free political speech.

The United States constitutional case-law in contrast regards defamation of public officials and figures as a mode of political speech entitled to the fullest degree of protection. In the *New York Times* case[33] an Alabama Commissioner of Police sued for defamation in an advertisement carried by the newspaper which, he contended, suggested that he was responsible for the harsh treatment of anti-segregation demonstrators. The Court held that a public official could not under the First Amendment recover damages for libel relating to his official conduct unless he proved malice, that is that the defendant knew the allegation was false or was reckless whether it was true or not. Having established that libel was within the coverage of the First Amendment, the Court proceeded to consider whether the state rule providing a defence of truth was adequate. Its weakness was that a critic might not be able to prove that his assertions were justified; owing to this uncertainty he might be deterred from publishing comments on official conduct, which he believed to be accurate and perhaps were objectively well founded. Because of this 'chilling effect', the Court concluded it was essential that the plaintiff have the burden of proving that the allegation was false and that the publisher knew it was. This is the crucial difference between the American constitutional rule and the common law. The latter assumes that the defendant will be able to show the truth of his speech in a court of law, while the *New York Times* rule perhaps more realistically appreciates the imperfections of the judicial process.[34]

---

[32] [1984] QB 1, 26–7 (Stephenson LJ).

[33] 376 US 254 (1964).

[34] This argument is made most fully in F. Schauer, 'Social Foundations of the Law of Defamation: A Comparative Analysis' (1980) 1 *Jo. Media Law and Practice* 3, 10–12.

The two absolutists, Black and Douglas JJ, would have gone even further than the Court's opinion and outlawed all libel actions for discussions of public officials and affairs, whether malicious or not. This would be much too extreme. To protect malicious or reckless allegations would be to tolerate a distortion of the democratic process, and could not be warranted under any rationale for the free speech principle.[35] It is probably more pertinent to ask whether the *New York Times* rule itself is not too solicitous of free speech interests in relation to the plaintiff's reputation, in view of the difficulty he will have in proving malice. The European Commission has recently approved the Austrian rule, which like the common law requires the press to show that the allegations are well founded; it argued that it would be unfair to expect the plaintiff to prove a negative, i.e. that the allegations of dishonesty were false.[36] The Austrian law of criminal defamation was, therefore, upheld under Article 10(2), at least in so far as it restricted personal attacks on politicians, rather than general criticism of their policies and attitudes.

Perhaps a more acceptable balance between the competing interests would be achieved by the imposition on the publisher of a negligence liability for untrue defamatory remarks about matters of public interest, the approach considered but rejected by the Faulks Committee. Harlan J. advocated this solution, for action brought by public figures, in two cases decided together three years after *New York Times*: a college football coach accused of fixing a football game and a former Army general alleged to have led resistance to school integration were 'public figures' who, in his view, should be able to recover damages if they showed that the press had engaged in extremely unreasonable behaviour, departing from the standards expected of a responsible press.[37] The majority of the Court was, however, prepared to apply the *New York Times* rule to 'public figures', people of note in whom the public had a reasonable interest because of their involvement in certain current issues. The subsequent decision in *Rosenbloom* then further extended the immunity to an action brought by an ordinary private person caught up in an event of general public interest; the focus was on the event rather than the notoriety or office of the individual concerned.[38]

This trend, however, has been halted by the ruling in *Gertz* v. *Robert*

---

[35] Nimmer, 'The Right to Speak', 949–52.
[36] *Lingens and Leitgens* v. *Austria* 8803/79 (1982) 4 EHRR 373.
[37] *Curtis Publishing Co.* v. *Butts, Associated Press* v. *Walker* 388 US 130 (1967).
[38] *Rosenbloom* v. *Metromedia, Inc.* 403 US 29 (1971).

Welch,[39] where the plaintiff, a Chicago lawyer representing the family of a person murdered by a policeman, was libelled in an extreme right-wing publication as a Communist and as responsible for the framing of the policeman. The majority of the Court first decided that Gertz was not a public figure: he was not well known in the community, and his participation in its affairs was not enough to make him such a figure. Reversing its earlier ruling, the Court then held that private individuals did not have to satisfy the *New York Times* test. The states were free to decide their own standards of liability provided they did not impose strict liability. Moreover, libel laws could only permit recovery where actual loss or injury was proved and no punitive damages could be awarded. In short, the common law has been limited by a constitutionally mandated scheme of fault liability with restrictions on the availability of damages.

There were dissents to the ruling, both by those favouring the application of the 'malice rule' established in the earlier cases, and by White J. who saw no constitutional justification for the modification of the common law rules governing libel actions by ordinary citizens. There was in fact one step missing in the Court's argument. *New York Times* and later cases had established that defamatory attacks on a public official or public figure were so closely connected with discussion of political and public affairs that they constituted 'speech' for the First Amendment. It had, however, never been held that libel of a private person (unless he had been caught up in a matter of public interest) was covered by the Amendment. The ruling in *Gertz* assumes that any defamatory remark, including one made in the course of a pub brawl and of no public interest whatsoever, is 'speech'. Of course, there is much to be said for the imposition of a negligence standard in defamation. In some ways the strict liability for libel is an anomaly in the law of torts. But this is no argument for making the reform a matter of constitutional law.

There are other difficulties in the American law. The difference between 'public figures' and private citizens was justified by the Court on the grounds that the former have thrust themselves into the public eye and that they have much greater opportunities through the press and media to reply to false statements.[40] There is clearly something to these points, but should they constitute decisive reasons for drawing important boundaries for the scope of free speech rules? Arguably, the character of the speech is more significant than the identity or characteristics of the

---

[39] 418 US 323 (1974).
[40] Ibid., 344–5.

plaintiff in this context, so that the *Rosenbloom* ruling discarded in *Gertz* is logical, albeit harsh on the particular individual. The fact that most, if not all, public officials and figures are able to reply to false rumours should be seen as mitigating the consequences of their inability to rely on libel actions, rather than justifying the formulation of the constitutional free speech rules. Another problem has been the scope of the 'public officials' or 'figures' rules: in particular, do they cover defamatory references to the past life of the individual before he became a public character? Here, the Court has adopted, sensibly in the case of a candidate for office, the principle that any biographical factor might be considered relevant to his election, and therefore no distinction should be drawn between current and previous conduct.[41] Perhaps this robust approach would be less appropriate for other public officials or figures, where arguably the plaintiff's past life is less relevant to his current reputation, and such speech is of relatively little public interest. Indeed such individuals may be more concerned to protect their privacy than their public standing and the principles discussed in the next section of the chapter are perhaps more pertinent than the libel rules. This suggests that the criterion for the determination of free speech immunity from libel should be the character of the particular speech concerning the particular plaintiff, rather than general characterization of the plaintiff as a 'public official' or 'public figure'.

As already mentioned, Article 5(2) of the *Grundgesetz* expressly limits freedom of expression where it conflicts with 'the right to inviolability of personal honour'. In practice the limits are primarily those imposed by the criminal law of insult and defamation. But the Constitutional Court in two major cases has held that a person's reputation is also covered by the constitutional right to the free development of personality (*Persön-lichkeitsrecht*) guaranteed by Article 2, and by Article 1 protecting the inviolable dignity of man (*Die Würde des Menschen*).[42] Under the balancing formula established in the *Luth* case,[43] the Court weighs the competing interests in freedom of expression and in personal reputation in the light of the particular facts of the case. The laws protecting individuals against defamation are not simply applied to limit the other

---

[41] *Monitor Patriot Co.* v. *Roy* 401 US 265 (1971).

[42] See the *Böll* case, 54 BVerfGE 208 (1980), where the complaint was brought by the novelist under art. 2 linked with art. 1, and the *Mephisto* case, 30 BVerfGE 173 (1971), where it succeeded under art. 1; art. 2 does not apply to protect the reputation of dead persons.

[43] 7 BVerfGE 198 (1958): see above, ch. V. s. 2.

party's free speech rights, but are themselves construed so as not unduly to restrict freedom of expression. The same balancing process takes place when two constitutional freedoms are weighed against each other. The famous *Mephisto* case nicely illustrates the Court's approach in this situation. The complainant publisher reissued *Mephisto*, a satirical novel by Klaus Mann portraying in a defamatory way the co-operation of a deceased actor with the Nazi regime. The actor's son's application to restrain this publication was upheld by the Hamburg Supreme Court, a decision which, the complainant alleged, violated his freedom of artistic expression guaranteed by Article 5(3) of the Basic Law. *Kunstfreiheit* is not subject to the limits set out in Article 5(2), including the right to personal honour, but the Constitutional Court held that the freedom must be considered in conjunction with the 'dignity of man' recognized in Article 1. The obligation to respect this dignity did not end with a person's death. In balancing the obligation against freedom of artistic expression, courts should consider the extent to which the publication was fabricated and the seriousness of the insults. Three members of the Constitutional Court found that the Hamburg judges had correctly assessed these factors, while the dissenters considered that the historical importance of the novel's theme outweighed the damage done to the deceased's memory. Judge Rupp-v. Brünneck even mentioned the *New York Times* decision to illustrate how a more appropriate balance between free speech and reputation interests should be achieved.[44]

This detailed consideration of the facts is characteristic in German cases. The balancing function is largely discharged by lower courts, subject to the guide-lines established by the Constitutional Court. One important element in determining whether speech should be immune from criminal libel proceedings (or against a constitutional complaint for a violation of the basic rights covered by Articles 1 and 2) is the character and subject-matter of the publication. So a conviction under Sections 186–7 of the Criminal Code (untrue allegations and defamation) for the publication of an article about the involvement of two politicians in the 1939 invasion of Poland was held contrary to Article 5; the Constitutional Court found that the lower court had failed to take proper account of the Article when it interpreted the leaflet as a libel, rather than as a contribution to political debate.[45] An incidental impact on individuals' reputation must be accepted as a consequence of vigorous political discussion. Moreover, in a recent case, where the Court held the

[44] 30 BVerfGE 173, 225 (1971).
[45] 43 BVerfGE 130 (1976).

characterization of the Bavarian Christian Social Union Party as a neo-Nazi party to be a fully protected expression of a political opinion, it emphasized that a person (and *a fortiori* a political party) to some extent forfeits the protection of the libel laws when he participates in political debate.[46] These principles are applied to any speech, e.g. a lively and intemperate exchange of views between art critics and a professor of sculpture, which contributes to the development of public opinion.[47] Free speech interests are entitled to much less weight in a purely private altercation.

A number of cases show that the Court will more readily give protection to expressions of opinion than to factual allegations.[48] The Criminal Code also distinguishes these varieties of libel and insult, penalizing particularly severely anyone who knowingly publishes untrue facts calculated to lower another's reputation.[49] Malicious assertions of this character are not covered at all by Article 5, and in a case brought by Heinrich Böll for violation of his rights under Article 2, the Court ruled that the use of inaccurate quotations to blacken the author's character was not covered by freedom of expression.[50] But the requirements of accuracy are not to be taken so strictly that they effectively undermine freedom of speech, and in some circumstances, it seems, the Court would hold the non-negligent publication of incorrect assertions to be covered by Article 5.[51] Moreover, it may sometimes be difficult to disentangle claims of fact from the political comment which is entitled to the highest degree of protection as an exercise of *Meinungsfreiheit*. The former then share the immunity from libel proceedings enjoyed by expressions of opinion.[52] In these cases, the Karlsruhe Court has, therefore, developed principles somewhat analogous to those applied by the United States Supreme Court. There is a margin of error for exaggerated claims, particularly for those involving an element of comment, while only those false factual allegations for which the publisher has no excuse fall wholly outside the scope of constitutional protection.

The Court is particularly tolerant of defamatory speech when it is an

---

[46] 61 BVerfGE 1, 13 (1982).
[47] 54 BVerfGE 129 (1980). Also see 60 BVerfGE 234 (1982) (defamatory attack on credit houses).
[48] For example, 42 BVerfGE 163 (1975); 54 BVerfGE 208 (1980); 61 BVerfGE 1 (1982).
[49] Criminal Code, s. 187.
[50] 54 BVerfGE 208, 219 (1980).
[51] Ibid., 220; 61 BVerfGE 1, 8–9 (1982).
[52] 42 BVerfGE 163 (1975); 61 BVerfGE 1, 9 (1982).

element in a reply to a personal attack, the so-called *Gegenschlag* theory. In the *Schmid-Spiegel* case,[53] a judge had been accused in an article in *Der Spiegel* of Communist sympathies and of unfitness for office. He wrote a vitriolic reply, on the basis of which the editor of the magazine and the author of the original article took civil proceedings for libel. Although both the article and the judge's reply contained significant factual inaccuracies, the latter was held immune from libel proceedings under Article 5. It was also covered by Section 193 of the Criminal Code, which affords a defence to a prosecution for defamation, when the remarks are made, *inter alia*, to protect justifiable interests. The section not only enables individuals to protect their own reputation, but is to be seen as implementing the fundamental freedom of speech. Neither the section nor Article 5 would, however, cover deliberate falsehood in these circumstances.[54]

The German case law occupies a position midway between those taken by English and United States law. Like the former, it draws a distinction between assertions of act and of opinion, conferring a higher degree of protection on the latter. Moreover, the defendant must prove the truth of an allegation if he is prosecuted under Section 186 of the Criminal Code for disseminating inaccurate and defamatory factual claims. On the other hand, in its willingness to grant some immunity for libels committed during the course of political and public debate and in its recognition that the publication of some exaggerations and inaccuracies should be tolerated, the Constitutional Court's approach is similar to that of the Supreme Court in Washington. But the Karlsruhe judges prefer to apply general principles flexibly in the light of the particular facts rather than to employ precise rules like that formulated in *New York Times* v. *Sullivan*.

In Germany and other civil law countries, libel is predominantly a criminal offence; civil actions for damages are relatively uncommon. This is the converse of the position in common law jurisdictions. Prosecutions for the offence are very rare in England, and may only be initiated against a newspaper proprietor or editor with the consent of a judge.[55] In exercising his discretion the judge will take into account the seriousness of the libel and the importance of the defamed person's position.[56] This unusual procedure is an example of an *ad hoc* balancing process in which the court weighs the state's interest in protecting the defamed person's

---

[53] 12 BVerfGE 113 (1961). Also see 24 BVerfGE 278 (1968).
[54] Schönke–Schröder, *Strafgesetzbuch-Kommentar*, 1284–5.
[55] Law of Libel Amendment Act 1888, s. 8.
[56] *Goldsmith* v. *Pressdram* [1977] QB 83; *Desmond* v. *Thorne* [1983] 1 WLR 163.

reputation against the value of free speech. Criminal proceedings are in fact normally initiated when there is some harm additional to the damage to reputation flowing from the libellous publication: perhaps there is a nuisance arising from repeated libels or there is some particular public interest in the protection of the reputation. In *Gleaves* v. *Deakin*,[57] the House of Lords emphasized that the libel must be 'serious' for it to constitute an offence, but did not lay down any criteria by which this should be determined.

In contradistinction to the tort of libel, truth is no defence to a criminal prosecution unless the defendant also shows that publication was for the public benefit. Largely for this reason Lord Diplock in *Gleaves* v. *Deakin* suggested that the offence (as presently defined) is probably an unjustifiable restriction on freedom of expression under Article 10 of the European Convention. Under Article 10(2) the state is required to show that a restriction is 'necessary', and it is in principle arguable that the imposition of the burden of proof on the accused in criminal libel is incompatible with this. We have seen that the Commission has recently approved the Austrian rule which requires the defendant in some circumstances to show the truth of the allegations, but the English requirement goes further than this and surely imposes an unacceptable restraint on freedom of speech.

Both the Faulks Committee in its review of defamation law and the Law Commission in a Working Paper have recommended that the offence of libel should be retained.[58] The latter, however, proposed that criminal proceedings should only be available for 'serious' or 'non-trivial' defamations where the accused knew or believed the statement to be false. Beyond the suggestion that the consent of the Director of Public Prosecutions to a prosecution should be mandatory, the Commission did not make any specific proposals to rule out proceedings against trivial defamation. The free speech principle requires not only the exclusion of criminal sanctions for libel which does not occasion significant harm to reputation, but also protection for political speech which only *incidentally* defames some public figure.[59] It is not clear that the Law Commission's recommendations would necessarily cover all publications of that character. On the other hand, the proposals to confine liability to cases where

---

[57] [1980] AC 477.
[58] Report of Faulks Committee, paras. 428–49; Law Commission Working Paper no. 84 (1982).
[59] As in *New York Times* v. *Sullivan* or in some German cases, e.g. 43 BVerfGE 130 (1976).

the publisher knew that his remarks were defamatory, and to provide a defence of truth (without the further element of public benefit) are to be welcomed.

3. INVASION OF PRIVACY

In *Time, Inc.* v. *Hill*,[60] the Supreme Court held an article, which in certain respects falsely depicted the plaintiff family's involvement in a notorious incident a few years previously and so invaded their privacy, to be covered by the First Amendment. Brennan J. laid down this principle:

... the constitutional protections for speech and press preclude the application of the New York [Right to Privacy] statute to redress false reports of matters of public interest in the absence of proof that the defendant published the report with knowledge of its falsity or in reckless disregard of the truth.[61]

As the article discussed the opening of a new stage play, based on the incident involving the Hill family, its subject was treated as a matter of public interest, and the fact that some of the details were inaccurate was considered immaterial in the absence of malice. The case was decided three years after *New York Times*, and shortly before the rulings extending the principle of that case to 'public figures'. Yet there was no discussion whether the First Amendment immunity from libel actions brought by public officials should in principle be applied to outlaw privacy actions by ordinary people caught up in an event which had temporarily attracted some publicity. The question is even more relevant now it is clear that the press may be liable in negligence for the libel of a private figure;[62] United States law seems to be less solicitous of privacy interests than it is of the right to reputation.

English law also fails to protect privacy, partly owing to a reluctance to institute new torts of uncertain scope, but also because of a fear that it would unduly fetter press freedom. But it is not at all clear that free speech considerations are as entitled to as much weight here as they are in libel actions. Many newspaper features which purport to describe the private lives of ordinary individuals do not really constitute 'speech' on any of the relevant arguments. The fact that the article excites public interest does not mean that it is 'of public interest'; certainly the argument from democracy, as Nimmer has pointed out in a leading law

---

[60] 385 US 374 (1967).
[61] Ibid., 387–8.
[62] See above, pp. 182–3.

review article, is inapplicable to this sort of material.[63] Comparable features about public officials and (some) public figures may, however, constitute 'speech', because they may disclose facts relevant to the public's assessment of their suitability for office or general worth as a 'public figure'. But in that event the feature also damages the plaintiff's reputation, always a matter of public estimation, so it becomes appropriate to apply the libel principles established in *New York Times* and *Gertz*. Further, a really private person is unable to rebut or reply to the offending article, first because he lacks the opportunities open to public personae, and second because an invasion of privacy can hardly be repelled in this way. The remedy for libel may be more 'speech', but this medicine can obviously not cure a loss of privacy.

Time, Inc. v. *Hill* involved the variety of privacy invasion known as the 'false light' cases. Much more commonly actions are brought for the damage sustained after the disclosure by the press of *true* private facts. There might appear to be a strong case for applying the free speech clause to true revelations, particularly where the disclosure harms the plaintiff's reputation and the libel rules might be relevant. But this would often be misconceived. The whole point of protecting privacy is to keep some information away from public exposure, even if it is true. As with false reports the crucial question is whether the publication is a form of 'speech', and here there may be a conflict between the conclusions suggested by the arguments from democracy and Mill's truth rationale. But the latter thesis does not really outlaw all restraints on the disclosure of true *facts*. Mill's argument, as we saw in Chapter I, applies more strongly to assertions of opinion rather than to propositions of fact, and more relevantly, the restrictions imposed through privacy actions are not framed to suppress false (or possibly true) beliefs.[64] So, the case for applying a free speech principle to invalidate actions for privacy is very weak, even where the disclosures are accurate. Perhaps the Supreme Court has recognized this now, for in dicta in *Cox Broadcasting* v. *Cohn*[65], White J. giving the Court's judgment thought it might be constitutionally lawful to restrain the truthful publication of private affairs unrelated to matters of public interest. But matters on the judicial record open to public inspection, like the names of rape victims, may be freely published, for they are necessarily matters of public interest.[66]

---

[63] Nimmer, 'The Right to Speak', 956–66.

[64] See ch. I, s. 2 (i).

[65] 420 US 469 (1975).

[66] This point is further discussed in the context of contempt of court below, ch. VIII, s. 1.

The difference betwen defamation and an invasion of privacy for free speech purposes is therefore that the former more often involves 'speech' which should be immune from regulation because it contributes to political and moral debate. As the German Constitutional Court recognized in a case where the press unsuccessfully claimed protection under Article 5 for a fabricated interview purportedly disclosing details of someone's private life, features of this character contribute nothing to the formation of public opinion.[67] This is so even if the revelations are accurate. The analogy between sedition and a defamatory attack on a political or a public figure, such as a union official or prominent employer is close, but it is far-fetched to draw one between political speech and, say, a salacious article about the sex life of a film star.

This conclusion does not of course resolve all the difficulties. Obviously there is an overlap between actions for defamation and for an invasion of privacy, and it may then be far from clear which free speech principles should apply: the broad immunity which should often be afforded libel or the much narrower one which might be permitted as a defence to the latter actions. How, for example, should an article revealing accurate details of a prominent politician's sexual peccadilloes twenty years ago be classified?[68] The United States Supreme Court would almost certainly hold this disclosure protected under the *New York Times* rule, for it would amount to defamation of a public figure. But the privacy arguments would suggest a different answer. It is surely right to apply the libel rule, at least where the right to free speech is constitutionally guaranteed and the courts recognize that political speech (including some libel) enjoys a special position. Perhaps it can tentatively be suggested that many difficulties here are attributable to the uncertain boundaries between libel and privacy. Moreover, the picture might be changed dramatically if the scope of the former tort were reduced by more realistic assessments of the factors relevant to a person's reputation. This point in its turn suggests that it may be better for a constitutional court to apply broad principles flexibly according to the character of the particular speech, rather than to formulate tight rules which follow the contours of the common law and thus reflect sharp distinctions between libel and the invasion of privacy.

---

[67] 34 BVerfGE 269 (1973).

[68] In *Wolston* v. *Reader's Digest Assoc.* 443 US 157 (1979), the Court held that a person who had failed twenty years before to reply to a grand jury subpoena during espionage investigations was not a 'public figure', so that the *New York Times* malice rule did not apply to defamation proceedings. It is far from clear in this sort of case whether libel or privacy free speech principles should apply.

VII

Public Order

EVEN the strongest advocates of free speech rights concede that restrictions may sometimes be justified in the interests of public order. Mill himself admitted this when he wrote that, '. . . opinions lose their immunity when the circumstances in which they are expressed are such as to constitute their expression a positive instigation to some mischievous act'. So, he continued, views on the iniquitous behaviour of corn-dealers could properly be punished if delivered to a mob assembled outside a merchant's house.[1] This proviso to the free speech principle may, however, not warrant the general, balancing approach now often adopted by courts and commentators to this problem of reconciling the interests (if that is what they are) in freedom of expression and in public order. Under this formula it is for the court retrospectively to assess the likelihood of a breach of the peace as it appeared *at the time of the police intervention* in order to determine the propriety of the restriction, for example, the dispersal of a public meeting. If the police have reasonable grounds for believing there is a danger to public order, it is right to curtail free speech. Inadequate attention may then be paid to the character of the speech suppressed—whether it was provocative and inflammatory—and to the objective likelihood of a breakdown of law and order, while there will almost inevitably be some deference to the judgment of the police, whose primary duty, of course, is to preserve the peace. To some extent legislation may compel this sort of approach, at any rate in a society where there is no constitutionally protected freedom of speech. But the judges in England have often shown a preference for public order even when this was not legally required, and on occasion despite the First Amendment the Supreme Court has adopted a similar stance.

This chapter is mainly concerned to explore, in the light of relevant British and American authorities, the ways in which an appropriate compromise may be struck. The position in Germany may be briefly mentioned. The Basic Law protects freedom of assembly (*Versammlungsfreiheit*) under Article 8: all Germans have the right to assemble

---

[1] J. S. Mill, *On Liberty* (Everyman edn., 1972), 114.

peaceably and without arms. There is no decision of the Constitutional Court on this provision, but leading commentaries indicate that the freedom is to be construed in the light of the purposes of Article 5, in particular the contribution of speech to the development of public opinion, and that therefore it would be wrong to allow violence and forcible demonstrations to be covered.[2] However, before the legal position in Britain and the United States is reviewed, some general arguments are considered, including the contention that free speech interests are not really implicated when restrictions are imposed to preserve the public peace.

1. SOME PRELIMINARY OBSERVATIONS

One perspective is that the law here has to deal with a conflict between two rights: the right of free speech, or more specifically of assembly and public meeting, and the right of the public to order and tranquillity. A classic expression of this is to be found in the statement of principles which prefaces Lord Scarman's Report on the Red Lion Square Disorders of 15 June 1974:[3]

A balance has to be struck, a compromise found that will accommodate the exercise of the right to protest within a framework of public order which enables ordinary citizens, who are not protesting, to go about their business and pleasure without obstruction or inconvenience ... the fact that the protesters are desperately sincere and are exercising a fundamental human right must not lead us to overlook the rights of the majority.

Of course in British law, neither right is a legal right in the sense of an enforceable claim, and as an earlier chapter has shown, there are considerable difficulties to the argument that free speech should entail wide claim-rights, for example, to demonstrate in the streets or to hold meetings in public places.[4] The suggestion by the National Council for Civil Liberties that there should be a statutory right to demonstrate probably represents in this context an attempt to give a little more weight in the balancing scales to free speech interests, rather than an argument that the right should generally, or always, prevail over public order requirements.[5] But if arguments about rights of free speech are tenden-

---

[2] See *Grundgesetz-Kommentar* (2nd edn., Munich, 1981), ed. I. von Münch, 382–3.
[3] Scarman Report (1975), Cmnd. 5919.
[4] See above, ch. III, s. 3.
[5] Evidence of the National Council for Civil Liberties to the Home Affairs Committee 1979–80, HC 756–II, 153. For a discussion of the merits of this proposal, see the Home

tious, the view that the majority, or any member of the majority, has a competing moral *right* to order and tranquillity seems wholly misconceived. Quite apart from doubts about whether it ever makes sense to talk of the rights of a group or society as a whole, it is difficult to give this particular 'right' any coherent content: what is it a right to be free from? Does it make sense to refer to a 'right to order' which might be invaded by an affray a few streets away?[6] In truth, propositions about the right of the majority in this context are really no more than emotive ways of saying what may be perfectly sensible things concerning the public interest.

While reference to competing 'rights' in this area seems far from helpful, there can be no doubt that the law here does have to strike compromises. The difficulty is where the line should be drawn: at the point implicitly indicated by Mill in the passage just mentioned, or at a place further towards the protection of public order? The police and magistrates are, of course, required to preserve the peace in situations where free speech concerns are entirely absent—pub brawls, football hooliganism, vandalism on trains. In other cases there may be an element of speech, but the occasion, for example, a race riot or a military parade by a private army, predominantly involves a course of conduct; here again there seems little to put in the scales against public order requirements. Where, however, there is a genuine and substantial element of communication, commitment to the value of free speech would seem to require a different approach. Society must then be prepared to take greater risks with the preservation of order than it is in situations where nobody is exercising freedoms of speech or assembly. This broadly is what acceptance of a free speech principle entails in this area. Thus it may well be perfectly reasonable to outlaw the possession of offensive weapons in public, on the ground that there is a strong (though not an irrebuttable) presumption that this necessarily creates a risk to public order, but it is harder to justify the proscription of offensive words on such a broad rationale.[7]

Office Green Paper, *Review of the Public Order Act 1936 and related legislation* (1980) Cmnd. 7891, paras. 24–8.

[6] A 'right' must surely refer to an interest which is not only generally protected against interference by the majority, but which is also capable of sufficiently precise definition that it is possible to determine when it is invaded. Thus, in contradistinction to the right 'to tranquillity and order', it makes sense to talk about an individual's right not to be assaulted and a property owner's right not to be disturbed in the enjoyment of his property. See R. M. Dworkin, *Taking Rights Seriously* (London, 1977), 90–2, 194–5.

[7] See the Prevention of Crime Act 1953, discussed in *Brownlie's Law of Public Order and National Security* (2nd edn., London, 1981, prepared by M. Supperstone), 148–61. For offensive words, see s. 2 of this chapter.

Where there is an actual breakdown of public order of more than minimal proportions, it is probably inevitable that the law treats political demonstrators and mere vandals alike. The Court of Appeal in *R.* v. *Caird*[8] rejected the argument, put forward as a plea in mitigation, that the appellants had only committed the offences of unlawful and riotous assembly from political motives—to demonstrate against a 'Greek week', the staging of which, they contended, supported the military regime in that country. Certainly this sort of contention is wholly unacceptable if put forward as a complete defence to such a charge, or as a suggestion that political demonstrators should be entitled to immunity from the general criminal law; it is perhaps more questionable whether it should be totally ignored for sentencing purposes. But in situations falling short of outbreaks of actual violence, both British and American law accommodate to some extent the interest of those wishing to exercise 'rights' of protest, even though their exercise creates some risk of disorder; the issue, to state it once more, is whether the accommodation adequately protects freedom of speech.

There are, however, two related arguments which deny that there is really any free speech problem at all in the case of most public order restrictions on meetings and processions. The first asserts that these forms of demonstration involve 'conduct' rather than 'pure speech', and therefore fall entirely outside the free speech principle. Second, it is said that public order rules, for example, those conferring powers on the police to order a group of people to disperse if an imminent breach of the peace is feared, or the laws against obstruction of the highway and nuisances, are not primarily aimed at the suppression of speech; any effect on the communication of opinion is incidental to the principal object of preserving the peace or some other related aim. These arguments are sometimes supported by the point that the political positions and attitudes of demonstrators can equally well be disseminated by more peaceful means—letters to the newspapers, books, and leaflets, and so only restrictions on the manner and form of speech, rather than on its content, are involved.

In a number of American cases in this area, remarks have been made suggesting that street demonstrations and meetings, and *a fortiori* all forms of picketing and sit-ins, should really be regarded as types of conduct, outside the protection of the First Amendment.[9] It is a position

---

[8] (1970) 54 Cr. App. Rep. 499.
[9] For example, see Black and Douglas JJ in *Gregory* v. *Chicago* 394 US 111, 118 and 124 (1969), and Black J. in *Cox* v. *Louisiana* 379 US 536, 577 (1965).

which naturally commended itself to absolutists, like Black J., who otherwise would have had considerable difficulty in approving any restrictions on such demonstrations. And in Britain, where in any case free speech interests are only protected by principles of common law and of statutory interpretation, there is little legal difficulty in the regulation of protest activity, or of conduct such as the wearing of political uniforms.[10] But, as the argument in Chapter II showed, distinctions between 'speech' and 'conduct' are easy to state, yet often hard to draw in particular contexts.[11] Intuitively it seems absurd not to recognize public meetings at which a series of speakers addresses the audience as a form of 'speech'; it would be almost as odd not to characterize in the same way a procession where the participants shout slogans and carry placards. In some cases, admittedly, the words used at the meeting or carried on the placards may be so emotive and abusive that on a restrictive view they hardly qualify as a mode of expression covered by the free speech provision; this issue is discussed later.[12] Legal doubts about the status of public meetings might be resolved by the specific constitutional recognition of separate rights of assembly and association, where the distinction between 'speech' and 'conduct' would be of little or no significance.[13] In fact, such recognition has not been of much importance in this context: the Supreme Court has not attached weight to the words, 'the right of the people peaceably to assemble', and (as already mentioned) while there is as yet no ruling of the German Constitutional Court on Article 8, it is unlikely that *Versammlungsfreiheit* will be held to cover activity which would not fall under Article 5 (freedom of expression).[14] At any rate it is doubtful whether any jurisdiction would recognize a constitutional right, say, to block entry into a factory during the course of a trade dispute under either a free speech or a separate freedom of assembly clause.

Frederick Schauer has argued very persuasively that free speech problems may only arise in this area if the purpose of the governmental restriction is to restrict expression, rather than to achieve some other end, such as public order, safety on the streets, or quiet in residential areas. He gives as an example the prohibition of a Communist march. This raises

---

[10] For the prohibition of uniforms denoting association with political organizations, see Public Order Act 1936, s. 1. There is an equivalent provision in German law: see Gesetz über Versammlungen, BGBl 1978 1, S. 1790, s. 3.

[11] See about, ch. II, s. 2.

[12] See below p. 200.

[13] For example, see the First Amendment to the US Constitution; art. 11 of the European Convention; art. 8 of the German Basic Law.

[14] See n. 2 above.

free speech issues if the reason for the order is the undesirability of extremist demonstrations, but does not so clearly involve them if the ban is imposed because the street is to be repaired on the day in question.[15] But, as this example itself shows, the argument can be used only to justify—or more strictly, remove from scrutiny on free speech grounds— restrictions which are temporary or limited to particular places. A permanent prohibition on all processions in a community can hardly be supported by reference to this argument. And a provision which permits the discriminatory treatment of some groups and political parties shows an illegitimate purpose on its face. These points justify the very limited scope of the power to ban processions under the British Public Order Act 1936: in certain carefully defined circumstances all processions, or processions of 'any class', may be banned for up to three months.[16] The provision does not allow permanent or discriminatory bans, and that is right because such restrictions would appear designed to abridge free speech.

But, as Schauer himself admits,[17] his distinction only carries convic- tion if the reason for giving free speech some measure of legal protection is suspicion of government, for then the purpose of the legal restrictions is crucial. If speech enjoys protection on some more positive rationale, such as the individual's right to autonomy or arguments from truth or participatory democracy, then the fact that it is restricted *incidentally* rather than deliberately is irrelevant; in effect the restriction is the same and it must be justified in relation to the competing free speech interest. In assessing the legitimacy of a regulation, the facts that it has been passed for some general social good, such as public order, that it does not discriminate between types of speech on a content basis, and that it restricts (or even bans) speech which shades imperceptibly into conduct are all arguments which can be used to support its validity. But none of these factors seems decisive in itself.

Most content-based restrictions on speech and assembly, purportedly justified on public order grounds, are rightly viewed with suspicion. If the Public Order Act 1936 were amended, as some suggest, to allow local authorities (admittedly with the Home Secretary's consent and on the application of a chief officer of police) to ban *specified* processions, there is a considerable danger that the power would be used totally to proscribe

---

[15] F. Schauer, *Free Speech: A Philosophical Enquiry* (Cambridge, 1982), 203–5.
[16] Public Order Act 1936, s. 3(2)–(3). German law exempts religious, funeral and wedding provisions from the general controls: BGBl 1978, 1, S. 1790, s. 17.
[17] Schauer, *Free Speech*, 204.

processions by particular organizations. The Home Affairs Committee of the House of Commons was probably correct for this reason not to recommend the creation of a power to ban marches where there was a likelihood of racial incitement.[18] This would almost certainly be exercised to outlaw National Front and other far right-wing demonstrations; however distasteful the views of these organizations may be, they are entitled to the same freedom of speech as those with more orthodox opinions, and the suppression of such views may be the first slide down the 'slippery slope' towards total government control of political discourse.

A further powerful argument against any amendment to the Public Order Act 1936, to permit the imposition of restrictions on particular organizations, is that it might encourage opponents of those groups to confront them violently, and thereby secure bans on their future activities. The opponents would then remain free to demonstrate themselves. Under the existing law their marches too may be curtailed for up to three months if they threaten serious disruption. This is one aspect of the familiar 'heckler's veto problem', the situation where peaceful demonstrations are broken up by opposing groups. Another aspect of this problem occurs when the police order the organizers of the (originally peaceful) meeting to disperse and they refuse. Whether, or in which precise circumstances, it is legitimate then to prosecute the organizers raises one of the most difficult issues in free speech jurisprudence. Not to allow any criminal charges in this situation may be to render impossible the preservation of the peace by the only means available. On the other hand, the indiscriminate imposition of criminal penalties here would enable the disrupters to succeed and would make a mockery of free speech.[19]

One way a legal system can solve this dilemma (at any rate partly) is in fact to draw a crude distinction between types of speech which might in some circumstances provoke a violent response and those which are merely offensive. People employing the former kind of language at a public meeting may be prosecuted if a breach of the peace occurs, whether or not they intend this consequence. Those using offensive or indecent words should not incur a similar risk of prosecution, though in English law at any rate there are residual police powers to preserve the peace, supported by criminal sanctions for failure to co-operate. Whether this distinction between provocative and offensive speech is justifiable,

---

[18] Fifth Report of the Home Affairs Committee 1979–80, HC 756, para. 51.
[19] For further discussion, see below, pp. 206–10.

and how it is drawn in the cases, forms the subject of section 2 of this chapter. The 'heckler's veto problem', most acute in those circumstances where the speaker does not incite his audience to violence, is discussed in section 3.

2. INFLAMMATORY SPEECH

In 1942 a unanimous Supreme Court held that to address a city marshal, 'You are a God damned racketeer' and 'a damned Fascist and the whole government of Rochester and Fascists or agents of Fascists', was to use insulting or 'fighting' words, wholly unprotected by the First Amendment.[20] Such words 'which by their very utterance inflict injury or tend to incite an immediate breach of the peace' did not communicate any ideas and were so valueless that, like libel and obscenity, they could not be regarded as 'speech' for the purposes of constitutional protection. In the *Chaplinsky* case, therefore, the Court approved the idea that a line should be drawn between, on the one hand, protected propositional speech and, on the other hand, provocative and insulting epithets.

Unfortunately the judgment of Murphy J. for the Court is unclear whether the latter type of language may be proscribed because it necessarily endangers public order or because it is intrinsically undesirable. On the facts of the case itself, an imminent breach of the peace was perhaps unlikely, though police officers have been known to retaliate to such unfriendly remarks in a hostile manner. In any case the Court did not seem too concerned with the particular circumstances of the incident; it was enough that the language used was of a character which *tended to* incite to a breach of the peace. The alternative interpretation is even more mysterious. In what sense do words *per se* inflict injury, unless of course they amount to a libel or an invasion of privacy? Notions of 'verbal assault' or 'hitting with words' are far from helpful, and only prompt a rephrasing of this question. Maybe the Court was going so far as to say that *offensive* remarks directed at a particular individual could be constitutionally proscribed simply because they hurt his sensibilities. The implications of this for any society which takes free speech seriously are considerable, and largely explain why the *Chaplinsky* ruling has fallen into disfavour.

It is, of course, understandable that laws should be enacted outlawing the use of unpleasant and offensive words in public. Few people enjoy the sound of foul language, particularly when directed at them, any more

---

[20] *Chaplinsky* v. *New Hampshire* 315 US 568 (1942).

than they like the sight of ugly buildings. But acceptance of the special value of freedom of speech entails that we should be more prepared to tolerate the former than the latter type of unpleasantness. What becomes important therefore is that the justifications, if any, for these restrictions on speech are explored. To some extent the points made in the discussion of group libel laws are also relevant here.[21] If the prosecution does not have to show that an imminent breach of the peace is likely to result from the offensive language, the public order rationale does not work. On the other hand, if the gravamen of the offence is the hurt to sensibilities of the person addressed, use of the criminal law is hardly compatible with respect for freedom of expression. Listeners would then have some sort of veto and the implications for freedom of political speech would be considerable. An alternative rationale for legal restrictions is that society has a legitimate interest in preserving the quality of language used in public debate. Violent and indecent language often, it is said, encourages the spread of dangerous, harmful ideas. As Alexander Bickel put it, '. . . a market-place without rules of civil discourse is no market-place of ideas, but a bullring'.[22] This argument goes well beyond the *Chaplinsky* case, since it would legitimate prohibitions on offensive speech, whether or not it is directed at a particular individual.

In fact the best justification for *Chaplinsky* is probably that the verbal communication there was simply not the sort of rational or intellectual 'speech' which it is the purpose of the First Amendment to protect. It did not form part of any dialogue, and was not made to elicit any considered response.[23] This particular argument concerning the meaning of 'speech' has been considered in Chapter II,[24] and nothing further need be said here. The other possible bases for the decision, outlined in the preceding paragraph, have now been repudiated by the Supreme Court in rulings which are relevant to public order and, therefore, deserve some consideration in this chapter.

In a line of decisions during the 1970s the Court narrowed the *Chaplinsky* principle so that it only applied to words which were likely to incite the person addressed to physical violence.[25] So statutes which had

[21] See above, ch. V, s. 4.

[22] *The Morality of Consent* (Yale, 1975), 77.

[23] See L. H. Tribe, *American Constitutional Law* (New York, 1978), 605–7.

[24] See above, ch. II, s. 1.

[25] For example, *Gooding* v. *Wilson* 405 US 518 (1972); *Rosenfeld* v. *New Jersey* 408 US 901 (1972); *Brown* v. *Oklahoma* 408 US 914 (1972); *Lewis* v. *New Orleans* II 415 US 130 (1974).

been construed by the state courts to cover abusive and offensive language, falling short of a tendency to provoke a breach of the peace, were ruled unconstitutional; it did not matter under this use of the 'overbreadth doctrine'[26] that, on the facts of the particular case, the appellant could have been properly convicted under a narrower, more precisely drafted, ordinance. Thus, in one leading case, the defendant, picketing an army induction centre, addressed a police officer: 'White son of a bitch, I'll kill you', and 'You son of a bitch, I'll choke you to death'.[27] The Court held it was wrong to convict him under a statute proscribing the use of 'opprobious words or abusive language, tending to cause a breach of the peace', as the Georgia courts had interpreted this to apply to any type of offensive language. In effect the Court ignored that part of the *Chaplinsky* judgment which held unprotected by the First Amendment words 'which by their very utterance inflict injury'.

The same general approach is also shown in cases in which the courts have insisted on strict proof that an outbreak of violence is likely to occur.[28] Close examination of the facts is therefore necessary to determine the constitutionality of a conviction under the 'fighting words' rule, though this scrutiny was singularly absent in *Chaplinsky* itself. Among the relevant factors are the character of the audience and the extent to which it might reasonably have anticipated the use of insulting or scurrilous language. According to Powell J., as the police are trained to use a high degree of restraint in the face of verbal provocation, abuse directed to them may not be punished, while identical language at a public meeting (particularly if women and children are present) might constitutionally be outlawed.[29] Interestingly a similar optimistic view of the capacity of police officers for self-control was shown in a Canadian case,[30] while an English court has, perhaps more realistically, held that a person can be convicted of insulting a policeman in such a way that a breach of the peace was likely.[31] It is surely correct to take into account the character of the audience in determining the likelihood of a breach of the peace (as the leading English case shows).[32] On a strict public order

[26] For the use of the doctrine in this area, see Tribe, *American Constitutional Law*, 710–16.

[27] *Gooding* v. *Wilson* 405 US 518 (1972).

[28] For example, *Terminiello* v. *Chicago* 337 US 1 (1949); *Edwards* v. *South Carolina* 372 US 229 (1963); *Hess* v. *Indiana* 414 US 105 (1973).

[29] *Lewis* v. *New Orleans* I 408 US 913 (1972).

[30] *R.* v. *Zwicker* (1938) 1 DLR 461, 463 (CC, Nova Scotia).

[31] *Simcock* v. *Rhodes* (1977) 66 Cr. App. Rep. 192 (DC).

[32] *Jordan* v. *Burgoyne* [1963] 2 QB 744 (DC).

approach, however, the fact that women and children are present at a public meeting should be irrelevant, since they might be presumed less likely to react violently to abusive and insulting language.

The Court has also rejected the argument that states may constitutionally regulate the quality of public debate by outlawing the use of indecent language, irrespective of whether it is likely to lead to a breach of the peace. In *Cohen* v. *California*[33] the appellant was convicted under a statute proscribing offensive conduct which disturbed the peace, when he wore a jacket bearing the words 'Fuck the Draft' in a court-house corridor. Harlan J. giving the Court's opinion rejected the application of the 'fighting words' doctrine, because there was no insult directed to any particular person. And there was no evidence that the appellant intended to provoke the public to violence or that this was at all likely on the facts. He then went on to consider whether offensive words could be constitutionally purged from public display and discourse. A vague fear that their use might induce some people to respond violently could not constitute any justification for such a prohibition; this would in effect confer a *de facto* power on the most sensitive members of the public. The stronger, general argument that the state has a legitimate concern to regulate the quality of the language used in public was also rejected. Harlan J.'s contention was that the style of speech cannot easily be divorced from its content; language conveys emotions as well as ideas, and it is as impermissible for the state to regulate the communication of the former as the latter.

The significance of this ruling extends far beyond the limits of public order jurisprudence. In the present context, however, it shows, together with the 'overbreadth' decisions discussed before it, that the Court will only tolerate the prohibition of *inflammatory* speech likely to cause an outbreak of violence and disorder. Admittedly Harlan J.'s judgment does leave open the possibility that, if there had been evidence that a large number of citizens were likely to react violently to Cohen's protest, the application of the statute might have been upheld. This interpretation is not, however, consistent with the overall spirit of his ruling, nor would it be in line with the 'heckler's veto' cases discussed in section 3 of this chapter. The justification for the Court's approach (assuming this view of it is correct) is that any wider prohibition would unduly restrict political protest. After all, there was really little difference between Chaplinsky's

---

[33] 403 US 15 (1971), discussed by D. A. Farber, 'Civilizing Public Discourse: An Essay on Professor Bickel, Justice Harlan and the Enduring Significance of *Cohen* v. *California* [1980] *Duke LJ* 283.

'fighting' talk and a seditious attack on local or central government, except the point that the former hardly formed part of a dialogue with the police officer. Where the speech is made in the course of a demonstration or meeting, the requirement that the language is insulting and that it is, therefore, more than merely offensive or annoying, is necessary to prevent the imposition of a heckler's veto by the unduly sensitive. A legislature, solicitous of the interests of free speech, should formulate an objective test in order to determine the type of speech which may be prohibited in the interests of public order, rather than a test which only takes into account the subjective reactions of the audience.

The British Parliament has made a laudable attempt to draft such a formula in section 5 of the Public Order Act 1936. This makes it an offence to use in a public place or at a public meeting 'threatening, abusive or insulting words or behaviour ... with intent to provoke a breach of the peace or whereby a breach of the peace is likely to be occasioned'. The leading case on the provision is *Jordan* v. *Burgoyne*.[34] There the defendant made a speech to a meeting of several thousand people in Trafalgar Square. When he suggested that 'Hitler was right' and that 'our real enemies, the people we should have fought, were not Hitler and the National Socialists of Germany but world Jewry and its associates in this country', there was complete disorder among the audience which included many Jews and Communists who were keen to stop the defendant's meeting. The Divisional Court allowed the prosecutor's appeal against the quarter sessions' acquittal of Jordan on the charge under section 5 of the 1936 Act. The lower court had taken the view that ordinary, reasonable people would not have reacted to Jordan's speech in a hostile manner. But the fact that an audience of a different character (an assembly of professors or divines?)[35] might have reacted in an entirely peaceable way—perhaps, by taking notes—was irrelevant. A speaker must take his audience as he finds it, and cannot argue that elements in the crowd are disposed to break his meeting up. This suggests that the case approves a heckler's veto and that, as Jordan contended, it marks a substantial inroad into free speech principles. However, Lord Parker CJ emphasized that the speaker must 'insult' his audience in the sense of 'hit [them] by words' for the offence to be committed. This phrase is reminiscent of the American 'fighting words' doctrine, though, of course, the British provision requires proof that a breach of the peace is probable.

---

[34] [1963] 2 QB 744. For a general discussion of this area of law, see D. G. T. Williams, *Keeping the Peace* (London, 1967), ch. 7.
[35] See Coleridge J. in *R.* v. *Aldred* (1909) 22 Cox C.C. 1, 3.

It was clear that Jordan had insulted the audience earlier in his speech, when he had referred to it as a 'red rabble' and 'far from wholesome', though it was not so apparent that it was these remarks, rather than the later non-insulting comments on the last war, which brought about the unrest.

The key question to be answered in determing the scope of the offence is this: how should the courts interpret 'threatening, abusive or insulting'? The interests of free speech require these words to be construed strictly, an obvious point reinforced by the fear that otherwise hecklers will too easily be able to impose a veto. In this context some decisions of lower courts are far from encouraging. For example, in 1969 demonstrators who shouted 'Remember Biafra' during the two minutes' silence at the Remembrance Day ceremony in Whitehall were convicted of using insulting words.[36] The fact that the crowd had become understandably restless was, however, irrelevant, unless the slogan was rightly held to be 'insulting'. Who, it may be asked, was insulted? Australian courts have held that the abuse or insults must be directed at persons present at the meeting or perhaps people associated with the audience.[37] This limitation must be correct, if the words are not to be emptied of any real meaning. It would be absurd, for example, if a political speech in England attacking the policies of the French government in the most intemperate terms could be treated as 'abusive' or 'insulting' merely because there were some ardent Francophiles in the audience. It should probably not make a difference if there were some Frenchmen present, because this sort of general political speech should not readily be treated as criminal. Yet the Divisional Court in one of its less impressive rulings decided that it was 'insulting' to people entering a club for United States servicemen to hand them leaflets opposing the Vietnam war and inviting American servicemen to desert.[38] As counsel for the defendant argued, it is hard to see how an invitation to consider a possible course of action could be regarded as an insult.

Some limits on the interpretation of section 5 have now been imposed by the House of Lords in *Brutus* v. *Cozens*.[39] The appellants had interrupted a tennis match at Wimbledon involving a South African

---

[36] See *Brownlie's Law of Public Order and National Security*, 9 n. 1.

[37] *Ex p. Breen* (1918) 18 SR (NSW) 1 (S. Ct. NSW), leave to appeal refused sub. nom. *Gumley* v. *Breen* (1918) 24 CLR 453 (H. C. of A.); *Lendrum* v. *Campbell* (1932) 32 SR (NSW) 499 (S. Ct. NSW).

[38] *Williams* v. *DPP* (1968) 112 Sol. J. 599.

[39] [1973] AC 854.

player in order to protest against the evils of apartheid. The disruption had prompted some spectators to react angrily. The magistrates held there had been no insulting behaviour, but on appeal the Divisional Court ruled there was an offence under section 5 of the 1936 Act because the appellants' conduct had affronted and offended the spectators. Lord Reid considered this approach misconceived. There is a distinction between 'insulting' a person on the one hand, and evincing disrespect or contempt for his rights on the other. The lower court's view, he pointed out, would have led to an undue restriction on vigorous public debate, merely because it offended some people. The meaning of 'insulting' was a question of fact for the magistrates, and the Divisional Court was wrong to give the term such a broad interpretation. The drawback to the Lords' ruling is that it will be virtually impossible to appeal from magistrates' rulings on the meaning of the key terms of the statute if they are regarded as deciding questions of fact.[40] Free speech will only be securely protected in this context if justices follow the approach indicated by Lord Reid.

A further limitation is that the prosecution must show it was the threatening, abusive, or insulting words which *caused* the breach of peace or made one likely.[41] Otherwise the heckler's veto could be imposed; a meeting might be broken up by a number of hooligans for reasons wholly unconnected with insults uttered by a speaker earlier in the meeting. To prosecute him under the Public Order Act in this circumstance would be to allow the disrupters a *de facto* censorship power. One robust view here is that the normal reaction of people in an audience who are insulted by an intemperate speech would be to walk away, so that only in extreme cases would it be right to conclude that the inflammatory speech actually caused the breach of the peace.[42] At all events the courts should insist on a close temporal connection between the abuse or insults and the likely disturbance. It should not be enough that in the long term the defendant's speeches may bring about an eventual breakdown of publc order.[43] In the United States the courts generally insist on proof of an

---

[40] *Brownlie's Law of Public Order and National Security*, 14–15.

[41] A. Dickey, 'Some Problems concerned with the Offence of Conduct Likely to Cause a Breach of the Peace' [1967] *Crim. LR* 265, 273–5.

[42] J. Feinberg, 'Limits to the Free Expression of Opinion', in *Philosophy of Law* (2nd edn., Belmont, California, 1980, ed. J. Feinberg and H. Gross), 191, 199–200. The argument for legal regulation is much stronger where the persons insulted are a 'captive audience'—see, e.g. *FCC* v. *Pacifica Foundation* 438 US 726 (1978), but this will rarely be true of public meetings, particularly in open spaces.

[43] See *R.* v. *Ambrose* (1973) 57 Cr. App. Rep. 538 (CA).

imminent breach of the peace as a result of the inflammatory speech in order to safeguard constitutionally protected speech.[44] This is justified in principle, because where there is a substantial period of time between the speech and the unlawful action, it cannot be right to punish the speaker rather than those who, after time for reflection, have acted in a disorderly or violent manner.[45]

Provided it is properly construed, section 5 of the Public Order Act draws a sensible and coherent line between speech which ought to be protected even though there is a risk to public order, and inflammatory speech which can appropriately be prohibited. The difficulty is that the courts have sometimes been inclined to give the provision a wide interpretation which unjustifiably restricts the communication of ideas and which may enable a hostile audience to impose a veto. On occasion the section appears to be used to control general disorderly behaviour, as in *Simcock* v. *Rhodes* when a member of a noisy group emerging late from a dance hall was convicted for telling a policeman to 'fuck off'.[46] This sort of language could as a matter of strict law be properly penalized under a statute or by-law prohibiting offensive words or disorderly behaviour,[47] but in principle such legislation surely goes too far in suppressing free speech (or conduct which communicates ideas and which, therefore, should be protected). The line should be drawn at the points indicated by the decisions in *Brutus* v. *Cozens* and *Cohen* v. *California*, in some respects closely comparable cases. The question, however, remains whether the police should have residual powers to disperse public meetings and arrest even the most pacific speakers, when there is no other way of preserving law and order.

3. THE HOSTILE AUDIENCE

Any simple solution to the hostile audience, or heckler's veto, problem is bound to cause dissatisfaction. The law must preserve the peace, but if it

---

[44] For example, *Brandenburg* v. *Ohio* 395 US 444 (1969), and *Hess* v. *Indiana* 414 US 105 (1973).

[45] See the argument of T. Scanlon, 'A Theory of Freedom of Expression', in *The Philosophy of Law* (Oxford, 1977, ed. R. M. Dworkin), 159–60, reprinted from (1972) 1 *Philos. and Pub. Affairs*, 204.

[46] (1977) 66 Cr. App. Rep. 192 (DC).

[47] See *Brownlie's Law of Public Order and National Security*, 192–4, discussing local statutes and by-laws. In New Zealand, such behaviour is covered by the Police Offences Act 1927, s. 3D—a statute equivalent to the Public Order Act 1936—which has been construed to outlaw forms of protest annoying or embarrassing to the majority: see *Melser* v. *Police* [1967] NZLR 437 (CA).

is preoccupied with this objective, it will inevitably confer censorship powers on bodies determined to break up a public meeting. Worse still, an alleged fear of disruption may induce the police to disperse a demonstration when the risk of violence is in fact relatively slight, and then if the convenor is prosecuted for obstructing the police (because he failed to stop the meeting) he will only be acquitted if the court holds the police action to be unreasonable. Courts, particularly magistrates, are reluctant to uphold a challenge to the exercise of police discretion in circumstances of apparent emergency. In any case, an acquittal does not enable the defendant retrospectively, as it were, to exercise his free speech rights; the time for the protest may have passed, the occasion for demonstration may be no longer relevant. In the face of these dilemmas, the law should look for imaginative solutions, which will reconcile the competing values as far as possible.

English law can in fact boast one decision which adopts an uncompromisingly pro-free speech position in these circumstances, the famous case of *Beatty* v. *Gillbanks*.[48] The Divisional Court refused to uphold binding-over orders which had been imposed on leaders of the Salvation Army in Weston-super-Mare for holding an unlawful assembly. On a number of previous occasions their procession had been broken up by their opponents, the Skeleton Army, and this time Beatty and some other leaders of the Salvationists were arrested when they refused to disperse a procession which the police feared would also be violently obstructed. Field J. held that the appellants had not caused any unlawful acts; the disturbances had not been the intended, or natural and necessary consequences of their processions. In a passage which has perhaps not received the attention it deserves, he added that the Skeleton Army would be less inclined to intervene when they appreciated that their obstruction would not terminate the Salvationist processions, but that if they did continue with their violent opposition, it was the police's duty to deal with them rather than with persons exercising lawful rights.[49]

The case remains both good law and highly controversial: it is still legitimate to question whether the Salvationists' intention was rightly characterized as entirely innocent. In any case, it is clear that it will be distinguished where the speeches or general behaviour of the defendant show an intention to provoke violence from opponents.[50] This type of conduct would also be caught by section 5 of the Public Order Act 1936,

---

[48] [1882] 9 QBD 308, (1882) 15 Cox C.C. 138.
[49] Ibid., 146, *per* Field J. (The passage does not appear in the Official Law Reports.)
[50] *Wise* v. *Dunning* [1902] 1 KB 167 (DC).

discussed in the previous section of the chapter. More importantly, preventive powers of the police to keep the peace now provide a basis for a criminal prosecution, even though the organizers of the meeting have no desire to provoke disruption. The authority for this is the highly unsatisfactory decision of the Divisional Court in *Duncan* v. *Jones*.[51] The appellant there started to address a small meeting outside an unemployed training centre in Deptford, London. Disturbance (of an unspecified sort) had followed a previous meeting conducted by her on the same spot a year before. Fearing a repetition of these troubles, the police asked her to move her meeting to a place 175 yards away; when she refused, she was charged with obstructing a police officer in the execution of his duty. Her conviction was upheld by the Divisional Court.

The judges can be criticized for their deliberate refusal to see the case in the context of rights or freedoms of public assembly, or to reconcile their conclusion with *Beatty* v. *Gillbanks*.[52] Of course, it can be said that the earlier decision was a ruling on the scope of unlawful assembly, while *Duncan* v. *Jones* concerned a minor summary offence (which now exists under the Police Act 1964). But the decision in effect outflanks the law on the freedom of non-provocative public assembly. Everything turns on whether the police *reasonably* apprehended a breach of the peace, a fragile basis for the protection of civil liberties. The court did not say whether a breach of the peace was to be apprehended as likely or only possible, or whether a *serious* breach had to be contemplated for the police to be justified in intervening. The relevance of the previous disturbance which had occurred over a year before these events was not discussed; in the United States such an occurrence would not be an adequate ground for refusing a permit to hold a meeting.[53] The police intervention was of course a variety of prior restraint, a feature which might have prompted more caution on the part of the Divisional Court. Finally, the court did not consider whether the police could have pursued any other course of action, which would have avoided this censorship.

Although this obstruction charge is now frequently used in demonstration cases, there is little subsequent authority refining the rule stated in *Duncan* v. *Jones*. In one case,[54] the Divisional Court made it clear that

[51] [1936] 1 KB 218.

[52] Lord Hewart CJ denied the case even touched the issue whether there is a right to hold a meeting which may be violently opposed, and Humphreys J. thought it had nothing to do with the law of unlawful assembly'.

[53] *Kunz* v. *New York* 340 US 290 (1951).

[54] *Piddington* v. *Bates* [1961] 1 WLR 162 (DC).

there must be a 'real possibility' of a breach of the peace before intervention is justified. Lord Parker CJ went on to suggest that oppressive and hostile picketing was enough to constitute a 'breach of the peace'; it did not matter that there was no clear threat of violence.[55] In any case, appellate courts are clearly reluctant to challenge the findings of magistrates, a factor which no doubt explains the dearth of reported cases in this area.

The result of these decisions is that hecklers are allowed to impose an effective veto on what would otherwise be peaceable public meetings. The police may—and indeed generally do—attempt to protect lawful demonstrations and processions by keeping their opponents at arms' length. But they equally may choose to intervene to disperse the meeting, if they think this course appropriate to keep the peace, even though nothing said there can be construed as inflammatory or provocative. This position contrasts sharply with some comparable American case-law, and there are other better solutions.

The leading Supreme Court ruling is that in *Feiner* v. *New York*.[56] A speaker at a street corner in Syracuse gathered a small crowd of both whites and blacks around him. He certainly provided them with good invective and entertainment: the President was described as a 'bum' and the local mayor as a 'champagne-sipping bum' who 'does not speak for the Negro people'. But when he advocated that the blacks should fight for equal rights, members of the crowd became restive. The police feared that a fight would break out, and after two requests to the speaker to stop, he was arrested for disorderly conduct. The majority of the Court upheld his conviction; he had incited to riot, and there was a clear and present danger of disorder. This is perfectly acceptable law, even though the majority's interpretation of the facts seems questionable. The interest of the case lies in the dissents of Black and Douglas JJ who did not think the record showed an intent on Feiner's part to cause violence. They thought the police's primary duty in the situation was to protect the speaker, if necessary by arresting members of the hostile audience. By adopting the opposite course, police censorship had been imposed.

There is perhaps no Supreme Court decision which clearly delimits the powers and duties of the police where there is a hostile audience on

---

[55] But see *R.* v. *Howell* [1982] QB 416 (CA), where it was held in a different context, that a threat of violence was required. In its recent report on Public Order offences (Law Com. no. 123, HC 85, 1983–4), the Law Commission concluded that the concept, 'breach of the peace', was too nebulous to use in the criminal law.

[56] 340 US 315 (1951).

the point of breaking up violently a lawful meeting.[57] But at least two Circuit Court cases indicate that their initial responsibility is to protect First Amendment rights so far as possible.[58] If a community has advance notice of a demonstration which is likely to be confronted by political opponents, it should ensure there are adequate police present at the meeting to safeguard freedom of speech and assembly. An order to disperse can only be justified as a last recourse when there is a clear and present, or imminent, danger of physical violence. Characteristically it has also been suggested that the police officers should observe certain procedural steps. The speaker should be warned before the final order to stop is issued (as happened in *Feiner*) and an explanation should be given for the police action.[59] This may be a counsel of perfection; in many cases it would be absurd to expect hard-pressed officers to behave with the deliberation and courtesy of a Chancery judge. But the American case-law is impressive in its commitment to preserve the values of free speech until it is clear beyond doubt that it should be subordinated on a particular occasion to public order. The British statutory provision creating the offence of obstructing a police officer in the execution of his duty, as construed in *Duncan* v. *Jones*, would be considered much too sweeping under the First Amendment, since it plainly enables the suppression of speech in circumstances which do not warrant it.

If the hostile audience problem cannot be satisfactorily solved at the moment when it becomes most acute, perhaps the law can seek to prevent the difficulty arising? One possibility would be for the authorities, as in Germany, to insist on advance notice of processions and public meetings, so that appropriate steps could be taken to ensure they take place peacefully.[60] The police would then have time to call up reinforcements, if necessary from neighbouring forces, for attendance along the route.[61]

---

[57] In *Gregory* v. *Chicago* 394 US 111 (1969), the majority of the Court held that the demonstrators could not constitutionally be convicted of 'disorderly conduct' for refusing to obey police requests to disperse when they were confronted by hostile opponents, since this had not been the basis of the charge. Black and Douglas JJ came close to ruling that demonstrators could never be convicted for such a refusal, as this would give the police censorship powers.

[58] *Sellers* v. *Johnson* 163 F. 2d. 877 (8th Cir., 1947); *Wolin* v. *Port of New York Authority* 392 F. 2d. 83 (2nd Cir., 1968).

[59] See the note, 'Hostile-Audience Confrontations: Police Conduct and First Amendment Rights' (1976) 75 *Mich. LR* 180, 196.

[60] In Germany at least 48 hours' notice is required, and one person must be designated as responsible for the meeting/procession: Gesetz über Versammlungen und Aufzüge, BGBl. 1978 1, S. 1790, s. 14.

[61] At present the availability of reinforcements is a criterion for determining whether it is necessary to apply for an order banning a procession under the Public Order Act 1936: 5th Report of the Home Affairs Committee 1979–80, HC 756, paras. 43–6.

Moreover, conditions could be imposed with regard to the time and place of the demonstration to minimize the risk of disorder by, for example, preventing its entrance into an area where its opponents are likely to gather in large numbers. A general notice requirement would also enable the police (or other suitable authority) to ban formally organized counter-demonstrations, though it would be naïve to claim this would always prevent clashes between rival groups.

The British Public Order Act 1936 contains some provisions along these lines. Passed largely to deal with the violence resulting from the Mosleyite demonstrations, section 3 first enables a chief officer of police to impose conditions on the organizers of a procession, including conditions as to its route, if he reasonably believes it may 'occasion serious public disorder'. Secondly, if he does not consider the use of these powers will be adequate to prevent such disorder, he can apply to the district council for an order prohibiting all or any class of public procession for a period up to three months; the council may make this order subject to the Home Secretary's consent.[62] In practice the power to ban has been exercised very rarely, even in the last few years when the number of street demonstrations and the cost of policing them have escalated dramatically.[63]

It was against the background of some major disturbances in the late 1970s that the Home Secretary initiated a review of the Public Order Act 1936, which in particular looked at the scope of these powers. The topic was also considered by the Home Affairs Committee of the House of Commons in 1979–80.[64] Although neither paper recommended radical changes, it is not surprising that some reforms were suggested. In particular, both the Home Office and the House of Commons Committee favoured a national provision, under which organizers of processions (and probably meetings) should give normally 72 hours advance notice of a demonstration, so the police could take appropriate steps to obviate risks to public order—often, in consultation with the organizers. The Home Affairs Committee was concerned that an inflexible requirement might prevent the organization of counter-demonstrations, so it suggested that 72 hours might be the usual minimum, 'or as soon as reasonably practicable after that time'.[65] But it is not at all clear why

---

[62] Public Order Act 1936, s. 3.

[63] It has been used altogether only eleven times since 1936: Home Office Review, *Review of Public Order Act*, para 31.

[64] See n 5 above.

[65] 5th Report of Home Affairs Committee, para. 35. Also see the discussion in the Scarman Report, paras. 127–30, which concluded that there was no need for a national notice requirement.

counter-demonstrations should be protected in this way. They create a serious risk of violence, as shown by the notorious Red Lion Square disorder in June 1974, when on the same date the Conway Hall was booked by both the National Front and a militant left-wing organization for public meetings. There is surely much to be said for conferring wide powers to ban counter-demonstrations, whenever there is reasonable belief in a risk of disorder. This, of course, entails a 'first come, first served' rule, and as a consequence some provisions would have to regulate the number of street processions which could be held by particular organizations. Otherwise some political groups could effectively exclude the freedom of others to assemble.

Another reform favoured in the two papers is the extension of these Public Order Act powers to meetings, at least when they are held on the highway or in open spaces.[66] It certainly seems anomalous that authorities at present have wider preventive powers over processions than over stationary meetings, until, of course, there is reasonable apprehension at the meeting itself of disorder, when the police can exercise the powers legitimated by *Duncan* v. *Jones*. Some minor, technical changes in the procedure for banning processions were also considered by the Home Office and by the Home Affairs Committee, but neither was enthusiastic about conferring wide powers to ban processions which are generally disruptive to community life, or an authority to confine them to particular reserved areas.

The exercise of these powers does constitute a form of prior restraint, and any extension in their scope should naturally be viewed with caution. But we saw in Chapter IV that it is not right to view every form of previous restraint with total hostility and that there are some arguments for their use in this context.[67] It does seem to be the case that a system of advance notice with power to regulate, or in some extreme cases to ban, meetings and processions may be the best means of reducing the scale of the hostile audience problem. The imposition of conditions as to route and time may obviate the need for total suppression by a police officer at a later stage. Furthermore, earlier decisions about the appropriate conditions can be taken in consultation with the organizers of the demonstration, who are therefore given an opportunity to co-operate in the effort to preserve public order; in contrast, intervention by the police

---

[66] Cmnd. 7891, paras. 74–80; HC 756, paras. 72–4.

[67] See above, ch. IV, s. 4. The German law on meetings and processions allows the authorities to ban them when they directly endanger public security and order: BGBl. 1978 I, S. 1790, s. 15.

during the course of the meeting may appear arbitrary to its convenors. It is also easier to formulate standards to regulate the exercise of preventive powers at this stage, and there is room for judicial review, though the courts have played a minimal part in controlling the use of the police powers under the Public Order Act 1936.[68]

A temporary ban on all public meetings in a Swiss town has been upheld by the European Commission.[69] The canton government feared a breakdown in public order from clashes between separatist organizations and pro-Federal groups. Interestingly, the Commission rejected in this case arguments that a ban on counter-demonstrations only, or police control exercised during the course of actual meetings, would obviously be such adequate measures that a total ban could not be justified; where a serious danger could be foreseen, the government had a wide margin of discretion in deciding what steps were necessary to meet it. Moreover, as the prohibition was only temporary, it could not be said to be a disproportionate measure. The Commission has also approved the exercise of the comparable powers under the Public Order Act 1936 for two months.[70]

It remains the case, however, that absolute bans should be imposed only as a last resort, and that the imposition of conditions with perhaps, if necessary, a prohibition on counter-demonstrations is preferable.[71] An inability to handle the hostile audience problem should not be used as a pretext to suppress all demonstrations, or to ban those of the organization which is alleged, sometimes rather disingenuously, to 'provoke' violence on the streets. There does indeed have to be a compromise between the interests of free speech and public order, but it should be struck at the points indicated in this chapter. It is not enough simply to balance the two interests as if they are of equal weight; commitment to a free speech principle demands that account is only taken of public order considerations when they are pressing and that the means used to maintain peace and order are not disproportionate.

---

[68] An unsuccessful attempt to challenge the reasonableness of a total ban on marches (except religious and traditional 1 May processions) was made by the Campaign for Nuclear Disarmament in *Kent* v. *Metropolitan Police Commssr.*, *The Times*, 15 May 1981.

[69] 8191/78, *Rassemblement Jurassien and Unité Jurassienne* v. *Switzerland* 17 D. & R. 93.

[70] 8440/78, *Christians against Racism and Fascism* v. *UK* 21 D. & R. 138.

[71] It was always contemplated that the power to ban processions under the 1936 Act would only be used in an emergency: Sir J. Simon, Home Secretary, 318 HC Deb. (5th ser.), col. 1719.

VIII

Free Speech and the Judicial Process

1. INTRODUCTION

WE know from one of Lord Atkin's most memorable pronouncements that: 'Justice is not a cloistered virtue: she must be allowed to suffer the scrutiny and the respectful even though outspoken comments of ordinary men.'[1] Indeed, it might appear obvious that free speech should be particularly securely protected when it publicizes or examines the workings of the legal process. But in fact this is one of those complicated areas of law where the values of free speech compete with other rights and interests, both individual and public, and it is, moreover, an area where British law has contrasted sharply with the approach in the United States and that now required under the European Convention. This is particularly apparent in the scope of contempt of court, that 'Proteus of the legal world, assuming an almost infinite diversity of forms'.[2] But divergent solutions also emerge in the treatment of related questions: to what extent is it permissible to place restrictions on the reporting of preliminary committal proceedings? Is it ever proper to prohibit publication of the names of parties to legal proceedings? And, to take finally an issue which has been raised recently in American cases, does the press have any right of access to attend criminal trials?

Civilized societies have for decades, in some instances centuries, attached paramount importance to the fairness of legal procedure. Whether or not the rules of natural justice (or due process) can be traced back to the hearing accorded Adam and Eve before their expulsion from the Garden of Eden,[3] they have certainly been enshrined in the common law long before judges began to pay even lip-service to the importance of freedom of expression. And inevitably practising lawyers and judges are much concerned with these rules. They are now commonly incorporated in Bills of Rights and written constitutions. Thus, the Sixth Amendment to the US Constitution confers on the accused in a criminal prosecution a

---

[1] *Ambard* v. *Att.-Gen. for Trinidad and Tobago* [1936] AC 322, 335 (PC).
[2] Moskovitz, 'Contempt of Injunctions, Civil and Criminal' (1943) 43 *Col. LR* 780.
[3] See *R.* v. *Univ. of Cambridge* (1723) 1 Str. 557.

'right to a speedy and public trial, by an impartial jury ... and to be informed of the nature and cause of the accusation'. The European Convention on Human Rights provides various specific procedural safeguards for persons charged with criminal offences. And the European Court has interpreted Article 6(1), which states, 'In the determination of his civil rights and obligations or of any criminal charge against him, everyone is entitled to a fair and public hearing within a reasonable time by an independent and impartial tribunal ...', to cover most civil proceedings.[4]

There is, therefore, both traditional and constitutional authority in many jurisdictions for protecting the right to a fair trial against government invasion. It is perhaps hardly surprising that it may be preferred where it comes into conflict with the more modern and abrasive interests of free speech. A decision to accord greater weight to a fair trial might be clearly taken in a constitution itself, though it is rare for such documents to rank competing civil liberties. In fact these issues are left to be resolved by the judiciary, as they are in a state such as Britain where courts decide on the basis of common law principles. An important preliminary question here is to what extent there is a genuine conflict between two rights: the right to a fair trial and to freedom of speech. Is it true that in some circumstances it is necessary to restrict speech in order to honour the guarantee of a fair trial by an impartial judiciary, or to serve some other interests connected with the proper administration of justice?

Law reports are in fact full of judicial observations to the effect that in many cases the interests of free speech and a fair trial, so far from conflicting, are quite compatible. This conclusion may indeed be considered implicit in the constitutional protection of a right to a *public* trial. It is vital for press and public to be admitted to court proceedings to prevent judicial arbitrariness and to protect the parties, and consequently to be free to circulate to other members of the public reports of these proceedings. Moreover, comment on the conduct of a trial and criticism of tribunal judgments can equally be considered to be conducive, rather than inimical, to the fair administration of justice. But in other situations, the press might jeopardize a fair trial—by, for example, giving publicity to irrelevant, but damaging evidence or to an accused's confession or previous convictions. Certain forms of verbal intimidation of parties and witnesses constitute clear cases of contempt of court. It may be easy to assimilate this pressure to physical intimidation or bribery and so treat it

[4] See the discussion in A. H. Robertson, *Human Rights in Europe* (Manchester, 1977), 68–72.

as falling entirely outside the scope of the free speech clause; but this cannot be done with any conviction in the case of a sustained press campaign designed to influence the course of litigation.

In other cases restrictions on free speech may be imposed, which are more difficult to justify in terms of safeguarding the fair administration of justice. One example is the variety of contempt of court known as 'scandalizing the court', discussed in section 2 of this chapter. Another is the new more or less absolute prohibition in British law of any disclosure of jury deliberations. An extraordinarily wide provision, introduced in the Contempt of Court Act 1981 against the government's wishes,[5] reverses a previous ruling that there was only a contempt when the disclosure tended to imperil the finality of jury verdicts or adversely to affect the attitude of prospective jurors.[6] On this pragmatic approach it was hard to see how any revelation of jury discussion relevant to the facts of the particular case, however insensitive and offensive such disclosure might be, could amount to a contempt. Conceivably the publication of deliberations which concluded in a guilty verdict might be thought to prejudice an appeal or a possible new trial, but this sort of assessment could only be made by a court in a specific contempt proceeding, and not by the legislature regardless of the particular circumstances. Now after the 1981 Act bona fide research into jury deliberations and, it may be thought, informed public discussion of the merits of the jury system are seriously impeded.

There are other categories of contempt where the proceedings, taken in respect of a forbidden publication, are only indirectly connected with the administration of justice and are also concerned to protect some other interest. For example, it may be a contempt in British law to publish the name of a party or witness when the judge has issued an order to stop this, because disclosure would endanger the life of the witness or national security.[7] Proceedings were successfully taken when a newspaper, contrary to the judge's direction, published the names of blackmail victims who had given evidence under pseudonym.[8] The court did make the point that to allow this disclosure might deter future victims from taking proceedings or giving evidence, but it is surely more plausible to justify

---

[5] The final version of s. 8(1) of the Act was introduced during the last stage of the Bill in the House of Lords, contrary to the advice of the Lord Chancellor, Lord Hailsham; see 422 HL Deb. (5th ser.) cols. 239–54.

[6] *Att.-Gen.* v. *New Statesman* [1981] 1 QB 1 (DC).

[7] *Att.-Gen.* v. *Leveller Magazine* [1979] AC 440.

[8] *R.* v. *Socialist Workers, Printers and Publishers* [1975] QB 636 (DC).

the sanction of contempt proceedings as necessary to protect the safety and privacy interest of the persons whose identity was concealed. The same factors also lie behind the legislative provision enabling rape complainants to bring prosecutions anonymously, though here there was evidence to suggest that women had been deterred from taking complaints to the police because they did not wish to attract publicity when the trial took place.[9] In all these cases, of course, the offending publication does violate a court order, and therefore the authority of the judiciary; but that does not justify the original order. The question remains whether there is good reason for penalizing the publication of information which has been acquired lawfully and which it may well be in the public interest to reveal. In the case of rape and probably blackmail victims there are persuasive arguments for allowing the restriction of free speech entailed by the non-disclosure orders, but similar arguments should probably not entitle a judge to forbid revelation of the names of, say, prominent politicians charged with acts of gross indecency![10]

There are, therefore, a number of restrictions imposed in British law on the reporting of judicial proceedings, some of them under the general law of contempt, others by specific legislative provision. And the object of these restraints is not the same in all cases: it may be to ensure a fair trial or to protect the authority of the judiciary, while in other situations the aim is to safeguard the anonymity of a person who might otherwise be deterred from taking part in legal proceedings. Unfortunately, there is not space here to do justice to all the relevant free speech issues connected with this complex area of law. One topical question, however, should be briefly discussed: is it compatible with freedom of speech to take contempt proceedings to enforce a solicitor's implied undertaking not to allow documents, disclosed on discovery, to be used for other purposes where the documents have already been read out in open court? In *Home Office* v. *Harman*,[11] the majority of the House of Lords, Lords

---

[9] Sexual Offences (Amendment) Act 1976, s. 4, implementing the recommendations in the Report of the Advisory Group on the Law of Rape (1975), Cmnd. 6352. The reform represents a legislative judgment that generally the interests of free speech should be subordinated here to other policies, but the judge in a particular case may remove the restriction if he is satisfied that this is in the public interest.

[10] Despite the conclusions of the Advisory Group (Cmnd. 6352, para. 171), the 1976 Act provides for the general anonymity of the accused in rape cases. The courts also have power under the Contempt of Court Act 1981, s. 11, to prohibit the publication of the name of a witness, who has given evidence anonymously, or (perhaps) the name of someone who has been mentioned during the course of the proceedings, where this is necessary for the administration of justice.

[11] [1983] 1 AC 280.

Scarman and Simon dissenting, found there was a contempt in these circumstances; the solicitor had allowed a journalist to see documents disclosed to her by the Home Office, on the basis of which he wrote a feature article about the special 'control unit' in Hull Prison. Lord Diplock, who gave the leading speech for the majority, denied that the case raised any free speech issue at all, a striking example of the restrictive framing of a question in order to achieve a particular answer. It also shows more pertinently how easy it is for judges to ignore free speech considerations when no constitution (or other authoritative text) requires that they be taken into account. For, as Lord Scarman pointed out in dissent, the case plainly demanded a balancing of freedom of expression and, it might be added, the public's interest in the receipt of the information against the litigant's interest in preserving the confidentiality of the documents. As they had already been read out in court and so become public knowledge, there was little, in Lord Scarman's view, to put in the scales against the presumption in favour of free expression. The solicitor has now taken the case to the European Commission, and it would be surprising if that body (and the European Court) did not find Britain to be in breach of Article 10;[12] there does not appear to be any pressing social justification in these circumstances for penalizing the solicitor's disclosure to the press of information which had already, in one sense, become available to members of the public (if they attended the court hearing).

The chapter will concentrate on three types of contempt which clearly raise major free expression issues: attacks on the judiciary, publications which are thought likely to prejudice a fair criminal trial, and thirdly, similar publications prejudging the issues in civil cases. The final section of the chapter deals with the question whether freedom of speech entails a right of access to attend trials.

2. ATTACKS ON THE JUDICIARY

The variety of contempt, colourfully described as 'scandalizing the court', which prohibits particularly vicious attacks on the judiciary, can be traced back in British law to the celebrated judgment of Wilmot J. in *Almon*'s case.[13] It is a contempt to accuse the judges of arbitrary and

---

[12] The Commission has held Ms Harman's application admissible.

[13] (1765) Wilm. 243, 97 ER 94. For a critical account of the background to this judgment, see Sir J. Fox, (1908) 24 LQR 184 and 266.

corrupt conduct because such an attack undermines their authority and public confidence in the proper administration of justice. The object is not to protect the judges personally, so comment on the character of a judge unrelated to his performance on the bench falls outside the scope of the offence. Proceedings have always been rare, and indeed at one time during the last years of the nineteenth century the view was expressed that this form of contempt procedure was obsolete.[14] Its use was also subject to criticism in Parliament; interestingly, Lord Fitzgerald in a debate in the Lords in 1883 argued that it unduly fettered press freedom and pointed approvingly to its absence from the criminal codes of the states in the USA.[15] But successful proceedings have been taken on a handful of occasions this century, perhaps most notoriously in a case where the *New Statesman* published an article suggesting that Dr Marie Stopes, the birth control advocate, could not expect a fair hearing in a libel action presided over by Mr Justice Avory, a Roman Catholic.[16] Lord Hewart CJ held that the allegation of unfairness and lack of impartiality lowered the judge's authority, even though it seems to have been conceded in argument that the article was not suggesting any deliberate bias.

It is clear, however, that reasonable and moderate criticism of judicial decisions does not constitute contempt. In the leading Privy Council ruling in *Ambard* v. *Att.-Gen. for Trinidad and Tobago*,[17] Lord Atkin distinguished the imputation of improper motives and malicious comment on the one hand from good faith criticism on the other. Both in his opinion and in that of Lord Denning MR in a modern Court of Appeal case,[18] emphasis was placed on the importance of the freedom, particularly on the part of the press, to comment on the administration of justice. In the later case, the Court also observed that the factual accuracy and good taste of the article were irrelevant; in this respect contempt law may not be so restrictive of hostile and inaccurate criticism as the law of libel. It is, therefore, not surprising that there has apparently been no successful application for this type of contempt since 1930.

This is not the case, however, in France. The French Penal Code was amended in 1958 to create a new offence of abuse of courts and tribunals,

---

[14] See *McLeod* v. *St Aubyn* [1899] AC 549, 561 *per* Lord Morris (PC). He suggested there was more justification for the offence in primitive communities.

[15] 277 HL Deb. (3rd ser.) cols. 1612–13.

[16] *R.* v. *New Statesman, ex parte DPP* (1928) 44 TLR 301.

[17] [1936] AC 322.

[18] *R.* v. *Metropolitan Police Commssr., ex parte Blackburn* [1968] 2 QB 150.

somewhat similar to the common law's 'scandalizing the court'.[19] Proceedings were brought under this provision when a Marxist journal published an attack on an arbitration board which had upheld the termination of the employment contracts of Peugeot workers; the decision was characterized as 'justice de classe'.[20] The state won its case. It appears that there is no need to show an intention to bring justice into disrepute, and moreover, in contrast to the position in modern British law, the form and extravagance of the article's wording may well be material. Proceedings in similar cases have also been brought relatively recently in Australia, Canada, and less surprisingly South Africa.[21] A Canadian case nicely illustrates one aspect of this type of contempt.[22] A Minister of Transport in Manitoba accused a magistrate of political bias in refusing to quash a criminal information laid against him: 'The fact that he [the magistrate] is a loyal Conservative and had been appointed by the Conservative administration can't be overlooked.' These remarks, coupled with a threat to take steps to have the magistrate removed, were regarded as calculated to lower his authority and therefore constituted a contempt. But from another perspective, the comments, however outrageous in tone, might be seen as the very stuff of political debate; in a genuine democracy, where there is necessarily a wide range of political beliefs, remarks such as those are unlikely to shake respect for the judiciary. Indeed, paradoxically they might in some circumstances enhance it!

But, of course, there are more fundamental arguments here. To hold that an attack on the political, religious, or, for that matter, racial attitudes of the judiciary constitutes a criminal contempt assumes that judges do and can reach their decisions in a wholly unprejudiced way. The premiss is highly controversial, particularly after the teachings of some Realist schools of jurisprudence that judges are necessarily influenced by their background and by their ideological beliefs.[23] More positively a serious commitment to free speech surely requires tolerance

---

[19] Art. 226. See L. Neville Brown, 'Outrage au tribunal' (1974) 15 *Les Cahiers de droit* 741, 752–3; B. van Niekerk, 'The Uncloistering of the Virtue—Freedom of Speech and the Administration of Justice' (1978) 95 *South African LJ* 362 and 534.

[20] *Schroedt* case, *Gaz. du Palais* 1963(2), 350.

[21] For example, *Att.-Gen. for New South Wales* v. *Mundey* [1972] 2 NSWLR 887 (NSW Sup. Ct.); *R.* v. *Murphy, ex parte Att.-Gen. of New Brunswick* (1969) 4 DLR (3d) 289; *State* v. *Van Niekerk* [1970] 3 SA 655 (T).

[22] *Re Borowski* (1971) 19 DLR (3d) 537 (Manitoba QB).

[23] See, for example, J. Frank, *Law and the Modern Mind* (Gloucester, Mass., 1930, republished 1970), especially ch. XII.

for any attack on the judiciary, whether directed at an individual or the bench collectively. Perhaps there is some case for proscribing malicious criticism, though this qualification is not made in the case of (non-defamatory) attacks on the other branches of government. A further point is that as the judiciary, unlike the legislature and executive, is not politically responsible, sustained criticism of the performance of a particular judge may be the only way to induce his resignation. The robust conclusion could, therefore, be reached that there can be no more room for this variety of contempt than there is for the offences of sedition or group libel in a free society, which takes seriously the value of public discussion of political issues.[24]

The Phillimore Committee on Contempt of Court, which reported in 1974, did question whether there was any need for this offence. It did not think it was acceptable to require a judge to bring a private action for libel to protect his reputation against intemperate criticism.[25] As Arthur Goodhart pointed out in an article in 1935,[26] the prospect of a judge being cross-examined before a jury on his political attitudes is hardly an enticing one. Instead the Committee recommended that a new, strictly defined offence should replace 'scandalizing the court', the advantages of this reform being the achievement of somewhat more certainty in the law and the abolition of the summary contempt procedure in this area. The Canadian Law Reform Commission made similar proposals in 1977.[27] A further problem then arises on which the Phillimore Committee and the English Law Commission have come to different conclusions: should the truth of a specific allegation concerning the integrity of a judge be a defence to a prosecution for the proposed offence? The Committee thought it should not, unless the defendant also showed that publication was for the public benefit, while the Law Commission felt that a true allegation of judicial corruption should never be penalized.[28] There are difficulties in both solutions. The former would require a jury to decide when it is in the public interest to make a true allegation about the integrity of a judge; some jurymen might find it easy here to adopt the Millian position that revelation of the truth is always for the public good! On the other hand, the Law Commission's proposal would lead to

[24] Ch. V, ss. 3 and 4.
[25] Report of the Committee on Contempt of Court (1974), Cmnd. 5794, para. 162.
[26] 'Newspapers and Contempt of Court in English Law' (1935) 48 *Harv. LR* 885.
[27] Working Paper no. 20 (1977).
[28] Report of Committee Contempt of Court, paras. 165–6; Report of the Law Commission, 'Offences Relating to Interference with the Course of Justice' (1979), Law Com. no. 96, para. 3. 68.

potentially embarrassing enquiries into the accuracy of the allegation every time a case was brought. Arguably this shows the difficulty inherent in a compromise solution. It is probably far better to stay with the present obsolescent law (as we have done in Britain) or to do away with the offence altogether.

The American courts have characteristically favoured the second alternative. In federal cases, the relevant statute has been narrowly construed so as to confine contempt to misbehaviour in or physically near to the court-room,[29] while in *Bridges* v. *California*, Black J. observed *obiter* that loss of respect for the judiciary was not a serious enough evil to justify abridgement by the states of free speech.[30] Even Frankfurter J., a consistent admirer of the British rules of contempt, held unconstitutional proceedings initiated in Florida when a newspaper published articles criticizing a judge for undue sensitivity to defendants accused of rape;[31] only comment affecting a *pending* decision could properly be proscribed without violating the First Amendment. American judges just do not accept the argument that public confidence in their authority and in the fair administration of justice will necessarily be shaken by hostile comment. It is the truth of the comment, not the mere fact that it is made, which may undermine such confidence; and if the remarks are true, the public should certainly be allowed to digest them.

The offence of scandalizing the court is now so unimportant in practice that it may appear fruitless to spend much space in debating its justification. But it is possible that newspaper editors are occasionally deterred from vigorous comment because of a slight risk of prosecution. In theoretical terms criticism of the judiciary should almost certainly be treated as a form of political speech, and therefore enjoy the highest degree of legal protection. The difference here between the British and American approaches partly reflects divergent perceptions of the functions and importance of the courts; it is natural for a society which fully accepts the political role of the judiciary to tolerate the most abusive criticism of them. On the other hand, in Britain such criticism of the legislature and its members is equally subject to the contempt powers of the Houses of Parliament.[32] So another explanation for the position in

---

[29] *Nye* v. *US* 313 US 33 (1940).

[30] 314 US 252, 270–1 (1941).

[31] *Pennekamp* v. *Florida* 328 US 331, 365–9 (1946).

[32] The use of the contempt power to punish criticism of the Houses of Parliament and their members is surely wholly unjustified in any society which tries to take free speech seriously: see the arguments in chs. V and VI.

this country is that respect for established institutions is still thought more important a value than freedom of expression.

3. PREJUDICE TO CRIMINAL TRIALS

In this and the following section of the chapter, we move into deeper waters. While the offence of scandalizing the court can only be justified by reference to the public interest in the administration of justice—courts have often repudiated the idea that contempt proceedings may be brought to protect the dignity of the individual judge—proceedings to restrain or punish the publication of matter which prejudices a fair trial clearly raise possible conflicts between two fundamental individual rights. This is most obvious in the case of criminal prosecutions, where the life and liberty of the accused may well be at stake. Juries, now rarely used in Britain in civil cases, are a priori more likely to be prejudiced by damaging newspaper articles about the accused than are judges; connected with this point is the argument that to tolerate publication in the press of incriminating information is to make nonsense of the rules of evidence (more important in criminal than civil cases), designed to shut out testimony which is prejudicial rather than probative.[33] These relatively precise contentions, together with rather vaguer arguments about the undesirability of trial by the media and the necessity for public confidence in the administration of justice, are said to justify the rigorous common law rules of contempt in this area. Although British law, as will be seen, has been somewhat relaxed by the recent Contempt of Court Act 1981, the general tendency here and in other Commonwealth countries is to give clear preference to the fair trial interest over free speech. The United States adopts a radically different approach, apparently denying that the conflict of values is as acute as it appears or alternatively seeking to resolve it by other means. In any case, the right of free speech is almost always given priority.

Before discussing the law of contempt, brief mention may be made of another area in which press freedom is restricted in Britain to protect the interest of the accused: the ban on reporting committal proceedings. Following the notorious Adams trial in 1957, where the judge, Devlin J., had criticized the prosecution for leading evidence at the committal stage, which was not then tendered at the trial, a Departmental Committee

---

[33] See the discussion by the Canadian Law Reform Commission, Working Paper no. 20 (1977), 37.

under Lord Tucker was set up to report on the publicity of examining magistrates' proceedings.[34] Its recommendation that only the bare essentials, and not the full details of the evidence submitted to the magistrates, should be reported when an accused is committed for trial was eventually implemented in 1967.[35] The statutory ban in essence represents a legislative judgment that revelation of the evidence may well prejudice the trial; there is no need, as there is in contempt proceedings, to show any such tendency in the particular case. The ban is, therefore, quite independent from the law of contempt.[36] There can be little doubt that the statute would be unconstitutional in the United States. Whether viewed as a prior restraint or as an ordinary penal provision, it would be regarded as much too broad, prohibiting indiscriminately the publication of quite harmless as well as possibly damaging material. Nor would the Supreme Court be impressed by the argument that the ban only *postpones* publication of the evidence until after the end of the trial; it is not permissible under the First Amendment to restrain, however temporarily, information reaching the public unless there are compelling reasons for tolerating the ban.[37] Although at first controversial, the restriction does not trouble the press in Britain too much, because the vast majority of these preliminary proceedings are uncontested, and the defendant is then committed for trial on the basis of written evidence.

The British common law of contempt, as the author of a leading textbook on the subject has pointed out, is concerned with the potential effect of the publication on the subsequent trial.[38] It is irrelevant whether it actually did prejudice the jury against the accused (or for or against one of the parties in a civil case). This concern is inevitable, of course, if the law is to intervene successfully before the trial has taken place; the court hearing the contempt proceedings at that stage can only estimate the likely or possible repercussions of the publication. But though the general approach may be understandable, its application in practice has not always been easy to support. Thus, in the *Thomson Newspapers* case,[39] the

---

[34] Report of the Committee on Examining Justices (1958), Cmnd. 479, especially paras. 41–3.

[35] Criminal Justice Act 1967, s. 3, now Magistrates' Courts Act 1980, s. 8.

[36] The relationship between the particular restrictions on reporting committal proceedings and the general powers of all courts to order a postponement of reporting under the Contempt of Court Act 1981, s. 4(s) was considered in *R. v. Horsham JJ, ex parte Farquharson* [1982] QB 762 (CA).

[37] See above, ch. IV, especially s. 1.

[38] See C. J. Miller, *Contempt of Court* (London, 1976), 70–1, 90–1. The discussion of many topics in this chapter is much indebted to this book.

[39] *R. v. Thomson Newspapers, ex parte Att.-Gen.* [1968] 1 WLR 1 (DC).

Sunday Times published an article about Michael Malik, the leader of a militant black organization, facing prosecution under the Race Relations legislation; it said nothing about the specific charges, but described him in a generally unflattering way and in such a manner that a link could be drawn between the article and the prosecution. The Divisional Court held that this was likely to prejudice a fair trial, and the publishers were found liable for contempt, although there was no evidence that they had been reckless, let alone that they had intended to prejudice the criminal proceedings. The Court, moreover, did not indicate why prejudice was likely in view both of the interval of time before the trial and the fact that the jury would be directed by the trial judge to consider their verdict on the evidence. If there was a good case for restricting free speech here (and it can be said that the article on Malik was of some considerable public interest), the Divisional Court did not substantiate it.

What must seem peculiar about the British approach, at least to an American observer, is that while the courts are willing to hold that prejudice is likely to result from a pre-trial publication, they are reluctant to rule that such a publication does actually prejudice the jury if the accused appeals against his conviction. So, Malik's appeal was rejected by the Court of Appeal because, it found, the evidence was so overwhelming that no prejudice could have affected the result.[40] In the *Savundranayagan* case,[41] the Court of Appeal came to the same conclusion, primarily because the trial took place a long time after the sensational television interview with the appellant (conducted when it was very much on the cards that he would be charged with insurance fraud). Salmon LJ here interestingly emphasized the importance of a free press and investigative journalism, but he also drew attention to the dangers of trial by television, a matter discussed later in the chapter. Admittedly, there is no logical contradiction between a ruling that a publication or interview is likely to prejudice a trial and a subsequent decision that it did not; in the light of these cases, it is surely difficult for a court to assert categorically that this sort of material necessarily influences juries and so must be penalized as a contempt.

British case-law does not stand alone in giving priority to the interests of a fair trial, particularly in criminal cases. The common law throughout the Commonwealth adopts the same approach, differing only in details, such as whether a contempt may be committed by an article published

---

[40] *R. v. Malik* [1968] 1 WLR 353 (CA).
[41] *R. v. Savundranayagan* [1968] 1 WLR 1761 (CA).

before the arrest or charge of a suspect.[42] Since 1958 the French Penal Code has contained a provision to similar effect; its introduction according to one commentator was influenced by British law.[43] It seems clear in all these jurisdictions that contempt may also be committed by a publication which had a definite tendency to prejudice a *judge* deciding a point of law or the sentence, or an appellate court.[44] Thus, in a New Zealand case,[45] contempt was found when a newspaper published an editorial, demanding that someone convicted of indecent assault 'should meet with the utmost rigour of the law when he comes up for sentence', a conclusion which sharply contrasts with the leading American case to be discussed shortly.

British law has recently been modified by the Contempt of Court Act 1981. This particular variety of contempt will now only be committed by a publication 'which creates a substantial risk that the course of justice in the proceedings in question will be seriously impeded or prejudiced',[46] an apparently more favourable rule to the press than the previous 'likely to prejudice' test. In fact the new formula, in essence that suggested by the Phillimore Committee, does not represent a radical improvement. In the only case concerned with the section to reach the House of Lords so far, Lord Diplock said that it was designed only to exclude remote risks of prejudice to a fair trial.[47] It might have been thought that the reform confined contempt to seriously damaging and incriminating publications, but Lord Diplock's interpretation, based on the understandable view that any prejudice to the accused is 'as serious as anything can be', indicates that this goal has not been achieved. What this may show is that it is difficult to formulate a satisfactory balancing test—that is, a test which requires the court to assess the seriousness of a harm before restricting free speech—in this indirect way.

---

[42] For example, in *R.* v. *Beaverbrook Newspapers* [1962] NI 15, the Northern Ireland High Court held the publication of an article about someone two days before he was arrested and charged with murder was a contempt, while in *James* v. *Robinson* (1963) 109 CLR 593, the High Court reached the opposite conclusion on similar facts. In Britain a contempt may now only be committed from the time an arrest has been made or a warrant for arrest has been issued: Contempt of Court Act 1981, Sch.1, para. 4, and see C J. Miller [1982] *Crim. LR* 71, 75.

[43] A. Vitu, 'Atteintes à l'autorité de la justice', 2 *Juris-Classeur Penal*, commentary on arts. 226–7.

[44] For example, *Re Truth and Sportsman Ltd* (1958) 61 SR (NSW) 484 (Sup. Ct. of NWS), and see the more cautious approach of the English Divisional Court in *R.* v. *Duffy ex parte Nash* [1960] 2 QB 188.

[45] *Att.-Gen.* v. *Tonks* [1939] NZLR 533.

[46] Contempt of Court Act 1981, s. 2(2).

[47] *Att.-Gen.* v. *English* [1983] 1 AC 116, 142.

Another major reform in the Contempt of Court Act 1981 offers more hope of protection for the press. Section 5 provides that a publication which forms part of a bona fide discussion of public affairs is not to be treated as a contempt if the risk of prejudice to particular legal proceedings is merely incidental to the discussion. Thus, in the *English* case,[48] the House of Lords held that an article endorsing the candidature at a by-election of a 'pro-life' candidate and implying that the tendency of modern medicine is to terminate the life of babies born with mental or physical handicaps did not amount to a contempt, when it was published during the trial of a doctor on a charge of murdering a mongoloid boy. What is particularly important is that Lord Diplock rejected the argument that, as the article could have omitted the prejudicial passages without losing its effectiveness, the protection of the section was forfeited; the test was not whether it was necessary to run the risk of prejudice, but whether the risk was incidental to the wider discussion of mercy killing. However, there is a strong suggestion in his speech that if the trial of the doctor had been specifically mentioned in the article, it would not have enjoyed the protection of the section.[49] But surely the risk of prejudice would have been just as incidental to the public discussion, which would have taken on a sharper focus in that event? Only if the predominant purpose or effect of the publication is seriously to prejudice a fair trial, should freedom of speech give way.

Even with these improvements, British law remains radically different from the approach of the American judges. The Supreme Court has consistently applied the 'clear and present danger' test to contempt proceedings, with the result that comment on a pending case is generally constitutionally protected. So a newspaper editorial urging a sentence of imprisonment on union members who had been convicted of assaulting non-union employees was held to be protected speech, despite a strong dissent by Frankfurter J.[50] Although prejudicial comment before a grand jury investigation has similarly been held protected by the First Amendment, there has, it seems, been no Supreme Court ruling on such comment published immediately before or during a jury trial.[51] But it is clear from a recent decision that a prior restraint, forbidding the press

---

[48] Ibid.

[49] Ibid., 143.

[50] *Bridges* v. *California* 314 US 252 (1941).

[51] *Wood* v. *Georgia* 370 US 375 (1962), a grand jury investigation. There is some state authority for extending the approach to jury trials, for example, *Baltimore Radio Show* v. *State* 67 A 2d. 497, 508–11 (Maryland CA, 1949). See the discussion in Z. Cowen, *Sir John Latham and Other Papers* (Oxford, 1965), 79–83.

and the media from disclosing details of an accused's confessions and incriminating statements to the police, will rarely, if ever, be countenanced.[52] Giving the Supreme Court's unanimous judgment, Burger CJ denied that pre-trial publicity, even of an adverse and pervasive character, necessarily led to an unfair trial. Without strong evidence that a jury would be prejudiced, conclusions about the impact on jurors of such publicity were merely speculative. Moreover, before issuing a 'gag order', a court should consider other alternative ways of protecting the defendant's rights, which would not interfere with freedom of the press: postponement of the trial, changing its venue, or screening of jurors to determine whether they were influenced by the pre-trial publicity. Although the question remains open whether a penal sanction for an already published article would be constitutional on similar facts, the stronger argument is surely that it would be treated in much the same way as a prior restraint. As has been contended in Chapter IV, it is far from clear why the latter remedy should in these circumstances be treated differently from a criminal prosecution.[53]

There is another striking contrast with the common law, at least as developed in Britain. The Supreme Court is willing on occasion to strike down a conviction for violation of the Due Process Clause of the Fourteenth Amendment, where the trial has been accompanied or preceded by significant prejudicial publicity. The best-known applications of this principle occurred in the two television trial cases, *Estes* v. *Texas*[54] and *Sheppard* v. *Maxwell*,[55] where there had been saturation coverage, which was held to have harassed the conduct of the defence and to have inevitably prejudiced the jury. A strong dissent by Stewart J. in the former case (where the evidence of prejudice on the facts was much thinner than in the latter) did point out the indirect impact this ruling might have on the exercise by the press of its First Amendment rights; and it is now established that there is no absolute ban on broadcast coverage of a criminal trial merely because there is a risk the jury will be prejudiced.[56] The position may therefore be the very opposite of that which prevails in Britain: the courts cannot use the contempt power to restrain or (probably) punish prejudicial statements, but are more ready than the British courts appear to be to reverse the criminal conviction. A

---

[52] *Nebraska Press Assoc.* v. *Stuart* 427 US 539 (1976).
[53] See above, ch. IV, s. 4.
[54] 381 US 532 (1965).
[55] 384 US 333 (1966).
[56] *Chandler* v. *Florida* 449 US 560 (1981).

leading commentary on the law in this country understandably prefers the common law approach,[57] but this choice is hard to reconcile with any serious commitment to freedom of speech.

The American position is not without its critics. Frankfurter J., generally in dissent, preferred the more pragmatic British rule.[58] This may be partly attributable to his general hesitation in applying the Bill of Rights against state decisions; the state judge was also in his view in a better position than the Supreme Court to determine what was necessary to ensure the proper administration of justice. But he was also more sceptical than his colleagues about the ability of the judiciary, let alone jurors, to resist media pressure. Other commentators have doubted the adequacy of the alternative steps which can be taken to insulate juries from prejudicial publicity.[59] In a country like England, which has a national press and is much smaller than many American states, moving the venue of a trial would be an inadequate safeguard. To postpone the trial while publicity dies down might be to prescribe a remedy more harmful than the disease. Lawyers on both sides of the Atlantic also share an instinctive horror of 'trial by newspaper', which probably goes beyond any fear of prejudice to the interests of the accused. Why this is so, and whether the horror is justified, will be discussed in section 4.

4. PREJUDICE TO CIVIL TRIALS

In civil cases in Britain, trial by jury is now very rare. Moreover, the personal liberty of the parties is not at stake. Some of the reasons for preferring the interests of a fair trial over those of free speech therefore do not apply, or at any rate apply so strongly in these cases as they do in criminal prosecutions. Despite this, in the famous *Sunday Times* case,[60] the House of Lords unanimously held that a newspaper article, assessing some of the issues in a pending (though dormant) negligence action against Distillers for the deformities caused by its thalidomide drug, constituted a contempt of court. This was primarily on the ground that it purported to prejudge the questions which would come before the trial

---

[57] Miller, *Contempt of Court*, 92.

[58] For example, see *Bridges* v. *California* 314 US 252, 294–5 (1941), and *State of Maryland* v. *Baltimore Radio Show* 338 US 912 (1950), where he appended a survey of the leading English cases to his opinion, concurring with some hesitation in the Court's denial of *certiorari* from a pro-free speech Maryland state decision, see n. 51 above.

[59] Donnelly and Goldfarb, 'Contempt by Publication in the United States', (1961) 24 MLR 239, 245–6.

[60] *Att.-Gen.* v. *Times Newspapers* [1974] AC 273.

court. Subsequently this ruling was held by the European Court to be a breach of Article 10 of the Convention,[61] and British law has accordingly been amended. There has been some debate whether the technical changes made by the Contempt of Court Act 1981—in particular, the rule that there may only be a contempt if the proceedings prejudiced are *active*, that is, in civil cases, set down for trial—adequately meet the requirements of the European Court's ruling. The more interesting question remains, however, whether there was anything really to justify the House of Lords decision.

The point of law was one on which there was very little authority. Some of the members of the House admitted that there was no real risk of the article influencing the tribunal, a High Court judge, or the witnesses, so that conventional 'prejudice' arguments would be irrelevant. Lords Diplock and Simon found it was a contempt to put pressure on a party to litigation to settle to the other's advantage, particularly where the pressure took the form of a press campaign which held that party up to obloquy and abuse. This principle was perhaps only repudiated by Lord Cross, but at any rate the majority ground for the decision was that the offending article would lead to public prejudgment of the negligence issue. In other words, trial by newspaper as such was proscribed. Some of the Law Lords tried to find rational justifications for what they intuitively felt to be the right result. In their view, trial by the media would lead to disrespect for the law; the functions of the courts would be usurped by newspapers and television; unpopular people and causes would fare badly if there were widespead press campaigns. Lord Morris preferred rhetoric: '. . . is it not contrary to the fitness of things that there should be unrestricted expressions of opinion as to whether the merits lie with one party to litigation rather than with another?'[62]

One or two of these arguments would appear on examination to collapse into the 'prejudice to a fair trial' justification, which is very hard to support in the context of a civil case, or the 'pressure principle', which was only openly advocated by two members of the House. Moreover, the view that the press is usurping the functions of the courts does not seem easy to sustain. The typical newspaper campaign will employ a range of moral and social, as well as legal, arguments and will rarely attempt to formulate conclusions of pure law, in which the public would generally not be very interested. The campaign against Distillers was as much directed to the moral issues as it was designed to draw attention to

---

[61] *Sunday Times* v. *United Kingdom* (1979) 2 EHRR 245.
[62] [1974] AC 273, 303.

questions of legal responsibility. And the press cannot make a legally binding award, so in this precise sense the functions of the courts cannot be usurped. There are perhaps two better arguments, touched on in one or two of the speeches, but never fully developed. The first is that in the long term trial by newspaper will undermine the authority of the judiciary, and the second is that parties have some sort of right to a dispassionate assessment of their litigation, wholly free from public discussion. I will take the latter of these arguments first.

Lord Diplock refers in his speech to the litigants' 'constitutional right to have their legal rights and obligations ascertained and enforced in courts of law'; the exercise of this right would be inhibited by public discussion of the merits of the case before the court pronounced on them.[63] To some extent this seems to be just another way of putting the case that there is a possible prejudice to a fair trial and a risk that the court's functions will be usurped, points which have already been found unconvincing. Alternatively, Lord Diplock might have had in mind some sort of independent right of access to the courts. But this also does not work. For a start there is no more a *constitutional* right in Britain to have legal rights determined by courts of law than there is such a right to free speech; more pertinently, it is far from clear how such a 'right' would be invaded by press discussion of the legal and moral issues involved in the case.

This leaves the argument based on protecting the authority of the judiciary, which formed the central theme of Lord Reid's speech and which also was the justification for the ruling canvassed before the European Court in Strasbourg. Public confidence in the administration of justice, and resort to the courts, might well, it is claimed, decline if it came to be believed that they were influenced by press campaigns. Ultimately it could be that people would use the media rather than the legal process to resolve their disputes. Perhaps this should not be dismissed as absolutely far-fetched. But the prospect is fortunately as unlikely as it is uninviting. The press has no inclination to take up more than a handful of causes, and in any case, as has just been pointed out, it cannot do more than persuade. The public will always have recourse to the courts when it believes it can obtain a coercive order reasonably promptly. In fact the very reason why the *Sunday Times* did wage a press campaign over the thalidomide affair, and why it was surely right to do so, was that recourse to the courts had already proved to be futile; in some of the cases, the writs in the negligence actions had been issued

[63] Ibid., 310.

several years before the offending article was written and there was no immediate prospect of a satisfactory settlement or a trial of these cases. For this reason, as well as the intense public interest in the saga, the *Sunday Times* case was an unfortunate one in which to invoke, as Lord Cross did, an absolute contempt rule, applicable no matter how remote the risk of prejudice, for the purpose of preventing 'a gradual slide towards trial by newspaper or television'.[64]

The conclusion which emerges from these paragraphs is that it is very hard to see any coherent justification for treating as a contempt of court an article prejudging issues in a forthcoming civil case. No important public interest seems to be served by the imposition of penal sanctions, let alone the issue of a prior restraint as in the *Sunday Times* case itself. If this is so, then we do not in this context even have to resolve the theoretical question whether it could ever be right to restrict free speech in order to achieve one of the aims supposedly pursued by the use of the contempt process. The question would only arise in practice if it were true that a number of press campaigns did undermine the authority of the courts; then, but only then, would it have to be decided whether it was right to give priority to the dissemination of information and opinion on matters of public interest or to the maintenance of confidence in the judiciary. The issue then would appear to be somewhat similar to that raised in the context of scandalizing the court; commitment to free speech would surely dictate its protection against the interests of established institutions and confidence in their processes. Further, one valuable function of the type of campaign that was conducted by the *Sunday Times* is to test public opinion concerning the quality of the legal process. Unless it can be shown that such a campaign does create a substantial risk of prejudicing a fair trial, there is no warrant for the use of contempt proceedings.[65]

This is in fact a more radical conclusion than that arrived at by the European Court. Article 10(2) of the Convention provides that the exercise of free expression may be subject to such restrictions 'as are prescribed by law and are necessary in a democratic society ... for maintaining the authority and impartiality of the judiciary'. With some hesitation the Court majority held that the common law of England

---

[64] Ibid., 323.

[65] This is now the position under the Contempt of Court Act 1981, s. 2(2), but it remains to be seen how the courts will apply this test in civil cases. The result in the *Sunday Times* case would now be different, because of the requirement that proceedings must be 'active', i.e. arrangements for the hearing must have been made, for the 'strict liability' rule to apply: see Contempt of Court Act 1981, s. 1(3) and Sch. 1, para. 12.

before the Lords' decision was sufficiently well established to satisfy the first condition, 'prescribed by law'. The Court then considered whether the House of Lords ruling had aims which fell within Article 10(2). It was not even argued that it could be justified in terms of maintaining the *impartiality* of the judiciary. But the Strasbourg judges did conclude that the ruling had the proper aim of maintaining judicial *authority* for the reasons given by the Lords and discussed in the preceding paragraphs. The wording of Article 10(2) does, of course, compel the Court to rule that it may in some circumstances be proper to restrict free speech to maintain the authority of the judiciary. It may be that it could not envisage circumstances, other than those which arose in the case, in which this aim would justify press restrictions. If so, the Court's approach was necessary to give the provision some content. I would suggest, however, that a press campaign urging refusal to comply with a court's judgment would be a much more appropriate occasion for applying this limb of Article 10(2).

However, this concession to the British government's argument was then virtually withdrawn in the third stage of the Court's reasoning. The majority held that the injunction restraining publication of the article was not in the circumstances *necessary* to preserve the authority of the judges. In view of the legitimate public interest in the thalidomide compensation controversy and the contemporaneous public (and Parliamentary) debate it had occasioned, the injunction which restrained in broad terms any public prejudgment of the legal issues was disproportionate to the aim. It did not satisfy a 'pressing social need'. Moreover, an absolute rule against trial by newspaper could not possibly be sustained, for it was inimical to the careful factual balancing required by the European Court. The Court's decision was by the slender majority of 11–9, and some of the minority arguments are relatively persuasive. In particular it is not easy to justify the Court's greater willingness to assess the reasonableness of the restriction in this case than in the earlier *Handyside* decision.[66] There is also much to be said for the minority's opinion that some discretion should be left to the national judges to determine whether a particular publication is likely to interfere with the administration of justice in that country, an outlook which echoes some of Frankfurter J.'s doubts about the wisdom of Supreme Court review of state decisions. These points perhaps reinforce the argument that it might have been better for the Court to hold that the aim of 'maintaining the judiciary's authority' was

[66] See below, ch. IX, s. 4.

wholly irrelevant. It could have reached that conclusion by construction of the Article, and so avoided review of the particular facts.

Despite these criticisms, the European Court's ruling should be recognised as a major contribution to the international jurisprudence of free speech. The majority judgment shows strong appreciation of the positive value of public discussion of issues relating to the administration of justice, a dimension of the *Sunday Times* case virtually ignored by the House of Lords. Emphasis was placed on the public's right to *receive* information, as much as on the media's responsibility to keep it informed. The Strasbourg judges pointed out that they did not have to balance two equal competing public interests: free speech and a fair trial. Article 10 enunciates a principle of free expression which is subject to narrow limitations. In that context, the absolute rule enunciated by the House of Lords, giving priority to the maintenance of judicial authority by banning any prejudgment of issues likely to come to court, could not possibly be sustained. Nor did the Court accept the argument that, while general discussion of the wide legal and moral issues was acceptable, comment on the liability of Distillers in the particular circumstances must be restrained; this distinction was artificial in a situation which had aroused such legitimate public interest. In so far as it is legitimate for a supra-national court to engage in such fine balancing, the task could not have been more sensitively discharged.

The question so strangely ignored in the *Sunday Times* case remains: can a contempt or other comparable law be justified in terms of preserving the *impartiality* of a judge, arbitrator, or other members of a tribunal. It is almost accepted as axiomatic that a judge cannot be prejudiced by pre-trial publicity. The Salmon Committee on the law of contempt as affecting Tribunals of Inquiry (which are composed of lay members with a High Court judge as chairman) regarded the risk of improper influence as minimal.[67] It is indeed most unlikely that a judge would be consciously swayed by any press campaign. But this may not be the point. Judges are as much subject as anyone to unconscious pressures, which may be created or reinforced by press publicity.[68] This is part of the teaching of the American Realist school of jurists. Of course, it does not logically follow from this assumption that it is right to restrict

---

[67] Report of the Interdepartmental Committee on the Law of Contempt as it affects Tribunals of Inquiry (1969), Cmnd. 4078, paras, 26–8.
[68] See Frankfurter J. in *Pennekamp* v. *Florida* 328 US 331, 357 (1946). The fact that in the USA many state judges are elected for short periods, rather than appointed for life, reinforces the point in the text.

media discussion of legal issues. It might be better to allow the fullest public debate, if only to counteract the private influence to which (on a Realist view) a judge will inevitably be subject from fellow lawyers and his social background. We are here in a world of psychological conjecture, which could perhaps be the subject of rational investigation. But until that produces results, it is probably better to protect free speech, and for civil cases that means absolute protection for pre-trial comment.

5. A RIGHT OF ACCESS TO THE COURTS

Recent American cases have raised the question whether there is a right of access on the part of the press or public to attend trials as an integral aspect of the freedom of speech. It hardly needs saying that the issue has rarely been discussed in these theoretical terms in Britain. But the common law has usually been hostile to the secret administration of justice behind closed doors. In the leading House of Lords decision, *Scott* v. *Scott*,[69] the principle was variously grounded on general arguments of liberty and on the policy that it is in the public interest to expose the workings of the courts to critical scrutiny. To insist on open proceedings is in the interests of justice, at least in the vast majority of cases.

It is here that theoretical questions may become practically important. If the justification for the general requirement of open trials is that this is conducive to the fair administration of justice, the rejoinder can be, and has been, made that in some cases the administration of justice requires rather that the proceedings be closed. This may be for a variety of reasons: witnesses may be embarrassed to give evidence in open court; the parties may be reluctant to pursue proceedings in certain types of litigation, particularly concerning family matters, if they are exposed to public gaze; the disclosure of evidence may destroy the whole point of the action, as in a trade secrets case. Alternatively, the interests of justice may have to give place to other matters of public concern, for example, national security or secrecy of defence installations. Thus, prosecutions for breach of the official secrets legislation or treason are sometimes heard wholly or partly in camera.[70] But as in other areas of free speech law, these balancing arguments may be less powerful if it can be successfully contended that a right of access to the courts necessarily flows from, or is in some way related to, the freedom of speech, which outweighs all but

---

[69] [1913] AC 417.
[70] For example, under Official Secrets Act 1920, s. 8(4).

the most compelling competing interests. If the press and other media have a right to communicate reports of legal proceedings, at least fair and accurate accounts, and the public has corresponding rights to be informed, these rights would be effectively rendered worthless if justice were frequently conducted behind closed doors.

In fact the legislatures and courts in both Britain and the United States often try to keep the two issues distinct. It does not follow from the fact that proceedings are legitimately conducted in camera that the press should not be free to publish a report of these proceedings. This is particularly true if it is published much later on the basis of information which has been acquired lawfully.[71] Conversely the press (and public) may be able to attend certain proceedings, the reporting of which is forbidden, at least for some time. But it is plausible nevertheless to claim that in most circumstances there is a close link between freedom of speech and the asserted right to attend judicial proceedings.

The arguments here have some similarity to those canvassed in Chapter III in the context of alleged rights of access to government information, the 'right to know'.[72] As in those situations, a right of access to the courts may conflict with the interests of other persons, in particular in this area the right to a fair trial or to preserve the confidentiality of trade secrets. There may also be theoretical difficulties concerned with the 'speech–conduct' distinction. Could it not be said, for example, that a claimed right to draw pictures or to take photographs of proceedings involves some element of 'conduct' in that a disturbance is created, quite separate from any harm entailed by the acquisition of information? Some members of the Supreme Court have argued that historically the court-room has been seen as a place which the public should be free to attend,[73] but it has been pointed out that there is no obvious reason why that custom should give rise to a legally protected right.[74] On the other hand, while in the case of government information, for example, concerning prison conditions, the political process is an alternative method for the acquisition and dissemination of knowledge, there is no such alternative to a right of access to the judicial process. The point is simply that the courts are not politically responsible. Moreover, the principal argument against recognition of rights of access to government information under a

---

[71] See below, p. 240.

[72] See above, ch. III, s. 5.

[73] *Richmond Newspapers* v. *Virginia* 448 US 555 (1980).

[74] R. M. Dworkin, 'Is the Press losing the First Amendment?', *New York Review of Books*, 4 Dec 1980, 49, 53.

free speech clause, that it would compel an unwilling speaker to disclose information, may not apply to an alleged right to attend trials. The accused may be perfectly willing to give his evidence in public (and for it to be fully reported), while only the government may oppose this. In that case there is a restraint on communication between parties who wish to transmit and receive information. It may finally be added that the courts themselves will find it easier to formulate this right of access than they will a general 'right to know'; this may be one reason why on both sides of the Atlantic they have been less willing to leave the area entirely to legislative regulation.

Closely connected with the argument whether a right of access to the courts can be asserted as a reasonable implication of a right to free speech is the question whether we are concerned here with individual freedoms or a special privilege of the press. While every individual, on a right-based thesis of free speech, has an equal right to exercise his freedom to say and write what he thinks, it cannot seriously be argued from this that he has a similar right to attend any trial. It would be quite impracticable for everyone to exercise such a right, and the theoretical basis for such rights-based theories—the equal entitlement of each individual to self-fulfilment—hardly justifies a right of access. But if the special protection afforded free speech and freedom of the press rests largely on the need for an informed citizenry in a participatory democracy, the case for conferring some special privileges on the press is strong. And among these privileges might be a right of access to attend courts. The case can alternatively be based on the separately protected 'freedom of the press', as it has been in Germany. The Constitutional Court has upheld a right of the press, exercisable by the editor or the paper's employees, to attend criminal trials, free from arbitrary exclusion.[75] The right to obtain information about the judicial process is necessary to enable the press to discharge its special responsibilities, though its exercise may be limited under Article 5(2) of the Basic Law, for example, in order to preserve good order in the court-room.[76]

But as Dworkin has pointed out, in so far as this case is utilitarian, it has the weakness that it may be balanced by the various policies which militate on occasion for closed hearings. These might quite frequently outweigh the policy argument for keeping trials open to the public and its representative, the press. For it is far from clear just how crucial it is to

---

[75] 50 BVerfGE 234 (1979).

[76] Ibid., 241–2. This right of access does however qualify the judge's freedom of action: see I. von Münch, *Grundgesetz-Kommentar* (Munich, 1980), vol. 1, 252–3.

know the detailed workings of the judicial process in every individual case, particularly when the parties (or in a criminal case, the accused) request proceedings in camera. Moreover, as Dworkin further argues, it is quite coherent for an informed democracy to tolerate trials behind closed doors whenever the parties consent and the judge permits under it clear rules. If anyone doubts that, he should consider the increasing use of arbitration, conducted in private and with no reporting of the proceedings, in Britain and other European countries.

Despite these theoretical reservations, it remains true that both the British and American legal systems are generally committed to open justice as a matter of fundamental principle. This is hardly surprising in the latter, but the traditional enthusiasm of the common law for the rule is a little strange in view of the attitude of the British courts in the areas of contempt law discussed earlier in this chapter. *Scott* v. *Scott*, decided by the Lords in 1913, is still the leading case; it was held that the High Court had no power, even if the parties requested it, to hear a nullity or other family suit in camera because of the embarrassing or indecent nature of the evidence. The Lords were only prepared to countenance a few exceptions to the general rule of open justice: wardship and lunatic cases, where the court's jurisdiction was administrative rather than judicial, and trade secrets litigation. Lord Loreburn considered that a hearing might be conducted in private where otherwise parties would reasonably be deterred from coming to court,[77] but this suggestion was not supported by other members of the House and has since been held to be wrong.[78] Though the principle enunciated in the case remains good, the actual result in *Scott* was subsequently reversed by legislation,[79] and there are now a number of statutory provisions requiring or enabling courts to conduct proceedings in private.

Many of these provisions govern magistrates' courts. When hearing committal proceedings, they must sit in open court (in the absence of a specific legislative rule to the contrary) unless they consider that the ends of justice would not be served by this.[80] Members of the public are not entitled to be present during domestic proceedings, e.g. affiliation and custody disputes, though the press do have a right to attend, subject to

[77] [1913] AC 417, 446.
[78] *B(orwise. P)* v. *Att.-Gen.* [1967] P. 119. The approval here of a rule which may have the effect of inhibiting parties from coming to court contrasts with the support for the 'pressure principle' of two members of the Lords in the *Sunday Times* case: above, s. 4 of this chapter.
[79] See now Matrimonial Causes Act 1973, s. 48(2).
[80] Magistrates' Courts Act 1980, s. 4(2).

the discretion of the magistrates to exclude them during the taking of indecent evidence if this is necessary in the interests of administration of justice or public decency.[81] There are similar provisions for juvenile court proceedings.[82] The High Court may sit in camera for cases under the Defence Contracts Act 1958, and, following recommendations in a Law Commission Report,[83] for legitimacy proceedings.[84] Further the public may not attend the hearing when a judge hears a case or application in chambers, as he may properly do in a variety of cases under the Rules of Court.

As already mentioned, it does not follow from the fact that a hearing is conducted in private, that there is no right to publish a report of these proceedings. In *Scott* itself, the Lords ruled that even if the nullity case had been rightly heard in camera, a subsequent report of the case would not necessarily constitute a contempt. Freedom to publish might be asserted not only by the press, but by one of the parties, seeking to correct a damaging impression created by the proceedings. On the other hand it would undermine the confidentiality of a hearing conducted in public if the press were free to report it simultaneously or very shortly after it was terminated. To some extent the law has been clarified by the Administration of Justice Act 1960, section 12 of which provides that: 'The publication of information relating to proceedings before any courts sitting in private shall not of itself be contempt of court', except in a number of specified cases, including wardship and adoption proceedings, trade secrets litigation, and cases where the court has sat in private for security reasons. The courts have refused to hold that these provisions enable contempt proceedings to be taken in respect of such publications where they could not have been under the common law, and in the leading case, the Court of Appeal ruled that it must be proved the press was aware its publication related to the private proceedings.[85] The judgments contained ringing declarations of the importance of a free press, and the undesirability of placing more restrictions on newspaper reporting than the strict wording of the Act justified.

There are also a number of circumstances where it is forbidden to publish reports of proceedings conducted *in public*, or to publish particulars other than the names of the parties, legal submissions, and

---

[81] Ibid., ss. 69(2) and (4).

[82] Children and Young Persons Act 1933, ss. 37 and 47(2).

[83] Report on the Powers of Appeal Courts to sit in Private and the Restrictions upon Publicity in Domestic Proceedings (1966), Cmnd. 3149.

[84] Matrimonial Causes Act 1973, s. 45(9).

[85] *In re F(orwise. A) (Publication of information)* [1977] Fam. 58 (CA).

rulings.[86] Sometimes an order may be made to postpone publication, as in the case of committal proceedings, an issue already discussed in section 2 of the chapter. The courts' powers to order such postponement have been radically increased by a controversial provision in the Contempt of Court Act 1981; under this an order may be made to avoid a substantial risk of prejudice to the administration of justice in the particular proceedings, or any other pending or imminent proceedings, and it may operate for the period the court thinks necessary to achieve this end.[87] The merits of these provisions, which would almost certainly be unconstitutional under the First Amendment, are not directly in issue here. They constitute prior restraints of a scope which is hard to justify. What is interesting is that they reinforce the point that, at any rate as a matter of existing British law, there is no necessary overlap between freedom of speech and access of the public to the courts. In these cases there are restrictions on the reporting of proceedings which are open to the press and members of the public, while in other situations a court may hear a case (or part of it) in private, but a subsequent report will not necessarily constitute a contempt. In *Att.-Gen.* v. *Leveller Magazine Ltd*,[88] the House of Lords held that the publication of the name of a witness who had given evidence to magistrates anonymously was not a contempt, as in the circumstances there was no evidence that the disclosure threatened the administration of justice; the Law Lords emphasized that it was not a contempt to publish details of a private hearing (or the name of a witness who had given evidence anonymously) merely because the publication violated a court order.

There are American cases which similarly reflect these distinctions. In *Landmark Communications* v. *Virginia*,[89] the Court unanimously invalidated a statute making it a crime to publish details of confidential proceedings before a state judicial review commission which heard complaints about members of the judiciary. The newspaper there published an accurate report on pending proceedings, identifying a particular judge. The Court agreed that confidentiality of such proceedings served legitimate state interests, but held the penal sanctions against third parties went further than necessary to protect them. Internal procedures to safeguard confidentiality should have been adequate. So here it is clear that while the press might properly be denied access, it

---

[86] Miller, *Contempt of Court*, 209–13.
[87] Contempt of Court Act 1981, s. 4(2).
[88] [1979] AC 440. See now Contempt of Court Act 1981, s. 11.
[89] 435 US 829 (1978).

could not constitutionally be punished for publishing information it had acquired. The same result has been reached in other cases involving the disclosure of the names of rape victims and juvenile offenders.[90] Two qualifications, however, should be entered. The first is that Stewart J. at least would base his concurrence in these rulings on the freedom of the press limb of the First Amendment. The second proviso is that the Courts' rulings do not in terms extend to protect the publication of information which has been *unlawfully* acquired. Suppose a journalist obtained admission to juvenile court proceedings by deceit, would (or should) his subsequent report be constitutionally immune from criminal sanction? Instinctively one may feel that a prosecution for publication would be appropriate here; on the other hand, the Court has said that the state's interest in rehabilitating juvenile offenders is not sufficiently substantial to justify penalties for such publication,[91] and it is difficult to see any basis for drawing a distinction between the communication of information which has been lawfully obtained and the communication of illegally obtained material.

The distinction between freedom to publish information which has already been acquired and a right of access to the court-room to acquire that information has been somewhat eroded now by the Supreme Court's decision in the *Richmond Newspapers* case.[92] In an earlier decision the majority of the Court had scrupulously refrained from determining whether there is a general First Amendment right to attend trials, when it refused to uphold a claimed right of access to a pre-trial judicial proceeding.[93] A bare majority of the Court had dismissed a newspaper's appeal from the trial judge's order excluding reporters from the proceedings; the parties had agreed that they should be closed in order to safeguard the accused's right to a fair trial. (The minority, however, had dissented on the basis of the Sixth Amendment's 'public trial' provision which was believed (rather oddly) to protect a right on the part of the *public* to attend trials as much as a right personal to the accused.) In the *Richmond* case the Court ruled, with only Rehnquist J. dissenting, that there is a First Amendment right of access to attend a criminal trial. The defendant had argued, without objection from the prosecution, that removal of the press was necessary to avoid irrelevant information being

---

[90] *Cox Broadcasting Corp.* v. *Cohn* 420 US 469 (1975); *Oklahoma Publishing Co.* v. *District Court* 430 US 308 (1977); *Smith* v. *Daily Mail Publishing Co.* 443 US 97 (1979).

[91] *Smith* v. *Daily Mail Publishing Co.* 443 US 97 (1979).

[92] 448 US 555 (1980).

[93] *Gannett* v. *De Pasquale* 443 US 368 (1979).

communicated to the jury during the course of the trial, but the Court reasoned that other safeguards, for example, removal of the jury from the court-room while the admissibility of evidence was being argued, would have been appropriate.

The justifications for finding a right of access implicit in freedom of speech have already been touched on. With varying degrees of emphasis the members of the Court saw the right, together with other rights to acquire information, as an integral aspect of the First Amendment, the purpose of which is to ensure the working of a participatory democracy. The presence of the public, and most particularly the press, serves to restrain possible abuses of judicial power and maintain popular confidence in the administration of justice. Some of the detailed arguments are less than convincing. Attention has already been drawn to the weak historical point that traditionally the court-room has been open to the public. History may prove to be an uncertain guide. In a subsequent case a majority of the Court struck down a Massachusetts statute requiring judges to exclude the press and public from the court-room when a victim under 18 gave evidence at a trial for specified sexual offences.[94] The majority applied the principles formulated in the *Richmond* case, but Burger CJ dissented here on the ground that historical tradition did permit proceedings to be closed to the public when a minor victim is concerned. Another point made in the *Richmond* case in favour of access to the trial was that freedom of speech entails a freedom to listen;[95] but the latter freedom is surely quite different from a right of the public to attend trials so that *unwilling* speakers, e.g. the defendant or witnesses, are in effect compelled to divulge information to it.

The key question, however, is this: is there really any good argument for holding a right to attend trials implicit in the First Amendment, when the Supreme Court has consistently refused to recognize press rights to acquire and gather information from government departments or other public institutions?[96] In these other cases the same arguments about the importance of an informed electorate can be deployed, but they have not been found persuasive enough to extend the scope of freedom of speech. Doubts concerning the correctness of the *Richmond* decision are reinforced by the point that it will be impracticable for more than a few people to exercise this First Amendment right to attend trials. Of course,

---

[94] *Globe Newspaper* v. *Sup. Ct. of County of Norfolk* 102 S. Ct. 2613 (1982).
[95] 448 US 555, 576 (1980).
[96] See above, ch. III, s. 5.

I am not arguing here against the open administration of justice. There are obviously powerful public policy reasons for it, and the accused (or parties) may have a right to a public trial as an aspect of due process. But these are not free speech arguments.

IX

Obscenity

I. INTRODUCTION

THE legitimacy of legal controls on pornography has almost certainly elicited more academic commentary than any other topic covered in this book. This depressing phenomenon (to some) may reflect our abiding interest in anything connected with sex. It is also attributable to the exceptionally wide range of controversial questions necessarily raised in any consideration of reform of obscenity laws. Mercifully this chapter is not concerned with all the issues discussed by such bodies as the United States President's Commission on Obscenity and the British Committee chaired by Bernard Williams, both of which have relatively recently recommended the relaxation of legal controls, particularly on written publications.[1] Neither body found it easy to reconcile the suppression of pornography with the value placed by society on freedom of speech. However, this chapter will show that the application of free speech principles to obscenity law is far from straightforward.

A crucial threshold question is whether, or to what extent, pornography should be immune from legal control, because it is a form of 'speech'. In the United States and Germany this is a legal issue for determination by the courts. If a pornographic magazine is 'speech', then it is covered by the First Amendment or Article 5 of the Basic Law, and its publication and distribution can only properly be regulated if the state is able to adduce powerful reasons for this course. For Britain the relevance of the free speech principle to the control of obscenity is a matter for philosophical argument and political debate. The report of the Williams Committee, for example, discusses how far Mill's free speech theory is applicable to pornography. Resolution of the question does indeed require some reference to the arguments for free speech protection considered in Chapter I. Moreover, some of the observations made in Chapter II on the meaning of 'speech' may also be pertinent. But one or two further points should be made before these ideas are developed.

---

[1] Report of the United States Commission on Obscenity and Pornography (Washington, 1970); Report of the Committee on Obscenity and Film Censorship ('The Williams Committee') (1979) Cmnd. 7772.

To conclude that pornography is not 'speech' for the purposes of the First Amendment or other equivalent constitutional provision is not to say that it may legitimately be outlawed. There may be other relevant constitutional arguments. For example, claims may be made on the basis of a constitution's specific provision for freedom of artistic expression, or as in West Germany, 'the right to the free development of . . . personality'.[2] To some extent, arguments from these freedoms may only reinforce the case for immunity which can be made under the speech clause itself; this is most obviously true when the freedom of artistic expression is conferred by the same Article which protects political and social speech. But the more radical claims now frequently made to support a right to obtain and read pornography extend well beyond the limits of freedom of speech. For example, it has been urged that the suppression of pornography, including live sex shows, violates general rights of moral autonomy, or more specific rights to choose one's sexual life-style.[3] Hitherto, these rights have not been recognized legally; the Supreme Court has gone as far as upholding a privacy right to read pornography in one's own home, but later cases show a marked reluctance to extend this to other situations.[4] It may be that ultimately these wide arguments will be thought to provide a better basis for a legal right of access to all types of pornography than the free speech principle. But they are no concern of this book.

Unfortunately, some proponents of a broad interpretation of the First Amendment to cover all pornography seem to confuse legitimate free speech contentions with these general libertarian claims. For example, some commentators, and the President's Commission, have thought it incompatible with the United States Constitution to ban pornography merely because its distribution may in the long term lower the moral tone of the community.[5] This conclusion, however, may depend on one or

---

[2] See German Basic Law, art. 2. Art 5(3) provides for freedom of art and science, research and teaching, as aspects of freedom of expression.

[3] See in particular, R. M. Dworkin, 'Is There a Right to Pornography?' (1981) 1 *Oxford Jo. Legal Stud.* 177. For some relevant case-law, see the German *Homosexuality Case* 6 BVerfGE 389 (1957), *Doe et al.* v. *Commonwealth's Attorney* 403 F. Supp. 1199 (1975), and 7215/75, *X* v. *UK* 19 D. & R. 66, in all of which the existence of a legal right to engage in homosexual behaviour was denied.

[4] *Stanley* v. *Georgia* 394 US 557 (1969) upholds the right to read pornography in the home, but the Court has refused to recognize a privacy right to receive such material by post (*US* v. *Reidel* 402 US 351 (1971)) or to import it for personal use (*US* v. *12 200 Ft. Reels* 413 US 123 (1973)).

[5] For example, L. Henkin, 'Morals and the Constitution: The Sin of Obscenity' (1963) 63 *Col. LR* 391; J. Feinberg, 'Pornography and the Criminal Law' (1979) 40 *U. Pitts. LR* 567; Report of the US Commission, 55.

other of two different assumptions: that there is a broad constitutional right for individuals to take their own moral decisions or that material, no matter how obscene, is 'speech'. These two arguments must be kept clearly separate.

Another common confusion is that between the *constitutionality* and the *wisdom* of legislation to control pornography. A judicial ruling that 'obscenity' is not constitutionally protected should not be taken to advocate its regulation as a matter of policy.[6] The decision is simply left to the legislature. There are a number of good arguments against attempting to suppress sexually explicit material which have nothing to do with constitutional rights; obscenity laws are difficult to enforce, the task may distract the police from more pressing matters, and intervention does interfere with some personal liberties, even if these do not have constitutional status.

Conversely a conclusion that even hard-core pornography is entitled to benefit from an entrenched right to freedom of speech, or a policy presumption in its favour, does not exhaust the legal argument. The state is still entitled to restrict its availability, or even to ban it altogether, if there is some compelling reason for this step. Only absolutists would deny this. But assessing these reasons, and weighing them against freedom of speech, pose difficult problems for judges, and may involve them in the distasteful work of reading the publication in issue. If it is legitimate (and prudent) to ban pornography, the decision which particular books or films should be proscribed is much better left to juries under general guidance from the trial judge—or perhaps as in New Zealand to a specialist tribunal—rather than to the appellate courts.

An institutional consideration of this character seems to have persuaded the Supreme Court in the leading case, *Roth* v. *United States*,[7] to rule that obscenity is wholly outside the area of constitutionally protected speech. On this approach the majority of the Court thought there was then no need for it to assess whether the *particular* publication presented a clear and present danger of likely anti-social conduct, a delicate inquiry which might entail reference to the book and to complex empirical evidence. But Harlan J., dissenting, thought the Court could not so easily escape careful scrutiny of the facts. For the courts must not only determine whether 'obscenity' is or is not protected 'speech'—which may appear to be an issue of abstract constitutional law—but must also decide

---

[6] But see the argument that the refusal to strike down legislation necessarily legitimates it: A. Bickel, *The Least Dangerous Branch* (New York, 1962), 29–33.

[7] 354 US 476 (1957).

what is 'obscene'. It is wrong, therefore, to hope that courts can entirely evade reflection on the purpose and application of pornography statutes merely by treating 'obscenity' as outside the area of protected speech.

Although, therefore, its resolution does not remove all difficulties, it is still important to answer the threshold question. It affects both the weight of the consideration which should be given to freedom of speech, and the character of the institutions by which the factors are weighed. If the free speech principle is applicable to all types of pornography, then the legislature should be reluctant to control it (*a fortiori* to ban it altogether), while courts with powers of constitutional review must subject such legislation to careful inspection to see whether it invades the protected freedom. On the other hand, if some forms of hard-core pornography are not 'speech', the legislature does have greater freedom to act. A further point is that the definition of 'obscenity' which can sensibly be applied in a predictable and coherent way by a constitutional court may differ from the more flexible test which can be devised by legislation for application by juries. It is this complex mixture of theoretical and institutional considerations which makes comparisons in this area both fascinating and difficult.

2. IS OBSCENITY 'SPEECH'?

One answer to the question in the title denies that there is any real difficulty. Granted that 'speech' includes writing and other forms of permanent representation (such as films and tapes), there is no reason why pornographic publications should not be regarded as types of 'speech' for constitutional or legislative policy purposes. The only distinction which would have to be drawn on this approach is the familiar one between speech and conduct. In fact, the Supreme Court has adopted a relatively broad view of 'speech' in the context of this difference: nude dancing, for example, has been held protected by the First Amendment.[8] There would still be a number of borderline cases — live sex shows accompanied by a commentary might pose some legal problems — but hard-core verbal and pictorial pornography would enjoy full constitutional protection.

This is not the position, however, in the United States or in the vast majority of other liberal countries, where political speech is generally unregulated. The point is that 'speech' is not in a legal or constitutional context given its broad dictionary meaning, but is treated as a term of art.

---

[8] *Schad* v. *Boro. of Mt Ephraim* 452 US 61 (1981), discussed in s. 6 of this chapter.

Certain types of expression, which in a literal sense are 'speech', are not so regarded for the purpose of defining the area of legal protection. As stated in Chapter II, perjury and fraudulent advertising, for example, have never qualified for constitutional protection from regulation.[9] The scope of 'freedom of speech' can only be determined by looking at the reasons for its special constitutional position.

The justifications for according freedom of speech a degree of special constitutional protection were discussed in Chapter I. We saw there that there are some difficulties in basing a free speech principle on arguments concerning fundamental rights to self-fulfilment and self-development.[10] These claims are too wide to be of much assistance in establishing a case for freedom of speech, for they equally can be used to support other rights and liberties that may be asserted. A background right to dignity or personal moral autonomy might appear in this context to justify the formulation (or implication from the text) of constitutional rights to unregulated sexual behaviour as well as of rights to distribute or read pornography. If the rationale is unhelpful in justifying the case for a special free speech principle, it follows that it is useless for determining the meaning of 'speech'. Indeed it does not matter much on this argument whether pornography is characterized as 'speech' or not, for its consumption would be immune from regulation on broad libertarian grounds.

The two other arguments for the free speech principle also cause difficulties in this context. The argument from democracy is more obviously applicable to political and social speech than to erotic literature, which contains no information or ideas. Admittedly some such writing might implicitly assert views of a vague political character about society or individual relationships. But much hard-core pornography makes no attempt at all to appeal to the intellect or reason. Nor does it assert any proposition that might be true, so as to make Mill's free speech theory pertinent. The intention of its publishers, and its effect, is merely to create sexual excitement, to provide material for the indulgence of fantasy. Indeed, there appears little significant distinction between the impact of a picture magazine, depicting sexual intercourse in close detail, and that of a plastic sex aid or a visit from a prostitute. Now it may be

---

[9] See above, ch. II, s. 1, and F. Schauer, *Free Speech: A Philosophical Inquiry* (Cambridge, 1982), 92. The discussion in this section owes much to ch. 12 of Schauer's book and to his article, 'Speech and "Speech"—Obscenity and "Obscenity": An Exercise in the Interpretation of Constitutional Language' (1977) 61 *Georgetown LR* 899.

[10] See above, ch. I, s. 2(ii).

that the public availability of all three means of taking pleasure should be immune from legal regulation. But that is not a free speech argument. A pornographic picture magazine no more involves communication than these other two means for achieving sexual satisfaction.

Powerful though it is, a number of points may be made against this case. First, it is clear in the United States and many other jurisdictions that 'speech' is not confined to intellectual and political discourse, but also includes literature and the visual arts. Some constitutions expressly recognize a right to artistic expression as part of the broader freedom of expression.[11] Although the free speech argument from truth might suggest that 'speech' can only cover the enunciation of propositions that might be true or false (and some Supreme Court dicta tend to support this),[12] the scope of constitutional protection is much wider. So, if political opinions and protest ('Fuck the Draft') are within the First Amendment,[13] why not construe it also to cover hard-core pornography which similarly reveals no truths, but may be presented elegantly and artistically? The assumption underlying this point is questionable: that no line can be drawn between non-propositional literature or other imaginative discourse on the one hand, and the truly obscene on the other. At least one prominent modern literary critic would disagree with this: 'Writing conceived as art is in most ways the antithesis of pornography. It implies detachment, a rigorous exercise of the critical faculty, and the constant reference to observable realism.'[14] Literature does communicate ideas, or (to put it another way) does appeal to reason and the intellect; no matter how erotic its content, it should not be treated as 'obscene' and should be regarded as protected 'speech'. The various definitions of 'obscenity' discussed later in this chapter show how the courts in different countries have attempted to draw this distinction.

Another difficulty is, of course, that serious works of literature and films may be banned under laws which are aimed at hard-core pornography of no intellectual or other merit whatsoever. Prosecutions have been brought against such significant works as Joyce's *Ulysses* and Lawrence's *Lady Chatterley's Lover*.[15] This danger seems to have influenced the conclusions of the Williams Committee which in 1979 proposed several

---

[11] For example, German Basic Law, art. 5(3).

[12] *Chaplinsky* v. *New Hampshire* 315 US 568, 572 (1942): see above, p. 39.

[13] *Cohen* v. *California* 403 US 15 (1971).

[14] W. Allen, 'The Writer and the Frontiers of Tolerance', in '*To Deprave and Corrupt* . . .', essays ed. J. Chandos (London, 1962), 146.

[15] See *US* v. '*Ulysses*' 5 F. Supp. 182, aff'd 72 F 2d. 705 (2nd Cir., 1934); *R.* v. *Penguin Books* [1961] Crim. LR 176.

changes to the British obscenity laws. It found Mill's arguments for freedom of speech hard to apply to pornography, particularly pictorial matter. But it also feared the risk of censorship of worth-while literature, and for that reason found that the importance of freedom of expression could not be ignored in framing appropriate legislation.[16] The Committee indeed suggested the abandonment of all controls on written matter where 'the argument about the survival of new ideas and perceptions applies most directly'.[17] An interesting comparative point is that although written materials may fall outside the protection of the First Amendment, in practice only pictorial pornography has been held 'obscene' by the Supreme Court in the United States.[18]

It would be silly to deny that there is inevitably *some* risk that serious innovative literature may be suppressed under obscenity laws, or more likely will not be published because of their 'chilling' or deterrent effect. The issue is whether this risk can be minimized so that it is trivial when weighed against the advantages of enabling the legislature to outlaw wholly worthless matter. In Britain (and other countries where there is no constitutional review by the courts), the only safeguards are political scrutiny of the legislation to ensure it is so carefully drafted as only to cover hard-core pornography of no merit at all, and the jury system under which decisions on obscenity are taken by twelve ordinary members of the community. Where the courts have powers of judicial review, there is an additional guaranteee that literature and art will never be affected.

These prophylactics do not satisfy the sceptics who doubt the ability of the legislature or the courts to formulate sufficiently precise standards. This doubt played a substantial part in the dissent of Brennan J. in the *Paris Adult Theatre* case.[19] He contended that an important aspect of the Court's test for 'obscenity'—whether the publication depicted, in a patently offensive way, ultimate sexual acts—imposed an impossible task on the judiciary. Its application to picture magazines would inevitably be unpredictable, and there would be a grave risk of abuse if it were applied to written material. The only answer to this is that courts always have to draw lines, and there is no immediately obvious reason why this should be harder in this area than in other aspects of free speech jurisprudence or, for that matter, in constitutional law generally. The natural distaste many judges may feel in examining and ruling on pornography only

---

[16] Williams Committee, paras. 5.15–5.25.
[17] Ibid., para. 5.25.
[18] See *Kaplan* v. *California* 413 US 115, 119 (1973).
[19] *Paris Adult Theatre* v. *Slaton* 413 US 49, 83–93 (1973).

reflects the quality of the material itself. Moreover, the constitutional definition of 'obscenity' should be sufficiently precise and narrow so as not to deter the publication of books of any literary merit even if this means that some hard-core pornography will escape prosecution.

A more radical approach is to deny that there can be any standards at all in this area, or—a slightly different criticism—to argue that any formulation of 'obscenity' compels the courts to distinguish between types of 'speech' on the basis of its content. But this begs the question whether pornography is 'speech' at all. To deny the coherence of any standards is surely cultural anarchy. When Douglas J., commenting on the supposedly incoherent notion of 'offensiveness' as applied to obscenity, said that, 'one of the most offensive experiences in my life was a visit to a nation where bookstalls were filled only with books on mathematics and books on religion',[20] he abandoned thought for invective. Standards have to be laid down in other contexts outside the First Amendment; presumably Douglas J. did not find the notion of 'offensiveness' impossible to apply in the fields of planning or zoning law.[21]

The case that 'obscenity' is not 'speech' for constitutional purposes depends, as has been said, on a distinction between the communication of ideas—an appeal to the mind—and the dissemination of matter which leads to erotic arousal and perhaps some sexual gratification. One subtle line of attack is to argue that sexually explicit material does convey an idea—that sex is fun, that it need have nothing to do with permanent relationships, that it is good to be erotically aroused whenever one wants, and so on—and that this can only be put across effectively by the distribution of what is conventionally described as hard-core pornography.[22] This novel use of 'The Medium is the Message' line of thought is buttressed by precedent from other areas of free speech jurisprudence. In particular, Harlan J.'s support for the protection of emotive political speech in *Cohen* v. *California* is frequently cited: '... much linguistic expression serves a dual communicative function: it conveys not only ideas of relatively precise, detached explication, but otherwise inexpressible emotions as well'.[23] That case can be distinguished, however, as dealing with a mode of communicating political speech, which is almost always entitled to constitutional protection in the United States (and

---

[20] Ibid., 71.
[21] A noted environmentalist, Douglas J. took a benevolent view of zoning regulations: *Village of Belle Terre* v. *Boraas* 416 US 1 (1974).
[22] D. A. J. Richards, 'Towards a Moral Theory of the First Amendment' (1974) 123 *U. Pa LR* 45.
[23] 403 US 15, 26 (1971).

enjoys some preferred position in other jurisdictions).[24] In this context it is important to appreciate the strength of public feelings on contemporary issues. Surely, however, freedom of speech does not always entail a right to communicate an idea by the most effective method? Otherwise there could be no objection to the use of loudspeakers and sound-tracks which may be the easiest way to spread information to a small community, but which is subject to local regulation.[25] The decisive objection, however, is that to concede a right to *effective* communication enables the speaker to cross the line between speech and action with impunity.[26] The most effective way of demonstrating hatred of the British establishment would be to shoot the Monarch or Prime Minister, but nobody would suggest this should be tolerated under a free speech principle. Pornography, like violence, may incidentally communicate an opinion in the most dramatic way possible, but this does not show it ought to be treated as 'speech'.

There is one other dimension to this issue which has so far not been properly explored in the legal commentaries. Almost all pornography, unlike most literature, is written to make money. The publisher has no intention of communicating information or opinions. While even the shabbiest politician wants his audience to react in a particular way, for instance, by believing what he has to say to them or voting for him at an election, the pedlar of porn is only interested that consumers purchase his wares. As far as he is concerned they can throw them away immediately afterwards. This feature of pornographic publication was emphasized by Warren CJ in his concurring judgments in the leading obscenity cases, *Roth* v. *United States* and *Alberts* v. *California*, decided together in 1957.[27] Subsequent cases have treated the distributor's marketing methods as an important factor: erotic literature advertised in an obscene way may fall outside the First Amendment.[28] (On the other hand, the British legislation regards the existence of a commercial motive as wholly irrelevant to a charge of publishing obscenity.)[29]

As a matter of principle then, purveyors of pornography can hardly

---

[24] See above, ch. V, s. 2.

[25] *Saia* v. *New York* 334 US 558 (1948); *Kovacs* v. *Cooper* 336 US 77 (1949).

[26] See Harlan J. in *US* v. *O'Brien* 391 US 367, 388 (1968); *Buckley* v. *Valeo* 424 US 1, 23–9 (1976). On the other hand this argument has been rejected in the street solicitation and canvassing cases, e.g., *Schneider* v. *State* 308 US 147 (1939).

[27] 354 US 476 (1957).

[28] For example, *Ginzburg* v. *US* 383 US 463 (1966).

[29] Obscene Publications AG 1959, s. 2. But it is only an offence to *possess* an obscene publication, if this is done for gain: Obscene Publications Act 1964.

claim they are exercising a right of free speech. That is why more emphasis than usual is placed on the rights of consumers in this context. Now we have seen earlier in this book that the recipient's interests in obtaining access to information (or the public interest in its communication to him) may be relevant to the protection of free speech rights, and indeed justify their recognition in particular cases where the speaker may have forfeited, or not be in a position to protect, his rights.[30] But it is difficult to characterize pornography as 'speech' solely because of the recipient's interest, when the speaker's claim to be exercising freedom of expression is so transparently bogus. Moreover, in some of the flag desecration cases, discussed in Chapter II, the Court has taken the defendant's intention into account in determining whether the action sufficiently involved the communication of an idea to be treated as 'speech' for the First Amendment.[31] There seems no reason to exclude it from consideration in deciding whether pornography is protected.

Whether 'obscenity' is characterized as 'speech' or not is, as has been emphasized earlier,[32] only the start of a court's inquiry. To recapitulate, if a pornographic publication is found to be within the ambit of constitutional protection, it must then be determined whether some compelling state interest or purpose justifies its suppression, or the restriction of its availability, in the particular circumstances. Alternatively, a court may be inclined to hold that really obscene matter is not 'speech', and that the legislature is constitutionally free to pass what measures it thinks appropriate. But obviously the court must first come to some conclusions concerning the character of 'obscenity' for this purpose. It cannot just accept the legislative characterization, for otherwise publications which obviously contain ideological and political discussion might be outlawed by a prudish legislature, merely because they happen to touch on sexual matters. The judges have to frame definitions of 'obscenity', against the background of their interpretation of constitutionally protected 'speech'. And their application of these standards to particular legislation to determine whether it passes constitutional muster will also depend to some extent on its interpretation. Constitutional courts cannot really therefore avoid consideration of the meaning and objects of anti-pornography statutes, whether 'obscenity' is regarded as 'speech' or not. There may be no necessary connection between the tests for determining whether hard-core pornography is 'speech' and the grounds for deciding

---

[30] See above, pp. 108, 112.
[31] See e.g., *Smith* v. *Goguen* 415 US 566 (1974); *Spence* v. *Washington* 418 US 405 (1974).
[32] See above, p. 245.

whether it should be outlawed,[33] but in practice the issues are closely related. In Britain and other countries, where the status of pornography as 'speech' is not a constitutional issue, the questions are really aspects of a single problem: the legislature must decide whether, taking into account the value of free speech, it is justifiable to restrict (or outlaw) pornography because it causes some evil which outweighs that value.

One straightforward example may illuminate these points. The United States Supreme Court, two years after *Roth* and *Alberts*, held that the film *Lady Chatterley's Lover* which advocated the desirability (in some circumstances) of adultery could not be constitutionally proscribed as 'obscene' and so fall outside the First Amendment.[34] The majority of the Court considered that the New York statute, requiring the state to refuse a licence for the exhibition of a film which portrayed acts of sexual immorality as desirable or acceptable, improperly restricted the circulation of ideas and opinions. 'Ideological obscenity', as it has sometimes been called, is rightly characterized as 'speech', because it does appeal to the intellect or to artistic sensitivity.[35] The fact that the ideas canvassed in the book or film are abhorrent or offensive to the vast majority of people is no more relevant than it would be in the case of political or social speech. The statute law of Britain and Commonwealth countries is also generally construed not to restrict this sort of sexual propaganda, though there is one Australian case holding the encouragement of sex orgies and the joys of single parenthood to be covered by an obscenity law.[36]

Commentators, and in their more reflective moods the courts, have suggested a number of rationales for the enactment of anti-pornography legislation. On some counts the possibilities come to five or six.[37] (What actually motivates the legislature and its members is one question which courts do not have to answer.) Three principal grounds for control are examined here. First, pornography may harm its consumers or induce them to cause harm to other groups or people. Second, its unlimited availabilty may in the long run lead to undesirable changes in the general

---

[33] This point is made by J. M. Finnis, '"Reason and Passion": The Constitutional Dialectic of Free Speech and Obscenity' (1967) 116 *U. Pa. LR* 222, 242.

[34] *Kingsley International Pictures Corp.* v. *Regents* 360 US 684 (1959).

[35] H. Kalven, 'The Metaphysics of the Law of Obscenity', [1960] *S. Ct. Rev.* 1, 28–34.

[36] *MacKay* v. *Gordon and Gotch (Australasia) Ltd* [1959] VR 420. And see Williams Committee Report, para. 3.25, for power of British Board of Film Censors to ban ideologically undesirable films.

[37] See the categories suggested by W. B. Lockhart and R. C. McLure, 'Why Obscene?', in '*To Deprave and Corrupt* . . .', 53, 57–8, and by R. G. Fox, *The Concept of Obscenity* (Melbourne, 1967), ch. X.

moral tone of society; this can be regarded as a variety of harm which the state is entitled to prevent, but the thesis is so different in character from that which emphasizes the likelihood of individual harms that it is treated separately. The third ground for regulation is that the material *offends* people. In its more defensible form, this is an argument for restrictions on the public display of pornography, rather than its total suppression, and is, therefore, one which free speech liberals find relatively acceptable.

3. SPECIFIC HARMS

The Williams Committee admitted that any presumption in favour of freedom of speech that may apply to obscene publications would be displaced if it were shown that they cause harm.[38] But the difficulty is to identify the harm they may occasion, and then to determine whether its prevention is compatible with any serious commitment to the protection of free speech. British law seems never to have been able to formulate a coherent answer to these questions. In the leading common law decision in *R. v. Hicklin*, Lord Cockburn CJ stated the familiar test for obscene libel, whether there is a tendency 'to deprave and corrupt those whose minds are open to ... immoral influences, and into whose hands a publication of this sort may fall'.[39] The essence of corruption according to this judgment is the suggestion of 'impure' thoughts, and the publication would be ruled obscene if it had this impact on any young or other vulnerable people who were likely to read it. The literary or other merits of the book were at this time wholly irrelevant, though Blackburn J. in the *Hicklin* case itself appreciated that many great works of literature were, therefore, exposed to prosecution.[40]

One major weakness of this formula was that the standard of acceptability might be assessed by reference to the effects a book would have on children. While few people, either then or now, doubt that young people should be protected from exposure to obscene literature, it is, as the Supreme Court ruled in one of its early pronouncements on the topic, intolerable that this risk should determine what adults can read.[41] Following the recommendation of the House of Commons Select Committee,[42] the modern British Obscene Publications Act 1959 has

---

[38] Para. 5.26.
[39] (1868) LR 3 QB 360, 371.
[40] Ibid., 374.
[41] *Butler v. Michigan* 352 US 380 (1957).
[42] (1958) HC 123.

substantially removed this possibility. The law now is that a work is obscene if it is 'such as to tend to deprave and corrupt persons who are likely, having regard to all the circumstances, to read, see or hear the matter ...'.[43] As interpreted by the Court of Appeal, this means that the jury must consider the effect on *a significant proportion* of the likely readers; the fact that the work may corrupt a few young or particularly vulnerable people who gain access to it is ignored.[44] A significant proportion may be much less than a half of the relevant group.[45] It is, therefore, a radically different test from that determining obscenity by reference to its impact on the typical man in the street, or as one American judge put it, 'a person with average sex instincts—what the French would call *l'homme moyen sensuel* ...'.[46] British law, therefore, emphasizes that there is no absolute test to determine 'obscenity'; rather there is a variable standard, the application of which depends on the probable readership or audience. The significance of the harm is assessed by reference to these particular people, not ordinary people in general.[47]

Of more importance, however, is the character of this harm. In fact there is some evidence that the courts paid little or no attention to the *Hicklin* formula before the passage of the 1959 legislation, and instead asked whether the publication was 'offensive' or 'indecent' in the ordinary meaning of these terms. Moreover, there is some Australian case-law which suggests that the question whether a publication corrupted the minds of its readers was relevant only if it had been first found that it was indecent, a position to some extent adopted to prevent the prosecution of classic works of literature.[48] Lord Wilberforce in the leading modern British case, *DPP* v. *Whyte*,[49] has, however, suggested that the Obscene Publications Act re-established the 'tendency to deprave and corrupt' formula as the central issue for decision. Now this phrase might refer to the mental and moral corruption of the publication's consumers, as Lord Cockburn CJ had ruled, or alternatively denote the instigation of anti-social acts, in particular sexual crimes. After *DPP* v. *Whyte* it is clear that the former meaning is the correct

---

[43] Obscene Publications Act 1959, s. 1(1).

[44] *R.* v. *Calder and Boyars Ltd* [1969] 1 QB 151.

[45] Lord Cross in *DPP* v. *Whyte* [1972] AC 849, 870.

[46] Woolsey J. in *US* v. '*Ulysses*' 5 F. Supp. 182, 184 (1933).

[47] Where magazines are kept for export, courts have to decide whether they may tend to corrupt foreigners: *Gold Star Publications* v. *DPP* [1981] 1 WLR 732 (HL).

[48] *R.* v. *Close* [1948] VR 445 (Full Ct. of Vict. SC); *Crowe* v. *Graham* 121 CLR 375, 392 *per* Windeyer J. (1969) (HC of A.).

[49] [1972] AC 849, 861.

interpretation. In that case the principal purchasers of what were admitted to be hard-core pornographic magazines were 'inadequate, pathetic, dirty-minded men, seeking cheap thrills—addicts to this type of material'.[50] The justices acquitted the respondents because such addicts could not be further corrupted; moreover, there was no evidence that the effect of the magazines went beyond the arousal of sexual fantasies. The majority of the Lords, allowing the prosecutor's appeal, concluded that the magistrates' decision was incompatible with the purpose of the 1959 Act. The legislation was designed to prevent corruption of mind and was equally concerned to stop the already depraved from further corruption. The argument that bad conduct must be induced was firmly rejected, though actual behaviour might in some cases provide necessary evidence to show mental corruption. The law, in this respect, has not really advanced from the *Hicklin* ruling.

Some members of the Lords were clearly unhappy with the interpretation they felt compelled to place on the 1959 legislation. There are, for example, considerable practical difficulties in applying the notion of mental corruption. More pertinently from the free speech perspective, it seems an extraordinarily broad basis on which to justify the suppression of publications, whether written or pictorial. Some great literature and works of art stimulate erotic fantasies, but should none the less be treated as 'speech'. The 'sexy thoughts' argument would justify the regulation of a much wider range of matter than the extreme hard-core pornography which may plausibly be excluded from the category of protected 'speech'.

The Williams Committee concluded that in practice courts still tend to assess publications in the light of contemporary standards of acceptability, despite the use of the 'deprave and corrupt' formula in the Obscene Publications Act.[51] Some remarks of Lord Reid in the *Knuller* case support this view.[52] On the other hand, one major feature of British obscenity law suggests that the notion of harm to the consumer through his moral corruption is still taken seriously. It may be a defence to an obscenity prosecution that the publication is so repulsive and disgusting that readers will be discouraged from indulging in the particular practices depicted. Failure to put the 'aversion' defence to jury results in reversal of a conviction.[53] Now this argument should be irrelevant if British law is really concerned, as some suggest, with the general decency of the

---

[50] Ibid., 870.
[51] Para. 2.6.
[52] [1973] AC 457.
[53] *R.* v. *Anderson* [1972] 1 QB 304 (CA).

material. In the United States the contention that the publication will sicken the average person has been rejected in cases where it is clearly designed to appeal to the perverse interests of a deviant group.[54] It is still treated as hard-core pornography, offensive to the community, and therefore outside the area of constitutionally protected speech. British law rather surprisingly may in this respect (at least in theory) be more liberal.

The principal utilitarian justification for obscenity law is that it prevents the dissemination of material which encourages the commission of sexual crimes and other overt undesirable behaviour. These may, therefore, be the harms that justify rebuttal of the presumption in favour of freedom of speech. It is conceivable that this is what legislatures have in mind when deciding to enact anti-pornography statutes, though the British rules of statutory interpretation prevent the courts inferring any such intention from whatever is said during the course of Parliamentary debates or stated in preparatory papers. At all events, the courts do not regard this as the main object of the Obscene Publications Act 1959. Nor has this argument played much part in the American decisions defining 'obscenity' for First Amendment purposes; there is no suggestion that the statute concerned must only suppress publications, the availability of which clearly does (or may) instigate the commission of sexual offences. Admittedly Burger CJ referred to the 'arguable correlation between obscene material and crime', when he gave the Court's judgment in the *Paris Adult Theatre* case.[55] In fact he need not have discussed the question at all, since it had already been ruled in this and the companion decision, *Miller* v. *California*, that matter judged 'obscene' by reference to other criteria was outside the First Amendment. The Court might then at most have had to decide whether the proscription of obscene material was sufficiently rational to withstand scrutiny under the weak 'rational classifications' test of the Fourteenth Amendment.[56] At all events Burger CJ thought that, although there was no conclusive proof of any causal connection between pornography and anti-social conduct, it was reasonable for a state legislature to act on the assumption that a link existed.

Any view about such a connection is of course highly controversial. Neither the United States President's Commission on Obscenity nor the

---

[54] *Mishkin* v. *US* 383 US 502 (1966).

[55] 413 US 49 (1973).

[56] For discussion of this principle, see P. G. Polyviou, *The Equal Protection of the Laws* (London, 1980), ch. 2.

Williams Committee found there was sufficient evidence to establish a causal relationship.[57] The latter body examined the arguments extremely carefully, including the claim that in Denmark, where restrictions on pornography had been abolished in the late 1960s, there had as a result been a marked fall in the incidence of sexual offences. The Committee, however, thought it premature to conclude there was a link between these phenomena. Indeed its twenty-five pages on the topic are a masterpiece of scepticism concerning any proposition in this area. What perhaps can be said is that the relationship (if any) between obscenity and conduct is better determined by a legislature than by a court, even by a court accustomed to considering sociological evidence. One advantage of the Supreme Court's refusal to classify some hard-core pornography as 'speech' is that it then does not have to rule whether the connection between the material and crime is sufficiently fully established to justify government intervention. This is a purely legislative question, subject perhaps to some judicial review under the 'reasonable classifications' test of the Fourteenth Amendment. And it follows from the uncertainty of the connection that constitutional courts are well advised not to define 'obscenity' as sexually explicit matter that causes undesirable conduct.

A number of other possible harms were considered by the Williams Committee.[58] One of them—the general damage to the moral tone of society—is considered in the next section of this chapter. Others relate to the physical and psychological harm which may be done to the people who participate in sexual activities which are filmed or photographed. The Committee was generally unimpressed by the argument that adult participants were necessarily injured, but in any event a direct prohibition on employment for this purpose would hardly raise free speech issues and could, subject to general claims about personal freedom, be properly regulated as 'conduct'. It is generally agreed on the other hand that children, whether as possible consumers or even more obviously as participants, do need protection.[59] Indeed the protection of young people is the principal aim underlying the German law restricting the availability of general, i.e. non-hard core, pornography. Section 184 of the Criminal Code prohibits the offer or supply of such material to all persons under eighteen, and further bans publication and sale by means,

[57] US Commission on Obscenity, 26–7; Williams Committee Report, paras. 6.1–6.59.
[58] Ibid., paras. 6.60–6.80.
[59] See the British Protection of Children Act 1978. A New York statute prohibiting the distribution of material showing children participating in sexual activity has been held constitutional: *New York* v. *Ferber* 102 S. Ct. 3348 (1982).

and in premises, to which the young have access.[60] This makes it harder for adults to obtain the material, but such restrictions are justified in view of the general difficulty that a supplier or retailer may have in checking the age of customers. For this reason, the Constitutional Court has upheld the ban (imposed under a special law for the protection of youth) on the supply by mail order of named pornographic magazines.[61] But the Court agreed with the lower court's conclusion that a comparable ban on the distribution of pictorial magazines advertising naturism was contrary to freedom of expression, which covered this type of 'ideological obscenity' (to use the American phrase).

Quite apart from any link between pornography and rape, it is frequently said that women generally are harmed by the mass availability of sex magazines. Produced almost exclusively for men, they insult women by implicitly treating them as sex objects. 'The fact that pornography is widely believed to be "sexual representations" or "depictions of sex" emphasizes only that the valuation of women as low whores is widespread and that the sexuality of women is perceived as low and whorish in and of itself.'[62] The feminist case is in effect that obscenity is a form of group libel, with women as the class victim.[63] Another analogy might be the law of blasphemy, which protects the religious sensibilities of Christians; it could be urged that pornography offends the feelings of women on a matter integrally connected with their self-identity in a somewhat similar manner. Perhaps this should not be pressed too far. The law of blasphemy may recently have been upheld by the European Commission,[64] but both it and group libel are almost certainly unconstitutional in the United States. It would be odd to justify the law of obscene libel on the basis of principles which carry so little conviction in these related areas. In any case, as the Williams Committee itself hinted, an answer to nasty speech in this area is more and better speech which upholds the dignity of women.[65]

My general conclusion is that it is difficult to identify a specific harm which might overcome the presumption in favour of free speech in this

---

[60] The text is set out and discussed in Schönke–Schröder, *Strafgesetzbuch-Kommentar* (20th edn., Munich, 1980), 1239–57.

[61] 30 BVerfGE 337 (1971).

[62] A. Dworkin, *Pornography: Men Possessing Women* (London, 1981), 201. For a discussion of the feminist arguments, see A. W. B. Simpson, *Pornography and Politics: The Williams Committee in Retrospect* (London, 1983), ch. 5.

[63] See ch. V, s. 4, for group libel.

[64] 8710/79, *Gay News* v. *UK* (1983) 5 EHRR 123.

[65] Para. 6.64.

area. The arousal of libidinous or sexy thoughts in particular individuals is hardly a significant enough evil to justify the law's intervention; moreover, to use this as a basis for legislation would legitimate the suppression of some great literature and is inimical to the free speech principle which protects the communication of ideas and artistic perceptions. There is too little evidence that the availability of pornography causes sexual offences to warrant its regulation on that ground, though few would dispute that this is potentially a harm which should be taken into account. So we must now turn to an argument of very broad sweep: the availability of some extreme hard-core pornography leads in the long term to significant changes in society's moral beliefs and conduct, which the state is entitled to prevent.

4. OBSCENITY AND THE MORAL TONE OF SOCIETY

Many liberals argue that it is important to outlaw incitement to racial hatred in order to show our abhorrence of discrimination, to make it clear that we constitute an integrated and harmonious society. It does not matter very much whether there are many prosecutions, nor does it trouble the law's advocates that there is little evidence to show that this type of inflammatory speech causes immediate outbreaks of violence or tension between racial groups. In the long term an unchecked flow of propaganda makes more likely the development in future generations of racialist attitudes with the incalculable dangers to the cohesion of society that they present.[66]

So, too, proponents of anti-pornography laws sometimes defend them on the ground that they reinforce balanced attitudes towards sexuality and reduce the risk of a decline into sexual anarchy and licentiousness. This view is not solely held by campaigners such as Mary Whitehouse and the Festival of Light, but has been entertained by such a distinguished constitutional lawyer as Professor Alexander Bickel. In 1971 he wrote in a passage quoted by Burger CJ in the *Paris Adult Theatre* case: '[The problem] concerns the tone of society, the mode, or to use terms that have perhaps greater currency the style and quality of life, now and in the future.'[67] Moreover, just as great books reflect the values of a civilized community and may ennoble and inspire generations, present and future, so the very existence of pornography lowers (it is claimed) our

[66] See ch. V, s. 4.
[67] 22 *The Public Interest*, quoted 413 US 49, 59 (1973).

sensitivities and debases society's moral outlook. The state has every right to eradicate it.

The strength of this argument in a way lies in its imprecision. Unlike the arguments concerning specific harms, it is difficult to puncture it by reference to the lack of evidence establishing a connection between pornography and moral change. The incidence of rape or individual moral corruption may be no greater now than in Victorian times, but the wider availability of pornography reflects and reinforces attitudes to sexual morality different from those held a century ago. And a community in which it was commonplace for people to read hard-core pornography (whether inside plain covers or not) when riding home from work on the underground would have a distinctive character, alien even to that of modern Britain. If the overwhelming majority of the people want to prevent the emergence of such a society, does adherence to the free speech principle stop it?

An easy answer to this is that it does not, because 'obscenity' is not 'speech'. That leaves it open to the political branches of government to determine the coherence and weight of the public's view. Courts with powers of judicial review, however, must initially define 'obscenity' in terms which cover, and only cover, pornographic material which can plausibly be regarded as having these debilitating effects on the future of society. There must be no risk that protected speech is suppressed or deterred by legal restraints, and this militates in favour of a narrow and precise definition of 'obscenity'. It seems to me that the recent history of United States law represents an attempt to arrive at an acceptable formula, allowing the legislatures of the states power to outlaw material which they find seriously incompatible with the moral tone of society. Some Commonwealth countries' law also appears to be influenced by this objective, and the same may in practice be true of British law, even though the 'deprave and corrupt' formula suggests that individual damage is the evil that is feared.

Under the formulation in *Miller* v. *California* (1973), 'obscenity' is limited to

works which, taken as a whole, appeal to the prurient interest in sex, which portray sexual conduct in a patently offensive way, and which taken as a whole, do not have serious literary, artistic, political, or scientific value.[68]

The first ingredient here—appeal to a prurient interest in sex—is arguably the most important, since it seems designed to capture those

[68] 413 US 15, 24 (1973).

non-rational, almost physical, features of pornography which render it inappropriate to be characterized as 'speech'. Yet the term is curiously ill-defined in the case-law of the Supreme Court. In the *Roth* case,[69] Brennan J. gave it the dictionary meaning of 'having a tendency to excite lustful thoughts', but this clearly is too wide. Lust may be one of the seven deadly sins, but its experience is virtually universal. Moreover, some serious works of literature may arouse such feelings. What seems to be indicated is material which is purely designed to excite sexual fantasies, largely as an aid to masturbation. Stewart J. prefers the simple term, hard-core pornography, 'without trying further to define it'.[70] Maybe the Canadian formula in the 1959 Criminal Code is as good an attempt as any to describe material which does not communicate ideas or information and which undermines contemporary values—at least as these are proclaimed in public: 'any publication a dominant characteristic of which is the undue exploitation of sex ...' is proscribed.[71] The Canadian Supreme Court has ruled that a search for the 'dominant characteristic' entails an inquiry into the author's or publisher's purposes, an approach incidentally which is fully consonant with suspicion of the commercial motive for most pornographic publication, while an 'undue exploitation' necessitates 'excessive emphasis on the theme for a base purpose'.[72]

German law also distinguishes between hard-core and general or plain pornography. Section 184(3) of the Criminal Code absolutely prohibits the distribution, public display, offer, or advertising of the former, which is defined as pornography depicting violence, abuse of children, or sexual activity with animals. Less objectionable matter (soft-core pornography) may be freely distributed, provided it is not made available to children or exposed to unwitting members of the public. More generally, pornography is not treated as a 'relative' concept (as in British law), the meaning of which depends on the character of its consumers. A leading commentary on the Criminal Code emphasizes the dissociation of sex from other aspects of human and cultural life as perhaps the key element in typical pornographic literature,[73] an approach which seems consistent with that adopted in the United States and by the Canadian Supreme Court.

---

[69] 354 US 476 (1957).
[70] *Ginzburg* v. *US* 383 US 463, 499 (1966).
[71] s. 159(8), discussed by W. S. Tarnopolsky, *The Canadian Bill of Rights* (Toronto, 1979), 195–201.
[72] *Brodie* v. *The Queen* [1962] SCR 681. For discussion of some comparable Australian cases, see G. A. Flick, *Civil Liberties in Australia* (Sydney, 1981), 236–44.
[73] Schönke–Schröder, *Kommentar*, 1241–4.

If the United States Supreme Court has not said enough about the first limb of its 'obscenity' formula, it has arguably written too much about the second: matters 'which portray sexual conduct in a patently offensive way'. Although in theory an additional requirement, in practice it assumes much more importance than the 'prurient interest in sex' condition. Originally formulated by Harlan J. in *Manual Enterprises* v. *Day*,[74] it first enjoyed the approval of a Court majority in the *Memoirs* case, where the right of Americans to read *Fanny Hill* was held to be constitutionally protected.[75] The justification for the use of this formula is probably that it enables contemporary moral judgments to be incorporated in the 'obscenity' test. At any rate the Supreme Court in *Miller* gave as examples of what could properly be regulated by the states under this head, 'patently offensive representations or descriptions of ultimate sexual acts, normal or perverted, actual or simulated', and 'patently offensive representations or descriptions of masturbation, excretory functions, and lewd exhibition of the genitals'. The desirability of precision, properly underlined by the Court, has of course encouraged states to formulate what is proscribed in embarrasing detail. Laws outlawing the depiction in film or photograph of the erect male organ, but implicitly permitting it to be shown flaccid do appear rather ridiculous. Their object is, however, commendable, and the only alternative, short of abandoning any attempt to draw distinctions and regulate the truly obscene, is to leave it all to jury discretion.

The Supreme Court has also consistently emphasized that the *average person* must find the material offensive under *contemporary community standards*. It is right to assess a publication by reference to its impact on an average person rather than on a particularly vulnerable or sensitive person (a sex maniac or a nun, for example), for otherwise the availability of reading matter would be determined by the standards of a small minority. In this respect United States law contrasts strongly with the requirement in the English Obscene Publications Act that only a significant proportion of likely readers need be depraved and corrupted. Theoretically it is possible for a publication to be successfully prosecuted in England merely because a large number of the sexual deviants at whom it is aimed are liable to be further corrupted by looking at it;[76] it is immaterial that ordinary people would find it inoffensive or just ridicu-

---

[74] 370 US 478 (1962).

[75] 383 US 413 (1966).

[76] Contrast the 'aversion' defence, above p. 257, where the English Act's concern with the reaction of likely readers may lead to more 'liberal' results.

lous. This result cannot occur in the United States if the law is applied properly.

The meaning of 'contemporary community standards', relevant to both the first two limbs of the obscenity formula, has, however, given rise to considerable difficulty. In *Miller*, it was decided that state law need not require the jury to assess the publication by reference to *national* standards, since this might compel a relatively conservative community to accept publications found tolerable in more permissive areas. The reasonable man on the Boise, Idaho omnibus is not the same person as the man who takes the last subway home in Manhattan. Later cases show that the states are not obliged to apply local or state-wide standards; the jury may assess the material, it seems, by the standards of more or less any community it chooses.[77] The juryman must not, however, decide on the basis of his own subjective reaction to the material. The state court may admit evidence of local community standards, though it is not obliged to do so. But evidence of what happened when other comparable publications were prosecuted is not admissible, though, of course, in principle it provides a rather good indication of what a section of the community thinks about such material. This rule incidentally also applies in Britain, where it has long been held that the character of other publications which are freely available is irrelevant to the question whether a particular article is obscene.[78]

The United States law in this area is really quite incoherent. It is particularly difficult to justify the 'local community standards' approach to the application of federal statutes. The posting of indecent material across state boundaries may be illegal in some parts of the country, but not in others because of the different attitudes of particular communities; the result, as Brennan J. has pointed out, will be to reduce what may safely be distributed to the highest common factor of what is aceptable thoughout the United States.[79] More fundamentally, it is hard to justify the use of inherently variable standards in the context of a federal constitution, under which citizens of all the states enjoy the same First Amendment rights. Burger CJ's argument that the meaning of 'prurient interest' and 'patently offensive' involves issues of fact, and that, therefore, a uniform approach is not required by the national Constitution seems a little naïve. The Canadian courts in contrast have adopted a national standards test to determine what is to be tolerated in the

---

[77] *Hamling* v. *US* 418 US 87 (1974); *Jenkins* v. *Georgia* 418 US 153 (1974).

[78] *R.* v. *Reiter* [1954] 2 QB 16 (DC).

[79] See his dissent in *Hamling* v. *US* 418 US 87, 141 (1974).

community.[80] Expert evidence which only shows local attitudes must be rejected.

Some of these issues have arisen for decision, admittedly in a radically different context, by the European Court of Human Rights.[81] *The Handyside* case raised the question whether the forfeiture proceedings taken in London under the Obscene Publications Act 1959 against the publishers of *The Little Red Schoolbook* violated Article 10 of the Convention. The publication urged the young people, to whom it was primarily addressed, to adopt a liberal attitude to sexual matters, and certain passages could be construed as advocating early sexual experience, which would be illegal in the case of children under sixteen. After deciding without hesitation that the publication was covered by Article 10—it was really 'ideological obscenity', rather than pornography—the Court went on to consider whether the proceedings were a 'necessary' measure 'for the protection of morals'. Here it ruled that each state has a margin of discretion in determining whether to restrict or suppress the circulation of books and magazines. While the European Court could supervise or review this determination, by, for example, ensuring that the measure was proportionate to the aim, the national authorities were in a better position to take the initial decision on the steps necessary to safeguard the morals of their community. The corollary is that there is no uniform degree of free expression throughout the European States which are parties to the Convention—at least in this particular area. Publications which circulate freely in Sweden or Denmark are, and may legitimately be, banned in the Republic of Ireland. Indeed the Court, quite logically in terms of its general approach, rejected the applicant's argument that *The Little Red Schoolbook* was circulating freely throughout the majority of the member states. Perhaps a little more surprisingly, it also did not take very seriously the contentions that the *Schoolbook* had not been prosecuted in other parts of the United Kingdom (while a prosecution in Scotland had failed), and that hard-core pornographic magazines, often available to children, were tolerated by the law enforcement authorities. These points do seem to undermine to some extent the British government's case that the forfeiture proceedings were 'necessary' to protect the morals of the young. Implicit in the Court's approach here is the view that the standards applied by each member State need not be *national*, but may be *local*.

---

[80] *R.* v. *Prairie Schooner News* (1970) 1 CCC(2d) 291; *R.* v. *Times Square Cinema* (1971) 4 CCC (2d) 229.
[81] *Handyside* v. *UK* Series A, no. 24; (1976) 1 EHRR 737.

The *Handyside* case raises broad questions (as do a number of European Court judgments) on the desirability and feasibility of common standards throughout the member states.[82] In effect the Court ruled that it would only require a common minimum degreee of free speech protection; beyond that it was open to each state to determine its own standards. This approach is more understandable in an international scheme for human rights protection than it is in the context of a federal constitution. More pertinently, the decision also raises the question whether this flexible approach is inevitable in areas such as obscenity law. Perhaps it is difficult to avoid. Any definition of 'obscenity' in terms of 'offensiveness to contemporary community values' necessarily raises questions about the size and character of the *community*, whose judgment is to be considered, as well as about the more obviously contentious concept of 'offensiveness'. The larger the community, the less likely that its members will share common values, except the fashionable faith in the virtues of pluralism. Small may be beautiful, but liberals should remember that it is easier for tiny communities to adopt restrictive attitudes on matters of moral and social behaviour.

The problem is then to find a coherent role and meaning for the concept of 'contemporary community standards', on the (admittedly controversial) assumption that it is relevant to the control of pornography. The American Supreme Court's approach, which is to use the concept as an element in the *definition* of 'obscenity' and therefore a factor in determining the scope of protected 'speech', together with its interpretation as referring to 'local' standards, is hard to reconcile with a national Bill of Rights which should be applicable uniformly throughout the country. Some conservatives who believe strongly that any society is entitled to proscribe material which the majority finds distasteful, particularly when it deals with sex, would of course use this difficulty as part of the argument against entrenched Bills of Rights. If the European Court were less accommodating to member states' standards in cases like *Handyside*, there would be much more unease in British legal circles about our participation in the Convention.

It is probably a mistake to incorporate a test such as 'offensiveness to contemporary community standards' into the definition of 'obscenity' for constitutional purposes. A definition in terms of sexually explicit mater-

[82] Compare *Sunday Times* v. *UK* Series A, no. 30, (1979) 2 EHRR 245, discussed above, ch. VIII, s. 4. See now 9615/81, *X* v. *UK* (1983) 5 EHRR 591, where the Commission upheld the seizure by British customs of pornographic articles designed for export, on the ground that this was a necessary measure to protect *British* moral standards!

ial, designed purely to appeal to a prurient interest in this matter can hardly be improved on. Hard-core pornography, moreover, can be identified without reference to (temporarily) prevailing standards. Schauer has in any case argued convincingly that the question whether the material is offensive to the majority of society is really irrelevant.[83] If it is wrong for the Court to take into account the degree of offensiveness or hurt occasioned to people when determining whether intemperate political discourse enjoys the coverage of the First Amendment, so it is in the case of sexually explicit material. The constitutional question is whether such material is 'speech' at all, and the degree of offensiveness has nothing to do with this; what matters is whether there is a genuine communication of ideas or information.

But where 'obscenity' is not 'speech', state legislatures may constitutionally incorporate an offensiveness test into their obscenity statutes. It does not matter then that it is formulated or applied differently from one area to another, since this is irrelevant to the question whether rights of free speech have been invaded. This reasoning incidentally provides another explanation why the European Court's approach in *Handyside* does not create the same problems as the apparently similar stance of the Supreme Court. The Strasbourg judges were not concerned with defining 'freedom of expression'—they were in any case satisfied that it included this sort of obscene literature—but with balancing the state's interest against that freedom. This process may properly entail weighing one state's interests differently from another's. Just as political speech may be inhibited in *times* of emergency, so *place* may be relevant when deciding whether to prohibit or restrict other types of speech.

One consequence of the suggested *constitutional* definition of 'obscenity', with the deletion of the formula 'offensive to contemporary community standards', is that a fixed, and more or less permanent, meaning, is attached to the concept. At first glance, this does not seem to accord with the undoubted truths that views of what is 'obscene' do change over time, and also that perceptions of what is unacceptable do vary from one community to another. Most legal systems appear to adopt some variable definition of pornography, whether they are based on an individual harm rationale (as in British law) or justified in terms of preserving the moral climate. The explanation lies, of course, in the difference between constitutional and legislative rules. A supreme court with powers of judicial review should frame a precise and restrictive

---

[83] F. Schauer, 'Response: Pornography and the First Amendment' (1979) 40 *U. Pittsb. LR* 605, 610.

definition of 'obscenity'; the judges must take into account the meaning of 'speech' and the purposes for which it is protected, though they must also bear in mind the reasons which prompted the legislature to intervene. Naturally the meaning of constitutional terms changes, but it cannot alter as rapidly as the formulation and construction of legislative provisions. Phrases such as 'contemporary community standards' are particularly ill-fitted for use by constitutional courts. But they are perfectly acceptable in valid obscenity legislation.

5. OBSCENITY, THE ARTS, AND LEARNING

One problem which has considerably exercised the framers of obscenity law on both sides of the Atlantic is how to treat works of artistic, literary, or scientific value which at the same time could be regarded as pornographic. The concern was also felt by some Victorian judges, and it weighed substantially with the House of Commons Committee, whose report led to the passage of the Obscene Publications Act 1959. Indeed the provision of the 'public good' defence in that Act is probably its most significant alteration to the common law. But it has not, according to the Williams Committee, been particularly successful, and that body did not foresee any role for it in the more liberal legal regime it was recommending.

From the perspective of freedom of speech, the purpose of any special measure of protection for works of literary or scholarly value is to ensure that publications which do communicate ideas and information are not banned. Arguably it is unnecessary to make any particular provision for such works in the definition of obscenity, for whatever 'obscenity' may be, it clearly does not include publications which are intended to inform or appeal to literary sensitivity. For example, a medical textbook showing close-up pictures of male and female genitals is designed to communicate and explain, and is 'speech'. The *Roth* definition of 'obscenity' in the United States did not in fact say anything about writing of literary or scholarly value, though Brennan J. stated that the entire absence of any social importance was one of the reasons why obscenity was not constitutionally protected.[84] It was not until the 1960s that the phrase, 'utterly without redeeming social value', became an essential element of the constitutional formula.[85] Its subsequent development will be discussed briefly after the comparable British law has been outlined.

[84] 354 US 476, 484 (1957).
[85] *Memoirs* v. *Massachusetts* 383 US 413 (1966).

The original Obscene Publications Bill introduced in 1956 and later Bills, like the United States formula, envisaged that literary, artistic, or scientific merit would be relevant to the general issue whether a publication was obscene or not. But after an amendment made during the Committee stage of the final Bill, these factors were incorporated in a special 'public good' defence, which is only relevant once a book has been found obscene. Section 4(1) of the 1959 Act provides:

A person shall not be convicted of an offence . . . if it is proved that publication of the article in question is justified as being for the public good on the grounds that it is in the interests of science, literature, art or learning, or of other objects of general concern.[86]

Expert evidence on the literary or other merits of the article is frequently admitted, almost always on the side of the defence. As construed by the courts, the jury must first rule on the 'obscenity' issue—does the article have a tendency to deprave and corrupt?—and then determine whether on balance publication is for the public good if the work has literary or other merits.[87] A familiar criticism is that this requires some mental gymnastics of Olympic proportions: is it possible that a book is both 'obscene' and yet has these qualities and, if so, how can these be balanced?

This aspect of British obscenity law is almost indefensible. The United States approach, also to be found in New Zealand and New South Wales, is much more coherent.[88] The best explanation is that British law is concerned (probably wrongly) with the specific harm that may be occasioned particular individuals, or groups of individuals, by the publication of pornography. It then is just plausible to ask the courts to balance this harm against the general good (to the rest of the less vulnerable community) which will flow from publication. In contrast it would make no sense at all to ask a jury to weigh the literary or other merits of a book against its general prurient appeal, the American approach to obscenity; a scholarly or artistic publication cannot have prurient appeal, at least to the average person.

Another related criticism of British law is that it assumes two readerships: those who are likely to be depraved and those wiser heads capable of appreciating the publication's merits. The élitist assumptions

---

[86] G. Robertson, *Obscenity* (London, 1979), 160–6.
[87] *R. v. Calder and Boyars Ltd* [1969] 1 QB 151 (CA).
[88] See the New Zealand Indecent Publications Act 1963, s. 11 and the New South Wales Indecent Articles and Classified Publications Act 1975, s. 24.

are also borne out by the use of expert witnesses, a feature of the law much attacked by the Williams Committee: 'It is as though informed persons, literary and artistic experts, are supposed to appear from the world of culture and inform the jury of how things stand there with the work under trial.'[89] Such testimony would suggest there could be general agreement about the importance of works of art, when in this context their value is likely to be particularly controversial. While the experience of the last twenty-five years shows that successful and established works are much more likely to enjoy the protection of section 4 than experimental literature, there is nothing inevitable about this, and the Williams Committee's protests here seem exaggerated. Some would argue that the jury should be more frequently helped with evidence concerning the tendency of a book to deprave and corrupt as well as on its redeeming merits, rather than be left to flounder on their own and to form necessarily impressionistic judgments.[90]

A major difficulty with section 4 is the meaning of 'other objects of general concern'. The House of Lords has ruled that the phrase refers to merits similar to those of science and literature, etc.; evidence that the publication might have beneficial effects in relieving sexual tensions could not be admitted, since a conclusion to that effect would be incompatible with the finding that it was obscene.[91] This is an inevitable consequence of the two-stage test the courts are required to apply. If the merits of a publication were considered in conjunction with its possible corrupting effects, it would be somewhat easier to argue that pornography, far from tending to deprave, had some therapeutic value. Such a claim might be no more far-fetched than the argument that the material has the very opposite consequence of sickening and disgusting its readers—the so-called 'aversion' defence.[92]

Supreme Court justices have rarely suggested that a work might have some redeeming value because it satisfied a pressing, psychological need of its consumers.[93] And the suggestion is most unlikely now to commend itself to a majority of the Court which formulated this aspect of the 'obscenity' test in the following terms: does the work, taken as a whole, lack serious literary, artistic, political, or social value?[94] This question

---

[89] Para. 8.23.

[90] Expert evidence may be tendered to show the impact of a publication on a special group; e.g., children: *DPP* v. *A&BC Chewing Gum Ltd* [1968] 1 QB 159 (DC).

[91] *R.* v. *Jordan* [1977] AC 699.

[92] See above, p. 257.

[93] But see Douglas J. in *Memoirs* v. *Massachusetts* (n. 85 above), 432.

[94] *Miller* v. *California* 413 US 15, 24 (1973).

represents a considerable tightening of the previous requirement that the work must utterly lack redeeming social value for it to be characterized as obscene. Understandably the development was vehemently criticized by Brennan J., who considered it a departure from the principles justifying a narrow definition of obscenity. Since the Court is concerned with the meaning of 'speech', it should be sufficient for the publication to have any non-trivial intellectual or artistic content. The *seriousness* of that content is surely irrelevant. Moreover, it would be wrong to accept Harlan J.'s suggestion that the value of the publication should be weighed against its prurient appeal, as if these were two distinct and separate features of a work.[95] As long as the work communicates an idea or perception which can be intellectually appreciated, it should be entitled to First Amendment protection. On this approach it is also quite irrelevant whether the material satisfies psychological needs and is overall beneficial to its consumers: the supply of sex aids, or the provision of prostitutes, would also satisfy these requirements, but nobody suggests that they are 'speech'.

6.   OBSCENITY AND OFFENSIVENESS

Most liberals find the idea of banning pornography on the grounds that it may cause particular individual harm to its readers or that it undermines the moral fabric of society wholly unacceptable. But they find more tolerable the proposition that the display of some types of pornography may be controlled in so far as it offends reasonable people. The exhibition of pornographic magazines would therefore be regulated as a public nuisance. The publications could still be obtained by the enthusiastic consumer, but he must be prepared to shop around for his purchases. The key point is that while the availability of obscene material may be *restricted* by this method of control, it is not entirely *suppressed*. But it may not always be easy to distinguish these two types of control.

It is perhaps too readily assumed that this approach evades the deficiencies of those previously considered in this chapter. In so far as some, if not all, pornography is to be regarded as 'speech', it is entitled to the same degree of constitutional protection as other types of communication. And in Britain, where freedom of speech is only one value to be taken into account by the legislature and the courts, it is as relevant in determining the restrictions that may be placed on obscenity as it is in defining the limits of political debate. Yet the Williams Committee was

---

[95] See his dissent in *Memoirs* v. *Massachusetts* (n. 85 above).

prepared to recommend restrictions on the availability of pornography which would not be countenanced for other types of publication. Can this be justified because much sexually explicit material offends reasonable people? It is commonplace that speech which offends the majority is the type which most needs the law's protection. One argument for the offensiveness principle which surely does not work is that the display of pornographic material on street bookstalls or hoardings invades a right of privacy which people somehow carry around with them when they are shopping or go for a Sunday promenade.[96] (There is almost certainly a right of privacy not to have obscene material sent to one's home, but this is incidental to the main argument.) Moreover, the public nuisance argument proves too much. Most people probably object to the appearance of skinheads, but nobody suggests this is any basis for legislation confining their movements to certain areas. And it would clearly not be acceptable for the local authority in a predominantly Conservative area to outlaw political advertising or leafleting by a left-wing minority, on the ground that this is offensive or a nuisance.

The Williams Committee's recommendation was for a restriction on material *offensive to reasonable people* by reason of the manner in which it portrays or deals with violence, sexual functions or the genital organs.[97] This confines the control to pornography and ensures that the law does not interfere with the availability of political speech. But the formula begs the question whether there is more reason for protecting the public from offence by sexually explicit material than from distress occasioned by other phenomena. The Committee offered two reasons for distinguishing restrictions on pornography from those that might be imposed on other types of speech: first, the restriction is not directed against the advocacy of any opinion, and second, it does not defeat the publisher's aims if pornography is only available to willing consumers.[98] Both points seem to be rather obliquely asserting that pornography is not really 'speech'; similar arguments have been touched on earlier in this chapter.[99] The liberal may reply with the arguments first, that whatever the purpose of the restrictions, they would in fact inhibit the availability of one type of 'speech', and second, that no other mode of expression can be so regulated as to ensure that the audience is confined to volunteers.

[96] D. N. MacCormick, 'Privacy and Obscenity', in *Censorship and Obscenity*, essays ed. R. Dhavan and C. Davies (London, 1978), 76.

[97] Paras. 9.29–9.38.

[98] Ibid., paras. 7.16–7.23.

[99] See above, s. 2.

Publishers want to have access to as wide a market as possible, even if only to make more money.

The truth is that if pornography is entitled to benefit from a presumption in favour of freedom of speech, it is little easier to justify its restriction on the basis of an offensiveness principle than it is to uphold a total ban. Implicit in the Williams Committee's approach is the view that obscenity is not fully 'speech', and that the public has a right to be protected from any offence it causes, though it does not enjoy any such freedom in respect of controversial political communication. Moreover, the offence which the Committee sought to prevent is not merely aesthetic. It did not consider it adequate to control the public display of pornography, which causes some visual offence; people should have the assurance that such matter does not exist, except in special premises. 'The problem lies not with indecent displays, but with displays of the indecent, and to control these, one needs to go beyond the content of the mere display itself to the character of the item being displayed.'[100] The offence is really moral, and it becomes a nice question whether the offensiveness principle, approved by the Williams Committee, does not shade into the 'moral tone of society' argument canvassed in section 4 of this chapter. This same ambiguity appears in the basis of the new statutory power given to lower authorities to control the number of sex shops in their area—to be discussed shortly.

The crucial point remains, however, that there is a difference between the total suppression of material and its restriction to separate premises which adults would only enter after due warning of the wares displayed there and from which children would be totally excluded. This second approach may be equally hard to justify in terms of free speech principles, but there are probably enough practical arguments to support it. It enables addicts to satisfy their craving, while a cynic might add that society thereby is able to combine muted moral disapproval with a measure of tolerance. A law based on the offensiveness principle is also probably easier to enforce than a total ban, the imposition of which encourages an underground market. One respect in which it might appear more liberal is that it is almost impossible to justify any restraint on purely *written* publications on this basis. Since an obscene book (without a lurid cover) does not appear to be any different from, say, the driest legal textbook, it cannot easily give offence. But as most written obscenity will have some ideological content—or perhaps some literary

---

[100] Williams Committee Report, para. 9.8. For a defence of this approach, see Simpson, *Pornography and Politics*, especially ch. 4.

value—it would probably also not be suppressed on any of the bases considered in this chapter, though the Supreme Court has held it to be subject to the 'obscenity' test laid down in *Miller*.[101] At any rate neither the Williams Committee nor the United States President's Commission on Obscenity thought there was any room for prohibiting the display of purely written material.

The offensiveness approach to the control of pornography has been adopted in countries such as France and Denmark, where it has more or less replaced the bans on publication of obscene or immoral material. In Germany too, apart from the absolute prohibition of hard-core pornography, the law is designed to prevent the unwanted intrusion of pornographic material on the public. Thus, it is an offence to post or provide such matter unsolicited, or to display it on news-stands or in shops, other than those specializing in pornography. It is also an offence to exhibit pornographic films for payment charged exclusively or principally for this performance—a requirement easily evaded and subject to much criticism.[102] There is, however, no immediate prospect that the English Obscene Publications Act will be replaced by such laws. Instead it has been supplemented by further restrictions such as the Indecent Displays (Control) Act 1981 which could be regarded as a partial enactment of the Williams Committee's proposals. This measure, introduced by a Conservative back-bencher, prohibits the display of any indecent matter in a 'public place'; this term is defined so as to include shops, except those to which admission is obtained by payment and those which display an adequate warning notice that the material inside may be regarded as indecent. The Act does not venture a definition of 'indecent'. There is, however, some authority on its meaning in other legislation, and it is clearly in British law a term of broader scope than 'obscene'.[103] The measure has obviously had some effect in inducing porn-shops to conceal their wares from passers-by. Further, it may have reduced the importance of the obscenity law as the primary means for protecting the public from exposure to immoral publications.

Another method of implementing the 'offensiveness' principle is to restrict the number of outlets which sell pornographic magazines and other similar material. This can be achieved by planning or licensing

---

[101] *Kaplan* v. *California* 413 US 115 (1973).

[102] See Schönke–Schröder, *Kommentar*, 1251. The provision has been upheld: 47 BVerfGE 117 (1977).

[103] For example, see *R.* v. *Stanley* [1965] 2 QB 327 (CCA), construing the words 'indecent' and 'obscene' in the Post Office Act 1953, s. 11.

controls, designed either to preserve the character of residential neighbourhoods or to prevent the development of seedy, red-light districts. The tactics necessary to achieve these two goals may in fact be incompatible: either porn-shops are confined to the commercial areas or they are dispersed throughout the particular community. There is, moreover, considerable danger that this type of restriction over a wide area may in effect amount to a total suppression of the availability of such material. Two American cases nicely illustrate some of the problems here. In *Young* v. *American Mini Theatres* the Court was asked to rule on the validity of a Detroit ordinance prohibiting the siting of 'adult motion picture theatres' and 'adult book stores' within 1,000 feet of any two other 'regulated uses', which included these theatres and book stores, as well as liquor stores and pawnshops.[104] Although the ordinance clearly affected films which might enjoy constitutional protection from total suppression, the Court by a bare majority held that this zoning ordinance was a valid measure for their regulation. Four members of the Court thought that it was proper to draw content-based distinctions in framing these regulations:

... even though the determination of whether a particular film fits that characterization turns on the nature of its content, we conclude that the city's interest in the present and future character of its neighbourhoods adequately supports its classification of motion pictures.[105]

The fifth member of the majority, Powell J., denied there was any content-discrimination in the Detroit measure, and in essence treated it as a land-use regulation which only incidentally affected First Amendment freedoms. On the other hand, the minority saw it as impermissibly distinguishing between sexually explicit material and other types of 'offensive' speech. Whether Stewart J. exaggerated in viewing the decision as 'an aberration', it is certainly unusual in approving content-based measures which restrict 'speech' on time, manner, and place grounds.

Perhaps the central question here is whether Powell J. was right in denying that there was any significant overall restriction on the showing of adult films. If Detroit residents had experienced difficulty in gaining access to adult movies, there would have been an improper abridgement of freedom of speech. This is shown by the contrasting decision in *Schad* v. *Borough of Mt Ephraim*, where a 7–2 majority invalidated a local ordinance which had been construed as prohibiting all live entertain-

[104] *Young* v. *American Mini Theatres* 427 US 50 (1976).   [105] Ibid., 71–2 *per* Stevens J.

ments in the town, including nude dancing.[106] The *Young* ruling was distinguished because it had only approved the dispersal of cinemas throughout the community, and had not banned a mode of speech altogether. It is not clear whether the majority in *Schad* would have come to the same conclusion had there been evidence that this entertainment was freely available in neighbouring communities.[107] Whether it should have done largely depends on the size of the town. A very small community, entirely residential, should probably be free, as two members of the Court suggested, entirely to ban certain types of entertainment on planning grounds. On the other hand, it is surely illegitimate for a large town, with a variety of commercial businesses, to outlaw adult films (or other forms of entertainment) and defend its position with the argument that residents can drive twenty miles into the suburbs or to another town for that sort of amusement. The test should be whether there is in substance a significant restriction on the ability of consumers to obtain access to their chosen pleasure. If there is, the measure in question is really a suppression of speech and should be justified by relevant arguments, not on the basis of planning or other time and place regulations.

British planning law does not allow local authorities to control the number of sex shops; a grocery store can be changed overnight into a pornography shop without planning permission.[108] The Williams Committee did not think the law should be reformed to enable local authorities to refuse permission for these developments, largely (it seems) because it feared they might exercise this power to exclude all porn-shops under public pressure. Nor did it consider that any special licensing system should be instituted.[109] New powers to control 'sex establishments' have now, however, been conferred on local authorities by legislation enacted in 1982.[110] Under widespread pressure from Members of Parliament, the government introduced a provision at the Report stage

---

[106] 452 US 61 (1981).

[107] Blackmun J. specifically repudiated any implication that a different result would have been reached if another nearby community allowed this type of entertainment. The same issue was touched on in the debates on the recent British 'sex shops' legislation; T. Higgins MP argued that a local authority should take the character of neighbouring areas into account when determining the suitability of 'sex shops' in its locality: 17 HC Deb. (6th ser.), cols. 423–4.

[108] But it is a change of use requiring planning permission if a shop begins to show sex films and thereby becomes a pornographic cinema: *SJD Properties Ltd* v. *Sec. of State for Environment* [1981] JPEL 673.

[109] Paras. 9.12–9.13.

[110] Local Government (Miscellaneous Provisions) Act 1982, s. 2 and Sch. 3.

of the Local Government (Miscellaneous Provisions) Bill enabling local councils to exercise licensing powers over sex shops and cinemas. A sex shop is defined broadly as premises used to a significant degree for sale of articles which are concerned primarily with the portrayal of, or designed to stimulate, sexual activity. If a local authority passes a resolution to this effect, all such premises will require a licence, and it can be refused if the council thinks there are too many premises of this kind in the locality or they are unsuitable in view of the locality's character or the particular use of neighbouring property. The most important aspect of these powers is that a council may ban *all* sex shops from a locality; moreover, there is no appeal from a decision to this effect. Although the Minister responsible for the Bill did not think authorities should exercise this power merely because it disapproved of sex shops, they are entitled to take account of the strength of local feeling in deciding whether it is appropriate for them to be situated in the area.[111] The only safeguard against a policy decision never to allow porn-shops within the authority's jurisdiction is judicial review, and it is not at all clear whether the courts would regard such a policy as illegal.

The 1982 'sex shops' provisions nicely illustrate the dangers to free speech of 'nuisance' legislation in this area. A measure, which purports to be merely concerned to limit numbers to preserve the character of particular localities on planning and related grounds, can easily be used to ban all outlets for pornographic material because of popular hostility. This reflects the essential ambiguity of the 'offensiveness' principle, which has already been touched on: is it primarily concerned with aesthetic distaste for publications, the display of which is visually unattractive, or does it really evince moral disapproval? The Williams Committee's approach in part adopts the latter stance, though its particular recommendations for the limits on the display of pornographic materials are compatible with the narrower position.

Local authority control is at least exercised by a politically responsible body, which should be aware of local community standards. Another remedy which may be used to redress offence is a civil action for nuisance, and in one recent English case an interlocutory injunction was granted to restrain the use of premises as a sex shop and cinema in a predominantly residential street in Victoria, London.[112] Vinelott J. held that a hard-core pornography business could amount to a nuisance because it was deeply repugnant to reasonable people, even though it was

[111] T. Raison, Minister of State Home Office, 17 HC Deb. (6th ser.), cols. 340–1
[112] *Laws* v. *Florinplace* [1981] 1 All ER 659.

carried on in a relatively decorous way; there was some evidence on the facts that the premises attracted undesirable people to the neighbourhood and thereby created a straightforward nuisance, but the decision also appears to support use of the tort action to restrain behaviour which is offensive to property-owners who merely *know* about it.[113] This goes well beyond the Williams Committee view that the sale of pornographic material is tolerable as long as it is confined to discreet premises which warn people not to enter unless they are looking for that matter. However, unlike the 'sex shops' legislation, the tort remedy could hardly be used to achieve a total ban in a wide area, and it would obviously not be granted to restrain the availability of pornography in commercial districts.

These last few pages have been rather critical of the coherence of the 'offensiveness' principle. This is partly a reaction against what seems to me the excessive enthusiasm for its adoption in preference to other approaches. There are admittedly persuasive arguments for attempting to restrict rather than wholly suppress material, which meets a need for a minority but which most people find disgusting and (perhaps rightly) disturbing. The lesson of American case law and the recent British legislation is that it is too easy to use the 'offensiveness' rationale to achieve bans over wide areas, and that this results in part from uncertainties inherent in the principle.

[113] Ibid., 666.

X

Freedom of Association

I. INTRODUCTION

FREEDOM of association is a relatively new member of the group of political liberties which are thought worthy of legal and constitutional protection in most Western democracies. Dicey in his classic work on British constitutional law at the end of the nineteenth century did not even mention the right, and it is not explicitly protected by the United States Constitution. It is, however, specifically covered by the West German Basic Law, the Constitution of the Republic of Ireland and the European Convention.[1] In West Germany and France there is also express protection for the establishment of political parties, on condition that they do not try to undermine democracy.[2] These provisions have been the subject of some recent litigation, which has often been of great political and social importance. Courts have been asked to decide, for example, whether the right of association entails a freedom not to associate (in particular 'the closed-shop question'), and how far it is legitimate for the state to regulate the electoral process and control the internal working of political parties.

Freedom of association is obviously related in some loose respects to freedom of speech. For example, a major objective of a political party or pressure group is to communicate ideas to the electorate, and therefore the rationale for protecting association rights in this context is similar to that which justifies a free speech principle. Historically there seems also to have been a close connection between the First Amendment rights to assemble and 'to petition the Government for a redress of grievances', and the newer freedom.[3] An association is after all in a sense a permanent assembly, with an organization, officers, and a formal constitution.

---

[1] Basic Law, art. 9; Constitution of Ireland, art. 40(b)(1)(iii); European Convention, art. 11. The German Constitutional Court has drawn attention to the recent origins of the freedom to form associations for the improvement of working conditions: see 50 BVerfGE 293, 366–7 (1979).

[2] Basic Law, art. 21; Constitution of the Fifth Republic, art. 4.

[3] D. Fellman, *The Constitutional Right of Association* (Chicago, 1963), ch. 1, and see *De Jonge* v. *Oregon* 299 US 353 (1937).

The relationship between these rights emerges clearly from Supreme Court rulings in the 1950s and 1960s when freedom of association was first held to be implicit in the First Amendment. In the European Convention, Article 11 in the same sentence protects freedom of assembly and freedom of association, including the right to form and join trade unions.[4]

On the other hand, freedom of association can equally be derived from freedom of contract; it is as much an economic and social liberty as a political one. Moreover, it can be justified by arguments which have little to do with the values underlying a free speech principle: the importance to a free society of independent institutions and the general desirability of voluntary partnership and shared activities. This point is connected with another important feature of the freedom; it may cover conduct which *ex hypothesi* falls outside the scope of free speech. Thus, the organization of a society and the compilation of its confidential membership lists involve activity which may well be designed not to communicate anything (at the relevant time) to the public. Yet this type of conduct has been held by the Supreme Court and the German Constitutional Court to be constitutionally protected.[5] In other cases, association rights may be used to claim privileges which could only with difficulty be obtained under a free speech principle, for example, access to facilities for speech.[6]

Naturally it is impossible to do justice to all aspects of association freedoms in this book. The connection between freedom of speech and of association is, however, worth some exploration. First, the closeness of this relationship may influence the scope of the latter right. In particular, it may be relevant here whether it is independently protected, as in the German Basic Law and under the European Convention, or whether it is derived from a freedom of speech and assembly provision as in the United States. Secondly, the existence of the connection with freedom of speech and belief seems to have influenced recent judicial rulings that freedom of association does (at any rate in some contexts) entail a right not to associate. Finally, the case law on freedom of association may in its turn shed some light on the scope and meaning of the free speech provision: if some political activity, for example, falls under a clause guaranteeing the right to form associations and political parties, it is

---

[4] For the differences between the right of assembly and the right of association in German law, see I. von Münch, *Grundgesetz-Kommentar* (Munich, 1982), vol. 1, 399–400.

[5] *NAACP* v. *Alabama* 357 US 449 (1958); 30 BVerfGE 227, 241 (1971).

[6] See below, pp. 286–7, and see the discussion in ch. III, s. 3.

clearly unnecessary (and perhaps incorrect) to subsume it under the former provision.

2. THE RELATIONSHIP WITH FREEDOM OF SPEECH

There is no doubt that an ability, free from onerous government restrictions, to form groups and societies enables their members more effectively to exercise their own free speech rights. Individuals may lack the self-confidence or the opportunities to communicate their views to those outside their family and friends. The press and broadcasting media cannot, or may not be prepared to, afford facilities to more than a relatively few individuals.[7] In practice, it is therefore very difficult for people other than professional politicians and pundits to speak to the national community. The existence of associations does enable ordinary people to communicate indirectly through their leaders and organizers in the same way that they are able to exercise vicarious political power through the ballot-box. This argument may constitute part of a philosophical justification for an independent right of association; more importantly, it may be the essential basis for the implication of the right in a free speech clause such as the First Amendment. This at any rate was the approach of Harlan J. in the first Supreme Court case unequivocally to recognize a right of association under that provision in the Bill of Rights, *NAACP* v. *Alabama*.[8] An Alabama statute requiring the organization to reveal the names and addresses of its members in that state was ruled unconstitutional for infringing that right, albeit indirectly.

Effective advocacy of both public and private points of view, particularly controversial ones, is undeniably enhanced by group association, as this Court has more than once recognised by remarking upon the close nexus between the freedoms of speech and assembly.[9]

Freedom of association was therefore treated as an integral aspect of the individual speech rights protected by the First and Fourteenth Amendments.

What was safeguarded in this case was, of course, not the speech of the association, but the very existence of the NAACP which was threatened indirectly by the disclosure law. But, even granted the strength of the arguments in the previous paragraph and the general political desirability

---

[7] See above, ch. III, s. 4.
[8] 357 US 449 (1958).
[9] Ibid., 460, *per* Harlan J.

of preserving such an important pressure group from control by a southern segregationist state, are the legal arguments for inferring a right of association from the terms of the constitutional text so overwhelming? It might be argued that access to a good education and a certain level of economic security are as important as the ability to form associations for ordinary people effectively to contribute to political debate; yet nobody has suggested that there is therefore a First Amendment entitlement to these goods. The case for deriving a freedom of association from its members' individual free speech rights is not as overwhelming as Harlan J. suggested in *NAACP* v. *Alabama*. There is, however, obviously a necessary connection between the freedom of a particular association to exist and *its own* freedom of expression. If there were any textual basis for ascribing free speech rights to clubs and societies, the inference of a wide-ranging freedom of association, protected against onerous state regulation, would be fairly straightforward. An analogy then would be provided by the 'freedom of the press' limb of the First Amendment. Under this provision laws, such as discriminatory tax legislation aimed at newspapers' ability to survive, are struck down.[10] Without newspapers there can be no freedom of the press at all, and the same point could be made to safeguard the existence and autonomy of associations, if it is clear that they enjoy the protection of the free speech limb of the First Amendment.

An implication of this last argument is that when a legal system derives freedom of association from a free speech clause, it might be as much concerned with the rights of the group or the society, as it is with the individual rights of the members. This is one dimension of the familiar debate whether association freedoms are primarily the rights of the *individuals* to form and join groups or are really rights of the *collectivity*, an issue which has some bearing on the closed-shop question discussed in the next section of the chapter. The American cases are not altogether clear on this broad issue, though in the majority of instances the right has been invoked to protect individuals, particularly against intrusive enquiries into their membership of various organizations. In the *NAACP* v. *Alabama* decision itself the Court clearly had an individual right in mind, for it specifically ruled that the association was entitled to assert the constitutional freedoms of its members:

We hold that the immunity from state scrutiny of membership lists which the Association claims on behalf of its members is here so related to the right of the

---

[10] *Grosjean* v. *American Press* 297 US 233 (1936).

members to pursue their lawful private interests privately and to associate freely with others in so doing . . .[11]

Further, the European Convention refers to the right of 'everyone . . . to freedom of association with others', which strongly suggests that the right is to be regarded as individual rather than collective.

The text of Article 9(1) of the German Basic Law indicates that the freedom is individual: 'All Germans shall have the right to form associations and societies.' But the Constitutional Court has repeatedly emphasized that *Vereinigungsfreiheit* protects the association itself as well as its individual members.[12] Some aspects of the freedom, for example the right to found and join an association, are individual in character, while others—the right to choose its constitutional structure and to formulate rules for the admission and expulsion of members—belong to the association.[13] The freedom to engage in certain activities to promote the aims of the association is collective, though individual members have a constitutional right to participate in this activity. The related *Koalitionsfreiheit*, guaranteed by Article 9(3), which covers employers' organizations and trades unions, is also treated as both an individual and a collective freedom—though the Constitutional Court's recent recognition of the right not to join a trade union perhaps suggests that the former aspect is primary.

Whatever the theoretical character of the right of association and its relationship to freedom of speech, it is clear that it may be claimed in circumstances where free speech rights are not seriously in issue. As already pointed out, it may protect certain types of organizational *activity*. Thus, in another case involving the NAACP, the Court struck down the application of a Virginia statute which had been construed to proscribe that organization's encouragement of prospective litigants to seek particular attorneys in order to pursue their actions in the courts.[14] Although Brennan J. for the majority did refer to litigation as a mode of political expression, he also characterized it in this context as a group activity which was a protected form of association. And Harlan J. in a dissent, joined by Clark and Stewart JJ, certainly considered the NAACP

---

[11] Harlan J. in *NAACP* v. *Alabama* 357 US 449, 466 (1958).

[12] See, for example, 13 BVerfGE 174, 175 (1963), 30 BVerfGE 227, 241 (1971), and 50 BVerfGE 293, 354 (1979).

[13] One of the most important collective rights is the freedom to enter collective bargaining agreements, which may be regulated but which must be respected in principle: 20 BVerfGE 312, 317 (1966); 50 BVerfGE 293, 369 (1979).

[14] *NAACP* v. *Button* 371 US 415 (1963).

was engaged in a course of conduct which the state could properly regulate. It may incidentally be mentioned that bans on the various activities of organizations are more common than the simple proscription of the organizations themselves. The reason for this is that the latter technique just invites the association to reorganize itself under a different name or in an altered form, and is therefore relatively ineffective. Both techniques of control can be found in British law. The former is exemplified by the Public Order Act 1936 which makes it an offence to take part in control or management of any quasi-military organization, defined broadly as a body organized to usurp the functions of the police or armed forces or to use force for achieving political objects.[15] On the other hand, the Prevention of Terrorism (Temporary Provisions) Act 1984 proscribes listed Irish nationalist groups, such as the IRA.[16]

A particularly interesting question on the scope of the freedom is whether it entails a right for a particular body to be recognized by the state for bargaining or consultation purposes. This goes well beyond anything which could seriously be claimed under a free speech clause; it is a claim-right rather than a privilege or liberty from interference, and correspondly imposes some sort of duty on the state to listen to the organization's demands.[17] On the other hand, a body which is totally ignored by the relevant authorities is hardly likely to attract members, and to that extent there is a very indirect fetter on the associational freedom of individuals. They will be under some inducement to join other associations which are recognized by the state. The European Court faced these issues in the *National Union of Belgian Police Case*,[18] where the applicant union complained that the Belgian authorities refused to accept it as one of the representative organizations it was prepared to consult on economic and social legislation. The Court admitted that some right to be heard on these questions was implicit in Article 11 of the Convention, but held that this did not require the bestowal of formal consultation rights; these were to be granted at the

---

[15] s. 2; see *R. v. Jordan and Tyndall* [1963] Crim. LR 124 (CCA).

[16] s. 1 and Sch. 1. The Home Secretary may, however, add to the Schedule 'any organization that appears to him to be concerned in terrorism occurring in the United Kingdom and connected with Northern Irish affairs, or in promoting or encouraging it': s. 1(4). A broad ban, proscribing 'organizations ... describing themselves as "republican clubs" or any like organization howsoever described' was upheld by a 3–2 majority of the Lords in *McEldowney* v. *Forde* [1971] AC 632, despite its vagueness. The regulation would almost certainly have been unconstitutional in the USA as an impermissibly broad infringement of First Amendment rights of association.

[17] See the discussion in ch. III, s. 1.

[18] (1975), 1 EHRR 578.

discretion of each member-state. A similar conclusion was reached in the *Swedish Engine Drivers' Union Case*,[19] in which it was argued unsuccessfully that the Swedish Collective Bargaining Office's refusal to negotiate with the Engine Drivers' Union was a breach of the Article. Again the Court ruled that a right to make representations preparatory to formal negotiation could be inferred from the concluding words of Article 11(1)—'. . . the right to form and to join trade unions for *the protection of his interests*'—but that no right to bargain was entailed. There is an equivalent recent ruling by the Supreme Court to the effect that a state body is under no First Amendment obligation to negotiate with a union about individual employees' grievances.[20]

Very similar questions have arisen outside the labour union context. The European Commission has ruled inadmissible a complaint by a student association that Article 11 was violated when the university authorities refused to accord it the same status which had been given the official student body.[21] In contrast the Supreme Court has held in *Healy* v. *James* that the denial of official recognition to a college political organization (suspected by the university authorities of holding militant left-wing views and being potentially dangerous to good order on the campus) did infringe the First Amendment freedom of association.[22] Without this recognition, the club would be unable to use campus facilities for meetings, or to advertise on notice-boards or in the college newspaper, and its ability to communicate with students would thereby be seriously jeopardized. Such disabilities were not offset by the continued freedom to hold meetings off the campus. The failure to recognize an organization amounts to a prior restraint, and this certainly influenced the Court in coming to its conclusion. But here it was in effect upholding a right of access to the use of facilities on campus, which might be difficult to justify on the case-law concerning the related freedom of speech.[23] Would an unorganized group of individuals have been afforded the same right, or a particular student who wished to talk about some pressing political matter? Moreover, the case might become a precedent for bolder claims; a club might argue for a right to the free use of the

---

[19] (1976), 1 EHRR 617.
[20] *Smith* v. *Arkansas State Highways Commission* 441 US 463 (1979).
[21] 6094/73, *Assoc. X.* v. *Sweden* 9 D. & R. 5.
[22] 418 US 169 (1972).
[23] See above, ch. III, s. 3, for rights of access to public fora for speech. The German Constitutional Court has refused to uphold a right under art. 9 of the *Grundgesetz* for unions to send representatives on to a firm's premises to canvass for members, where the representatives are not employed by the firm: 57 BVerfGE 220 (1980).

telephone and posting facilities, or sabbatical leave from studies for its officers, so as more effectively to organize. *Healy* v. *James* may be rightly decided, but the Court might have more carefully considered the relation of free speech principles to its decision on freedom of association.

If assertions of a right to be recognized appear to emphasize the collective right over the individual, the most common form of restriction in the United States—registration and disclosure laws—is more obviously aimed at individuals' freedom of association. We have already seen that the Supreme Court had an individual right in mind in the *NAACP* v. *Alabama* case.[24] A few other leading cases may be mentioned. In *Shelton* v. *Tucker*[25] an Arkansas law requiring schoolteachers to disclose every organization to which they had belonged or contributed for the previous five years was struck down as impermissibly fettering their freedom of association. The scope of the statute went well beyond the provisions a state might have thought reasonable to ensure that teachers were competent to discharge their duties. Although requirements to register and file membership lists imposed on Communist organizations have been upheld,[26] a provision of the same Subversive Activities Control Act 1950 prohibiting any member of such a body from working in any defence facility was ruled unconstitutional.[27] The section was too broad, as it applied whether or not the employee was working in a sensitive area, and irrespective whether he was an active member of the Communist Party or of any similar organization. The rule is that 'mere knowing membership without a specific intent to further the unlawful aims of an organization is not a constitutionally adequate basis for exclusion . . .'.[28] In all these cases (and there have been many others) the Court protected freedom of association on much the same grounds as it has safeguarded the freedom of speech of public employees, dismissed from service because of some controversial publication or communication.[29] The disclosure statute or other law restricting employment to, say, non-Communists improperly discourages freedom of association; the fetter is indirect, but still real, and as oppressive as a direct ban on the organization.

In some ways the most interesting question in these cases is not

---

[24] See n. 11 above.
[25] 364 US 479 (1960).
[26] *Communist Party* v. *Subversive Activities Control Board* 367 US 1 (1961).
[27] *US* v. *Robel* 389 US 258 (1967).
[28] *Keyishian* v. *Board of Regents* 385 US 589, 606 *per* Brennan J. (1967).
[29] For example, see *Pickering* v. *Board of Education* 391 US 563 (1968); *Givhan* v. *Board of Education of Western Line Construction School Dist.* 439 US 410 (1979).

whether freedom of association can properly be inferred from the First Amendment freedom of speech, or even whether it is entitled to the same degree of protection, but whether either right should be fully protected when the government acts as employer rather than as a legislator for all citizens. The same question arises when restrictions are imposed by a local school or education authority on the views that may be expressed by a schoolteacher when he is on the premises, or on the books that are available in the school library; then the public body is also acting as an educator (and perhaps as employer) rather than simply as a general law-making authority.[30] It can be argued that normal constitutional principles should not apply when the speech or association rights of particular people are restricted by contract or local regulation. It may be contrary to a free speech provision to outlaw racialist language altogether, but it is surely reasonable for a school to ban its use by teachers in class. This may be partly because the arguments for the application of the free speech clause (or principle) are relatively weak in this environment; the educational process necessarily assumes that some propositions and arguments are more likely to be true than others, and the case for the free speech principle from democracy does not apply very strongly where the audience is too young to vote.[31] From the teacher's point of view, it can be said that to some extent free speech rights are voluntarily ceded with regard to expression in the class-room. However, speech and association rights exercised outside the school or other place of employment should remain unaffected by contractual restrictions, unless these limitations are absolutely necessary to protect the government employer's interests.

The legitimacy of these employment restrictions is most frequently discussed in the context of civil servants' political activities, ranging from speaking in public on matters of controversy to canvassing at elections. The British rules, imposed by Treasury circular, have recently been revised following the recommendations of the Armitage Committee Report on civil servants' political activity.[32] As before, civil servants are divided into three groups: first, the politically free group entitled to engage in any political activity when not on duty or on government premises, secondly, an intermediate group free to engage in political

---

[30] See *Board of Education, Island Trees Free School Dist. no. 26* v. *Pico* 102 S. Ct. 2799 (1982), discussed above, pp. 82 and 110.

[31] For a vigorous attack on the view that schools are a 'public forum' for unrestricted speech, see J. Tussmann, *Government and the Mind* (New York, 1977), especially ch. III. But see *Tinker* v. *Des Moines School District* 393 US 503 (1969) above, p. 41 for a decision applying the free speech clause to protest in the class-room.

[32] Report of the Committee on the Political Activities of Civil Servants (1978), Cmnd. 7057.

activity with departmental permission, and thirdly, the politically restricted group who are wholly debarred from engaging in national political activity, but who may participate in local politics with permission. The criteria for granting permission now largely concern the duties of the particular applicant; consent will be given unless his work is so sensitive that its discharge would be affected by the appearance of political bias. Thus, staff employed in giving policy advice to Ministers or in assisting the public (for example, with social security or tax matters) are more restricted than those whose work is not so public. These rules do, of course, constitute a variety of prior restraint, but the criteria for granting or withholding permission are at least published and there is also now a right of appeal to the Civil Service Appeal Board.[33]

The restrictions do not draw any distinction between speech and association. A civil servant (outside the first group) may be prevented from speaking in public or writing to the press as well as from actively participating in national or local politics. (There does not, however, appear to be any rule against joining a political party, as long as this is not made too public!) Trade union activity by civil servants enjoys some immunity from the general rules, though it must often be hard to distinguish from party political work. The object of the code is apparently to allow the maximum freedom to government employees consistent with Ministerial and public confidence in their political impartiality. But it is surely questionable whether this formula adequately protects the free speech interests of civil servants and the public; the restrictions apply to all public disclosure of the formers' views, and not just their expression within a particular environment, as in the schoolteacher case. Moreover, limits should probably only be imposed where confidence in the employees' impartiality would otherwise *reasonably* (or necessarily) be shaken. It is always open for a Minister or head of department to dismiss or transfer an employee because he cannot be trusted to implement government policy or do his work impartially, but there is surely no need to have rules which require in effect these steps to be taken just because a civil servant expresses his opinion or engages in (non-disruptive) associational activity. The case for some further relaxation of the rules in the interests of civil servants may in fact be somewhat stronger here than in the case of the disclosure of official information where it is the recipients' interest in the communication which is more important.[34]

[33] To some extent the procedural objections to a system of prior restraints have been met: above, ch. IV, s. 1.

[34] See above, ch. V, s. 5, for the restrictions imposed by official secrecy laws.

One authority does suggest that the United States courts may be more solicitous of pure speech than association rights in this context. A provision of the 1939 Hatch Act prohibits federal employees from taking an 'active part in political management or in political campaigns', a phrase construed by the Civil Service Commission to cover, for example, fund-raising and campaigning for elective office, but to exclude the mere expression in private or public of political views. A majority of the Court in *Civil Service Commission* v. *Letter Carriers*[35] upheld this prohibition. Freedom of association is not absolute, and the government has a legitimate interest in preserving the impartiality of the civil service and in preventing employees from influencing or being influenced by other government officials. The restrictions were applied equally to all political activity, irrespective of party or view, and did not cover pure political speech, though the three dissenters thought the distinction between this and the prohibited activity impossible to draw satisfactorily. Whatever the merits of the particular decision, it does seem reasonable to distinguish fundamental freedoms to speak and write from the more active modes of political campaigning, which are probably more likely to compromise the impartiality of the government employees.

The distinction between speech and association rights has recently been affirmed in the leading case, *Buckley* v. *Valeo*.[36] Here the restriction was general, rather than a particular rule imposed by contract or local regulation. The Supreme Court was faced with challenges to the constitutionality of some provisions of the Federal Election Campaign Act 1971, in particular those limiting *contributions* to candidates' campaigns and those limiting *expenditure* in their support. While the latter were regarded as an illegitimate restriction on the quantity and range of political speech (a matter more fully discussed in Chapter II),[37] the contribution limitations were upheld. Contributions were treated by the Court more as a form of political association than a mode of speech, because 'the transformation of contributions into political debate involves speech by someone other than the contributor';[38] then applying the principles formulated in the *Letter Carriers* decision, it ruled that the restrictions were justifiable in order to prevent bribery of candidates. Contributors were still free to express themselves by speech-making and

---

[35] 413 US 549 (1973).

[36] 424 US 1 (1976), discussed by D. D. Polsby, 'Buckley v. Valeo: The Special Nature of Political Speech' [1976] *Sup. Ct. Rev.* 1.

[37] See above, ch. II, s. 3.

[38] 424 US 1, 21 (1976).

publication, and there was no restriction on membership of political parties and pressure groups.[39] It is clear that a stricter approach was adopted by the Court to the expenditure provisions, because of their characterization as a mode of 'speech'. Again this differential treatment can be justified, if the Court's characterization is considered acceptable. It would have been better, however, if both the payment of contributions and the incurring of expenditure had been categorized as associational activity or conduct which Congress could legitimately regulate in the interests of a fair electoral process.[40]

3. FREEDOM NOT TO ASSOCIATE

One of the most difficult civil liberties questions in the last decade or two has been whether the positive freedom to associate entails a negative freedom not to associate, or more accurately perhaps whether a right not to associate is implicit in constitutions, which protect, *inter alia*, freedoms of belief, speech, and association. The Universal Declaration of Human Rights expressly outlaws compulsory association, but this is very unusual; other international covenants, the European Convention and the German Basic Law contain no such provision.[41] But this hardly exhausts the argument, even if it is clear (as it is with the European Convention) that the omission was deliberate. Constitutions are rightly not construed literally, nor can much reliance be placed on the intentions (actual or presumed) of the framers. But there is also little to be said for the view that somehow a freedom not to associate is as a matter of logic 'necessarily complementary to, a correlative of and inseparable from' the right to association, though this stance has been adopted by some members of the European Court in the recent closed-shop case.[42]

As with any difficult question on the meaning and scope of freedom of speech, there are limits to the usefulness of dictionaries or purely logical argument. It is surely more helpful to ask why and in whose interest freedom to associate is protected, so that the relevant provisions can be construed in the light of their purposes. And since the construction of the constitution as a whole should be consistent and coherent, it is proper to

[39] Ibid., 28.
[40] See the arguments of J. Skelly Wright, 'Politics and the Constitution: Is Money Speech?' (1976) 85 *Yale LJ* 1001.
[41] Universal Declaration of Human Rights 1948, art. 20. Cf. International Covenant on Civil and Political Rights 1966, art. 22, European Convention, art. 11, and German Basic Law, art. 9.
[42] *Young, James and Webster* v. *UK* (1982) 4 EHRR 38.

ask whether any light on the meaning of freedom of association is thrown by the scope of related liberties, such as freedom of speech. In this context the issue whether the right is primarily individual or collective in character is particularly relevant. If its purpose is mainly to protect the interests of private organizations as a counterweight to the authority of the state, and in the trade union context to enable unions to bargain effectively with employers, there is a strong argument for denying any complementary freedom not to associate, for its recognition would effectively weaken the collective right of the association.[43] As already mentioned, these justifications for recognition of a right to associate have little or nothing to do with free speech; further they may even be incompatible with the protection of individual rights of expression, belief, and opinion. The other view is that freedom of association is really protected to secure more fully and render more effective individuals' rights to speak, assemble, protest, and so on. This seems to be the predominant approach of the United States cases, such as *NAACP* v. *Alabama*, and (as already mentioned) is suggested by the text of Article 11 of the European Convention, and for that matter, the Universal Declaration and the International Covenant on Civil and Political Rights. A case can then be made that to compel someone to join an association, political party, or trade union against his will, or even to pay some dues to enable the organization to carry on its activities, is incompatible with his individual rights of belief, opinion, and perhaps speech. Compulsory membership of an organization, it is said, requires the person implicitly to associate himself with aims he disagrees with, and so can no more be justified than, say, a requirement to salute the flag.[44]

Of course, this argument is not decisive. Just as freedom of speech and the positive freedom of association are not absolute rights, so equally a freedom not to associate may be restricted, where compelling state interests justify this course. In the trade union context, for example, it can be strongly urged that solidarity in the work-place is more important than the objections to union membership of a few individuals, whether they are based on conscientious or broad political grounds. But it may remain crucial to determine whether there is a right not to associate even if it is not absolute, for the burden then falls on the state to justify the

---

[43] For arguments in defence of the closed shop in Britain, see the Royal Commission on Trades Unions (1968), Cmnd. 3623, paras. 588–617, especially 592–3. Also see P. Davies and M. R. Freedland, *Labour Law: Cases and Materials* (2nd edn., London, 1984), 633–7.

[44] *West Virginia Board of Education* v. *Barnette* 319 US 624 (1943), discussed above, ch. II, s. 5.

existence of rules enabling compulsory membership of a union or other association. We should now look at some case-law from various jurisdictions to see how courts have applied these general arguments.

Two recent Supreme Court decisions have formulated under the First Amendment an emerging freedom not to associate with particular political parties, an important right in a system rife with patronage. In *Elrod* v. *Burns*[45] the applicants were Republican non-civil service employees in the Sheriff's office, Cook County, Illinois; they brought an action to stop their dismissal by the newly elected Sheriff, a step which was threatened on the sole ground that they were not affiliated with or sponsored by the Democrats. By a majority of 5–3 the Court held that their First Amendment rights of belief and association had been violated. Brennan J., giving the Court's opinion, cited the *Barnette* flag-salute case and the ruling in *Keyishian* (precluding loyalty oath requirements) in support of this conclusion. He recognized that the group association interests of the Democrats—the efficiency of the administration and loyalty of its employees—were possibly endangered by the decision, but in so far as there was a conflict of First Amendment interests, the rights of the individuals were to be preferred.

This last point also raises the question, explicitly canvassed by Stewart J. in his dissent in the later case, *Branti* v. *Finkel*,[46] whether the protection of the applicants in this sort of situation did not compel the Democrats (in these two cases) to associate with the Republicans who could not lawfully be dismissed. The Democrats' freedom of association might be infringed in this way. If this were the case, there would be a violation of an individual right, whatever the decision, and the Court should probably decide the case on purely utilitarian grounds. The same argument can be made (and was put by the British government in its submissions to the European Court in the *Railway Closed-Shop case*)[47] to justify compulsory membership of trade unions: if non-unionists are protected from dismissal for failure to join the union, are not union members compelled against their will to work with and hence associate with them? The answer to this ingenious conundrum is that to be required to work with someone or share the same office is not the same as

---

[45] 427 US 347 (1976).

[46] 445 US 507 (1980). The majority of the Court applied the *Elrod* v. *Burns* principle to assistant public defenders, who were regarded as 'non-confidential employees' immune from dismissal on the ground that they were of a different party from the Public Defender.

[47] (1982) 4 EHRR 38, discussed by A. Staines, 'Constitutional Protection and the European Convention on Human Rights—an Irish Joke?' (1981) 44 *MLR* 149, 153–6.

being required to *associate with* him. Democrats' individual rights of association are not violated merely because they have to employ, or work in the same premises as, Republicans, but the latters' freedom is invaded if they are required to register as a Democrat or contribute to that party's funds, because these requirements would impose formal institutional links.[48]

This distinction also applies in the trade union cases. The union members' freedom to associate is not infringed if they are required to work with non-unionists (though admittedly the effectiveness of the union as a bargaining agent may be significantly reduced). But their freedom would be infringed if they were obliged to accept someone against their wishes as a member of their union. It follows, as Lord Diplock recently said in *Cheall* v. *APEX*, that 'there can be no right of an individual to associate with other individuals who are not willing to associate with him'.[49] A similar point arose in a leading German case. The *Mitbestimmungsgesetz* of 1976 provided, among other things, for employee representation on the supervisory board of directors of companies (with more than 2,000 employees). The law was attacked on a number of grounds under Articles 9(1) and 9(3) of the *Grundgesetz*: one of the contentions was that such representation interfered with the *Vereinigungsfreiheit* of shareholders and other members of a company by requiring them to associate in this way with worker-representatives. But the Karlsruhe Court pointed out that this did not really impinge on the essential freedoms under Article 9 of shareholders; they remained free to found companies and to leave them and, moreover, were not required to accept the representatives as members of the company itself.[50] In other words not every form of forced co-operation violates 'freedom of association'; it is crucial to elucidate the meaning of this concept in the light of its functions in order to determine its scope.[51]

The American patronage cases do not perhaps really say much about the relationship between freedom of speech and the controversial right

---

[48] The distinction between formal and informal association seems to be supported by two European Commission decisions; 8317/78, *McFeeley* v. *UK* (1981) 3 EHRR 161, and 9054/80, *X* v. *UK* (1983) 5 EHRR 260. On the other hand, in *Democratic Party of US* v. *Wisconsin* 450 US 107 (1981), a majority of the Court found the First Amendment freedom of association of Democrats was violated by the state's requirement of an open primary election (an election in which non-registered Democrats could vote for delegates at the party's convention), although this requirement imposed only a temporary formal link between the party and those choosing to vote.

[49] [1983] 2 AC 180, 190–1.

[50] 50 BVerfGE 293, 356–7 (1979).

[51] See ch. II *passim* for this point in the context of free speech.

not to associate; the mainspring for the inference of the latter is primarily the right of personal belief formulated in the *Barnette* case,[52] which itself was derived from a broad reading of the First Amendment. The German Constitutional Court after some hesitation has held that a freedom to leave or remain outside an association or union is covered by Article 9; but nothing has been said in support of this conclusion, apart perhaps from the observation that these are essential aspects of a *Freiheitsrecht*.[53] But some of the trade union cases, both in Europe and the United States, do illustrate the possible connection between free speech and a right not to associate. The majority of the Supreme Court in the Republic of Ireland has held that the closed shop is incompatible with the freedom of expression which is expressly protected by the Constitution:

> The right to express freely convictions and opinions . . . must include the right to hold such convictions and opinions and the right not to be forced to join a union or association professing, forwarding, and requiring its members to subscribe to contrary opinions.[54]

A similar approach, albeit in a more cautious form, has now been adopted by a majority of the European Court of Human Rights.

In *Young, James and Webster* v. *UK*,[55] the applicants argued that the application of the British trade union legislation allowing their dismissal from employment by British Rail for failure to join unions specified in a 'closed-shop' agreement violated Article 11 of the Convention. The majority of the Court accepted this without committing itself to the view that in all circumstances the Article protected a negative freedom of association; in this case, the applicants' freedom was violated because they were required to join a particular union or be dismissed from their employment, a dilemma which was particularly onerous as the applicants (or two of them) had conscientious objections to union membership and the requirement to join had not been imposed when they were first employed. Article 11, in the view of the majority, is to be construed in the light of Articles 9 and 10, since the protection of freedom of thought, conscience and religion, and freedom of expression is one of the objects of the freedom of association covered by the former provision. Six concur-

---

[52] See n. 44 above.

[53] 50 BVerfGE 293, 367 (1979).

[54] *Educational Company of Ireland* v. *Fitzpatrick (no. 2)* (1961) IR 345, 393 *per* Kingsmill Moore J.

[55] See n. 42 above. For the present British law imposing substantial limits on the closed shop and formulating in effect a right not to join a union where the objector has grounds of 'conscience or deeply held personal conviction', see Employment Act 1980, s. 3.

ring judges were prepared to go further and rule the closed shop illegal in all circumstances, whether or not the applicant had conscientious or political reservations about joining the union. Significantly the three dissenters (from Scandinavia) emphasized the collective character of the right of association and made no mention of Articles 9 and 10.

Whatever the merits of the ruling—and I think on balance it can be justified on the ground that freedom of association must at least entail some choice of union, a choice which was denied to the applicants—the nexus between freedom of opinion and freedom of association is perhaps not quite as clear as the Court assumed. At any rate there was room for more argument in the judgments. Let us take the case of an inactive trade union member, who merely pays his general union subscription without the political levy and who never participates in meetings or (so far as he can avoid it) protest activity. He remains free to form his own opinions and to express his convictions in any way he chooses. Admittedly he contributes to union funds and this does enable the union to do various things which he may disapprove of; but this is only equivalent to compelled speech on the *Barnette* principle, if the payment of money to subsidize another's expression is treated as equivalent to 'speech', which we have seen from the discussion of *Buckley* v. *Valeo* is highly controversial.[56] Another way of viewing the nexus is to argue that the individual is somehow taken as subscribing to the expression and activities of the trade union merely because he is a member, who could with others exercise control over its conduct if he so chose. This is a complex matter. Much may depend on the general understanding of the relationship; is it believed by the public, or (perhaps) should it reasonably be believed, that A, B, and C, members of a large trade union, are calling for a strike because the executive or the president of that union has urged industrial action? The usual derisive view of a trade union block vote at a Labour Party conference where a million or so votes may be cast, say, for or against unilateral disarmament, indicates that the public are not easily confused in this way. Association with any club or union inevitably compromises its members, even if they joined voluntarily, in that they may to some extent be loosely regarded as supporting the group view. But this falls well short of identifying the association's views with their own. In short it is almost certainly better to base a right not to associate on the argument that compulsory association interferes with the individual's freedom to form or join other organizations (including one whose

[56] See above, ch. II, s. 3.

object is to break up a closed shop), than it is to justify it on the basis that otherwise the related freedoms of speech and belief will be infringed.

This scepticism was expressed in the dissent of Frankfurter and Harlan JJ in one of the handful of American cases on the topic, *International Association of Machinists* v. *Street*.[57] The plaintiffs contested the legality of a union-shop agreement under which all railway employees had to be members of a union, which spent a portion of the compulsory dues on general political campaigning. While the majority held as a matter of construction that the Act only compelled the payment of dues to defray the necessary costs of collective bargaining and related expenditure, Black and Douglas JJ considered the statute violated the First Amendment freedoms of association and speech on the basis of the arguments already considered. But the two dissenters were surely right to point out that members of the union remained free to express in any way they liked disagreement with its political stance and that, therefore, there was no real infringement of freedom of speech.

The constitutional nettle has now been grasped by the whole Court in *Abood* v. *Detroit Board of Education*.[58] A Michigan statute allowed an 'agency-shop' agreement under which all local government workers, even though they were not members of the relevant union, were required to pay a sum equivalent to the union dues to that body. Some schoolteachers refused to pay these dues, first, because they objected to much of the union's general political work and, second, because they were opposed to collective bargaining in the public sector. The second ground was rejected by the majority of the Court, following earlier cases,[59] but it accepted that to compel payment of contributions towards the general political expenditure was to violate the plaintiffs' First Amendment freedoms. The Court applied the principles of *Elrod* v. *Burns* to trade unions, at least so far as political expenditure is concerned, and also the holding in *Buckley* v. *Valeo* that the payment of contributions was a form of 'speech' or 'association'. Other members of the Court, concurring in the result, were prepared to go further and hold that any compulsory payment to a union in the public sector, whether used to defray the costs of collective bargaining with the public authority or not, was an

[57] 367 US 740 (1961).
[58] 431 US 209 (1977). Maunz-Dürig, *Kommentar zum Grundgesetz* (Munich, 1981), para. 233 of treatment of art. 9, suggests the requirement to pay dues of this character violates a non-member's negative *Koalitionsfreiheit*.
[59] *Railway Employees' Dept.* v. *Hanson* 351 US 225 (1956); *International Machinists* v. *Street*, above, n. 57.

unconstitutional infringement of free speech and freedom of associa-tion.[60]

The distinction between payments for strict union purposes such as collective bargaining and for general political causes may seem attractive initially, but it is hard to apply in practice and to justify in theory: the exaction of each type of payment equally compromises the reluctant contributor's beliefs. At all events, free speech arguments, as distinct from broader contentions about the rights of belief and association, did not play a significant part in the Court's reasoning. Nor, as the discussion in this chapter has shown, should they have done. The relationship between freedom of speech and positive freedom of association is far from clear; that between the former and the controversial right not to associate is necessarily even more obscure. The short conclusion of this chapter is that it is much better for freedom of association to be explicitly covered by a separate constitutional provision rather than derived from other rights such as freedom of speech. Naturally, the meaning of any provision covering freedom of association will be influenced by the free speech clause of the Constitution and vice versa, but that is because of the general principle that a constitution should be interpreted as a unity, rather than because there is necessarily a close connection between the two freedoms.

---

[60] See the judgments of Powell J. (with whom Burger CJ and Blackmun J. concurred) and Rehnquist J.

XI

Some Conclusions

1. FREEDOM OF SPEECH AS A CONSTITUTIONAL RIGHT

As we saw in Chapter I, a number of justifications have been put forward for the free speech principle, although each of them on its own is far from convincing. The argument from democracy, that is the case that much political and social discussion should be immune from government suppression because it enables people to participate fully and knowledgeably in public affairs and to deal with government on a level of equality, is perhaps the most persuasive. But it needs reformulation to protect expression from regulation by a temporary political majority; further, it fails to explain or justify the protection now afforded in many Western democracies to some commercial and literary speech, including much soft-core pornography. Other rationales for the free speech principle, in particular the rights-based argument from its importance to self-fulfilment and development, may be more relevant for non-political speech. Moreover, some of the different arguments may be more readily applicable to the expression of opinions, while others fit better the dissemination of information.

Whatever the weaknesses of the particular arguments may be in the context of one or other variety of speech, cumulatively they constitute a powerful case for recognition of the principle that the regulation of expression should be subject to special restraints. These, however, need not be imposed by a constitution. It is possible to trust that a government will be restrained by political tradition, or by a set of legislative principles, not enforceable by the courts. Indeed, this is the expectation in Britain, where all politicians and many commentators would claim that freedom of speech is respected, although it is not given constitutional protection. The case for constitutional guarantees rests on further contentions, touched on in various places throughout this book, if rarely explicitly stated: first, that the legislature and government are not to be relied on always to respect the freedom, and second, that the courts in the absence of a constitutional text are unable to give adequate weight to the freedom when it conflicts with other public values and interests. This case, of course, is not confined to freedom of speech; it applies equally to rights of privacy, freedom from arbitrary search and seizure, and all the other civil liberties that may be periodically threatened, albeit with the best of intentions, by governments anxious to respond to popular pressure.

Readers will naturally disagree on whether the case for constitutional protection of freedom of speech and other fundamental freedoms in Britain is a good one. Something more on this subject is said in the following section of this chapter. What the discussion of various areas of free speech jurisprudence in this book does show is that constitutional courts are generally relatively cautious in their interpretation of a free speech clause. Both the United States Supreme Court and the German Constitutional Court are more inclined to give full protection to political speech, admittedly a term which embraces a wide range of discourse, than they are to commercial speech and obscenity. For the most part they are reluctant to uphold positive rights of access, for example, to appear on the media or to use public premises for meetings, and prefer to regard the freedom as a set of liberties (or immunities) from government interference.[1] The Supreme Court is hostile to prior restraints, but does not wholly rule them out: in some areas of law they are used regularly, although the courts have imposed procedural constraints.[2] The European Court and Commission of Human Rights have, if anything, been even less willing to uphold the bolder free speech claims. There are, of course, good reasons to expect supra-national tribunals to exercise a degree of restraint: they are not enforcing a federal Bill of Rights or exercising an appellate jurisdiction over the national courts, but rather ensuring for the most part that certain minimum standards are met. In time the European Court may with an expansion in its work-load adopt a more 'interventionist' stance. It is possible to detect signs of this in its *Sunday Times* judgment, particularly when this is compared with the earlier *Handyside* ruling, which had emphasized the discretion of national legislatures and courts.[3]

But even well-established constitutional courts in national jurisdictions are wise to construe a free speech clause fairly narrowly. In particular, they are right to accord political speech a preferred position and not to give any, or any significant degree of, protection to commercial advertising or hard-core pornography. And with some qualifications, as I argued in Chapter III, it is correct to construe the clause generally only

---

[1] See the discussion in ch. III, esp. ss. 3 and 4.
[2] See ch. IV.
[3] For the *Sunday Times* case, see ch. VIII, s. 4, and for the *Handyside* case, ch. IX, s. 4.

to cover liberties to speak, and not also rights of access—especially not rights to acquire information from an unwilling speaker. These conclusions will disappoint those who wish to advocate the recognition of more radical claims. But quite apart from the general point that constitutional courts should not unnecessarily invite criticism by upholding extremely controversial free speech claims in borderline areas (for example, by holding forms of civil disobedience and protest to be covered by the clause),[4] there are powerful institutional reasons for a cautious approach by the judiciary. They are not, for instance, the appropriate body to formulate positive constitutional rights of access to the media or to acquire information. This is largely because such rights may require detailed regulation which is better left to the judgment of a specialist administrative body, admittedly subject to judicial review for abuse of its discretion. When the Supreme Court begins to fashion particular remedies, as it has done, for example, to achieve school integration, it invites the criticism that it is exceeding its competence.[5] This is, however, not in all contexts a decisive argument. The constitutional text read as a whole may require a court to recognize some positive rights in the free speech area—to achieve equality of access to the media among political parties—and, further, the court may be able to uphold the right in principle, while leaving the drafting of the remedy to the legislature or the appropriate administrative body.[6] The role of the judiciary is here to state the free speech right in outline, but not to act as a substitute legislature.

It may become even more important to sound this note of caution in the years to come. Constitutional courts and the European Human Rights institutions will be called on to construe freedom of expression provisions in new contexts and circumstances arising from technological developments in communications. The mass availability of video recordings and the rapid development of cable television networks—to take but two examples—have already begun to create legal free speech problems, which can probably only be solved satisfactorily on an international

---

[4] *US* v. *O'Brien* 391 US 367 (1968), considered in ch. II, s. 2.

[5] For example, the Court's formulation of guidelines for specific remedies such as busing to achieve school integration (*Swann* v. *Charlotte-Mecklenburg Board of Education* 402 US 1 (1971)) has been subject to much criticism on these lines. For a general critique of judicial competence in this area, see D. L. Horowitz, *The Court and Social Policy* (Brookings Institution, 1977).

[6] This point is discussed in ch. III, s. 4: the members of the Court favouring a *constitutional* right of access to the media would leave its detailed formulation to the Federal Communications Commission.

scale.[7] Other problems have recently arisen within national boundaries, to which the application of traditional free speech principles by the courts is far from obvious; an important illustration of this is provided by the Supreme Court rulings that the First Amendment precludes legislative controls on the amount of money spent on election and referendum campaigns. In Chapter II, it was argued that the Court did not really substantiate its conclusion that the expenditure of money should be treated as 'speech' for the purposes of constitutional protection.[8] I do not resile from that position at all, but it is right to recognize that *Buckley* v. *Valeo* and the other election law cases, as well as the line of cases on access to the broadcasting media, create baffling free speech problems, which cannot easily be resolved by recourse to principles formulated, say, fifty to sixty years ago. The courts' traditional hostility (at least in the United States) to government censorship or to suppression and regulation of speech on the basis of its content or viewpoint does not really afford much guidance on how the issues of 'mass speech' should be decided. For example, do limitations on expenditure at elections, designed to prevent the wealthier candidates and their campaign groups drowning out the voices of those less well endowed, restrict or rather enhance speech? And should a constitutional court approach such measures with suspicion merely because it is government which has framed them, and regard its claim that there is no discrimination against the content of any particular type of speech as possibly disingenuous?[9]

I have argued throughout this book, and again in this chapter, that too much may be claimed for the legal repercussions of entrenchment in a constitution of the free speech principle. Courts should certainly set their face against any content-based suppression of speech, particularly in the area of political speech, and they should further leave writers, speakers, and publishers a wide margin of error, as it were, so that some expression of a doubtful constitutional status should be immune from regulation. The danger of suppression of speech which ought to be covered and protected by the free speech clause is a worse evil by far than the toleration on occasion of publications that could legitimately be proscribed. For this reason, the United States libel rule, allowing the press

---

[7] These problems are discussed in the Directorate of Human Rights' Report, *Council of Europe Activities in the Mass Media Field*, DH-MM (83) 1.

[8] ch. II, s. 3.

[9] These issues are discussed by L. A. Powe, 'Mass Speech and the Newer First Amendment' [1982] *Sup. Ct. Rev.* 243.

freedom to publish even careless, though not malicious, defamatory criticism of 'public figures', is preferable to the common law rules, for it removes the risk that some important political speech will not be distributed for fear of the tort action.[10] The same argument justifies, as I have said in Chapters II and IX, the coverage of emotive, non-rational political abuse (except where it provokes public disorder) and much soft-core pornography which on its own is wholly worthless. In all these cases the arguments for the free speech principle and the general desirability of independent checks by the courts on government regulation which may contravene that principle point in the same direction—to a justification for application by the judges of the free speech clause. But the indications are not so clear when the use of this clause to uphold some claim, say, for access to the media or to government premises to gather information, is harder to justify by reference to the underlying free speech principles and involves the courts in the task of framing a remedy that stretches their competence. Judicial intervention is even harder to support when the government—or still more, an independent administrative agency—is trying to promote or enhance free speech, as arguably the US government was in the controversial election cases.[11] There may be a tension in some of these situations between the solution suggested by a serious construction of the free speech clause in the light of relevant underlying political principles on the one hand, and that intimated by a general suspicion of government on the other.

The usual conservative approach of the Supreme Court and the German Constitutional Court to the hard questions concerning the meaning and character of a free speech clause seems on balance to be correct. New areas of free speech law are developed gradually and slowly, as in the case of the extension of coverage to commercial speech and obscenity, and the courts should always be prepared to reconsider their bolder decisions when difficulties in the more radical approach emerge. In some areas, as I have already emphasized, it is wiser to leave as much as possible to other agencies, for them to work out the implications of the free speech clause in legislation and regulation, subject naturally to the ordinary process of judicial review. But just as it is possible to claim too much for the consequences of a constitutional freedom of speech clause, so it may be possible to claim too little.

---

[10] See the discussion in ch. VI, especially s. 2.

[11] *Buckley* v. *Valeo* 424 US 1 (1976), *Common Cause* v. *Schmitt* 512 F. Supp. 489, discussed in ch. II, s. 3.

2.   A 'FREE SPEECH CLAUSE' FOR BRITAIN?

In many of the areas of law considered in this book, we have seen that the law does not protect freedom of speech as fully in Britain as it does in the other jurisdictions discussed. This is for the most part inevitable in the absence of a written constitution or Bill of Rights, which would enable the courts to strike down legislation infringing the freedom. If there were a constitutional free speech provision, legislation creating the offence of incitement to racial hatred, the Incitement of Disaffection Act 1934, and perhaps the Obscene Publications Act 1959 and section 2 of the Official Secrets Act 1911, would be suspect under it. Equally importantly, many areas of common law which implicate freedom of speech would have to be reformulated; among them are the law of libel and contempt of court. In the absence of a constitutional or strong free speech principle, it is difficult for the judiciary to give much weight to the interests of free expression when they are exercising judicial review over administrative decisions (for example, controlling the exercise of police or local authority discretion in banning processions under the Public Order Act 1936), or when they are interpreting Acts of Parliament.[12] Admittedly, there are some significant exceptions, for instance Lord Reid's speech in *Cozens* v. *Brutus*,[13] but they are striking largely because they are so exceptional. Generally, however, free speech is just a factor to be given some weight in common law litigation, but easily trumped by competing public and private interests.

Many commentators and, one suspects, a large number of lawyers find this position perfectly satisfactory. And their attitude is reinforced if attention is drawn to some of the United States cases where the claims of free speech are pressed very far. Most English lawyers do find the American approach, as evidenced, for instance, by its hostility to almost all prior restraints and its refusal to countenance restriction on pre-trial publicity even in criminal cases, alien and unacceptable. However, it is surely important to set against these impressions the overall picture that emerges from this book. The Supreme Court balances the relevant public or governmental interest in, say, public order or the protection of youth

---

[12] See, for example, the discussion in ch. III, s. 3, of the British courts' inability to develop a right of equal opportunity to hold public meetings in the absence of a strong (let alone a constitutional) free speech principle. The same point is perhaps also pertinent to the recent decision of the Divisional Court, *R.* v. *Broadcasting Complaints Commission, ex parte Owen, The Times*, 26 Jan. 1985, refusing to compel the Commission to consider the SDP's complaint that it (and the Liberals) were treated unfairly by the television authorities.

[13] [1973] AC 854, fully discussed in ch. VII, s. 2.

against the constitutionally guaranteed freedom of speech, and if the former is pressing or compelling enough, a limit will be upheld. An absolutist position has never enjoyed more than the support of a small minority of the Court. As pointed out in the previous section of this chapter, the Court has usually resisted the recognition of the more radical free speech claims—to rights of access, the use of government and public facilities for meetings, or to enter property to acquire information. Nor need a British constitutional court adopt the same approach as the Supreme Court in its more liberal periods, as under Warren CJ. The examples of the West German Constitutional Court and the European Court of Human Rights are probably more instructive for the possible implications of entrenchment of a free speech clause in this country.

This observation is hardly surprising. One point, already made in Chapter I, is that the texts of both the free speech provision and the documents as a whole (that is, the German Basic Law and the European Convention) are much more precise and afford the judges much more guidance than the comparable United States texts. The courts in the European jurisdictions enjoy, therefore, much less discretion in their interpretation and development of freedom of speech, and it is clear in particular that the freedom is to be balanced against other interests—set out in some detail in the European Convention. Any British Bill of Rights is much more likely to be modelled on these provisions than the two-centuries-old Amendments to the US Constitution. Indeed, the most probable alternative to the perpetuation of the present constitutional position—always the strongest bet in the British context, it must be said—is the incorporation into British law of the European Convention. The growing familiarity of lawyers in London with the Convention, reference to which is now frequently made in leading civil liberties cases even though this is to little effect, is another factor supporting the view put forward at the end of the last paragraph.

The question whether Britain ought to take free speech more seriously by adopting an appropriate constitutional clause is, of course, just one aspect of the intermittent debate on whether a Bill of Rights—entrenched or not, tailor-made or taken from the European Convention—is a good thing. The general issue is not the subject of this book. But we have seen that British law cannot protect free speech as adequately as those countries with a suitable constitutional provision, and in particular that our law of contempt was found incompatible with Article 10 of the European Convention in the *Sunday Times* case.[14] (The

[14] See ch. VIII, s. 4.

argument that we already have a Bill of Rights, which is enforceable only in Strasbourg, is too familiar to require restatement here.) If there is a good case for a free speech principle, then the argument for its constitutional protection in a Bill of Rights which prevails against inconsistent legislation seems to me overwhelming. The short reason for that conclusion is that not even British governments are to be trusted to uphold free speech when it suits their convenience or (to be fair) their assessment of the public interest to prefer some other value. If evidence is called for, then one would refer to the passage of the Official Secrets Act in a day in July 1911 (though admittedly the relationship of this measure to the free speech principle is a little problematic),[15] or the ready acceptance by governments of strict rules, legal and conventional, under which Ministers and former Ministers may not publish Cabinet and other high-level political discussions until a time when they have ceased to be of great public interest.[16]

But are the British judges more likely to uphold freedom of speech than the politicians? Their record in areas of common law, where it would be possible to give some weight to the freedom in formulating rules and decisions, is far from impressive; too often in libel and contempt of court cases, and in actions for injunctions to restrain a breach of confidence, free speech arguments are either ignored or belittled. And it can be argued that when senior judges sit as members of the Judicial Committee of the Privy Council to construe Commonwealth constitutional provisions modelled on the European Convention, they rarely appreciate the distinctive character of constitutional interpretation. As a result, it is said, provisions are too often construed literally and narrowly to the detriment of fundamental liberties.[17] Powerful though

---

[15] For the passage of the 1911 Bill, see D. Williams, *Not in the Public Interest* (London, 1965), 25–6. The relationship of official secrecy laws and free speech is considered in ch. V, s. 5.

[16] See ch. IV, s. 3, for a discussion of the *Crossman Diaries* case and the government's acceptance of the Radcliffe Committee Report recommending extra-legal restrictions on these publications.

[17] See, for example, the powerful criticisms of D. Pannick, *Judicial Review of the Death Penalty* (London, 1982), 15–20. The decisions of the Committee in free speech cases are too few to afford any indication of a general approach to this area: in addition to *Att.-Gen.* v. *Antigua Times* [1976] AC 16, criticized in ch. IV, s. 1, see *Olivier* v. *Buttigieg* [1967] 1 AC 115, where a Maltese government circular prohibiting employees from taking an anti-clerical paper into their place of work was held contrary to freedom of expression, and *Francis* v. *Chief of Police* [1973] AC 761, where it was held, after discussion of the United States cases on loudspeakers (*Saia* v. *New York* 334 US 558 (1948) and *Kovacs* v. *Cooper* 336 US 77 (1949)) that control on their use under a permit system was not contrary to the freedom.

these arguments are, they do not in my view amount to a persuasive case against a free speech provision in particular, or a Bill of Rights in general. The British courts' customary reluctance to take general principles seriously, evidenced in so many of the areas of law discussed in this book, would surely be abandoned if they were required to apply a Bill of Rights. And Privy Council cases do not really indicate how the judiciary would handle free speech litigation, where counsel would cite relevant European decisions; these would be of great weight if the constitutional provisions incorporated, or were modelled on, the Convention. It has always seemed to me perverse that so many legal and political commentators claim with so much relish that British judges, unlike their American or European brethren, are somehow incapable of making sense of a Bill of Rights. I am a little more optimistic.[18] I wish I could be as hopeful that the courts in this country will ever have the opportunity to justify this faith.

---

[18] It would be understandable, but I think irrational, to revise this attitude in the light of the judge's direction to the jury in the recent *Ponting* case, where 'the interests of the State' (see Official Secrets Act 1911, s.2) were in effect equated with those of the government.

Index